5|00

Philosophy:
Basic Readings

Other books by the same author:

Philosophy: The Basics
(3rd edition 1999)

Philosophy: The Classics
(1998)

Thinking from A to Z
(1996)

Philosophy:
Basic Readings

ROUTLEDGE

Edited by Nigel Warburton

First published 1999
by Routledge
11 New Fetter Lane,
London EC4P 4EE

Simultaneously published
in the USA and Canada
by Routledge
29 West 35th Street,
New York, NY 10001

Typeset in Times and Frutiger by
The Florence Group, Stoodleigh, Devon

Printed and bound in Great Britain
by TJ International Ltd, Padstow,
Cornwall

*British Library Cataloguing in
Publication Data*
A catalogue record for this book is
available from the British Library

*Library of Congress Cataloging in
Publication Data*
Warburton, Nigel
    Philosophy: basic readings / edited
by Nigel Warburton
        p.   cm.
    1. Philosophy.   I. Title
BD21.W34   1999   98–41074
100-dc21

ISBN 0–415–18719–2 (hbk)
ISBN 0–415–18720–6 (pbk)

Contents

CONTENTS

Section Three: Politics

Section Four: The external world

Section Five: Science

Section Six: Mind

Section Seven: Art

Preface

Preface

Philosophy can be an exhilarating subject to study. At its best it challenges previously unquestioned beliefs, develops transferable thinking skills, and gives students a chance to interact with the ideas of some of the greatest thinkers known to humanity. One reason for it being such a stimulating subject is that it is anything but a spectator sport: in order to study it you have to do it. You have to enter into the debate rather than observe it from the sidelines. Unfortunately many anthologies of readings in philosophy kill the subject for the reader: worthy but dull articles are the staple of introductory philosophy courses and textbooks. Much of the standard material used to introduce philosophy to beginning students gives the impression that it is little more than a sophisticated form of nit-picking. I hope my selection of readings here counteracts that impression. My aim has been to select writing that will repay study, and which is, above all, interesting. Part of the point of this anthology is to demonstrate philosophy in action.

I have deliberately kept my introductions to readings brief: too often with collections of this kind it is simpler just to read the summary of the article given in the introduction and to dispense with reading the article itself. The point of my introductions is to aid the reader, not provide him or her with an excuse not to read the article. Above all studying philosophy should

involve thinking and critical reading rather than regurgitation and learning by rote. I have provided a range of readings which will, I hope, encourage this approach.

Inevitably the difficulty of the readings varies. In some cases, such as the readings by David Hume, this is due in large part to the eighteenth-century prose style; in other cases difficulty comes from the abstraction characteristic of much philosophical writing. Philosophy is not the obscure and esoteric subject it is sometimes made out to be, but it is not always easy to read philosophical writings. It often requires closer attention and greater critical engagement than that demanded by other types of writing.

This book follows the structure of my book *Philosophy: The Basics* (3rd edn, Routledge, 1999) though it can be used independently of it. The area headings should be self-explanatory. My aim has not been comprehensive coverage of all the central topics in philosophy, but rather interesting coverage of a selection of topics.

Nigel Warburton,
Oxford, 1998

What is philosophy?

Introduction

1

*What makes someone
a philosopher?*
Mary Warnock

Many students coming to philosophy for the first time are unclear about the nature of the subject they are studying. What is distinctive about philosophy and about being a philosopher? What singles it out from other subjects? Here Mary Warnock (1924–) isolates several important features of any philosopher worthy of the name. Professional recognition is unimportant: what matters is that a philosopher is someone who thinks at a high level of generality, has 'explanatory ambition' and, most importantly, provides arguments in support of his or her views. These are the distinguishing marks of a true philosopher.

From *Women Philosophers*, edited by Mary Warnock

'What makes someone a philosopher, apart from being deemed such by a university?' First, I think, a writer must be concerned with matters of a high degree of generality, and must be at home among abstract ideas. It is not enough to seek the truth, for truth can be established with regard to particular facts; it can be the aim of historians, or of novelists who seek imaginatively to tell things, in some sense, as they are. A philosopher would doubtless also claim to be seeking the truth, but would be interested in whatever lies behind the particular facts of experience, the details of history; a philosopher is concerned with the underlying meaning of the language that we habitually and unthinkingly use, the categories into which we sort our experience. Thus he or she would claim not only to seek the truth, but to seek a truth, or theory, that will explain the particular and the detailed and the everyday.

One very great philosopher who exemplified these characteristics was the eighteenth-century Scotsman David Hume. He never held any academic post (though he once unsuccessfully tried for one); most of his writings were of that particularly Scottish kind, the essay; and his essays were on a variety of social, political and economic subjects. But his great philosophical work, the *Treatise of Human Nature*, which he completed when he was only twenty-six years old, was designed to establish the foundations of a genuinely empirical science of human nature. From these foundations, he hoped, could be built up an account of all human knowledge, including scientific knowledge, and all morality, including political morality. Here was generality, and indeed vast explanatory ambition. Hume also satisfied another criterion by which to judge a true philosopher: he was concerned not merely with stating his views, but with arguing for them. This concern has almost always led, among philosophers, to a passionate interest in one another's work; to dissenting from, and if possible refuting, the arguments of other philosophers; to expounding theories by means of dialogue, spoken or written. Sometimes, as in the case of Plato, Berkeley or Hume, these dialogues were fictional; sometimes they were real, and took the form, as in Descartes's case, of replies to objections, or the exchange of letters. Philosophers are by nature talkers or correspondents; only rarely do they prefer to sit and think, isolated from their kind.

2

Analytic philosophy

D. H. Mellor

Philosophers seem to spend more time studying apparent nonsense than do some other thinkers. Why is this? The answer reveals important facts about the nature of philosophy, at least about the nature of philosophy within the tradition known as analytic philosophy. Here D. H. Mellor (1938–) outlines his view about what philosophy is and why it matters.

From D. H. Mellor, *Matters of Metaphysics*

Bishop Berkeley said in 1710, in the introduction to *The Principles of Human Knowledge*, 'Upon the whole, I am inclined to think that the far greater part, if not all, of those difficulties which have hitherto amused philosophers, and blocked up the way to knowledge, are entirely owing to ourselves – that we have first raised a dust and then complain we cannot see' (para. 3).

Those remarks of Berkeley's seem to me just as true now as they were in 1710. Indeed matters are in some ways worse now than they were then. For one thing, philosophers today are too rarely amused by the difficulties that block the way to knowledge. They should be amused, because philosophy has to deal amongst other things with the limits of what makes sense: that is, with the boundary between sense and nonsense, which is the very stuff of humour. Take this example from Lewis Carroll's *Through the Looking-Glass*:

> 'Who did you pass on the road?' the King went on, holding out his hand to the Messenger for some more hay.
> 'Nobody', said the Messenger.
> 'Quite right', said the King: 'this young lady saw him too. So of course Nobody walks slower than you.'
> 'I do my best', the Messenger said in a sullen tone. 'I'm sure nobody walks much faster than I do!'

'He can't do that', said the King, 'or else he'd have been here first.'

(ch. VII)

It takes a philosopher to see *why* this is funny, to see why it's nonsense to talk of Nobody as if he and she (Nobody is both male and female . . .) were a being of some kind. The reason is, of course, that although the word 'Nobody' looks like the name of some being, it really isn't a name at all: it's a way of saying that there was *not* a being who walked either slower or faster than the Messenger. Now that's a pretty trivial piece of philosophical analysis, which anyone could do: but as we shall see, there is much more serious (and more misleading) nonsense than Lewis Carroll's around, which it takes rather more analysis to expose and explain.

To expose nonsense, however, we must first detect it: we need a nose for nonsense. And, as Ramsey said of Wittgenstein's proposition that philosophy itself is nonsense, 'we must then take seriously that it is nonsense, and not pretend, as Wittgenstein does, that it is important nonsense' (Ramsey 1929: 1).[1] Now I don't think philosophy is nonsense, but I do think it includes taking the fact of nonsense seriously and saying why it's nonsense. To do that, however, we need to be suitably amused by jokes like the one about Nobody, and to distinguish taking them seriously from pretending they're important. But not all philosophers are suitably amused. Some I fear lack the serious sense of humour, and with it the nose for nonsense, that good philosophy needs. And that is a serious defect. For without a nose for nonsense, philosophers run a real risk of talking nonsense themselves, and (unlike Lewis Carroll) of persuading themselves and others that it's important nonsense.

None of this would matter much if philosophy were read and judged only by other philosophers, as mathematics is by mathematicians, who can, on the whole, tell when their colleagues are talking nonsense. But it isn't, even though perhaps it should be, since philosophy is really no more of a spectator sport than mathematics is – by which I mean that it's not like poetry, for example, which you needn't be a poet to judge, whereas you do need to be a philosopher to judge philosophy, just as you need to be a mathematician to judge mathematics. Of course philosophy, like mathematics, is also read by outsiders who don't want to judge it, but rather to take it on trust and use it, just as physicists use mathematics. But not many outsiders want philosophy to do physics with: on the whole, they want it to provide a kind of secular substitute for religion. In other words, they want their philosophers to be gurus. And the last thing disciples want in gurus is a sense of humour: it's inimical to the air of authority which attracts disciples to gurus in the first place. So when philosophical gurus raise a dust by talking important-sounding nonsense, their disciples, far from *complaining* that they cannot see, are all the more impressed by the profound obscurity of the proffered view. In philosophy, therefore, as in religion and medicine, a gullible public will often give much fame and fortune to mystery-mongers.

What has all this to do with *analytic* philosophy? Well, to pursue Berkeley's metaphor, philosophical analysis is, as even my trivial example of it illustrates, a kind of intellectual sprinkler system, whose function is to lay the conceptual dust which obscures our view of the world. This indeed is one of its primary objects: to detect and dissipate the bogus mysteries which nonsense generates, like Lewis Carroll's little mystery about Nobody, so that the world's real mysteries can be more clearly seen and thereby – we hope – better appreciated and understood.

In this sense, good philosophy has always been analytic. Analysis is more a matter of technique than of doctrine, and it is as evident in Plato, Aristotle, Aquinas, Leibniz, Hume, Kant and Mill as in any modern analytic philosopher. What if anything distinguishes analytic philosophy, so-called, is that it not only uses analytic techniques, but is explicitly concerned to develop and assess them: not of course as ends in themselves, but as means to philosophical understanding. But not of course the only means, since an analyst always needs non-analytic material to analyse. Analysis can no more provide a complete philosophy on its own than – for example – democracy can provide a complete politics: because, obviously, accepting the principle of majority rule doesn't tell you whom or what to vote for, or why. No political democrat, in other words, can *just* be a democrat; and in much the same way, no philosophical analyst can *just* be an analyst. Which is not of course to deny that analysis matters, just as democracy matters; nor to deny that it can conflict with philosophical nonsense (like the being of Nobody), just as democracy can conflict with political nonsense (like the one-party state).

But whereas everyone can feel that democracy matters, and can more or less see why, it is less obvious to non-philosophers why philosophical analysis matters. If philosophy in general is not really a spectator sport, what can analytic philosophy, in particular, offer to the rest of society? Well, I could say, for a start, that it offers, because it demands and encourages, a socially desirable temperament. A nose for nonsense isn't only an asset in philosophy. A sense of humour, and hence of proportion, is a powerful antidote to political and religious fanaticism. An insistence on explicit discursive understanding where it can be had, as opposed to obscure intimations of ineffable insight, is a great deterrent to charlatanism of all kinds. A commitment to truth, and hence to basing one's beliefs on evidence rather than on wishful thinking (however high-minded), is essential not only to good science, but to all serious attempts to acquire knowledge and understanding about anything, including ourselves. And the feeling for reason which analysis gratifies helps to combat a recurrent tendency to elevate feeling at the expense of reason, as if they were opposed, and as if we didn't need both.

Society, however, is not only indebted to the temperament that analytic philosophy fosters. The results of analysis too have had many uses outside philosophy itself, although I don't wish to exaggerate them, or to accept that they provide its main justification: philosophy, like mathematics, has a value of its own, independent of its applications. Still, those applications are remarkable enough: ranging from the invention of computers (based on analyses of the concepts of mathematical proof and truth) to debates on abortion, which turn on concepts of life and of humanity whose analysis is far too important to be left to people with particular religious (or anti-religious) axes to grind.

But besides all this, I think analytic philosophy serves society most distinctively when it increases our understanding by clarifying concepts that concern everyone, whether they are philosophers or not.

Note

1   See Frank P. Ramsey, 'Philosophy', in D. H. Mellor (ed.) *Philosophical Papers* (Cambridge: Cambridge University Press, 1990), pp. 1–7.

3

The method of philosophy

A. J. Ayer

How does a philosopher set about working on a philosophical problem? In this extract from his book *The Problem of Knowledge* (1956), A. J. Ayer (1910–88) describes the method of philosophy as he sees it, taking the question 'What is knowledge?' as an illustration of how a philosopher goes about investigating a concept.

From A. J. Ayer, *The Problem of Knowledge*

It is by its methods rather than its subject-matter that philosophy is to be distinguished from other arts or sciences. Philosophers make statements which are intended to be true, and they commonly rely on argument both to support their own theories and to refute the theories of others; but the arguments which they use are of a peculiar character. The proof of a philosophical statement is not, or only very seldom, like the proof of a mathematical statement; it does not normally consist in formal demonstration. Neither is it like the proof of a statement in any of the descriptive sciences. Philosophical theories are not tested by observation. They are neutral with respect to particular matters of fact.

This is not to say that philosophers are not concerned with facts, but they are in the strange position that all the evidence which bears upon their problems is already available to them. It is not further scientific information that is needed to decide such philosophical questions as whether the material world is real, whether objects continue to exist at times when they are not perceived, whether other human beings are conscious in the same sense as one is oneself. These are not questions that can be settled by experiment, since the way in which they are answered itself determines how the result of any experiment is to be interpreted. What is in dispute in such cases is not whether, in a given set of circumstances, this or that event will happen, but rather how anything at all that happens is to be described.

This preoccupation with the ways things are, or are to be, described is often represented as an enquiry into their essential nature. Thus philosophers are given to asking such questions as What is mind? What sort of a relation is causality? What is the nature of belief? What is truth? The difficulty is then to see how such questions are to be taken. It must not be supposed, for instance, that a philosopher who asks What is mind? is looking for the kind of information that a psychologist might give him. His problem is not that he is ignorant of the ways in which people think and feel, or even that he is unable to explain them. Neither should it be assumed that he is simply looking for a definition. It is not as if philosophers do not understand how words like 'mind' or 'causality' or 'truth' are actually used. But why, then, do they ask such questions? What is it that they are trying to find out?

The answer to this, though not indeed the whole answer, is that, already knowing the use of certain expressions, they are seeking to give an analysis of their meaning. This distinction between the use of an expression and the analysis of its meaning is not easy to grasp. Let us try to make it clear by taking an example. Consider the case of knowledge. A glance at the dictionary will show that the verb 'to know' is used in a variety of ways. We can speak of knowing, in the sense of being familiar with, a person or a place, of knowing something in the sense of having had experience of it, as when someone says that he has known hunger or fear, of knowing in the sense of being able to recognize or distinguish, as when we claim to know an honest man when we see one or to know butter from margarine. I may be said to know my Dickens, if I have read, remember, and can perhaps also quote his writings, to know a subject such as trigonometry, if I have mastered it, to know how to swim or drive a car, to know how to behave myself. Most important of all, perhaps, are the uses for which the dictionary gives the definition of 'to be aware or apprized of', 'to apprehend or comprehend as fact or truth', the sense, or senses, in which to have knowledge is to know that something or other is the case.

All this is a matter of lexicography. The facts are known, in a sense, to anyone who understands the English language, though not everyone who understands the English language would be competent to set them out. The lexicographer, *pace* Dr Johnson, is required to be something more than a harmless drudge. What he is not required to be is a philosopher. To possess the information which the dictionary provides, about the accredited uses of the English word 'to know', or the corresponding words in other languages, is no doubt a necessary qualification for giving an analysis of knowledge; but it is not sufficient. The philosopher who has this information may still ask What is knowledge? and hesitate for an answer.

We may discover the sense of the philosopher's question by seeing what further questions it incorporates, and what sorts of statement the attempt to answer it leads him to make. Thus, he may enquire whether the different cases in which we speak of knowing have any one thing in common; whether, for example, they are alike in implying the presence of some special state of mind. He may maintain that there is, on the subjective side, no difference in kind between knowing and believing, or, alternatively, that knowing is a special sort of mental act. If he thinks it correct to speak of acts of knowing, he may go on to enquire into the nature of their objects. Is any limitation to be set upon them? Or, putting it another way, is there anything thinkable that is beyond the reach of human knowledge? Does knowing make a difference to what is known? Is it necessary to distinguish between the sorts of things that can be known directly and those that can be known only indirectly? And, if so, what are the relationships between them? Perhaps it is philosophically misleading to talk of knowing objects at all. It may be possible to show that what appears to be an instance of knowing some object always comes down to knowing that something is the case. What is known, in this sense, must be true, whereas what is believed may very well be false. But it is also possible to believe what is in fact true without knowing it. Is knowledge then to be distinguished by the fact that if one knows that something is so, one cannot be mistaken? And in that case does it follow that what is known is necessarily true, or in some other way indubitable? But, if this does follow, it will lead in its turn to the conclusion that we commonly claim to know much more than we really do; perhaps even to the paradox that we do not know anything at all: for it may be contended that there is no statement whatsoever that is not in itself susceptible to doubt. Yet surely there must be something wrong with an argument that would make knowledge unattainable. Surely some of our claims to knowledge must be capable of being justified. But in what ways can we justify them? In what would the processes of justifying them consist?

I do not say that all these questions are clear, or even that they are all coherent. But they are instances of the sort of question that philosophers ask.

4

The value of philosophy
Bertrand Russell

Almost anyone who studies philosophy will sooner or later encounter disparaging remarks about the subject, such as that it is just hair-splitting and irrelevant – a subject best pursued by those who want to live in an ivory tower. Here Bertrand Russell (1872–1970) responds to such remarks with a robust defence of the value of philosophy. Philosophy has value not because it is likely to provide definitive answers to the questions it asks, but rather because the questions themselves are profound and important ones. Philosophical contemplation removes us from our narrow everyday concerns and takes us to a realm of generality which can put our lives into a new perspective.

From Bertrand Russell, *The Problems of Philosophy*

It is the more necessary to consider this question [What is the value of philosophy and why it ought to be studied?] in view of the fact that many men, under the influence of science or of practical affairs, are inclined to doubt whether philosophy is anything better than innocent but useless trifling, hair-splitting distinctions, and controversies on matters concerning which knowledge is impossible.

This view of philosophy appears to result, partly from a wrong conception of the ends of life, partly from a wrong conception of the kind of goods which philosophy strives to achieve. Physical science, through the medium of inventions, is useful to innumerable people who are wholly ignorant of it; thus the study of physical science is to be recommended, not only, or primarily, because of the effect on the student, but rather because of the effect on mankind in general. Thus utility does not belong to philosophy. If the study of philosophy has any value at all for others than students of philosophy, it must be only indirectly, through its effects upon the lives of those who study it. It is in these effects, therefore, if anywhere, that the value of philosophy must be primarily sought.

But further, if we are not to fail in our endeavour to determine the value of philosophy, we must first free our minds from the prejudices of what are wrongly called 'practical' men. The 'practical' man, as this word is often used, is one who recognizes only material needs, who realizes that men must have food for the body, but is oblivious of the necessity of providing food for the mind. If all men were well off, if poverty and disease had been reduced to their lowest possible point, there would still remain much to be done to produce a valuable society; and even in the existing world the goods of the mind are at least as important as the goods of the body. It is exclusively among the goods of the mind that the value of philosophy is to be found; and only those who are not indifferent to these goods can be persuaded that the study of philosophy is not a waste of time.

Philosophy, like all other studies, aims primarily at knowledge. The knowledge it aims at is the kind of knowledge which gives unity and system to the body of the sciences, and the kind which results from a critical examination of the grounds of our convictions, prejudices, and beliefs. But it cannot be maintained that philosophy has had any very great measure of success in its attempts to provide definite answers to its questions. If you ask a mathematician, a mineralogist, a historian, or any other man of learning, what definite body of truths has been ascertained by his science, his answer will last as long as you are willing to listen. But if you put the same question to a philosopher, he will, if he is candid, have to confess that his study has not achieved positive results such as have been achieved by other sciences. It is true that this is partly accounted for by the fact that, as soon as definite knowledge concerning any subject becomes possible, this subject ceases to be called philosophy, and becomes a separate science. The whole study of the heavens, which now belongs to astronomy, was once included in philosophy; Newton's great work was called 'the mathematical principles of natural philosophy'. Similarly, the study of the human mind, which was a part of philosophy, has now been separated from philosophy and has become the science of psychology. Thus, to a great extent, the uncertainty of philosophy is more apparent than real: those questions which are already capable of definite answers are placed in the sciences, while those only to which, at present, no definite answer can be given, remain to form the residue which is called philosophy.

This is, however, only a part of the truth concerning the uncertainty of philosophy. There are many questions – and among them those that are of the profoundest interest to our spiritual life – which, so far as we can see, must remain insoluble to the human intellect unless its powers become of quite a different order from what they are now. Has the universe any unity of plan or purpose, or is it a fortuitous concourse of atoms? Is consciousness a permanent part of the universe, giving hope of indefinite growth in wisdom, or is it a transitory accident on a small planet on which life must ultimately become impossible? Are good and evil of importance to the universe or only to man? Such questions are asked by philosophy, and variously answered by various philosophers. But it would seem that, whether answers be otherwise discoverable or not, the answers suggested by philosophy are none of them demonstrably true. Yet, however slight may be the hope of discovering an answer, it is part of the business of philosophy to continue the consideration of such questions, to make us aware of their importance, to examine all the approaches to them, and to keep alive that speculative interest in the universe which is apt to be killed by confining ourselves to definitely ascertainable knowledge.

Many philosophers, it is true, have held that philosophy could establish the truth of certain answers to such fundamental questions. They have supposed that what is of most importance in religious beliefs could be proved by strict demonstration to be true. In order to judge of such attempts, it is necessary to take a survey of human knowledge, and to form an opinion as to its methods and its limitations. On such a subject it would be unwise to pronounce dogmatically; but if the investigations of our previous chapters have not led us astray, we shall be compelled to renounce the hope of finding philosophical proofs of religious beliefs. We cannot, therefore, include as part of the value of philosophy any definite set of answers to such questions. Hence, once more, the value of philosophy must not depend upon any supposed body of definitely ascertainable knowledge to be acquired by those who study it.

The value of philosophy is, in fact, to be sought largely in its very uncertainty. The man who has no tincture of philosophy goes through life imprisoned in the prejudices derived from common sense, from the habitual beliefs of his age or his nation, and from convictions which have grown up in his mind without the co-operation or consent of his deliberate reason. To such a man the world tends to become definite, finite, obvious; common objects rouse no questions, and unfamiliar possibilities are contemptuously rejected. As soon as we begin to philosophize, on the contrary, we find, as we saw in our opening chapters, that even the most everyday things lead to problems to which only very incomplete answers can be given. Philosophy, though unable to tell us with certainty what is the true answer to the doubts which it raises, is able to suggest many possibilities which enlarge our thoughts and free them from the tyranny of custom. Thus, while diminishing our feeling of certainty as to what things are, it greatly increases our knowledge as to what they may be; it removes the somewhat arrogant dogmatism of those who have never travelled into the region of liberating doubt, and it keeps alive our sense of wonder by showing familiar things in an unfamiliar aspect.

Apart from its utility in showing unsuspected possibilities, philosophy has a value – perhaps its chief value – through the greatness of the objects which it contemplates, and the freedom from narrow and personal aims resulting from this contemplation. The life of the instinctive man is shut up within the circle of his private interests: family and friends may be included, but the outer world is not regarded except as it may help or hinder what comes within the circle of instinctive wishes. In such a life there is something feverish and confined, in comparison with which the philosophic life is calm and free. The private world of instinctive interests is a small one, set in the midst of a great and powerful world which must, sooner or later, lay our private world in ruins. Unless we can so enlarge our interests as to include the whole outer world, we remain like a garrison in a beleaguered fortress, knowing that the enemy prevents escape and that ultimate surrender is inevitable. In such a life there is no peace, but a constant strife between the insistence of desire and the powerlessness of will. In one way or another, if our life is to be great and free, we must escape this prison and this strife.

One way of escape is by philosophic contemplation. Philosophic contemplation does not, in its widest survey, divide the universe into two hostile camps – friends and foes, helpful and hostile, good and bad – it views the whole impartially. Philosophic contemplation, when it is unalloyed, does not aim at proving that the rest of the universe is akin to man. All acquisition of knowledge is an enlargement of the Self, but this enlargement is best attained when it is not directly sought. It is obtained when the desire for knowledge is alone operative, by a study which does not wish in advance that its objects should have this or that character, but adapts the Self to the characters which it finds in its objects. This enlargement of Self is not obtained when, taking the Self as it is, we try to show that the world is so similar to this Self that knowledge of it is possible without any admission of what seems alien. The desire to prove this is a form of self-assertion and, like all self-assertion, it is an obstacle to the growth of Self which it desires, and of which the Self knows that it is capable. Self-assertion, in philosophic speculation as elsewhere, views the world as a means to its own ends; thus it makes the world of less account than Self, and the Self sets bounds to the greatness of its goods. In contemplation, on the contrary, we start from the not-Self, and through its greatness the boundaries of Self are enlarged; through the infinity of the universe the mind which contemplates it achieves some share in infinity.

For this reason greatness of soul is not fostered by those philosophies which assimilate the universe to Man. Knowledge is a form of union of Self and not-Self; like all union, it is impaired by dominion, and therefore by any attempt to force the universe into conformity with what we find in ourselves. There is a widespread philosophical tendency towards the view which tells us that Man is the measure of all things, that truth is man-made, that space and time and the world of universals are properties of the mind, and that, if there be anything not created by the mind, it is unknowable and of no account for us. This view, if our previous discussions were correct, is untrue; but in addition to being untrue, it has the effect of robbing philosophic contemplation of all that gives it value, since it fetters contemplation to Self. What it calls knowledge is not a union with the not-Self, but a set of prejudices, habits, and desires, making an impenetrable veil between us and the world beyond. The man who finds pleasure in such a theory of knowledge is like the man who never leaves the domestic circle for fear his word might not be law.

The true philosophic contemplation, on the contrary, finds its satisfaction in every enlargement of the not-Self, in everything that magnifies the objects contemplated, and thereby the subject contemplating. Everything, in contemplation, that is personal or private, everything that depends upon habit, self-interest, or desire, distorts the object, and hence impairs the union which the intellect seeks. By thus making a barrier between subject and object, such personal and private things become a prison to the intellect. The free intellect will see as God might see, without a *here* and *now*, without hopes and fears, without the trammels of customary beliefs and traditional prejudices, calmly, dispassionately, in the sole and exclusive desire of knowledge – knowledge as impersonal, as purely contemplative, as it is possible for man to attain. Hence also the free intellect will value more the abstract and universal knowledge into which the accidents of private history do not enter, than the knowledge brought by the senses, and dependent, as such knowledge must be, upon an exclusive and personal point of view and a body whose sense-organs distort as much as they reveal.

The mind which has become accustomed to the freedom and impartiality of philosophic contemplation will preserve something of the same freedom and impartiality in the world of action and emotion. It will view its purposes and desires as parts of the whole, with the absence of insistence that results from seeing them as infinitesimal fragments in a world of which all the rest is unaffected by any one man's deeds. The impartiality which, in contemplation, is the unalloyed desire for truth, is the very same quality of mind which, in action, is justice, and in emotion is that universal love which can be given to all, and not only to those who are judged useful or admirable. Thus contemplation enlarges not only the objects of our thoughts, but also the objects of our actions and our affections: it makes us citizens of the universe, not only of one walled city at war with all the rest. In this citizenship of the universe consists man's true freedom, and his liberation from the thraldom of narrow hopes and fears.

Thus, to sum up our discussion of the value of philosophy: Philosophy is to be studied, not for the sake of any definite answers to its questions, since no definite answers can, as a rule, be known to be true, but rather for the sake of the questions themselves; because these questions enlarge our conception of what is possible, enrich our intellectual imagination, and diminish the dogmatic assurance which closes the mind against speculation; but above all because, through the greatness of the universe which philosophy contemplates, the mind also is rendered great, and becomes capable of that union with the universe which constitutes its highest good.

God

5

The wager

Blaise Pascal

In this famous passage from his *Pensées*, Blaise Pascal (1623–63), philosopher and mathematician, sets out an ingenious argument designed to persuade a rational agnostic that he or she should believe in God. The reasoning he offers is based on the assumption that a rational gambler will aim to maximize potential winnings and minimize potential losses. Not only does Pascal provide the gambler with reasons to believe in God, but he also sketches a strategy for acquiring such a belief, even if the gambler is psychologically disposed not to believe in God.

From Blaise Pascal, *Pensées*

If there is a God, he is infinitely beyond our comprehension, since, being indivisible and without limits, he bears no relation to us. We are therefore incapable of knowing either what he is or whether he is. That being so, who would dare to attempt an answer to the question? Certainly not we, who bear no relation to him.

Who then will condemn Christians for being unable to give rational grounds for their belief, professing as they do a religion for which they cannot give rational grounds? They declare that it is a folly, *stultitiam*, in expounding it to the world, and then you complain that they do not prove it. If they did prove it they would not be keeping their word. It is by being without proof that they show they are not without sense. 'Yes, but although that excuses those who offer their religion as such, and absolves them from the criticism of producing it without rational grounds, it does not absolve those who accept it.' Let us then examine this point, and let us say: 'Either God is or he is not.' But to which view shall we be inclined? Reason cannot decide this question. Infinite chaos separates us. At the far end of this infinite distance a coin is being spun which will come down heads or tails. How will you wager? Reason cannot make you choose either, reason cannot prove either wrong.

Do not then condemn as wrong those who have made a choice, for you know nothing about it. 'No, but I will condemn them not for having made this particular choice, but any choice, for, although the one who calls heads and the other one are equally at fault, the fact is that they are both at fault: the right thing is not to wager at all.'

Yes, but you must wager. There is no choice, you are already committed. Which will you choose then? Let us see: since a choice must be made, let us see which offers you the least interest. You have two things to lose: the true and the good; and two things to stake: your reason and your will, your knowledge and your happiness; and your nature has two things to avoid: error and wretchedness. Since you must necessarily choose, your reason is no more affronted by choosing one rather than the other. That is one point cleared up. But your happiness? Let us weigh up the gain and the loss involved in calling heads that God exists. Let us assess the two cases: if you win you win everything, if you lose you lose nothing. Do not hesitate then; wager that he does exist. 'That is wonderful. Yes, I must wager, but perhaps I am wagering too much.' Let us see: since there is an equal chance of gain and loss, if you stood to win only two lives for one you could still wager, but supposing you stood to win three?

You would have to play (since you must necessarily play) and it would be unwise of you, once you are obliged to play, not to risk your life in order to win three lives at a game in which there is an equal chance of losing and winning. But there is an eternity of life and happiness. That being so, even though there were an infinite number of chances, of which only one were in your favour, you would still be right to wager one in order to win two; and you would be acting wrongly, being obliged to play, in refusing to stake one life against three in a game, where out of an infinite number of chances there is one in your favour, if there were an infinity of infinitely happy life to be won. But here there is an infinity of infinitely happy life to be won, one chance of winning against a finite number of chances of losing, and what you are staking is finite. That leaves no choice; wherever there is infinity, and where there are not infinite chances of losing against that of winning, there is no room for hesitation, you must give everything. And thus, since you are obliged to play, you must be renouncing reason if you hoard your life rather than risk it for an infinite gain, just as likely to occur as a loss amounting to nothing.

For it is no good saying that it is uncertain whether you will win, that it is certain that you are taking a risk, and that the infinite distance between the certainty of what you are risking and the uncertainty of what you may gain makes the finite good you are certainly risking equal to the infinite good that you are not certain to gain. This is not the case. Every gambler takes a certain risk for an uncertain gain, and yet he is taking a certain finite risk for an uncertain finite gain without sinning against reason. Here there is no infinite distance between the certain risk and the uncertain gain: that is not true. There is, indeed, an infinite distance between the certainty of winning and the certainty of losing, but the proportion between the uncertainty of winning and the certainty of what is being risked is in proportion to the chances of winning or losing. And hence if there are as many chances on one side as on the other you are playing for even odds. And in that case the certainty of what you are risking is equal to the uncertainty of what you may win; it is by no means infinitely distant from it. Thus our argument carries infinite weight, when the stakes are finite in a game where there are even chances of winning and losing and an infinite prize to be won.

This is conclusive and if men are capable of any truth this is it.

'I confess, I admit it, but is there really no way of seeing what the cards are?' – 'Yes. Scripture and the rest, etc.' – 'Yes, but my hands are tied and my lips are sealed; I am being forced to wager and I am not free; I am being held fast and I am so made that I cannot believe. What do you want me to do then?' – 'That is true, but at least get it into your head that, if you are unable to believe, it is because of your passions, since reason impels you to believe and yet you cannot do so. Concentrate then not on convincing yourself by multiplying proofs of God's existence but by diminishing your passions. You want to find faith and you do not know the road. You want to be cured of unbelief and you ask for the remedy: learn from those who were once bound like you and who now wager all they have. These are people who know the road you wish to follow, who have been cured of the affliction of which you wish to be cured: follow the way by which they began. They behaved just as if they did believe, taking holy water, having masses said, and so on. That will make you believe quite naturally, and will make you more docile.' – 'But that is what I am afraid of.' – 'But why? What have you to lose? But to show you that this is the way, the fact is that this diminishes the passions which are your great obstacles. . . .'

End of this address

'Now what harm will come to you from choosing this course? You will be faithful, honest, humble, grateful, full of good works, a sincere, true friend. . . . It is true you will not enjoy noxious pleasures, glory and good living, but will you not have others?

'I tell you that you will gain even in this life, and that at every step you take along this road you will see that your gain is so certain and your risk so negligible that in the end you will realize that you have wagered on something certain and infinite for which you have paid nothing.'

'How these words fill me with rapture and delight! – ,

'If my words please you and seem cogent, you must know that they come from a man who went down upon his knees before and after to pray to this infinite and indivisible being, to whom he submits his own, that he might bring your being also to submit to him for your own good and for his glory: and that strength might thus be reconciled with lowliness.'

Custom is our nature. Anyone who grows accustomed to faith believes it, and can no longer help fearing hell, and believes nothing else.

6

Proofs of God
Martin Gardner

Does God exist? This is a profoundly important question. Philosophers of religion have traditionally produced arguments that are designed either to prove or to disprove God's existence. In the article that follows, Martin Gardner (1914–) considers and rejects the most familiar traditional arguments for God's existence. He denies that these arguments can provide a suitable foundation for belief in God. Instead he adopts an attitude known as fideism: the view that belief in God should be achieved by an act of faith rather than as the conclusion to a logical proof.

From Martin Gardner, *Whys of a Philosophical Scrivener*

Are there purely logical arguments for God, arguments so convincing that if an intelligent atheist understood them he or she would become a theist? There are no such arguments. In Lecture 18 of his *Varieties of Religious Experience*, William James summed up the situation in a few sentences that could have been written last week:

> The arguments for God's existence have stood for hundreds of years with the waves of unbelieving criticism breaking against them, never totally discrediting them in the ears of the faithful, but on the whole slowly and surely washing out the mortar from between their joints. If you have a God already whom you believe in, these arguments confirm you. If you are atheistic, they fail to set you right.

A long line of distinguished thinkers, fully capable of understanding the arguments yet remaining unconvinced, is testimony to the flabbiness of those 'proofs.' But, you may respond, is there not also a long line of equally distinguished theists who firmly believed God's existence *could* be established by unaided reason?

Yes, and now I must explain why I qualified 'logical' by saying there are no 'purely' logical arguments. There indeed are partly logical arguments. If you make certain posits, posits unsupported by logic or science, the traditional proofs do make a kind of sense. From my fideist perspective, the posits required to confer validity on the proofs are not rational but emotional. They are made in response to deeply felt needs. Grant these emotive posits and the proofs become compelling, but the posits themselves are from the heart, not the head.

Logical and mathematical systems also require posits, but they are not posits based on passions. We believe in the truth of the Pythagorean theorem, for example, because we can prove it within the formal system of Euclidean geometry and because its truth can be empirically confirmed with physical models. If we could draw a triangle and find that the sum of its interior angles was 90 degrees, our trust in the theorems of Euclidean geometry would be shaken, but of course we cannot draw such a triangle any more than we can produce five pebbles by adding two pebbles to two pebbles. Given the formal system of Euclidean geometry, it follows with iron logic that the angles of every triangle must have a sum of 180 degrees, just as it follows from the formal system of arithmetic that the sum of two and two must be four. Even in the interior of a sun, Bertrand Russell once said, there are three feet in a yard.

The posits that confer plausibility on the traditional proofs of God are of an altogether different sort. Consider the familiar argument from first cause. If every event has a prior cause, we seem to be faced with either believing in a first cause (Aristotle's unmoved mover) that is self-caused or uncaused, or accepting chains of causes that go back forever in time.

Now whenever Thomas Aquinas encountered an infinite regress in one of his proofs of God he simply dismissed it as absurd. But why absurd? This is precisely the spot at which a subliminal emotion stealthily slips into the argument. An endless regress is absurd only to someone who finds it ugly or disturbing. There is nothing *logically* absurd about an infinite regress. We may feel uncomfortable with the infinite set of integers, but who wants to deny that the sequence goes to infinity in both positive and negative directions? Fractions in the sequence ½, ⅓, ¼, ⅕ ... get smaller and smaller but the sequence never ends with a smallest fraction. The proof by first cause may be emotionally satisfying in its escape from the anxiety generated by an infinite regress, but clearly it is logically flawed.

The same applies to a closely related variant of the argument. We allow the universe to be infinite in time, but insist that the entire sequence of events cannot be uncaused or self-caused. Again, it is emotionally satisfying to many people, perhaps to most people, to hang a beginningless universe on a higher peg, but without this emotion the argument proves nothing. If God, the transcendent peg, is declared to be self-caused or uncaused, we are merely evading the mystery of being, not solving it. Would it not be simpler, as David Hume suggested, to allow the entire universe to be uncaused or self-caused, like one of Saul Steinberg's cartoons that shows a man, pen in hand, drawing himself on the page? For many people it is impossible to think of the universe doing this, but the difficulty springs from an emotion, not from reason. There is nothing irrational about the thought. Every person, Bertrand Russell somewhere says, has a mother. This doesn't entail that the human race had a mother. Every integer has a predecessor. This doesn't entail that the infinite sequence of negative integers had a predecessor.

The teleological argument, or argument from design – that patterns in nature imply a Patternmaker – has been and still is the most popular of all traditional proofs of God. Before Darwin it was constantly invoked with reference to the marvelously adapted parts of living things. We all know how those arguments have been weakened by evolution. It is no longer possible to think of the wondrous structure of a human eye, or even the patterns of such lifeless things as galaxies and solar systems, as having histories analogous to the making of a watch.

This does not, of course, deny that most people, when they contemplate the grandeur of the starry heavens or the humbler patterns of flowers and snow crystals, may experience a strong feeling that behind such marvelous order there must be something like a human intelligence. Even Immanuel Kant, who demolished the logical force of the design argument in his *Critique of Pure Reason*, granted the proof's strong emotional power:

> This proof always deserves to be mentioned with respect. It is the oldest, the clearest, and the most accordant with the common reason of mankind. It enlivens the study of nature, just as it itself derives its existence and gains ever new vigour from that source. It suggests ends and purposes, where our observation would not have detected them by itself, and extends our knowledge of nature by means of the guiding-concept of a special unity, the principle of which is outside nature. This knowledge again reacts on its cause, namely, upon the idea which has led to it, and so strengthens the belief in a supreme Author [of nature] that the belief acquires the force of an irresistible conviction.
>
> It would therefore not only be uncomforting but utterly vain to attempt to diminish in any way the authority of this argument. Reason, constantly upheld by this ever-increasing evidence, which, though empirical, is yet so powerful, cannot be so depressed through doubts suggested by subtle and abstruse speculation, that it is not at once aroused from the indecision of all melancholy reflection, as from a dream, by one glance at the wonders of nature and the majesty of the universe – ascending from height to height up to the all-highest, from the conditioned to its conditions, up to the supreme and unconditioned Author [of all conditioned being].

One could easily fill a book with colorful extracts from writers who have testified to the persuasiveness of the proof by design. Here, for instance, are the thoughts of Charlotte Brontë's Jane Eyre, alone on the moor:

Night was come, and her planets were risen: a safe, still night; too serene for the companionship of fear. We know that God is everywhere; but certainly we feel His presence most when His works are on the grandest scale spread before us: and it is in the unclouded night-sky, where His worlds wheel their silent course, that we read clearest His infinitude, His omnipotence, His omnipresence. I had risen to my knees to pray for Mr. Rochester. Looking up, I, with tear-dimmed eyes, saw the mighty Milky-way. Remembering what it was – what countless systems there swept space like a soft trace of light – I felt the might and strength of God. Sure was I of His efficiency to save what He had made: convinced I grew that neither earth should perish, nor one of the souls it treasured. I turned my prayer to thanksgiving: the Source of Life was also the Savior of spirits. Mr. Rochester was safe: he was God's and by God would he be guarded. I again nestled to the breast of the hill; and ere long, in sleep, forgot sorrow.

Listen to Sir Isaac Newton, speaking iambic pentameters in Alfred Noyes's *Watchers of the Sky*:

Was the eye contrived by blindly moving atoms,
Or the still-listening ear fulfilled with music
By forces without knowledge of sweet sounds?
Are nerves and brain so sensitively fashioned
That they convey these pictures of the world
Into the very substance of our life,
While That from which we came, the Power that made us,
Is drowned in blank unconsciousness of all?

Whittaker Chambers's *Witness* provides a final example, one that might have come straight from the pen of the eighteenth-century English theologian William Paley:

But I date my break [with the Communist Party] from a very casual happening. I was sitting in our apartment on St. Paul Street in Baltimore. It was shortly before we moved to Alger Hiss's apartment in Washington. My daughter was in her high chair. I was watching her eat. She was the most miraculous thing that had ever happened in my life. I liked to watch her even when she smeared porridge on her face or dropped it meditatively on the floor. My eye came to rest on the delicate convolutions of her ear – those intricate, perfect ears. The thought passed through my mind: 'No, those ears were not created by any chance coming together of atoms in nature (the Communist view). They could have been created only by immense design.' The thought was involuntary and unwanted. I crowded it out of my mind. But I never wholly forgot it or the occasion. I had to crowd it out of my mind. If I had completed it, I should have had to say: Design presupposes God. I did not then know that, at that moment, the finger of God was first laid upon my forehead.

I find nothing in this passage to ridicule. Why should not the ear of a loved child be as good an example of God's design as anything in the universe? The inner ear is no less complex than the eye. Both are far more intricate than the watch Paley used in his famous proof. The argument's emotive force is not in the least diminished by the truth of evolution. In fact it is augmented. Cosmic evolution implies that the elementary particles that came into existence during the first few minutes of the big bang had mathematical properties that would permit them, billions of years later, to form microscopic eggs which would grow to become you and me. I cannot imagine anyone reading *Witness* without being impressed by the authenticity of Chambers's religious experience.

Since the development of organic chemistry, a new version of the argument from the design of living things has been advanced by a number of scientists and thinkers who have no quarrel with biological evolution. The argument focuses instead on the probability that life could arise spontaneously in earth's primeval seas. Presumably life began several billion years ago when carbon-based molecules, shuffling for millions of years in an organic soup, happened to form a self-replicating microorganism. The probability of this occurring by blind chance, so goes the reasoning, is so incredibly low that intervention by a deity is needed to explain how life started.

Pierre Leconte du Noüy gave this argument in two of his widely read books of the forties. More recently, Sir Fred Hoyle and his associate N. Chandra Wickramsinghe have refined the argument in their book *Evolution from Space*. They estimate the odds against blind chance producing a single self-replicating microorganism to be 10 to the power of 40,000 (1 followed by 40,000 zeros) to 1. Unable to make the leap to a God outside the universe, Hoyle and his friend (who was raised a Buddhist) settle for what they call an 'intelligence' within the universe that is constantly fabricating microorganisms in interstellar gas. These tiny life-forms are pushed around the cosmos by the pressure of starlight. Comets carry them to the planets, where they flourish and evolve if conditions are suitable.

Long before the discovery of the molecules and atoms, and before the development of evolutionary cosmology, Francis Bacon expressed the same emotion. In the following passage from his essay 'On Atheism,' Bacon contrasts Democritus's particle theory of matter with the four-elements theory of Aristotle and the Schoolmen:

> For it is a thousand times more credible that four mutable elements and one immutable fifth essence, duly and eternally placed, need no God, than that an army of infinite small portions or seeds, unplaced, should have produced this order and beauty without a divine marshal.

David Hume considered the design argument at such length that it is not easy to say anything about it that Hume did not say. Even evolution enters the argument in Hume's *Dialogues Concerning Natural Religion* when Philo insists that the universe is more like a growing tree than a watch or a knitting-loom. Because a tree knows nothing about the ordering of its parts, why should we assume a universal mind behind what today we call the 'tree' of evolution?

Few scientists take Hoyle's new science-fiction theology seriously. Its weakest point is that there are no compelling reasons for assuming that when organic molecules shuffle together, either in organic soups or in outer space, they combine by blind chance alone. Rather they combine by what Isaac Asimov once called 'unblind chance' – chance constrained by natural laws about which we as yet know nothing. Because of our vast ignorance, there are no ways to make reasonable probability estimates.

A more subtle recent variant of the design argument centers on the nature of the big bang. Physicists see no reason why this explosion could not have produced a universe in which certain basic constants, such as Planck's constant or the fine-structure constant or the rate of the universe's expansion, would have been other than what they are. But let some of these constants deviate ever so slightly from what they are and we get a possible universe in which not even stars could congeal, let alone planets and microorganisms. Therefore . . .

I find this argument for God as logically fragile as the old design arguments before Darwin. For all we know, as physicist John Wheeler has taught us, billions of big bangs may be constantly taking place in hyperspace and throughout eternity, explosions that manufacture universes in which all possible combinations of constants occur. As the old song goes, 'We're here because we're here because we're here because we're here.' The argument that God had to fine-tune the fireball to create a cosmos capable of producing intelligent life is compelling only to those who shrink from contemplating an infinity of lifeless universes, who find it more comforting to suppose that a superior intelligence guided our big bang to form just the universe it did.

Note that Wheeler's vision provides the atheist with a way of escaping Hoyle's probability estimate even if we grant that organic molecules combine by blind chance. The odds against life in any one universe may be low, but there is no limit to the number of universes that can live and die if time and space are endless. No matter how low the odds, eventually there will be a universe in which the rare event occurs, and so here we are!

My remarks are not intended to disparage what cosmologists call the 'anthropic principle.' According to this principle we can 'explain' certain properties of the earth, solar system, galaxy, universe, even the original fireball, by asking what sort of conditions are necessary to account for the existence now of cosmologists. Only the name of the principle is new. To chess problemists it is no more than the application to cosmology of 'retrograde analysis.' Given a position on the chessboard with, say, one piece removed, you can sometimes deduce the nature of the missing piece by reasoning backward through the game.

The principle appeals to physicists with solipsistic urges because it seems to say, though of course it does not, that somehow our consciousness makes the universe what it is. 'We have found a strange footprint on the shores of the unknown,' wrote Sir Arthur Stanley Eddington in the often-quoted last paragraph of his *Space, Time and Gravitation*. (By 'strange footprint' he meant the strange way our universe is put together.) 'We have devised profound theories . . . to account for its origin. At last, we have succeeded in reconstructing the creature that made the footprint. And Lo! it is our own.'

This may seem profound, but when expressed with less poetry and ambiguity it becomes trivial. 'Imagine an ensemble of universes of all sorts,' say Robert Dicke and P. J. E. Peebles in their contribution to *General Relativity: An Einstein Centenary Survey*. 'It should be no surprise that ours is not an 'average' one, for conditions on the average may well be hostile. We could only be present in a universe that happens to supply our needs.'

Dicke and Peebles describe a game of Russian roulette played by thousands of persons. From a large supply of guns each player randomly selects a gun that may or may not be loaded. At the end of the game a statistician makes a retrograde analysis and concludes 'that there is a high probability of the randomly selected unloaded guns being drawn by the survivors of the game.'

The Russian roulette analogy surely demolishes any effort to invoke the anthropic principle as an argument for God. Of course you may assume, if you like, that a Creator carefully selected our particular unloaded-gun universe in preference to loaded ones, but an assumption is not a proof. Roger Penrose, in the book cited above, imagines God looking over a large map on which each point represents the plan for a possible world, then sticking a pin in the map to cause a universe to explode into reality. Maybe only one such universe is chosen. Maybe God creates millions of universes by stabbing the map in many spots, perhaps even stabbing at random, or stabbing simultaneously with a billion hands. It is a celestial game in which the Creator entertains himself (and others?) by experimenting with myriads of possible worlds to see how each works out.

Whatever the scenario, the argument from the fine-tuning of the fireball to the existence of a Great Tuner seems to me no different in essence from the early arguments based on design in nature, and which today sound like Irish bulls. If water did not expand when it freezes, ice would form from the bottom up in lakes, thus killing all fish. If the earth's axis did not tilt at just the angle it does, our seasons would be either too mild or too severe for life (see Dante's *Paradiso*, Canto 10). If the earth's orbit were closer to or farther from the sun, its surface would be too hot or too cold to support life. Meteors would destroy our cities if they were not burned out by the earth's atmosphere. James, in Lecture 20 of *Varieties*, cites dozens of other amusing examples from theological rhetoric. Even the youthful Kant was not immune to such reasoning. In his monograph *On the Only Demonstrative Proof of the Existence of God* (which he later repudiated), Kant extolls the earth's atmosphere for (among other things) producing twilight, a slow transition to darkness that is easy on the eyes. Presumably if daylight went out like a snuffed candle we would have less reason to believe in God.

Such arguments have been interminably caricatured by skeptics. Dr Pangloss, in Voltaire's *Candide*, observes how carefully the nose is made to support spectacles. Freud, in his witty book on wit, quotes Jules Michelet: 'How beautifully everything is arranged in nature. As soon as the child comes into the world, it finds a mother who is ready to care for it.' How providential that polar wastes are in regions where nobody lives! How pleasant that Washington and Lincoln were born on holidays!

The old argument from common consent – that because so many people have believed in God belief must be true – obviously is not logically convincing, though it does have a crude kind of merit. The fact that so many persons, especially persons of towering intellect, have believed in God should at least give an atheist pause, just as a tone-deaf person might suspect there is something of value in music because so many admirable people profess to enjoy it. But this, too, is clearly an emotive argument. It does no more than demonstrate what all atheists know, that for large numbers of people a belief in God or gods satisfies deep longings.

It is easy to turn the design proof upside down and argue that the chaos and evil in the world suggest the nonexistence of God – an old argument that C. S. Lewis once called the 'argument from undesign.' It is particularly forceful when applied to natural evils which beset human life, such as earthquakes and plagues, but it applies to lower forms of life as well. Long before Darwin it was apparent that an anatomical design of great benefit to one species could hardly be called beneficial to the species it preyed upon.

'To the grub under the bark,' wrote James in *Pragmatism*, 'the exquisite fitness of the woodpecker's organism to extract him would certainly argue a diabolical designer.' In 1964 a pair of ants in Johnny Hart's comic strip *B.C.* made the same point. 'It's wonderful to be alive, to exist! What magnificent purpose has put me here? Is it to elevate the species? Is it to discover the secret of creation? Am I here to inspire my kind? Am I king? Prince? Prophet?' Says the other ant: 'Try anteater food!'

On this score, for now, I will add only the old thought that even if one finds the argument from design valid, it offers no assurance that the Designer had anything more in mind than to design a plaything. Every now and then some whimsical mechanic constructs a large, intricate piece of machinery with thousands of gears, levers, pulleys, chains, shafts, lights, and so on, designed only to run, not to *do* anything. Perhaps the entire universe is just such a joke, a vast cosmic jest fabricated by a god who had no motive except to amuse himself and his friends. It could even be a diabolical joke perpetrated by a demon god. Part of the joke is to place intelligent beings in a universe designed to arouse in them false hopes that they are in the hands of a benevolent God who will reward them with a future life.

The proof of God that I find the least defensible is Saint Anselm's famous ontological argument. C. S. Lewis, in his poem 'Abecedarium Philosophicum,' summed up Descartes's version this way:

D for Descartes who said 'God couldn't be
So complete if he weren't. So he is Q.E.D.'

The proof does indeed establish that if we form a concept of God as the most supreme being we can imagine, we cannot avoid adding existence to the concept. Clearly an existing God is superior to one who doesn't exist. But I agree with those critics who fail to see how we are logically compelled to make the ontological leap from a concept of an existing God to the assurance that the concept represents something outside our mind. I am aware that the argument continues to have distinguished advocates who defend it tirelessly and, to my mind, tiresomely: Norman Malcolm, Richard Campbell, my former teacher Charles Hartshorne, and several others. I can only say that I have never found the argument expressed in such a way that I could not find at some juncture a gap crossable only by an emotive jump.

Kant saw the fallacy of the proof quite clearly, but because he expressed it in a terminology easily misunderstood, he has often been unfairly belabored. When Kant said existence is not a predicate, and that a hundred real thalers contain not a thaler more than a hundred possible thalers, he meant only that the *concept* of a hundred thalers is not altered by one's belief, or by the discovery through experience, that thalers actually exist.

Suppose I express my idea of a blue apple by painting a picture of five blue apples. I point to it and say, 'This represents five blue apples.' If I later learn that blue apples actually exist I can point to the same picture and say, 'This represents five real blue apples.' Even if I fail to discover that blue apples exist I can point to the picture and say, 'This represents five imaginary blue apples.' In all three cases the picture remains the same. The concept of five real apples contains not an apple more than the concept of five possible apples. The idea of a unicorn does not acquire additional horns if real unicorns exist. In Kant's terminology you do not add a new property to a concept by expressing your belief that the concept corresponds to an actual object outside your brain.

Of course it is all a matter of words. In other epistemological languages it is quite acceptable to say that existence is a predicate. But to suppose that Kant did not realize it is better to have real money in your pocket than imaginary money is to suppose Kant to have been a moron, which he wasn't. 'My financial position,' Kant wrote, 'is, however, affected very differently by a hundred real thalers than it is by the mere concept of them.' When you think you have found a statement by a great philosopher that is obviously absurd, it is a good bet you have not understood the statement. A surprising recent example of such a failure to do homework occurs in Mortimer Adler's *How to Think About God*. Adler chastises Kant severely for falling into a childish blunder:

> Is not a hundred dollars in my pocket better than an imaginary hundred dollars by virtue of its enabling me to buy things with it? Is not a really existent umbrella or raincoat better than an imaginary one so far as protection from the rain is concerned?

As a lifelong champion of the Great Books – his friend Robert Hutchins liked to call him the Great Bookie – Adler above all should not have supposed that Kant was unaware of the value of real money and real umbrellas.

I shall waste no time on trivial variants of the ontological argument that reduce it to such tautologies as that Being must exist, or that if there is a necessarily existing perfect Being, that Being must necessarily exist. Nor do I wish to deny that in thinking through various forms of the ontological argument, a believer in God is led to *feel* that the highest possible Being must exist, but of course the proof claims to be more than that. It claims that the sentence 'There is no God' is as self-contradictory as 'A triangle has four sides.' Not even Aquinas could accept this, and although the argument still mesmerizes a few metaphysicians, I agree with the vast majority of thinkers who see the proof as no more than linguistic sleight-of-hand. There is no existing thing, said Hume, including the entire cosmos, whose nonexistence entails logical contradiction. The thought that everything would be much simpler if nothing existed at all may stab us with anxiety, but there is nothing logically inconsistent in the thought.

Karl Barth wrote a cantankerous and (to me) funny book about Anselm's proof. The book has the following thesis: The ontological argument proves nothing, but it serves to deepen a believer's understanding of God. Some medieval Schoolmen, Bonaventure in particular, said much the same thing, and although I cannot fault this thesis, it certainly is not what Anselm or most later defenders of his proof intended the proof to say. We can rephrase Barth's thesis as follows. For believers in God it is emotionally intolerable that their concept of a perfect God, so sublime and so satisfying, does not include belief in the actual existence of God. Hermann Lotze in his *Microcosmos* (Book 9, chapter 4) put it crisply: 'We *feel* the impossibility of God's nonexistence.' (Italics mine.)

When Barth's book on Anselm appeared in an English translation in 1962 it was reviewed by John Updike, a great admirer of Barth and a former Barthian. I agree with Updike that Barth wrote more about his own theology than about Anselm's. As you inch your way through Barth's curious monograph, Updike writes, you anticipate 'the gigantic leap that lies ahead, from existence as a concept to existence as a fact – from *esse in intellectu* to *esse in re*. Then a strange thing happens. Anselm takes the leap, and Barth does not, yet he goes on talking as if he had never left Anselm's side.'

Indeed, Barth ends by accepting the traditional criticisms of the proof, but admiring it nonetheless because it shows, as Updike puts it, 'we cannot pray to or believe in a God whom we recognize as a figment of our own imaginations.' In Barth's words: 'God is the One who manifests himself in the command not to imagine a greater than he.' Is this all that Anselm meant? Updike does not think so, nor do I, nor did Étienne Gilson, who criticized Barth's book along similar lines.

I repress the urge to devote more pages to the classic proofs of God, and to their refutations by Hume, Kant, Mill, and many others. Let me capsule my own view: In every proof I find an explicit or implicit emotional leap that springs from a desire or a fear or both, a leap that occurs at some point between the proof's links. As fully rational arguments, instances of what Kant called pure reason, the proofs are invalid. As partly rational, given certain emotional posits, they express deeply felt convictions in persuasive, reasonable ways, and for this reason they continue to flourish. Actually, this view is not far from that of many Schoolmen who maintained that without special illumination from God, a special grace, it is not possible to find the proofs convincing. Given prior faith, the proofs dramatize the intensity of our hunger for God. They deepen and strengthen our belief in God.

A curious position held by a few Christian thinkers is that although no logically flawless demonstration of God's existence has yet been formulated, one may believe by faith that such a formulation is possible. The scriptural authority for this, quoted endlessly by medieval theologians, is Saint Paul's statement: 'For the invisible things of him from the creation of the world are clearly seen, being understood by the things that are made, even his eternal power and Godhead. ...' (Romans 1: 20) 'It may be that there are true demonstrations,' wrote Blaise Pascal in his *Pensées*, 'but it is not certain. Thus this proves nothing but that it is not certain that all is uncertain, to the glory of skepticism.' Kant, near the end of his *Critique of Pure Reason*, attributes the hope for a perfect proof to 'certain excellent and thoughtful men,' including his Swiss contemporary, the philosopher Johann Georg Sulzer, who wrote mainly about aesthetics. Kant adds, 'I am certain that this will never happen.'

In spite of Pascal's doubts and Kant's certainty, the hope for a valid proof of God, not yet devised, continues to haunt Mortimer Adler. Back in the thirties, when Adler was teaching at the University of Chicago, he believed so firmly in all five of Aquinas's proofs of God that he made strenuous efforts to persuade his students to accept them. Then he began to have doubts. They were first expressed in technical detail in an article on 'The Demonstration of God's Existence' in a *Festschrift* issue of *The Thomist* (January 1943) honoring his friend Jacques Maritain. In this paper Adler argued that all five proofs are seriously flawed. He tried to outline a valid proof that had the form: If things exist, God exists: things exist, therefore God exists. Kant put it this way in his *Critique of Pure Reason*: 'If anything exists, an absolutely necessary being must also exist. Now I, at least, exist. Therefore an absolutely necessary being exists.'

Unfortunately, as Adler says in his autobiography *Philosopher at Large* (1977): 'The demonstration, I admitted, left a number of difficulties still to be resolved. This amounted to saying that although God's existence might be demonstrated in the future, it had not yet been accomplished. ...'

Adler's criticism of Aquinas provoked vigorous adverse reactions among Thomists. 'My greatest disappointment,' Adler tells us, 'occurred when I learned that I had even failed to make any headway in changing Maritain's mind on the subject.' Indeed, in his book *Approaches to God*, Maritain warns against Adler's viewpoint.

Adler is still searching for the elusive proof. In *How to Think About God* he repeats the usual objections to the traditional arguments, finding all the arguments invalid. Then in chapter 14 he defends what he calls a 'truly cosmological argument' that goes as follows. If the cosmos as a whole needs to be explained, and if it can't be explained by natural causes, then God must have caused it. The second *if* is the troublesome one. In his next chapter Adler argues that the second premise is the same as saying it is impossible for the cosmos to cease to exist and be replaced by nothingness. According to Adler, our cosmos is one of many possible worlds; hence it is possible for it not to exist. Because it does exist, we must assume either that God created it out of nothing (in which case God exists) or that the world has always existed. In the latter case Adler gives his reasons for believing that the continued existence of the cosmos requires God as a 'preservative cause.' He admits his argument does not furnish certitude that God exists, but he thinks it establishes God's existence either 'beyond a reasonable doubt,' or at least it shows that there is a 'preponderance of reasons' for believing God exists.

The God that Adler thinks he has established as probable is, Adler recognizes, only an impersonal abstraction, not a God to whom one can pray. The argument tells us nothing about whether God cares about us, or will provide us with life after death. These are among those beliefs that demand, Adler says, the leap of faith.

I find it depressing that Adler's long 'dogmatic slumber,' as Kant described his own earlier thinking about the proofs before Hume awakened him, and his admiration for Étienne Gilson (to whose memory *How to Think About God* is dedicated), still hold Adler back from the simple step to fideism that would dissolve his difficulties. Even among Roman Catholic thinkers, increasing numbers no longer feel obliged to establish God's existence even by probable reasoning, or to hope that some day a flawless proof will come to light.

For Kierkegaard, whose fideism so strongly influenced Barth and Unamuno and Heidegger, the desire to find rational evidence for God betrays a weakness of faith. In his *Concluding Unscientific Postscript*, Kierkegaard draws a parallel with a young woman who is so unsure of her love for a man that she keeps trying to find remarkable traits in him that will revive her fading emotion. Is it not an insult to God, Kierkegaard asks, to try to prove him? Is it not like standing in the presence of a mighty king and demanding irrefutable evidence that he exists?

Atheists will, of course, find all this absurd. But those who make the leap of faith are not only certain of God's existence, they see all Nature as a manifestation of God even though God remains invisible. They 'prove' God inwardly, writes Kierkegaard, through worship and prayer and submission to God's will. To all those who demand logical proofs or physical wonders, God 'craftily' hides himself. 'A poor wretch of an author, whom a later investigator drags out of the obscurity of oblivion may indeed be very glad that the investigator succeeds in proving his existence – but an omnipresent being can only by a thinker's pious blundering be brought to this ridiculous embarrassment.' The most interesting references in the bibliography at the back of Adler's book are the books not there.

Apparently he has been totally uninfluenced by any of the great Jewish, Christian, or philosophical fideists.

The hope for a valid proof of God strikes me as strangely similar to Bertrand Russell's youthful hope that someday he, or someone else, would discover a logical justification for induction. In his last great book, *Human Knowledge, Its Scope and Limits*, Russell abandoned this hope for the view that induction can be justified only by making certain posits about the structure of the external world. Put simply, induction works because the world is what it is. John Stuart Mill said essentially the same thing. Induction works because nature is orderly. Naturally we learn about the world's order only by induction, but Russell finally concluded that this is not a vicious circle, and he tried to go beyond Mill by specifying a minimum set of posits about nature's structure that would permit induction to work as well as it obviously does.

To my way of thinking, the hope for a logical justification of God's existence is as futile as the hope for a logical justification of induction. With respect to both questions, I believe only pragmatic answers can be given. Is it not the height of human pride and folly to suppose that our finite little brains can construct a proof that the world must be built just the way it is, or a proof that there must be a God who built it?

One way of justifying induction pragmatically was put forth by Hans Reichenbach. If there is any way at all to learn something about the structure of the world, that way is by induction; hence induction is justified. One could similarly argue that if there is a God who has chosen to be indemonstrable by either reason or science, then if we are to know God at all, it can only be through faith.

Please do not suppose from these remarks that I wish to defend an argument, often employed by theists, that a scientist's belief in an ordered world is comparable to a believer's faith in God. The popular American Baptist preacher Harry Emerson Fosdick put it this way in his book *Adventurous Religion* (1926):

> I am sure that the faith by which one thus orders and unifies his spiritual world, although it is more difficult of demonstration, is essentially the same kind of faith as that by which the scientist in his realm is conquering chaos.

The same point has been elaborated by innumerable philosophers. Josiah Royce, for instance, wrote in chapter 9 of *The Religious Aspect of Philosophy* (1885):

> To make the parallel a little clearer, we may say that science postulates the truth of the description of the world that, among all the possible descriptions, at once includes the given phenomena and

attains the greatest simplicity: while religion assumes the truth of the description of the world that, without falsifying the given facts, arouses the highest moral interest and satisfies the highest moral needs.

All this has often been said, but it has not always been clearly enough joined with the practical suggestion that if one gives up one of these two faiths, he ought consistently to give up the other. If one is weary of the religious postulates, let him by all means throw them aside. But if he does this, why does he not throw aside the scientific postulates, and give up insisting upon it that the world is and must be rational?

In his article on faith in the *Encyclopedia Britannica* (fourteenth edition), the Cambridge philosopher Frederick Robert Tennant draws the same parallel between the faith of a theist and the faith of a scientist. Induction, he writes, rests on 'human hope, sanguine expectation, faith in the unseen. ... Our very rationality of the world, which science would read and expound, is at bottom an idea of faith.' Tennant puts it even more preposterously in his masterwork, *Philosophical Theology* (1928): 'The electron and God are equally ideal positings of faith-venture, rationally indemonstrable, invisible; and the 'verifications' of the one idea, and of the other, follow lines essentially identical. ...' Even William James, in his essay on 'The Sentiment of Rationality,' favors the same inept analogy.

Is not the flaw obvious? There may well be no purely rational demonstration that induction must always work, but the patterns we find in nature are so strongly confirmed that we cannot disregard them without risking our lives. The quickest way to get from a high floor to the street is to jump out a window, but our 'faith' in the laws of gravity and the fragility of our bodies make this an irrational act for anyone who cares to stay alive. On the other hand, an atheist gets along quite well, thank you, without believing in God. It only obscures the nature of faith to liken it to the inescapable necessity of believing in causal laws.

We know what it means to say induction works. What does it mean to say that belief in God works? To fideists it can mean only this – that belief in God is so emotionally rewarding, and the contrary belief so desolate, they cannot not believe. Beneath the *credo quia absurdum*, as Unamuno said, is the *credo quia consolans*. I believe because it consoles me. The true water of life, says our Spanish brother, is that which assuages our thirst.

7

Evil and omnipotence

J. L. Mackie

There is no greater challenge to belief in the existence of an all-powerful benevolent God than the Problem of Evil. How could such a God tolerate the widespread evil that exists in the world? Such a God would know that evil occurs, must be able to prevent it, and surely wants to eradicate it. Yet evil continues to occur. J. L. Mackie (1917–81) sees the problem as one of logic: those who believe in such a God and in the existence of evil have inconsistent beliefs. Here he demonstrates the nature of this inconsistency and the failings of traditional theodicies (attempts to explain the existence of evil within a theistic framework). For an attempt to meet this challenge, see the reading following this one, 'Why God allows evil'.

From *The Philosophy of Religion*, edited by Basil Mitchell

The traditional arguments for the existence of God have been fairly thoroughly criticized by philosophers. But the theologian can, if he wishes, accept this criticism. He can admit that no rational proof of God's existence is possible. And he can still retain all that is essential to his position, by holding that God's existence is known in some other, non-rational way. I think, however, that a more telling criticism can be made by way of the traditional problem of evil. Here it can be shown, not that religious beliefs lack rational support, but that they are positively irrational, that the several parts of the essential theological doctrine are inconsistent with one another, so that the theologian can maintain his position as a whole only by a much more extreme rejection of reason than in the former case. He must now be prepared to believe, not merely what cannot be proved, but what can be *disproved* from other beliefs that he also holds.

    The problem of evil, in the sense in which I shall be using the phrase, is a problem only for someone who believes that there is a God who is both omnipotent and wholly good. And it is a logical problem, the problem of clarifying and reconciling a number of beliefs: it is not a scientific problem that might be solved by further observations, or a practical problem that might be solved by a decision or an action. These points are obvious; I mention them only because they are sometimes ignored by theologians, who sometimes parry a statement of the problem with such remarks as 'Well, can you solve the problem yourself?' or 'This is a mystery which may be revealed to us later' or 'Evil is something to be faced and overcome, not to be merely discussed.'

In its simplest form the problem is this: God is omnipotent; God is wholly good; and yet evil exists. There seems to be some contradiction between these three propositions, so that if any two of them were true the third would be false. But at the same time all three are essential parts of most theological positions: the theologian, it seems, at once *must* adhere and *cannot consistently* adhere to all three. (The problem does not arise only for theists, but I shall discuss it in the form in which it presents itself for ordinary theism.)

However, the contradiction does not arise immediately; to show it we need some additional premises, or perhaps some quasi-logical rules connecting the terms 'good', 'evil', and 'omnipotent'. These additional principles are that good is opposed to evil, in such a way that a good thing always eliminates evil as far as it can, and that there are no limits to what an omnipotent thing can do. From these it follows that a good omnipotent thing eliminates evil completely, and then the propositions that a good omnipotent thing exists, and that evil exists, are incompatible.

A. Adequate solutions

Now once the problem is fully stated it is clear that it can be solved, in the sense that the problem will not arise if one gives up at least one of the propositions that constitute it. If you are prepared to say that God is not wholly good, or not quite omnipotent, or that evil does not exist, or that good is not opposed to the kind of evil that exists, or that there are limits to what an omnipotent thing can do, then the problem of evil will not arise for you.

There are, then, quite a number of adequate solutions of the problem of evil, and some of these have been adopted, or almost adopted, by various thinkers. For example, a few have been prepared to deny God's omnipotence, and rather more have been prepared to keep the term 'omnipotence' but severely to restrict its meaning, recording quite a number of things that an omnipotent being cannot do. Some have said that evil is an illusion, perhaps because they held that the whole world of temporal, changing things is an illusion, and that what we call evil belongs only to this world, or perhaps because they held that although temporal things *are* much as we see them, those that we call evil are not really evil. Some have said that what we call evil is merely the privation of good, that evil in a positive sense, evil that would really be opposed to good, does not exist. Many have agreed with Pope that disorder is harmony not understood, and that partial evil is universal good. Whether any of these views is *true* is, of course, another question. But each of them gives an adequate solution of the problem of evil in the sense that if you accept it this problem does not arise for you, though you may, of course, have *other* problems to face.

But often enough these adequate solutions are only *almost* adopted. The thinkers who restrict God's power, but keep the term 'omnipotence', may reasonably be suspected of thinking, in other contexts, that his power is really unlimited. Those who say that evil is an illusion may also be thinking, inconsistently, that this illusion is itself an evil. Those who say that 'evil' is merely privation of good may also be thinking, inconsistently, that privation of good is an evil. (The fallacy here is akin to some forms of the 'naturalistic fallacy' in ethics, where some think, for example, that 'good' is just what contributes to evolutionary progress, and that evolutionary progress is itself good.) If Pope meant what he said in the first line of his couplet, that 'disorder' is only harmony not understood, the 'partial evil' of the second line must, for consistency, mean 'that which, taken in isolation, falsely appears to be evil', but it would more naturally mean 'that which, in isolation, really is evil'. The second line, in fact, hesitates between two views, that 'partial evil' isn't really evil, since only the universal quality is real, and that 'partial evil' is really an evil, but only a little one.

In addition, therefore, to adequate solutions, we must recognize unsatisfactory inconsistent solutions, in which there is only a half-hearted or temporary rejection of one of the propositions which together constitute the problem. In these, one of the constituent propositions is explicitly rejected, but it is covertly re-asserted or assumed elsewhere in the system.

B. Fallacious solutions

Besides these half-hearted solutions, which explicitly reject but implicitly assert one of the constituent propositions, there are definitely fallacious solutions which explicitly maintain all the constituent propositions, but implicitly reject at least one of them in the course of the argument that explains away the problem of evil.

There are, in fact, many so-called solutions which purport to remove the contradiction without abandoning any of its constituent propositions. These must be fallacious, as we can see from the very statement of the problem, but it is not so easy to see in each case precisely where the fallacy lies. I suggest that in all cases the fallacy has the general form suggested above: in order to solve the problem one (or perhaps more) of its constituent propositions is given up, but in such a way that it appears to have been retained, and can therefore be asserted without qualification in other contexts. Sometimes there is a further complication: the supposed solution moves to and fro between, say, two of the constituent propositions, at one point asserting the first of these but covertly abandoning the second, at another point asserting the second but covertly abandoning the first. These fallacious solutions often turn upon some equivocation with the words 'good' and 'evil', or upon some vagueness about the way in which good and evil are opposed to one another, or about how much is meant by 'omnipotence'. I propose to examine some of these so-called solutions, and to exhibit their fallacies in detail. Incidentally, I shall also be considering whether an adequate solution could be reached by a minor modification of one or more of the constituent propositions, which would, however, still satisfy all the essential requirements of ordinary theism.

1. 'Good cannot exist without evil' or 'Evil is necessary as a counterpart to good.'

It is sometimes suggested that evil is necessary as a counterpart to good, that if there were no evil there could be no good either, and that this solves the problem of evil. It is true that it points to an answer to the question 'Why should there be evil?' But it does so only by qualifying some of the propositions that constitute the problem.

First, it sets a limit to what God can do, saying that God *cannot* create good without simultaneously creating evil, and this means either that God is not omnipotent or that there are *some* limits to what an omnipotent thing can do. It may be replied that these limits are always presupposed, that omnipotence has never meant the power to do what is logically impossible, and on the present view the existence of good without evil would be a logical impossibility. This interpretation of omnipotence may, indeed, be accepted as a modification of our original account which does not reject anything that is essential to theism, and I shall in general assume it in the subsequent discussion. It is, perhaps, the most common theistic view, but I think that some theists at least have maintained that God can do what is logically impossible. Many theists, at any rate, have held that logic itself is created or laid down by God, that logic is the way in which God arbitrarily chooses to think. (This is, of course, parallel to the ethical view that morally right actions are those which God arbitrarily chooses to command, and the two views encounter similar difficulties.) And *this* account of logic is clearly inconsistent with the view that God is bound by logical necessities – unless it is possible for an omnipotent being to bind himself, an issue which we shall consider later, when we come to the Paradox of Omnipotence. This solution of the problem of evil cannot, therefore, be consistently adopted along with the view that logic is itself created by God.

But secondly, this solution denies that evil is opposed to good in our original sense. If good and evil are counterparts, a good thing will not 'eliminate evil as far as it can'. Indeed, this view suggests that good and evil are not strictly qualities of things at all. Perhaps the suggestion is that good and evil are related in much the same way as great and small. Certainly, when the term 'great' is used relatively as a condensation of 'greater than so-and-so', and 'small' is used correspondingly, greatness and smallness are counterparts and cannot exist without each other. But in this sense greatness is not a quality, not an intrinsic feature of anything; and it would be absurd to think of a movement in favour of greatness and against smallness in this sense. Such a movement would be self-defeating, since relative greatness can be promoted only by a simultaneous promotion of relative smallness. I feel sure that no theists would be content to regard God's goodness as analogous to this – as if what he supports were not the *good* but the *better*, and as if he had the paradoxical aim that all things should be better than other things.

This point is obscured by the fact that 'great' and 'small' seem to have an absolute as well as a relative sense. I cannot discuss here whether there is absolute magnitude or not, but if there is, there could be an absolute sense for 'great', it could mean of at least a certain size, and it would make sense to speak of all things getting bigger, of a universe that was expanding all over, and therefore it would make sense to speak of promoting greatness. But in *this* sense great and small are not logically necessary counterparts: either quality could exist without the other. There would be no logical impossibility in everything's being small or in everything's being great.

Neither in the absolute nor in the relative sense, then, of 'great' and 'small' do these terms provide an analogy of the sort that would be needed to support this solution of the problem of evil. In neither case are greatness and smallness *both* necessary counterparts *and* mutually opposed forces or possible objects for support or attack.

It may be replied that good and evil are necessary counterparts in the same way as any quality and its logical opposite: redness can occur, it is suggested, only if non-redness also occurs. But unless evil is merely the privation of good, they are not logical opposites, and some further argument would be needed to show that they are counterparts in the same way as genuine logical opposites. Let us assume that this could be given. There is still doubt of the correctness of the metaphysical principle that a quality must have a real opposite: I suggest that it is not really impossible that everything should be, say, red, that the truth is merely that if everything were red we should not notice redness, and so we should have no word 'red'; we observe and give names to qualities only if they have real opposites. If so, the principle that a term must have an opposite would belong only to our language or to our thought, and would not be an onto-logical principle, and, correspondingly, the rule that good cannot exist without evil would not state a logical necessity of a sort that God would just have to put up with. God might have made everything good, though *we* should not have noticed it if he had.

But, finally, even if we concede that this *is* an ontological principle, it will provide a solution for the problem of evil only if one is prepared to say, 'Evil exists, but only just enough evil to serve as the counterpart of good.' I doubt whether any theist will accept this. After all, the *onto-logical* requirement that non-redness should occur would be satisfied even if all the universe, except for a minute speck, were red, and, if there were a corresponding requirement for evil as a counterpart to good, a minute dose of evil would presumably do. But theists are not usually willing to say, in all contexts, that all the evil that occurs is a minute and necessary dose.

2. 'Evil is necessary as a means to good.'

It is sometimes suggested that evil is necessary for good not as a coun-terpart but as a means. In its simple form this has little plausibility as a solution of the problem of evil, since it obviously implies a severe restric-tion of God's power. It would be a *causal* law that you cannot have a certain end without a certain means, so that if God has to introduce evil as a means to good, he must be subject to at least some causal laws. This certainly conflicts with what a theist normally means by omnipotence. This view of God as limited by causal laws also conflicts with the view that causal laws are themselves made by God, which is more widely held than the corresponding view about the laws of logic. This conflict would, indeed, be resolved if it were possible for an omnipotent being to bind himself, and this possibility has still to be considered. Unless a favourable answer can be given to this question, the suggestion that evil is necessary as a means to good solves the problem of evil only by denying one of its constituent propositions, either that God is omnipotent or that 'omnipo-tent' means what it says.

3. 'The universe is better with some evil in it than it could be if there were no evil.'

Much more important is a solution which at first seems to be a mere variant of the previous one, that evil may contribute to the goodness of a whole in which it is found, so that the universe as a whole is better as it is, with some evil in it, than it would be if there were no evil. This solution may be developed in either of two ways. It may be supported by an aesthetic analogy, by the fact that contrasts heighten beauty, that in a musical work, for example, there may occur discords which somehow add to the beauty of the work as a whole. Alternatively, it may be worked out in connection with the notion of progress, that the best possible organization of the universe will not be static, but progressive, that the gradual overcoming of evil by good is really a finer thing than would be the eternal unchallenged supremacy of good.

In either case, this solution usually starts from the assumption that the evil whose existence gives rise to the problem of evil is primarily what is called physical evil, that is to say, pain. In Hume's rather half-hearted presentation of the problem of evil, the evils that he stresses are pain and disease, and those who reply to him argue that the existence of pain and disease make possible the existence of sympathy, benevolence, heroism, and the gradually successful struggle of doctors and reformers to overcome these evils. In fact, theists often seize the opportunity to accuse those who stress the problem of evil of taking a low, materialistic view of good and evil, equating these with pleasure and pain, and of ignoring the more spiritual goods which can arise in the struggle against evils.

But let us see exactly what is being done here. Let us call pain and misery 'first order evil' or 'evil (1)'. What contrasts with this, namely, pleasure and happiness, will be called 'first order good' or 'good (1)'. Distinct from this is 'second order good' or 'good (2)' which somehow emerges in a complex situation in which evil (1) is a necessary component – logically, not merely causally, necessary. (Exactly *how* it emerges does not matter: in the crudest version of this solution good (2) is simply the heightening of happiness by the contrast with misery, in other versions it includes sympathy with suffering, heroism in facing danger, and the gradual decrease of first order evil and increase of first order good.) It is also being assumed that second order good is more important than first order good or evil, in particular that it more than outweighs the first order evil it involves.

Now this is a particularly subtle attempt to solve the problem of evil. It defends God's goodness and omnipotence on the ground that (on a sufficiently long view) this is the best of all logically possible worlds, because it includes the important second order goods, and yet it admits that real evils, namely first order evils, exist. But does it still hold that good and evil are opposed? Not, clearly, in the sense that we set out originally: good does not tend to eliminate evil in general. Instead, we have a modified, a more complex pattern. First order good (e.g. happiness) *contrasts with* first order evil (e.g. misery): these two are opposed in a fairly mechanical way; some second order goods (e.g. benevolence) try to maximize first order good and minimise first order evil; but God's goodness is not this, it is rather the will to maximize *second* order good. We might, therefore, call

God's goodness an example of a third order goodness, or good (3). While this account is different from our original one, it might well be held to be an improvement on it, to give a more accurate description of the way in which good is opposed to evil, and to be consistent with the essential theist position.

There might, however, be several objections to this solution.

First, some might argue that such qualities as benevolence – and *a fortiori* the third order goodness which promotes benevolence – have a merely derivative value, that they are not higher sorts of good, but merely means to good (1), that is, to happiness, so that it would be absurd for God to keep misery in existence in order to make possible the virtues of benevolence, heroism, etc. The theist who adopts the present solution must, of course, deny this, but he can do so with some plausibility, so I should not press this objection.

Secondly, it follows from this solution that God is not in our sense benevolent or sympathetic: he is not concerned to minimize evil (1), but only to promote good (2), and this might be a disturbing conclusion for some theists.

But, thirdly, the fatal objection is this. Our analysis shows clearly the possibility of the existence of a *second* order evil, an evil (2) contrasting with good (2) as evil (1) contrasts with good (1). This would include malevolence, cruelty, callousness, cowardice, and states in which good (1) is decreasing and evil (1) increasing. And just as good (2) is held to be the important kind of good, the kind that God is concerned to promote, so evil (2) will, by analogy, be the important kind of evil, the kind which God, if he were wholly good and omnipotent, would eliminate. And yet evil (2) plainly exists, and indeed most theists (in other contexts) stress its existence more than that of evil (1). We should, therefore, state the problem of evil in terms of second order evil, and against this form of the problem the present solution is useless.

An attempt might be made to use this solution again, at a higher level, to explain the occurrence of evil (2): indeed the next main solution that we shall examine does just this, with the help of some new notions. Without any fresh notions, such a solution would have little plausibility: for example, we could hardly say that the really important good was a good (3), such as the increase of benevolence in proportion to cruelty, which logically required for its occurrence the occurrence of some second order evil. But even if evil (2) could be explained in this way, it is fairly clear that there would be third order evils contrasting with this third order good: and we should be well on the way to an infinite regress, where the solution of a problem of evil, stated in terms of evil (n), indicated the existence of an evil ($n + 1$), and a further problem to be solved.

4. 'Evil is due to human free will.'

Perhaps the most important proposed solution of the problem of evil is that evil is not to be ascribed to God at all, but to the independent actions of human beings, supposed to have been endowed by God with freedom of the will. This solution may be combined with the preceding one: first order evil (e.g. pain) may be justified as a logically necessary component in second order good (e.g. sympathy) while second order evil (e.g. cruelty) is not *justified*, but is so ascribed to human beings that God cannot be held responsible for it. This combination evades my third criticism of the preceding solution.

The free will solution also involves the preceding solution at a higher level. To explain why a wholly good God gave men free will although it would lead to some important evils, it must be argued that it is better on the whole that men should act freely, and sometimes err, than that they should be innocent automata, acting rightly in a wholly determined way. Freedom, that is to say, is now treated as a third order good, and as being more valuable than second order goods (such as sympathy and heroism) would be if they were deterministically produced, and it is being assumed that second order evils, such as cruelty, are logically necessary accompaniments of freedom, just as pain is a logically necessary pre-condition of sympathy.

I think that this solution is unsatisfactory primarily because of the incoherence of the notion of freedom of the will: but I cannot discuss this topic adequately here, although some of my criticism will touch upon it.

First I should query the assumption that second order evils are logically necessary accompaniments of freedom. I should ask this: if God has made men such that in their free choices they sometimes prefer what is good and sometimes what is evil, why could he not have made men such that they always freely choose the good? If there is no logical impossibility in a man's freely choosing the good on one, or on several occasions, there cannot be a logical impossibility in his freely choosing the good on every occasion. God was not, then, faced with a choice between making innocent automata and making beings who, in acting freely, would sometimes go wrong: there was open to him the obviously better possibility of making beings who would act freely but always go right. Clearly, his failure to avail himself of this possibility is inconsistent with his being both omnipotent and wholly good.

If it is replied that this objection is absurd, that the making of some wrong choices is logically necessary for freedom, it would seem that 'freedom' must here mean complete randomness or indeterminacy, including randomness with regard to the alternatives good and evil, in other words that men's choices and consequent actions can be 'free' only if they are not determined by their characters. Only on this assumption can God escape the responsibility for men's actions; for if he made them as they are, but did not determine their wrong choices, this can only be because the wrong choices are not determined by men as they are. But then if freedom is randomness, how can it be a characteristic of *will*? And, still more, how can it be the most important good? What value or merit would there be in free choices if these were random actions which were not determined by the nature of the agent?

I conclude that to make this solution plausible two different senses of 'freedom' must be confused, one sense which will justify the view that freedom is a third order good, more valuable than other goods would be without it, and another sense, sheer randomness, to prevent us from ascribing to God a decision to make men such that they sometimes go wrong when he might have made them such that they would always freely go right.

This criticism is sufficient to dispose of this solution. But besides this there is a fundamental difficulty in the notion of an omnipotent God creating men with free will, for if men's wills are really free this must mean that even God cannot control them, that is, that God is no longer omnipotent. It may be objected that God's gift of freedom to men does not mean that he *cannot* control their wills, but that he always *refrains* from controlling their wills. But why, we may ask, should God refrain from controlling evil wills? Why should he not leave men free to will rightly, but intervene when he sees them beginning to will wrongly? If God could do this, but does not, and if he is wholly good, the only explanation could be that even a wrong free act of will is not really evil, that its freedom is a value which outweighs its wrongness, so that there would be a loss of value if God took away the wrongness and the freedom together. But this is utterly opposed to what theists say about sin in other contexts. The present solution of the problem of evil, then, can be maintained only in the form that God has made men so free that he *cannot* control their wills.

This leads us to what I call the Paradox of Omnipotence: can an omnipotent being make things which he cannot subsequently control? Or, what is practically equivalent to this, can an omnipotent being make rules which then bind himself? (These are practically equivalent because any such rules could be regarded as setting certain things beyond his control and *vice versa*.) The second of these formulations is relevant to the suggestions that we have already met, that an omnipotent God creates the rules of logic or causal laws, and is then bound by them.

It is clear that this is a paradox: the questions cannot be answered satisfactorily either in the affirmative or in the negative. If we answer 'Yes', it follows that if God actually makes things which he cannot control, or makes rules which bind himself, he is not omnipotent once he has made them: there are *then* things which he cannot do. But if we answer 'No', we are immediately asserting that there are things which he cannot do, that is to say that he is already not omnipotent.

It cannot be replied that the question which sets this paradox is not a proper question. It would make perfectly good sense to say that a human mechanic has made a machine which he cannot control: if there is any difficulty about the question it lies in the notion of omnipotence itself.

This, incidentally, shows that although we have approached this paradox from the free will theory, it is equally a problem for a theological determinist. No one thinks that machines have free will, yet they may well be beyond the control of their makers. The determinist might reply that anyone who makes anything determines its ways of acting, and so determines its subsequent behaviour: even the human mechanic does this by his *choice* of materials and structure for his machine, though he does not know all about either of these: the mechanic thus determines, though he may not foresee, his machine's actions. And since God is omniscient, and since his creation of things is total, he both determines and foresees the ways in which his creatures will act. We may grant this, but it is beside the point. The question is not whether God *originally* determined the future actions of his creatures, but whether he can *subsequently* control their actions, or whether he was able in his original creation to put things beyond his subsequent control. Even on determinist principles the answers 'Yes' and 'No' are equally irreconcilable with God's omnipotence.

Before suggesting a solution of this paradox, I would point out that there is a parallel Paradox of Sovereignty. Can a legal sovereign make a law restricting its own future legislative power? For example, could the British parliament make a law forbidding any future parliament to socialize banking, and also forbidding the future repeal of this law itself? Or could the British parliament, which was legally sovereign in Australia in, say, 1899, pass a valid law, or series of laws, which made it no longer sovereign in 1933? Again, neither the affirmative nor the negative answer is really satisfactory. If we were to answer 'Yes', we should be admitting the validity of a law which, if it were actually made, would mean that parliament was no longer sovereign. If we were to answer 'No', we should be admitting that there is a law, not logically absurd, which parliament cannot validly make, that is, that parliament is not now a legal sovereign. This paradox can be solved in the following way. We should distinguish between first order laws, that is laws governing the actions of individuals and bodies other than the legislature, and second order laws, that is laws about laws, laws governing the actions of the legislature itself. Correspondingly, we should distinguish between two orders of sovereignty, first order sovereignty (sovereignty (1)) which is unlimited authority to make first order laws, and second order sovereignty (sovereignty (2)) which is unlimited authority to make second order laws. If we say that parliament is sovereign we might mean that any parliament at any time has sovereignty (1), or we might mean that parliament has both sovereignty (1) and sovereignty (2) at present, but we cannot without contradiction mean both that the present parliament has sovereignty (2) and that every parliament at every time has sovereignty (1), for if the present parliament has sovereignty (2) it may use it to take away the sovereignty (1) of later parliaments. What the paradox shows is that we cannot ascribe to any continuing institution legal sovereignty in an inclusive sense.

The analogy between omnipotence and sovereignty shows that the paradox of omnipotence can be solved in a similar way. We must distinguish between first order omnipotence (omnipotence (1)), that is unlimited power to act, and second order omnipotence (omnipotence (2)), that is unlimited power to determine what powers to act things shall have. Then we could consistently say that God all the time has omnipotence (1), but if so no beings at any time have powers to act independently of God. Or we could say that God at one time had omnipotence (2), and used it to assign independent powers to act to certain things, so that God thereafter did not have omnipotence (1). But what the paradox shows is that we cannot consistently ascribe to any continuing being omnipotence in an inclusive sense.

An alternative solution to this paradox would be simply to deny that God is a continuing being, that any times can be assigned to his actions at all. But on this assumption (which also has difficulties of its own) no meaning can be given to the assertion that God made men with wills so free that he could not control them. The paradox of omnipotence can be avoided by putting God outside time, but the free will solution of the problem of evil cannot be saved in this way, and equally it remains impossible to hold that an omnipotent God *binds himself* by causal or logical laws.

Conclusion

Of the proposed solutions of the problem of evil which we have examined, none has stood up to criticism. There may be other solutions which require examination, but this study strongly suggests that there is no valid solution of the problem which does not modify at least one of the constituent propositions in a way which would seriously affect the essential core of the theistic position.

Quite apart from the problem of evil, the paradox of omnipotence has shown that God's omnipotence must in any case be restricted in one way or another, that unqualified omnipotence cannot be ascribed to any being that continues through time. And if God and his actions are not in time, can omnipotence, or power of any sort, be meaningfully ascribed to him?

8

Why God allows evil
Richard Swinburne

As its title suggests, this piece is an attempt to explain how a benevolent and all-powerful God could possibly tolerate evil. Richard Swinburne (1934–) presents a series of arguments intended to show that the presence of evil, both natural and moral, in no way counts as evidence against the existence of God. Swinburne's position is a direct response to the sorts of arguments used by J. L. Mackie in the previous reading.

From Richard Swinburne, *Is there a God?*

This world is a clearly providential world in this sense – that we humans can have a great influence on our own destiny, and on the destiny of our world and its other inhabitants; and it is very good for us that it is like that. And yet animals and humans suffer (through natural processes of disease and accident), and they cause each other to suffer (we hurt and maim each other and cause each other to starve). The world, that is, contains much evil. An omnipotent God could have prevented this evil, and surely a perfectly good and omnipotent God would have done so. So why is there this evil? Is not its existence strong evidence against the existence of God? It would be unless we can construct what is known as a theodicy, an explanation of why God would allow such evil to occur. I believe that that can be done, and I shall outline a theodicy in this chapter. I emphasize that in this chapter in writing that God would do this or that, I am not taking for granted the existence of God, but merely claiming that, if there is a God, it is to be expected that he would do certain things, including allowing the occurrence of certain evils; and so, I am claiming, their occurrence is not evidence against his existence. [. . .]

The problem of evil is not that of the absence of various good states. [. . .] however much good God creates, he could create more; and he does not in general have any obligation to create. That is why death is not in itself an evil; death is just the end of a good state, life (and in any case one of which God may choose to give us more – by giving us a life after death). Death may be an evil if it comes prematurely, or causes great grief to others; but in itself it is not an evil. But there are plenty of evils, positive bad states, which God could if he chose remove. I divide these into moral evils and natural evils. I understand by 'natural evil' all evil which is not deliberately produced by human beings and which is not allowed by human beings to occur as a result of their negligence. Natural evil includes both physical suffering and mental suffering, of animals as well as humans; all the trail of suffering which disease, natural disasters, and accidents unpredictable by humans bring in their train. 'Moral evil' I understand as including all evil caused deliberately by humans doing what they ought not to do (or allowed to occur by humans negligently failing to do what they ought to do) *and* also the evil constituted by such deliberate actions or negligent failure. It includes the sensory pain of the blow inflicted by the bad parent on his child, the mental pain of the parent depriving the child of love, the starvation allowed to occur in Africa because of negligence by members of foreign governments who could have prevented it, and also the evil of the parent or politician deliberately bringing about the pain or not trying to prevent the starvation.

Moral evil

The central core of any theodicy must, I believe, be the 'free-will defence', which deals – to start with – with moral evil, but can be extended to deal with much natural evil as well. The free-will defence claims that it is a great good that humans have a certain sort of free will which I shall call free and responsible choice, but that, if they do, then necessarily there will be the natural possibility of moral evil. (By the 'natural possibility' I mean that it will not be determined in advance whether or not the evil will occur.) A God who gives humans such free will necessarily brings about the possibility, and puts outside his own control whether or not that evil occurs. It is not logically possible – that is, it would be self-contradictory to suppose – that God could give us such free will and yet ensure that we always use it in the right way.

Free and responsible choice is not just free will in the narrow sense of being able to choose between alternative actions, without our choice being causally necessitated by some prior cause. I have urged ... that humans do have such free will. But humans could have that kind of free will merely in virtue of being able to choose freely between two equally good and unimportant alternatives. Free and responsible choice is rather free will (of the kind discussed) to make significant choices between good and evil, which make a big difference to the agent, to others, and to the world.

Given that we have free will, we certainly have free and responsible choice. Let us remind ourselves of the difference that humans can make to themselves, others, and the world. Humans have opportunities to give themselves and others pleasurable sensations, and to pursue worthwhile activities – to play tennis or the piano, to acquire knowledge of history and science and philosophy, and to help others to do so, and thereby to build deep personal relations founded upon such sensations and activities. And humans are so made that they can form their characters. Aristotle famously remarked: 'we become just by doing just acts, prudent by doing prudent acts, brave by doing brave acts.' That is, by doing a just act when it is difficult – when it goes against our natural inclinations (which is what I understand by desires) – we make it easier to do a just act next time. We can gradually change our desires, so that – for example – doing just acts becomes natural. Thereby we can free ourselves from the power of the less good desires to which we are subject. And, by choosing to acquire knowledge and to use it to build machines of various sorts, humans can extend the range of the differences they can make to the world; they can build universities to last for centuries, or save energy for the next generation; and by co-operative effort over many decades they can eliminate poverty. The possibilities for free and responsible choice are enormous.

It is good that the free choices of humans should include *genuine* responsibility for other humans, and that involves the opportunity to benefit *or* harm them. God has the power to benefit or to harm humans. If other agents are to be given a share in his creative work, it is good that they have that power too (although perhaps to a lesser degree). A world in which agents can benefit each other but not do each other harm is one where they have only very limited responsibility for each other. If my responsibility for you is limited to whether or not to give you a camcorder, but I cannot cause you pain, stunt your growth, or limit your education, then I do not have a great deal of responsibility for you. A God who gave agents only such limited responsibilities for their fellows would not have given much. God would have reserved for himself the all-important choice of the kind of world it was to be, while simply allowing humans the minor choice of filling in the details. He would be like a father asking his elder son to look after the younger son, and adding that he would be watching the elder son's every move and would intervene the moment the elder son did a thing wrong. The elder son might justly retort that, while he would be happy to share his father's work, he could really do so only if he were left to make his own judgements as to what to do within a significant range of the options available to the father. A good God, like a good father, will delegate responsibility. In order to allow creatures a share in creation, he will allow them the choice of hurting and maiming, of frustrating the divine plan. Our world is one where creatures have just such deep responsibility for each other. I can not only benefit my children, but harm them. One way in which I can harm is that I can inflict physical pain on them. But there are much more damaging things which I can do to them. Above all I can stop them growing into creatures with significant knowledge, power, and freedom; I can determine whether they come to have the kind of free and responsible choice which I have. The possibility of humans bringing about significant evil is a logical consequence of their having this free and responsible choice. Not even God could give us this choice without the possibility of resulting evil.

Now, [. . .] an action would not be intentional unless it was done for a reason – that is, seen as in some way a good thing (either in itself or because of its consequences). And, if reasons alone influence actions, that regarded by the subject as most important will determine what is done; an agent under the influence of reason alone will inevitably do the action which he regards as overall the best. If an agent does not do the action which he regards as overall the best, he must have allowed factors other than reason to exert an influence on him. In other words, he must have allowed desires for what he regards as good only in a certain respect, but not overall, to influence his conduct. So, in order to have a choice between good and evil, agents need already a certain depravity, in the sense of a system of desires for what they correctly believe to be evil. I need to *want* to overeat, get more than my fair share of money or power, indulge my sexual appetites even by deceiving my spouse or partner, want to see you hurt, if I am to have choice between good and evil. This depravity is itself an evil which is a necessary condition of a greater good. It makes possible a choice made seriously and deliberately, because made in the face of a genuine alternative. I stress that, according to the free-will defence, it is the natural possibility of moral evil which is the necessary condition of the great good, not the actual evil itself. Whether that occurs is (through God's choice) outside God's control and up to us.

Note further and crucially that, if I suffer in consequence of your freely chosen bad action, that is not by any means pure loss for me. In a certain respect it is a good for *me*. My suffering would be pure loss for me if the only good thing in life was sensory pleasure, and the only bad thing sensory pain; and it is because the modern world tends to think in those terms that the problem of evil seems so acute. If these were the only good and bad things, the occurrence of suffering would indeed be a conclusive objection to the existence of God. But we have already noted the great good of freely choosing and influencing our future, that of our fellows, and that of the world. And now note another great good – the good of our life serving a purpose, of being of use to ourselves and others. Recall the words of Christ, 'it is more blessed to give than to receive' (as quoted by St Paul (Acts 20: 35)). We tend to think, when the beggar appears on our doorstep and we feel obliged to give and do give, that that was lucky for him but not for us who happened to be at home. That is not what Christ's words say. They say that *we* are the lucky ones, not just because we have a lot, out of which we can give a little, but because we are privileged to contribute to the beggar's happiness – and that privilege is worth a lot more than money. And, just as it is a great good freely to choose to do good, so it is also a good to be used by someone else for a worthy purpose (so long, that is, that he or she has the right, the authority, to use us in this way). Being allowed to suffer to make possible a great good is a privilege, even if the privilege is forced upon you. Those who are allowed to die for their country and thereby save their country from foreign oppression are privileged. Cultures less obsessed than our own by the evil of purely physical pain have always recognized that. And they have recognized that it is still a blessing, even if the one who died had been conscripted to fight.

And even twentieth-century man can begin to see that – sometimes – when he seeks to help prisoners, not by giving them more comfortable quarters, but by letting them help the handicapped; or when he pities rather than envies the 'poor little rich girl' who has everything and does nothing for anyone else. And one phenomenon prevalent in end-of-century Britain draws this especially to our attention – the evil of unemployment. Because of our system of social security, the unemployed on the whole have enough money to live without too much discomfort; certainly they are a lot better off than are many employed in Africa or Asia or Victorian Britain. What is evil about unemployment is not so much any resulting poverty but the uselessness of the unemployed. They often report feeling unvalued by society, of no use, 'on the scrap heap'. They rightly think it would be a good for them to contribute; but they cannot. Many of them would welcome a system where they were obliged to do useful work in preference to one where society has no use for them.

It follows from that fact that being of use is a benefit for him who is of use, and that those who suffer at the hands of others, and thereby make possible the good of those others who have free and responsible choice, are themselves benefited in this respect. I am fortunate if the natural possibility of my suffering if you choose to hurt me is the vehicle which makes your choice really matter. My vulnerability, my openness to suffering (which necessarily involves my actually suffering if you make the wrong choice), means that you are not just like a pilot in a simulator, where it does not matter if mistakes are made. That our choices matter tremendously, that we can make great differences to things for good or ill, is one of the greatest gifts a creator can give us. And if my suffering is the means by which he can give you that choice, I too am in this respect fortunate. Though of course suffering is in itself a bad thing, my good fortune is that the suffering is not random, pointless suffering. It is suffering which is a consequence of my vulnerability which makes me of such use.

Someone may object that the only good thing is not *being* of use (dying for one's country or being vulnerable to suffering at your hands), but *believing* that one is of use – believing that one is dying for one's country and that this is of use; the 'feel-good' experience. But that cannot be correct. Having comforting beliefs is only a good thing if they are true beliefs. It is not a good thing to believe that things are going well when they are not, or that your life is of use when it is not. Getting pleasure out of a comforting falsehood is a cheat. But if I get pleasure out of a true belief, it must be that I regard the state of things which I believe to hold to be a good thing. If I get pleasure out of the true belief that my daughter is doing well at school, it must be that I regard it as a good thing that my daughter does well at school (whether or not I believe that she is doing well). If I did not think the latter, I would not get any pleasure out of believing that she is doing well. Likewise, the belief that I am vulnerable to suffering at your hands, and that that is a good thing, can only be a good thing if being vulnerable to suffering at your hands is itself a good thing (independently of whether I believe it or not). Certainly, when my life is of use and that is a good for me, it is even better if I believe it and get comfort therefrom; but it can only be even better if it is already a good for me whether I believe it or not.

But though suffering may in these ways serve good purposes, does God have the right to allow me to suffer for your benefit, without asking my permission? For surely, an objector will say, no one has the right to allow one person A to suffer for the benefit of another one B without A's consent. We judge that doctors who use patients as involuntary objects of experimentation in medical experiments which they hope will produce results which can be used to benefit others are doing something wrong. After all, if my arguments about the utility of suffering are sound, ought we not all to be causing suffering to others in order that those others may have the opportunity to react in the right way?

There are, however, crucial differences between God and the doctors. The first is that God as the author of our being has certain rights, a certain authority over us, which we do not have over our fellow humans. He is the cause of our existence at each moment of our existence and sustains the laws of nature which give us everything we are and have. To allow someone to suffer for his own good or that of others, one has to stand in some kind of parental relationship towards him. I do not have the right to let some stranger suffer for the sake of some good, when I could easily prevent this, but I do have *some* right of this kind in respect of my own children. I may let the younger son suffer *somewhat* for his own good or that of his brother. I have this right because in small part I am responsible for the younger son's existence, his beginning and continuance. If I have begotten him, nourished, and educated him, I have some limited rights over him in return; to a *very limited* extent I can use him for some worthy purpose. If this is correct, then a God who is so much more the author of our being than are our parents has so much more right in this respect. Doctors do have over us even the rights of parents.

But secondly and all-importantly, the doctors *could* have asked the patients for permission; and the patients, being free agents of some power and knowledge, could have made an informed choice of whether or not to allow themselves to be used. By contrast, God's choice is not about how to use already existing agents, but about the sort of agents to make and the sort of world into which to put them. In God's situation there are no agents to be asked. I am arguing that it is good that one agent A should have deep responsibility for another B (who in turn could have deep responsibility for another C). It is not logically possible for God to have asked B if he wanted things thus, for, if A is to be responsible for B's growth in freedom, knowledge, and power, there will not be a B with enough freedom and knowledge to make any choice, before God has to choose whether or not to give A responsibility for him. One cannot ask a baby into which sort of world he or she wishes to be born. The creator has to make the choice independently of his creatures. He will seek on balance to benefit them – all of them. And, in giving them the gift of life – whatever suffering goes with it – that is a substantial benefit. But when one suffers at the hands of another, often perhaps it is not enough of a benefit to outweigh the suffering. Here is the point to recall that it is an additional benefit to the sufferer that his suffering is the means whereby the one who hurt him had the opportunity to make a significant choice between good and evil which otherwise he would not have had.

Although for these reasons, as I have been urging, God has the right to allow humans to cause each other to suffer, there must be a limit to the amount of suffering which he has the right to allow a human being to suffer for the sake of a great good. A parent may allow an elder child to have the power to do some harm to a younger child for the sake of the responsibility given to the elder child; but there are limits. And there are limits even to the moral right of God, our creator and sustainer, to use free sentient beings as pawns in a greater game. Yet, if these limits were too narrow, God would be unable to give humans much real responsibility; he would be able to allow them only to play a toy game. Still, limits there must be to God's rights to allow humans to hurt each other; and limits there are in the world to the extent to which they can hurt each other, provided above all by the short finite life enjoyed by humans and other creatures – one human can hurt another for no more than eighty years or so. And there are a number of other safety-devices in-built into our physiology and psychology, limiting the amount of pain we can suffer. But the primary safety limit is that provided by the shortness of our finite life. Unending unchosen suffering would indeed to my mind provide a very strong argument against the existence of God. But that is not the human situation.

So then God, without asking humans, has to choose for them between the kinds of world in which they can live – basically either a world in which there is very little opportunity for humans to benefit or harm each other, or a world in which there is considerable opportunity. How shall he choose? There are clearly reasons for both choices. But it seems to me (just, on balance) that his choosing to create the world in which we have considerable opportunity to benefit or harm each other is to bring about a good at least as great as the evil which he thereby allows to occur. *Of course* the suffering he allows is a bad thing; and, other things being equal, to be avoided. But having the natural possibility of causing suffering makes possible a greater good. God, in creating humans who (of logical necessity) cannot choose for themselves the kind of world into which they are to come, plausibly exhibits his goodness in making for them the heroic choice that they come into a risky world where they may have to suffer for the good of others.

Natural evil

Natural evil is not to be accounted for along the same lines as moral evil. Its main role rather, I suggest, is to make it possible for humans to have the kind of choice which the free-will defence extols, and to make available to humans specially worthwhile kinds of choice.

There are two ways in which natural evil operates to give humans those choices. First, the operation of natural laws producing evils gives humans knowledge (if they choose to seek it) of how to bring about such evils themselves. Observing you catch some disease by the operation of natural processes gives me the power either to use those processes to give that disease to other people, or through negligence to allow others to catch it, or to take measures to prevent others from catching the disease. Study of the mechanisms of nature producing various evils (and goods) opens up for humans a wide range of choice. This is the way in which in fact we learn how to bring about (good and) evil. But could not God give us the requisite knowledge (of how to bring about good or evil) which we need in order to have free and responsible choice by a less costly means? Could he not just whisper in our ears from time to time what are the different consequences of different actions of ours? Yes. But anyone who believed that an action of his would have some effect because he believed that God had told him so would see all his actions as done under the all-watchful eye of God. He would not merely believe strongly that there was a God, but would know it with real certainty. That knowledge would greatly inhibit his freedom of choice, would make it very difficult for him to choose to do evil. This is because we all have a natural inclination to wish to be thought well of by everyone, and above all by an all-good God;

that we have such an inclination is a very good feature of humans, without which we would be less than human. Also, if we were directly informed of the consequences of our actions, we would be deprived of the choice whether to seek to discover what the consequences were through experiment and hard co-operative work. Knowledge would be available on tap. Natural processes alone give humans knowledge of the effects of their actions without inhibiting their freedom, and if evil is to be a possibility for them they must know how to allow it to occur.

The other way in which natural evil operates to give humans their freedom is that it makes possible certain kinds of action towards it between which agents can choose. It increases the range of significant choice. A particular natural evil, such as physical pain, gives to the sufferer a choice – whether to endure it with patience, or to bemoan his lot. His friend can choose whether to show compassion towards the sufferer, or to be callous. The pain makes possible these choices, which would not otherwise exist. There is no guarantee that our actions in response to the pain will be good ones, but the pain gives us the opportunity to perform good actions. The good or bad actions which we perform in the face of natural evil themselves provide opportunities for further choice – of good or evil stances towards the former actions. If I am patient with my suffering, you can choose whether to encourage or laugh at my patience; if I bemoan my lot, you can teach me by word and example what a good thing patience is. If you are sympathetic, I have then the opportunity to show gratitude for the sympathy; or to be so self-involved that I ignore it. If you are callous, I can choose whether to ignore this or to resent it for life. And so on. I do not think that there can be much doubt that natural evil, such as physical pain, makes available these sorts of choice. The actions which natural evil makes possible are ones which allow us to perform at our best and interact with our fellows at the deepest level.

It may, however, be suggested that adequate opportunity for these great good actions would be provided by the occurrence of moral evil without any need for suffering to be caused by natural processes. You can show courage when threatened by a gunman, as well as when threatened by cancer; and show sympathy to those likely to be killed by gunmen as well as to those likely to die of cancer. But just imagine all the suffering of mind and body caused by disease, earthquake, and accident unpreventable by humans removed at a stroke from our society. No sickness, no bereavement in consequence of the untimely death of the young. Many of us would then have such an easy life that we simply would not have much opportunity to show courage or, indeed, manifest much in the way of great goodness at all. We need those insidious processes of decay and dissolution which money and strength cannot ward off for long to give us the opportunities, so easy otherwise to avoid, to become heroes.

God has the right to allow natural evils to occur (for the same reason as he has the right to allow moral evils to occur) – up to a limit. It would, of course, be crazy for God to multiply evils more and more in order to give endless opportunity for heroism, but to have *some* significant opportunity for real heroism and consequent character formation is a benefit for the person to whom it is given. Natural evils give to us the knowledge to make a range of choices between good and evil, and the opportunity to perform actions of especially valuable kinds.

There is, however, no reason to suppose that animals have free will. So what about their suffering? Animals had been suffering for a long time before humans appeared on this planet – just how long depends on which animals are conscious beings. The first thing to take into account here is that, while the higher animals, at any rate the vertebrates, suffer, it is most unlikely that they suffer nearly as much as humans do. Given that suffering depends directly on brain events (in turn caused by events in other parts of the body), then, since the lower animals do not suffer at all and humans suffer a lot, animals of intermediate complexity (it is reasonable to suppose) suffer only a moderate amount. So, while one does need a theodicy to account for why God allows animals to suffer, one does not need as powerful a theodicy as one does in respect of humans. One only needs reasons adequate to account for God allowing an amount of suffering much less than that of humans. That said, there is, I believe, available for animals parts of the theodicy which I have outlined above for humans.

The good of animals, like that of humans, does not consist solely in thrills of pleasure. For animals, too, there are more worthwhile things, and in particular intentional actions, and among them serious significant intentional actions. The life of animals involves many serious significant intentional actions. Animals look for a mate, despite being tired and failing to find one. They take great trouble to build nests and feed their young, to decoy predators and explore. But all this inevitably involves pain (going on despite being tired) and danger. An animal cannot intentionally avoid forest fires, or take trouble to rescue its offspring from forest fires, unless there exists a serious danger of getting caught in a forest fire. The action of rescuing despite danger simply cannot be done unless the danger exists – and the danger will not exist unless there is a significant natural probability of being caught in the fire. Animals do not choose freely to do such actions, but the actions are nevertheless worthwhile. It is great that animals feed their young, not just themselves; that animals explore when they know it to be dangerous; that animals save each other from predators, and so on. These are the things that give the lives of animals their value. But they do often involve some suffering to some creature.

To return to the central case of humans – the reader will agree with me to the extent to which he or she values responsibility, free choice, and being of use very much more than thrills of pleasure or absence of pain.

There is no other way to get the evils of this world into the right perspective, except to reflect at length on innumerable very detailed thought experiments (in addition to actual experiences of life) in which we postulate very different sorts of worlds from our own, and then ask ourselves whether the perfect goodness of God would require him to create one of these (or no world at all) rather than our own. But I conclude with a very small thought experiment, which may help to begin this process. Suppose that you exist in another world before your birth in this one, and are given a choice as to the sort of life you are to have in this one. You are told that you are to have only a short life, maybe of only a few minutes, although it will be an adult life in the sense that you will have the richness of sensation and belief characteristic of adults. You have a choice as to the sort of life you will have. You can have either a few minutes of very considerable pleasure, of the kind produced by some drug such as heroin, which you will experience by yourself and which will have no effects at all in the world (for example, no one else will know about it); or you can have a few minutes of considerable pain, such as the pain of childbirth, which will have (unknown to you at the time of pain) considerable good effects on others over a few years. You are told that, if you do not make the second choice, those others will never exist – and so you are under no moral obligation to make the second choice. But you seek to make the choice which will make *your* own life the best life for *you* to have led. How will you choose? The choice is, I hope, obvious. You should choose the second alternative.

For someone who remains unconvinced by my claims about the relative strengths of the good and evils involved – holding that, great though the goods are, they do not justify the evils which they involve – there is a fall-back position. My arguments may have convinced you of the greatness of the goods involved sufficiently for you to allow that a perfectly good God would be justified in bringing about the evils for the sake of the good which they make possible, if and only if God also provided compensation in the form of happiness after death to the victims whose sufferings make possible the goods. Someone whose theodicy requires buttressing in this way will need an independent reason for believing that God does provide such life after death if he is to be justified in holding his theodicy. .... While believing that God does provide at any rate for many humans such life after death, I have expounded a theodicy without relying on this assumption. But I can understand someone thinking that the assumption is needed, especially when we are considering the worst evils. (This compensatory afterlife need not necessarily be the everlasting life of Heaven.)

It remains the case, however, that evil is evil, and there is a substantial price to pay for the goods of our world which it makes possible. God would not be less than perfectly good if he created instead a world without pain and suffering, and so without the particular goods which those evils make possible. Christian, Islamic, and much Jewish tradition claims that God has created worlds of both kinds – our world, and the Heaven of the blessed. The latter is a marvellous world with a vast range of possible deep goods, but it lacks a few goods which our world contains, including the good of being able to reject the good. A generous God might well choose to give some of us the choice of rejecting the good in a world like ours before giving to those who embrace it a wonderful world in which the former possibility no longer exists.

9

Of miracles
David Hume

Miracles are often cited as evidence in support of the idea that God exists, or even as conclusive proof that he or she does. Few of us witness miracles; we must instead rely on the testimony of those who do. They tell us about them, or write down, what they saw and we either believe them or are sceptical, looking for more plausible explanations of what happened. In the following essay, the great eighteenth-century philosopher David Hume (1711–76) presents an argument which leads to the conclusion that it is always more rational to doubt the truth of testimony of miracles than it is to believe it. One response to such a position, assuming that Hume is right, might be that at a certain point rational argument is useless: religion involves a leap of faith which is in a sense irrational.

From David Hume, *Enquiry Concerning Human Understanding*

_____

Part I

Though experience be our only guide in reasoning concerning matters of fact; it must be acknowledged, that this guide is not altogether infallible, but in some cases is apt to lead us into errors. One, who in our climate, should expect better weather in any week of June than in one of December, would reason justly, and conformably to experience; but it is certain, that he may happen, in the event, to find himself mistaken. However, we may observe, that, in such a case, he would have no cause to complain of experience; because it commonly informs us beforehand of the uncertainty, by that contrariety of events, which we may learn from a diligent observation. All effects follow not with like certainty from their supposed causes. Some events are found, in all countries and all ages, to have been constantly conjoined together: Others are found to have been more variable, and sometimes to disappoint our expectations; so that, in our reasonings concerning matter of fact, there are all imaginable degrees of assurance, from the highest certainty to the lowest species of moral evidence.

A wise man, therefore, proportions his belief to the evidence. In such conclusions as are founded on an infallible experience, he expects the event with the last degree of assurance, and regards his past experience as a full *proof* of the future existence of that event. In other cases; he proceeds with more caution: He weighs the opposite experiments: He considers which side is supported by the greater number of experiments: to that side he inclines, with doubt and hesitation; and when at last he fixes his judgement, the evidence exceeds not what we properly call *probability*. All probability, then, supposes an opposition of experiments and observations, where the one side is found to overbalance the other, and to produce a degree of evidence, proportioned to the superiority. A hundred instances or experiments on one side, and fifty on another, afford a doubtful expectation of any event; though a hundred uniform experiments, with only one that is contradictory, reasonably beget a pretty strong degree of assurance. In all cases, we must balance the opposite experiments, where they are opposite, and deduct the smaller number from the greater, in order to know the exact force of the superior evidence.

To apply these principles to a particular instance; we may observe, that there is no species of reasoning more common, more useful, and even necessary to human life, than that which is derived from the testimony of men, and the reports of eye-witnesses and spectators. This species of reasoning, perhaps, one may deny to be founded on the relation of cause and effect. I shall not dispute about a word. It will be sufficient to observe that our assurance in any argument of this kind is derived from no other principle than our observation of the veracity of human testimony, and of the usual conformity of facts to the reports of witnesses. It being a general maxim, that no objects have any discoverable connexion together, and that all the inferences, which we can draw from one to another, are founded merely on our experience of their constant and regular conjunction; it is evident, that we ought not to make an exception to this maxim in favour of human testimony, whose connexion with any event seems, in itself, as little necessary as any other. Were not the memory tenacious to a certain degree; had not men commonly an inclination to truth and a principle of probity; were they not sensible to shame, when detected in a falsehood: Were not these, I say, discovered by *experience* to be qualities, inherent in human nature, we should never repose the least confidence in human testimony. A man delirious, or noted for falsehood and villany, has no manner of authority with us.

And as the evidence, derived from witnesses and human testimony, is founded on past experience, so it varies with the experience, and is regarded either as a *proof* or a *probability*, according as the conjunction between any particular kind of report and any kind of object has been found to be constant or variable. There are a number of circumstances to be taken into consideration in all judgements of this kind; and the ultimate standard, by which we determine all disputes, that may arise concerning them, is always derived from experience and observation. Where this experience is not entirely uniform on any side, it is attended with an unavoidable contrariety in our judgements, and with the same opposition and mutual destruction of argument as in every other kind of evidence. We frequently hesitate concerning the reports of others. We balance the opposite circumstances, which cause any doubt or uncertainty; and when we discover a superiority on any side, we incline to it; but still with a diminution of assurance, in proportion to the force of its antagonist.

This contrariety of evidence, in the present case, may be derived from several different causes; from the opposition of contrary testimony; from the character or number of the witnesses; from the manner of their delivering their testimony; or from the union of all these circumstances. We entertain a suspicion concerning any matter of fact, when the witnesses contradict each other; when they are but few, or of a doubtful character; when they have an interest in what they affirm; when they deliver their testimony with hesitation, or on the contrary, with too violent asseverations. There are many other particulars of the same kind, which may diminish or destroy the force of any argument, derived from human testimony.

Suppose, for instance, that the fact, which the testimony endeavours to establish, partakes of the extraordinary and the marvellous; in that case, the evidence, resulting from the testimony, admits of a diminution, greater or less, in proportion as the fact is more or less unusual. The reason why we place any credit in witnesses and historians, is not derived from any *connexion*, which we perceive *a priori*, between testimony and reality, but because we are accustomed to find a conformity between them. But when the fact attested is such a one as has seldom fallen under our observation, here is a contest of two opposite experiences; of which the one destroys the other, as far as its force goes, and the superior can only operate on the mind by the force, which remains. The very same principle of experience, which gives us a certain degree of assurance in the testimony of witnesses, gives us also, in this case, another degree of assurance against the fact, which they endeavour to establish; from which contradiction there necessarily arises a counterpoize, and mutual destruction of belief and authority.

I should not believe such a story were it told me by Cato, was a proverbial saying in Rome, even during the lifetime of that philosophical patriot. The incredibility of a fact, it was allowed, might invalidate so great an authority.

The Indian prince, who refused to believe the first relations concerning the effects of frost, reasoned justly; and it naturally required very strong testimony to engage his assent to facts, that arose from a state of nature, with which he was unacquainted, and which bore so little analogy to those events, of which he had had constant and uniform experience. Though they were not contrary to his experience, they were not conformable to it.

But in order to encrease the probability against the testimony of witnesses, let us suppose, that the fact, which they affirm, instead of being only marvellous, is really miraculous; and suppose also, that the testimony considered apart and in itself, amounts to an entire proof; in that case, there is proof against proof, of which the strongest must prevail, but still with a diminution of its force, in proportion to that of its antagonist.

A miracle is a violation of the laws of nature; and as a firm and unalterable experience has established these laws, the proof against a miracle, from the very nature of the fact, is as entire as any argument from experience can possibly be imagined. Why is it more than probable, that all men must die; that lead cannot, of itself, remain suspended in the air; that fire consumes wood, and is extinguished by water; unless it be, that these events are found agreeable to the laws of nature, and there is required a violation of these laws, or in other words, a miracle to prevent them? Nothing is esteemed a miracle, if it ever happen in the common course of nature. It is no miracle that a man, seemingly in good health, should die on a sudden: because such a kind of death, though more unusual than any other, has yet been frequently observed to happen. But it is a miracle, that a dead man should come to life; because that has never been observed in any age or country. There must, therefore, be a uniform experience against every miraculous event, otherwise the event would not merit that appellation. And as a uniform experience amounts to a proof, there is here a direct and full *proof*, from the nature of the fact, against the existence of any miracle; nor can such a proof be destroyed, or the miracle rendered credible, but by an opposite proof, which is superior.

The plain consequence is (and it is a general maxim worthy of our attention), 'That no testimony is sufficient to establish a miracle, unless the testimony be of such a kind, that its falsehood would be more miraculous, than the fact, which it endeavours to establish; and even in that case there is a mutual destruction of arguments, and the superior only gives us an assurance suitable to that degree of force, which remains, after deducting the inferior.' When anyone tells me, that he saw a dead man restored to life, I immediately consider with myself, whether it be more probable, that this person should either deceive or be deceived, or that the fact, which he relates, should really have happened. I weigh the one miracle against the other; and according to the superiority, which I discover, I pronounce my decision, and always reject the greater miracle. If the falsehood of his testimony would be more miraculous, than the event which he relates; then, and not till then, can he pretend to command my belief or opinion.

Part II

In the foregoing reasoning we have supposed, that the testimony, upon which a miracle is founded, may possibly amount to an entire proof, and that the falsehood of that testimony would be a real prodigy: But it is easy to shew, that we have been a great deal too liberal in our concession, and that there never was a miraculous event established on so full an evidence.

For *first*, there is not to be found, in all history, any miracle attested by a sufficient number of men, of such unquestioned good-sense, education, and learning, as to secure us against all delusion in themselves; of such undoubted integrity, as to place them beyond all suspicion of any design to deceive others; of such credit and reputation in the eyes of mankind, as to have a great deal to lose in case of their being detected in any falsehood; and at the same time, attesting facts performed in such a public manner and in so celebrated a part of the world, as to render the detection unavoidable: All which circumstances are requisite to give us a full assurance in the testimony of men.

Secondly. We may observe in human nature a principle which, if strictly examined, will be found to diminish extremely the assurance, which we might, from human testimony, have, in any kind of prodigy. The maxim, by which we commonly conduct ourselves in our reasonings, is, that the objects, of which we have no experience, resemble those, of which we have; that what we have found to be most usual is always most probable; and that where there is an opposition of arguments, we ought to give the preference to such as are founded on the greatest number of past observations. But though, in proceeding by this rule, we readily reject any fact which is unusual and incredible in an ordinary degree; yet in advancing farther, the mind observes not always the same rule; but when anything is affirmed utterly absurd and miraculous, it rather the more readily admits of such a fact, upon account of that very circumstance, which ought to destroy all its authority. The passion of *surprise* and *wonder*, arising from miracles, being an agreeable emotion, gives a sensible tendency towards the belief of those events, from which it is derived. And this goes so far, that even those who cannot enjoy this pleasure immediately, nor can believe those miraculous events, of which they are informed, yet love to partake of the satisfaction at second-hand or by rebound, and place a pride and delight in exciting the admiration of others.

With what greediness are the miraculous accounts of travellers received, their descriptions of sea and land monsters, their relations of wonderful adventures, strange men, and uncouth manners? But if the spirit of religion join itself to the love of wonder, there is an end of common sense; and human testimony, in these circumstances, loses all pretensions to authority. A religionist may be an enthusiast, and imagine he sees what has no reality: he may know his narrative to be false, and yet persevere in it, with the best intentions in the world, for the sake of promoting so holy a cause: or even where this delusion has not place, vanity, excited by so strong a temptation, operates on him more powerfully than on the rest of mankind in any other circumstances; and self-interest with equal force. His auditors may not have, and commonly have not, sufficient judgement to canvass his evidence: what judgement they have, they renounce by principle, in these sublime and mysterious subjects: or if they were ever so willing to employ it, passion and a heated imagination disturb the regularity of its operations. Their credulity increases his impudence: and his impudence overpowers their credulity.

Eloquence, when at its highest pitch, leaves little room for reason or reflection; but addressing itself entirely to the fancy or the affections, captivates the willing hearers, and subdues their understanding. Happily, this pitch it seldom attains. But what a Tully or a Demosthenes could scarcely effect over a Roman or Athenian audience, every *Capuchin*, every itinerant or stationary teacher can perform over the generality of mankind, and in a higher degree, by touching such gross and vulgar passions.

The many instances of forged miracles, and prophecies, and supernatural events, which, in all ages, have either been detected by contrary evidence, or which detect themselves by their absurdity, prove sufficiently the strong propensity of mankind to the extraordinary and the marvellous, and ought reasonably to beget a suspicion against all relations of this kind. This is our natural way of thinking, even with regard to the most common and most credible events. For instance: There is no kind of report which rises so easily, and spreads so quickly, especially in country places and provincial towns, as those concerning marriages; insomuch that two young persons of equal condition never see each other twice, but the whole neighbourhood immediately join them together. The pleasure of telling a piece of news so interesting, of propagating it, and of being the first reporters of it, spreads the intelligence. And this is so well known, that no man of sense gives attention to these reports, till he find them confirmed by some greater evidence. Do not the same passions, and others still stronger, incline the generality of mankind to believe and report, with the greatest vehemence and assurance, all religious miracles?

Thirdly. It forms a strong presumption against all supernatural and miraculous relations, that they are observed chiefly to abound among ignorant and barbarous nations; or if a civilized people has ever given admission to any of them, that people will be found to have received them from ignorant and barbarous ancestors, who transmitted them with that inviolable sanction and authority, which always attend received opinions. When we peruse the first histories of all nations, we are apt to imagine ourselves transported into some new world; where the whole frame of nature is disjointed, and every element performs its operations in a different manner, from what it does at present. Battles, revolutions, pestilence, famine and death, are never the effect of those natural causes, which we experience. Prodigies, omens, oracles, judgements, quite obscure the few natural events, that are intermingled with them. But as the former grow thinner every page, in proportion as we advance nearer the enlightened ages, we soon learn, that there is nothing mysterious or supernatural in the case, but that all proceeds from the usual propensity of mankind towards the marvellous, and that, though this inclination may at intervals receive a check from sense and learning, it can never be thoroughly extirpated from human nature.

It is strange, a judicious reader is apt to say, upon the perusal of these wonderful historians, *that such prodigious events never happen in our days*. But it is nothing strange, I hope, that men should lie in all ages. You must surely have seen instances enough of that frailty. You have yourself heard many such marvellous relations started, which, being treated with scorn by all the wise and judicious, have at last been abandoned even by the vulgar. Be assured, that those renowned lies, which have spread and flourished to such a monstrous height, arose from like beginnings; but being sown in a more proper soil, shot up at last into prodigies almost equal to those which they relate.

It was a wise policy in that false prophet, Alexander, who though now forgotten, was once so famous, to lay the first scene of his impostures in Paphlagonia, where, as Lucian tells us, the people were extremely ignorant and stupid, and ready to swallow even the grossest delusion. People at a distance, who are weak enough to think the matter at all worth enquiry, have no opportunity of receiving better information. The stories come magnified to them by a hundred circumstances. Fools are industrious in propagating the imposture; while the wise and learned are contented, in general, to deride its absurdity, without informing themselves of the particular facts, by which it may be distinctly refuted. And thus the impostor above mentioned was enabled to proceed, from his ignorant Paphlagonians, to the enlisting of votaries, even among the Grecian philosophers, and men of the most eminent rank and distinction in Rome: nay, could engage the attention of that sage emperor Marcus Aurelius; so far as to make him trust the success of a military expedition to his delusive prophecies.

The advantages are so great, of starting an imposture among an ignorant people, that, even though the delusion should be too gross to impose on the generality of them (*which, though seldom, is sometimes the case*) it has a much better chance for succeeding in remote countries, than if the first scene had been laid in a city renowned for arts and knowledge. The most ignorant and barbarous of these barbarians carry the report abroad. None of their countrymen have a large correspondence, or sufficient credit and authority to contradict and beat down the delusion. Men's inclination to the marvellous has full opportunity to display itself. And thus a story, which is universally exploded in the place where it was first started, shall pass for certain at a thousand miles distance. But had Alexander fixed his residence at Athens, the philosophers of that renowned mart of learning had immediately spread, throughout the whole Roman empire, their sense of the matter; which, being supported by so great authority, and displayed by all the force of reason and eloquence, had entirely opened the eyes of mankind. It is true; Lucian, passing by chance through Paphlagonia, had an opportunity of performing this good office. But, though much to be wished, it does not always happen, that every Alexander meets with a Lucian, ready to expose and detect his impostures.

I may add as a *fourth* reason, which diminishes the authority of prodigies, that there is no testimony for any, even those which have not been expressly detected, that is not opposed by an infinite number of witnesses; so that not only the miracle destroys the credit of testimony, but the testimony destroys itself. To make this the better understood, let us consider, that, in matters of religion, whatever is different is contrary; and that it is impossible the religions of ancient Rome, of Turkey, of Siam, and of China should, all of them, be established on any solid foundation. Every miracle, therefore, pretended to have been wrought in any of these religions (and all of them abound in miracles), as its direct scope is to establish the particular system to which it is attributed; so has it the same force, though more indirectly, to overthrow every other system. In destroying a rival system, it likewise destroys the credit of those miracles, on which that system was established; so that all the prodigies of different religions are to be regarded as contrary facts, and the evidences of these prodigies, whether weak or strong as opposite to each other.

. . . .

The wise lend a very academic faith to every report which favours the passion of the reporter; whether it magnifies his country, his family, or himself, or in any other way strikes in with his natural inclinations and propensities. But what greater temptation than to appear a missionary, a prophet, an ambassador from heaven? Who would not encounter many dangers and difficulties, in order to attain so sublime a character? Of if, by the help of vanity and a heated imagination, a man has first made a convert of himself, and entered seriously into the delusion; who ever scruples to make use of pious frauds, in support of so holy and meritorious a cause?

The smallest spark may here kindle into the greatest flame; because the materials are always prepared for it. The *avidum genus auricularum*, the gazing populace, receive greedily, without examination, whatever sooths superstition, and promotes wonder.

How many stories of this nature have, in all ages, been detected and exploded in their infancy? How many more have been celebrated for a time, and have afterwards sunk into neglect and oblivion? Where such reports, therefore, fly about, the solution of the phenomenon is obvious; and we judge in conformity to regular experience and observation, when we account for it by the known and natural principles of credulity and delusion. And shall we, rather than have a recourse to so natural a solution, allow of a miraculous violation of the most established laws of nature?

I need not mention the difficulty of detecting a falsehood in any private or even public history, at the place, where it is said to happen; much more when the scene is removed to ever so small a distance. Even a court of judicature, with all the authority, accuracy, and judgement, which they can employ, find themselves often at a loss to distinguish between truth and falsehood in the most recent actions. But the matter never comes to any issue, if trusted to the common method of altercation and debate and flying rumours; especially when men's passions have taken part on either side.

In the infancy of new religions, the wise and learned commonly esteem the matter too inconsiderable to deserve their attention or regard. And when afterwards they would willingly detect the cheat, in order to undeceive the deluded multitude, the season is now past, and the records and witnesses, which might clear up the matter, have perished beyond recovery.

No means of detection remain, but those which must be drawn from the very testimony itself of the reporters: and these, though always sufficient with the judicious and knowing, are commonly too fine to fall under the comprehension of the vulgar.

Upon the whole, then, it appears, that no testimony for any kind of miracle has ever amounted to a probability, much less to a proof; and that, even supposing it amounted to a proof, it would be opposed by another proof; derived from the very nature of the fact, which it would endeavour to establish. It is experience only, which gives authority to human testimony; and it is the same experience, which assures us of the laws of nature. When, therefore, these two kinds of experience are contrary, we have nothing to do but substract the one from the other, and embrace an opinion, either on one side or the other, with that assurance which arises from the remainder. But according to the principle here explained, this substraction, with regard to all popular religions, amounts to an entire annihilation; and therefore we may establish it as a maxim, that no human testimony can have such force as to prove a miracle, and make it a just foundation for any such system of religion.

I beg the limitations here made may be remarked, when I say, that a miracle can never be proved, so as to be the foundation of a system of religion. For I own, that otherwise, there may possibly be miracles, or violations of the usual course of nature, of such a kind as to admit of proof from human testimony; though, perhaps, it will be impossible to find any such in all the records of history. Thus, suppose, all authors, in all languages, agree, that, from the first of January 1600, there was a total darkness over the whole earth for eight days: suppose that the tradition of this extraordinary event is still strong and lively among the people: that all travellers, who return from foreign countries, bring us accounts of the same tradition, without the least variation or contradiction: it is evident, that our present philosophers, instead of doubting the fact, ought to receive it as certain, and ought to search for the causes whence it might be derived. The decay, corruption, and dissolution of nature, is an event rendered probable by so many analogies, that any phenomenon, which seems to have a tendency towards that catastrophe, comes within the reach of human testimony, if that testimony be very extensive and uniform.

But suppose, that all the historians who treat of England, should agree, that, on the first of January 1600, Queen Elizabeth died; that both before and after her death she was seen by her physicians and the whole court, as is usual with persons of her rank; that her successor was acknowledged and proclaimed by the parliament; and that, after being interred a month, she again appeared, resumed the throne, and governed England for three years: I must confess that I should be surprised at the concurrence of so many odd circumstances, but should not have the least inclination to believe so miraculous an event. I should not doubt of her pretended death, and of those other public circumstances that followed it: I should only assert it to have been pretended, and that it neither was, nor possibly could be real. You would in vain object to me the difficulty, and almost impossibility of deceiving the world in an affair of such consequence; the wisdom and solid judgement of that renowned queen; with the little or no advantage which she could reap from so poor an artifice: All this might astonish me; but I would still reply, that the knavery and folly of men are such common phenomena, that I should rather believe the most extraordinary events to arise from their concurrence, than admit of so signal a violation of the laws of nature.

But should this miracle be ascribed to any new system of religion; men, in all ages, have been so much imposed on by ridiculous stories of that kind, that this very circumstance would be a full proof of a cheat, and sufficient, with all men of sense, not only to make them reject the fact, but even reject it without farther examination. Though the Being to whom the miracle is ascribed, be, in this case, Almighty, it does not, upon that account, become a whit more probable; since it is impossible for us to know the attributes or actions of such a Being, otherwise than from the experience which we have of his productions, in the usual course of nature. This still reduces us to past observation, and obliges us to compare the instances of the violation of truth in the testimony of men, with those of the violation of the laws of nature by miracles, in order to judge which of them is most likely and probable. As the violations of truth are more common in the testimony concerning religious miracles, than in that concerning any other matter of fact; this must diminish very much the authority of the former testimony, and make us form a general resolution, never to lend any attention to it, with whatever specious pretence it may be covered.

Lord Bacon seems to have embraced the same principles of reasoning. 'We ought,' says he, 'to make a collection or particular history of all monsters and prodigious births or productions, and in a word of every thing new, rare, and extraordinary in nature. But this must be done with the most severe scrutiny, lest we depart from truth. Above all, every relation must be considered as suspicious, which depends in any degree upon religion, as the prodigies of Livy: And no less so, every thing that is to be found in the writers of natural magic or alchimy, or such authors, who seem, all of them, to have an unconquerable appetite for falsehood and fable.'

I am the better pleased with the method of reasoning here delivered, as I think it may serve to confound those dangerous friends or disguised enemies to the *Christian Religion*, who have undertaken to defend it by the principles of human reason. Our most holy religion is founded on *Faith*, not on reason; and it is a sure method of exposing it to put it to such a trial as it is, by no means, fitted to endure. To make this more evident, let us examine those miracles, related in scripture; and not to lose ourselves in too wide a field, let us confine ourselves to such as we find in the *Pentateuch*, which we shall examine, according to the principles of these pretended Christians, not as the word or testimony of God himself, but as the production of a mere human writer and historian. Here then we are first to consider a book, presented to us by a barbarous and ignorant people, written in an age when they were still more barbarous, and in all probability long after the facts which it relates, corroborated by no concurring testimony, and resembling those fabulous accounts, which every nation gives of its origin. Upon reading this book, we find it full of prodigies and miracles. It gives an account of a state of the world and of human nature entirely different from the present: Of our fall from that state: Of the age of man, extended to near a thousand years: Of the destruction of the world by a deluge: Of the arbitrary choice of one people, as the favourites of heaven; and that people the countrymen of the author: Of their deliverance from bondage by prodigies the most astonishing imaginable: I desire any one to lay his hand upon his heart, and after a serious consideration declare, whether he thinks that the falsehood of such a book, supported by such a testimony, would be more extraordinary and miraculous than all the miracles it relates; which is, however, necessary to make it be received, according to the measures of probability above established.

What we have said of miracles may be applied, without any variation, to prophecies; and indeed, all prophecies are real miracles, and as such only, can be admitted as proofs of any revelation. If it did not exceed the capacity of human nature to foretell future events, it would be absurd to employ any prophecy as an argument for a divine mission or authority from heaven. So that, upon the whole, we may conclude, that the *Christian Religion* not only was at first attended with miracles, but even at this day cannot be believed by any reasonable person without one. Mere reason is insufficient to convince us of its veracity: And whoever is moved by *Faith* to assent to it, is conscious of a continued miracle in his own person, which subverts all the principles of his understanding, and gives him a determination to believe what is most contrary to custom and experience.

10

Viruses of the mind
Richard Dawkins

In this provocative article the zoologist Richard Dawkins (1941–) argues that religious beliefs are a kind of virus, not unlike a computer virus. They are parasitic on human beings, self-replicating, and extremely difficult to eradicate. Unlike scientific ideas, which are testable, precise and independent of cultural milieu, religious beliefs are usually untestable, imprecise and largely the product of a particular kind of upbringing. Religious faith is a kind of disease. The young need protection against it.

From *Dennett and His Critics*, edited by Bo Dahlbom

The haven all memes depend on reaching is the human mind, but a human mind is itself an artifact created when memes restructure a human brain in order to make it a better habitat for memes. The avenues for entry and departure are modified to suit local conditions, and strengthened by various artificial devices that enhance fidelity and prolixity of replication: native Chinese minds differ dramatically from native French minds, and literate minds differ from illiterate minds. What memes provide in return to the organisms in which they reside is an incalculable store of advantages – with some Trojan horses thrown in for good measure . . .

Daniel Dennett, Consciousness Explained

1 Duplication fodder

A beautiful child close to me, six and the apple of her father's eye, believes that Thomas the Tank Engine really exists. She believes in Father Christmas, and when she grows up her ambition is to be a tooth fairy. She and her schoolfriends believe the solemn word of respected adults that tooth fairies and Father Christmas really exist. This little girl is of an age to believe whatever you tell her. If you tell her about witches changing princes into frogs she will believe you. If you tell her that bad children roast forever in hell she will have nightmares. I have just discovered that without her father's consent this sweet, trusting, gullible six-year-old is being sent, for weekly instruction, to a Roman Catholic nun. What chance has she?

A human child is shaped by evolution to soak up the culture of her people. Most obviously, she learns the essentials of their language in a matter of months. A large dictionary of words to speak, an encyclopedia of information to speak about, complicated syntactic and semantic rules to order the speaking, all are transferred from older brains into hers well before she reaches half her adult size. When you are preprogrammed to absorb useful information at a high rate, it is hard to shut out pernicious or damaging information at the same time. With so many mindbytes to be downloaded, so many mental codons to be duplicated, it is no wonder that child brains are gullible, open to almost any suggestion, vulnerable to subversion, easy prey to Moonies, scientologists and nuns. Like immune-deficient patients, children are wide open to mental infections that adults might brush off without effort.

DNA, too, includes parasitic code. Cellular machinery is extremely good at copying DNA. Where DNA is concerned, it seems to have an eagerness to copy, like a child's eagerness to imitate the language of its parents. Concomitantly, DNA seems eager to be copied. The cell nucleus is a paradise for DNA, humming with sophisticated, fast, and accurate duplicating machinery.

Cellular machinery is so friendly towards DNA duplication that it is small wonder cells play host to DNA parasites – viruses, viroids, plasmids and a riff-raff of other genetic fellow travelers. Parasitic DNA even gets itself spliced seamlessly into the chromosomes themselves. 'Jumping genes' and stretches of 'selfish DNA' cut or copy themselves out of chromosomes and paste themselves in elsewhere. Deadly oncogenes are almost impossible to distinguish from the legitimate genes between which they are spliced. In evolutionary time, there is probably a continual traffic from 'straight' genes to 'outlaw', and back again (Dawkins 1982). DNA is just DNA. The only thing that distinguishes viral DNA from host DNA is its expected method of passing into future generations. 'Legitimate' host DNA is just DNA that aspires to pass into the next generation via the orthodox route of sperm or egg. 'Outlaw' or parasitic DNA is just DNA that looks to a quicker, less cooperative route to the future, via a sneezed droplet or a smear of blood, rather than via a sperm or egg.

For data on a floppy disc, a computer is a humming paradise just as cell nuclei hum with eagerness to duplicate DNA. Computers and their associated disc and tape readers are designed with high fidelity in mind.

As with DNA molecules, magnetized bytes don't literally 'want' to be faithfully copied. Nevertheless, you can write a computer program that takes steps to duplicate itself. Not just duplicate itself within one computer but spread itself to other computers. Computers are so good at copying bytes, and so good at faithfully obeying the instructions contained in those bytes, that they are sitting ducks to self-replicating programs: wide open to subversion by software parasites. Any cynic familiar with the theory of selfish genes and memes would have known that modern personal computers, with their promiscuous traffic of floppy disks and e-mail links, were just asking for trouble. The only surprising thing about the current epidemic of computer viruses is that it has been so long in coming.

2 Computer viruses: a model for an informational epidemiology

Computer viruses are pieces of code that graft themselves into existing, legitimate programs and subvert the normal actions of those programs.

. . . .

DNA viruses and computer viruses spread for the same reason: an environment exists in which there is machinery well set up to duplicate and spread them around and to obey the instructions that the viruses embody. These two environments are, respectively, the environment of cellular physiology and the environment provided by a large community of computers and data-handling machinery. Are there any other environments like these, any other humming paradises of replication?

3 The infected mind

I have already alluded to the programmed-in gullibility of a child, so useful for learning language and traditional wisdom, and so easily subverted by nuns, Moonies and their ilk. More generally, we all exchange information with one another. We don't exactly plug floppy disks into slots in one another's skulls, but we exchange sentences, both through our ears and through our eyes. We notice each other's styles of moving and of dressing and are influenced. We take in advertising jingles, and are presumably persuaded by them, otherwise hard-headed businessmen would not spend so much money polluting the air with them.

Think about the two qualities that a virus, or any sort of parasitic replicator, demands of a friendly medium, the two qualities that make cellular machinery so friendly towards parasitic DNA, and that make computers so friendly towards computer viruses. These qualities are, firstly, a readiness to replicate information accurately, perhaps with some mistakes that are subsequently reproduced accurately; and, secondly, a readiness to obey instructions encoded in the information so replicated.

Cellular machinery and electronic computers excel in both these virus-friendly qualities. How do human brains match up? As faithful duplicators, they are certainly less perfect than either cells or electronic computers. Nevertheless, they are still pretty good, perhaps about as faithful as an RNA virus, though not as good as DNA with all its elaborate proofreading measures against textual degradation. Evidence of the fidelity of brains, especially child brains, as data duplicators is provided by language itself. Shaw's Professor Higgins was able by ear alone to place Londoners in the street where they grew up. Fiction is not evidence for anything, but everyone knows that Higgins's fictional skill is only an exaggeration of something we can all do. Any American can tell Deep South from Mid West, New England from Hillbilly. Any New Yorker can tell Bronx from Brooklyn. Equivalent claims could be substantiated for any country. What this phenomenon means is that human brains are capable of pretty accurate copying (otherwise the accents of, say, Newcastle would not be stable enough to be recognized) but with some mistakes (otherwise pronunciation would not evolve, and all speakers of a language would inherit identically the same accents from their remote ancestors). Language evolves, because it has both the great stability and the slight changeability that are prerequisites for any evolving system.

The second requirement of a virus-friendly environment – that it should obey a program of coded instructions – is again only quantitatively less true for brains than for cells or computers. We sometimes obey orders from one another, but also we sometimes don't. Nevertheless, it is a telling fact that, the world over, the vast majority of children follow the religion of their parents rather than any of the other available religions. Instructions to genuflect, to bow towards Mecca, to nod one's head rhythmically towards the wall, to shake like a maniac, to 'speak in tongues' – the list of such arbitrary and pointless motor patterns offered by religion alone is extensive – are obeyed, if not slavishly, at least with some reasonably high statistical probability.

Less portentously, and again especially prominent in children, the 'craze' is a striking example of behavior that owes more to epidemiology than to rational choice. Yo-yos, hula hoops and pogo sticks, with their associated behavioral fixed actions, sweep through schools, and more sporadically leap from school to school, in patterns that differ from a measles epidemic in no serious particular. Ten years ago, you could have traveled thousands of miles through the United States and never seen a baseball cap turned back to front. Today, the reverse baseball cap is ubiquitous. I do not know what the pattern of geographical spread of the reverse baseball cap precisely was, but epidemiology is certainly among the professions primarily qualified to study it. We don't have to get into arguments about 'determinism;' we don't have to claim that children are compelled to imitate their fellows' hat fashions. It is enough that their hat-wearing behavior, as a matter of fact, *is* statistically affected by the hat-wearing behavior of their fellows.

Trivial though they are, crazes provide us with yet more circum-stantial evidence that human minds, especially perhaps juvenile ones, have the qualities that we have singled out as desirable for an informational parasite. At the very least the mind is a plausible *candidate* for infection by something like a computer virus, even if it is not quite such a para-site's dream-environment as a cell nucleus or an electronic computer.

It is intriguing to wonder what it might feel like, from the inside, if one's mind were the victim of a 'virus.' This might be a deliberately designed parasite, like a present-day computer virus. Or it might be an inadvertently mutated and unconsciously evolved parasite. Either way, especially if the evolved parasite was the memic descendant of a long line of successful ancestors, we are entitled to expect the typical 'mind virus' to be pretty good at its job of getting itself successfully replicated.

Progressive evolution of more effective mind-parasites will have two aspects. New 'mutants' (either random or designed by humans) that are better at spreading will become more numerous. And there will be a ganging up of ideas that flourish in one another's presence, ideas that mutu-ally support one another just as genes do and as I have speculated computer viruses may one day do. We expect that replicators will go around together from brain to brain in mutually compatible gangs. These gangs will come to constitute a package, which may be sufficiently stable to deserve a collective name such as Roman Catholicism or Voodoo. It doesn't too much matter whether we analogize the whole package to a single virus, or each one of the component parts to a single virus. The analogy is not that precise anyway, just as the distinction between a computer virus and a computer worm is nothing to get worked up about. What matters is that minds are friendly environments to parasitic, self-replicating ideas or infor-mation, and that minds are typically massively infected.

Like computer viruses, successful mind viruses will tend to be hard for their victims to detect. If you are the victim of one, the chances are that you won't know it, and may even vigorously deny it. Accepting that a virus might be difficult to detect in your own mind, what tell-tale signs might you look out for? I shall answer by imagining how a medical text-book might describe the typical symptoms of a sufferer (arbitrarily assumed to be male).

(1) The patient typically finds himself impelled by some deep, inner conviction that something is true, or right, or virtuous: a conviction that doesn't seem to owe anything to evidence or reason, but which,

nevertheless, he feels as totally compelling and convincing. We doctors refer to such a belief as 'faith.'

(2) Patients typically make a positive virtue of faith's being strong and unshakable, *in spite of* not being based upon evidence. Indeed, they may feel that the less evidence there is, the more virtuous the belief (see below).

This paradoxical idea that lack of evidence is a positive virtue where faith is concerned has something of the quality of a program that is self-sustaining, because it is self-referential (see the chapter, 'On viral sentences and self-replicating structures' in Hofstadter, 1985). Once the proposition is believed, it automatically undermines opposition to itself. The 'lack of evidence is a virtue' idea would be an admirable sidekick, ganging up with faith itself in a clique of mutually supportive viral programs.

(3) A related symptom, which a faith-sufferer may also present, is the conviction that 'mystery,' *per se*, is a good thing. It is not a virtue to solve mysteries. Rather we should enjoy them, even revel in their insolubility.

Any impulse to solve mysteries could be seriously inimical to the spread of a mind virus. It would not, therefore, be surprising if the idea that 'mysteries are better not solved' was a favored member of a mutually supporting gang of viruses. Take the 'Mystery of the Transubstantiation.' It is easy and non-mysterious to believe that in some symbolic or metaphorical sense the eucharistic wine turns into the blood of Christ. The Roman Catholic doctrine of transubstantiation, however, claims far more. The 'whole substance' of the wine is converted into the blood of Christ; the appearance of wine that remains is 'merely accidental,' 'inhering in no substance' (Kenny 1986, p. 72). Transubstantiation is colloquially taught as meaning that the wine 'literally' turns into the blood of Christ. Whether in its obfuscatory Aristotelian or its franker colloquial form, the claim of transubstantiation can be made only if we do serious violence to the normal meanings of words like 'substance' and 'literally.' Redefining words is not a sin but, if we use words like 'whole substance' and 'literally' for this case, what word are we going to use when we really and truly *want* to say that something did actually happen? As Anthony Kenny observed of his own puzzlement as a young seminarian, 'For all I could tell, my typewriter might be Benjamin Disraeli transubstantiated. . . .'

Roman Catholics, whose belief in infallible authority compels them to accept that wine becomes physically transformed into blood despite all appearances, refer to the 'mystery' of the transubstantiation. Calling it a mystery makes everything OK, you see. At least, it works for a mind well prepared by background infection. Exactly the same trick is performed in the 'mystery' of the Trinity. Mysteries are not meant to be solved, they are meant to strike awe. The 'mystery is a virtue' idea comes to the aid of the Catholic, who would otherwise find intolerable the obligation to believe the obvious nonsense of the transubstantiation and the 'three-in-one.' Again, the belief that 'mystery is a virtue' has a self-referential ring. As Hofstadter might put it, the very mysteriousness of the belief moves the believer to perpetuate the mystery.

An extreme symptom of 'mystery is a virtue' infection is Tertullian's '*Certum est quia impossibile est*' ('It is certain because it is impossible'). That way madness lies. One is tempted to quote Lewis Carroll's White Queen who, in response to Alice's 'One can't believe impossible things' retorted 'I daresay you haven't had much practice . . . When I was your age, I always did it for half-an-hour a day. Why, sometimes I've believed as many as six impossible things before breakfast.' Or Douglas Adams's Electric Monk, a labor-saving device programmed to do your believing for you, which was capable of 'believing things they'd have difficulty believing in Salt Lake City' and which, at the moment of being introduced to the reader, believed, contrary to all the evidence, that everything in the world was a uniform shade of pink. But White Queens and Electric Monks become less funny when you realize that these virtuoso believers are indistinguishable from revered theologians in real life. 'It is by all means to be believed, because it is absurd' (Tertullian again). Sir Thomas Browne (1635) quotes Tertullian with approval, and goes further: 'Methinks there be not impossibilities enough in religion for an active faith.' And 'I desire to exercise my faith in the difficultest point; for to credit ordinary and visible objects is not faith, but perswasion.'

I have the feeling that something more interesting is going on here than just plain insanity or surrealist nonsense, something akin to the admiration we feel when we watch a ten-ball juggler on a tightrope. It is as though the faithful gain prestige through managing to believe even more ridiculous things than their rivals succeed in believing. Are these people testing – exercising – their believing muscles, training themselves to believe impossible things so that they can take in their stride the merely improbable things that they are ordinarily called upon to believe?

While I was writing this, the *Guardian* (July 29, 1991) fortuitously carried a beautiful example. It came in an interview with a rabbi undertaking the bizarre task of vetting the kosher-purity of food products right back to the ultimate origins of their minutest ingredients. He was currently agonizing over whether to go all the way to China to scrutinize the menthol that goes into cough sweets. 'Have you ever tried checking Chinese menthol . . . it was extremely difficult, especially since the first letter we sent received the reply in best Chinese English, 'The product contains no kosher' . . . China has only recently started opening up to kosher investigators. The menthol should be OK, but you can never be absolutely sure unless you visit.' These koshner investigators run a telephone hotline on which up-to-the-minute red-alerts of suspicion are recorded against chocolate bars and cod-liver oil. The rabbi sighs that the green-inspired trend away from artificial colors and flavors 'makes life miserable in the kosher field because you have to follow all these things back.' When the interviewer asks him why he bothers with this obviously pointless exercise, he makes it very clear that the point is precisely that there *is* no point:

> That most of the Kashrut laws are divine ordinances without reason given is 100 per cent the point. It is very easy not to murder people. Very easy. It is a little bit harder not to steal because one is tempted occasionally. So that is no great proof that I believe in God or am fulfilling His will. But, if He tells me not to have a cup of coffee with milk in it with my mincemeat and peas at lunchtime, that is a test. The only reason I am doing that is because I have been told to so do. It is doing something difficult.

Helena Cronin has suggested to me that there may be an analogy here to Zahavi's handicap theory of sexual selection and the evolution of signals (Zahavi 1975). Long unfashionable, even ridiculed (Dawkins 1976), Zahavi's theory has recently been cleverly rehabilitated (Grafen 1990a, 1990b) and is now taken seriously by evolutionary biologists (Dawkins 1989). Zahavi suggests that peacocks, for instance, evolve their absurdly burdensome fans with their ridiculously conspicuous (to predators) colors, precisely *because* they are burdensome and dangerous, and therefore impressive to females. The peacock is, in effect, saying: 'Look how fit and strong I must be, since I can afford to carry around this preposterous tail.'

To avoid misunderstanding of the subjective language in which Zahavi likes to make his points, I should add that the biologist's convention of personifying the unconscious actions of natural selection is taken for granted here. Grafen has translated the argument into an orthodox Darwinian mathematical model, and it works. No claim is here being made about the intentionality or awareness of peacocks and peahens. They can be as sphexish or as intentional as you please (Dennett 1983, 1984). Moreover, Zahavi's theory is general enough not to depend upon a Darwinian underpinning. A flower advertising its nectar to a 'skeptical' bee could benefit from the Zahavi principle. But so could a human salesman seeking to impress a client.

The premise of Zahavi's idea is that natural selection will favor skepticism among females (or among recipients of advertising messages generally). The only way for a male (or any advertiser) to authenticate his boast of strength (quality, or whatever it is) is to prove that it is true by shouldering a truly costly handicap – a handicap *that only a genuinely strong* (high-quality, etc.) male could bear. It may be called the principle of costly authentication. And now to the point. Is it possible that some religious doctrines are favored not *in spite of* being ridiculous but precisely *because* they are ridiculous? Any wimp in religion could believe that bread *symbolically* represents the body of Christ, but it takes a real, red-blooded Catholic to believe something as daft as the transubstantiation. If you can believe that you can believe anything, and (witness the story of Doubting Thomas) these people are trained to see that as a virtue.

Let us return to our list of symptoms that someone afflicted with the mental virus of faith, and its accompanying gang of secondary infections, may expect to experience.

(4)   The sufferer may find himself behaving intolerantly towards vectors of rival faiths, in extreme cases even killing them or advocating their deaths. He may be similarly violent in his disposition towards apostates (people who once held the faith but have renounced it); or towards heretics (people who espouse a different – often, perhaps significantly, only very slightly different – version of the faith). He may also feel hostile towards other modes of thought that are potentially inimical to his faith, such as the method of scientific reason which may function rather like a piece of anti-viral software.

The threat to kill the distinguished novelist Salman Rushdie is only the latest in a long line of sad examples. On the very day that I wrote this, the Japanese translator of *The Satanic Verses* was found murdered, a week after a near-fatal attack on the Italian translator of the same book. By the way, the apparently opposite symptom of 'sympathy' for Muslim 'hurt,' voiced by the Archbishop of Canterbury and other Christian leaders (verging, in the case of the Vatican, on outright criminal complicity) is, of course, a manifestation of the symptom we diagnosed earlier: the delusion that faith, however obnoxious its results, has to be respected simply because it *is* faith.

Murder is an extreme, of course. But there is an even more extreme symptom, and that is suicide in the militant service of a faith. Like a soldier ant programmed to sacrifice her life for germ-line copies of the genes that did the programming, a young Arab or Japanese is taught that to die in a holy war is the quickest way to heaven. Whether the leaders who exploit him really believe this does not diminish the brutal power that the 'suicide mission virus' wields on behalf of the faith. Of course suicide, like murder, is a mixed blessing: would-be converts may be repelled, or may treat with contempt a faith that is perceived as insecure enough to need such tactics.

More obviously, if too many individuals sacrifice themselves the supply of believers could run low. This was true of a notorious example of faith-inspired suicide, though in this case it was not 'kamikaze' death in battle. The Peoples' Temple sect became extinct when its leader, the Reverend Jim Jones, led the bulk of his followers from the United States to the Promised Land of 'Jonestown' in the Guyanan jungle where he persuaded more than 900 of them, children first, to drink cyanide. The macabre affair was fully investigated by a team from the *San Francisco Chronicle* (Kilduff and Javers 1978).

> Jones, 'the Father,' had called his flock together and told them it was time to depart for heaven.
> 'We're going to meet,' he promised, 'in another place.'
> The words kept coming over the camp's loudspeakers.
> 'There is great dignity in dying. It is a great demonstration for everyone to die.'

Incidentally, it does not escape the trained mind of the alert sociobiologist that Jones, within his sect in earlier days, 'proclaimed himself the only person permitted to have sex' (presumably his partners were also permitted). 'A secretary would arrange for Jones's liaisons. She would call up and say, "Father hates to do this, but he has this tremendous urge and could you please . . .?"' His victims were not only female. One 17-year-old male follower, from the days when Jones's community was still in San Francisco, told how he was taken for dirty weekends to a hotel where Jones received a 'minister's discount for Rev. Jim Jones and son.' The same boy said: 'I was really in awe of him. He was more than a father. I would have killed my parents for him.' What is remarkable about the Reverend Jim Jones is not his own self-serving behavior but the almost superhuman gullibility of his followers. Given such prodigious credulity, can anyone doubt that human minds are ripe for malignant infection?

Admittedly, the Reverend Jones conned only a few thousand people. But his case is an extreme, the tip of an iceberg. The same eagerness to be conned by religious leaders is widespread. Most of us would have been prepared to bet that nobody could get away with going on television and saying, in all but so many words, 'Send me your money, so that I can use it to persuade other suckers to send me their money too.' Yet today, in every major conurbation in the United States, you can find at least one television evangelist channel entirely devoted to this transparent confidence trick. And they get away with it in sackfuls. Faced with suckerdom on this awesome scale, it is hard not to feel a grudging sympathy with the shiny-suited conmen. Until you realize that not all the suckers are rich, and that it is often widows' mites on which the evangelists are growing fat. I have even heard one of them explicitly invoking the principle that I now identify with Zahavi's principle of costly authentication. God really appreciates a donation, he said with passionate sincerity, only when that donation is so large that it hurts. Elderly paupers were wheeled on to testify how much happier they felt since they had made over their little all to the Reverend whoever it was.

(5)   The patient may notice that the particular convictions that he holds, while having nothing to do with evidence, do seem to owe a great deal to epidemiology. Why, he may wonder, do I hold *this* set of convictions rather than *that* set? Is it because I surveyed all the world's faiths and chose the one whose claims seemed most convincing? Almost certainly not. If you have a faith, it is statistically overwhelmingly likely that it is the same faith as your parents and grandparents had. No doubt soaring cathedrals, stirring music, moving stories and parables, help a bit. But by far the most important variable determining your religion is the accident of birth. The convictions that you so passionately believe would have been a completely different, and largely contradictory, set of convictions, if only you had happened to be born in a different place. Epidemiology, not evidence.

(6)   If the patient is one of the rare exceptions who follows a different religion from his parents, the explanation may still be epidemiological. To be sure, it is *possible* that he dispassionately surveyed the world's faiths and chose the most convincing one. But it is statistically more probable that he has been exposed to a particularly potent infective agent – a John Wesley, a Jim Jones or a St Paul. Here we are talking about horizontal transmission, as in measles. Before, the epidemiology was that of vertical transmission, as in Huntington's Chorea.

(7)   The internal sensations of the patient may be startlingly reminiscent of those more ordinarily associated with sexual love. This is an extremely potent force in the brain, and it is not surprising that some viruses have evolved to exploit it. St Teresa of Avila's famously orgasmic vision is too notorious to need quoting again. More seriously, and on a less crudely sensual plane, the philosopher Anthony Kenny provides moving testimony to the pure delight that awaits those that manage to believe in the mystery of the transubstantiation. After describing his ordination as a Roman Catholic priest, empowered by laying on of hands to celebrate Mass, he goes on that he vividly recalls

> the exaltation of the first months during which I had the power to say Mass. Normally a slow and sluggish riser, I would leap early out of bed, fully awake and full of excitement at the

thought of the momentous act I was privileged to perform. I rarely said the public Community Mass: most days I celebrated alone at a side altar with a junior member of the College to serve as acolyte and congregation. But that made no difference to the solemnity of the sacrifice or the validity of the consecration.

It was touching the body of Christ, the closeness of the priest to Jesus, which most enthralled me. I would gaze on the Host after the words of consecration, soft-eyed like a lover looking into the eyes of his beloved . . . Those early days as a priest remain in my memory as days of fulfilment and tremulous happiness; something precious, and yet too fragile to last, like a romantic love-affair brought up short by the reality of an ill-assorted marriage.

(Kenny 1986: 101–2)

Dr Kenny is affectingly believable that it felt to him, as a young priest, as though he was in love with the consecrated host. What a brilliantly successful virus! On the same page, incidentally, Kenny also shows us that the virus is transmitted contagiously – if not literally then at least in some sense – from the palm of the infecting bishop's hand through the top of the new priest's head:

If Catholic doctrine is true, every priest validly ordained derives his orders in an unbroken line of laying on of hands, through the bishop who ordains him, back to one of the twelve Apostles . . . there must be centuries-long, recorded chains of layings on of hands. It surprises me that priests never seem to trouble to trace their spiritual ancestry in this way, finding out who ordained their bishop, and who ordained him, and so on to Julius II or Celestine V or Hildebrand, or Gregory the Great, perhaps.

(Kenny 1986: 101)

It surprises me, too.

4 Is science a virus?

No. Not unless all computer programs are viruses. Good, useful programs spread because people evaluate them, recommend them and pass them on. Computer viruses spread solely because they embody the coded instructions: 'Spread me.' Scientific ideas, like all memes, are subject to a kind of natural selection, and this might look superficially virus-like. But the selective forces that scrutinize scientific ideas are not arbitrary or capricious. They are exacting, well-honed rules, and they do not favor pointless self-serving behavior. They favor all the virtues laid out in textbooks of standard methodology: testability, evidential support, precision, quantifiability, consistency, intersubjectivity, repeatability, universality, progressiveness, independence of cultural milieu, and so on. Faith spreads despite a total lack of every single one of these virtues.

You may find elements of epidemiology in the spread of scientific ideas, but it will be largely descriptive epidemiology. The rapid spread of a good idea through the scientific community may even look like a description of a measles epidemic. But when you examine the underlying reasons you find that they are good ones, satisfying the demanding standards of scientific method. In the history of the spread of faith you will find little else but epidemiology, and causal epidemiology at that. The reason why person *A* believes one thing and *B* believes another is simply and solely that *A* was born on one continent and *B* on another. Testability, evidential support and the rest aren't even remotely considered. For scientific belief, epidemiology merely comes along afterwards and describes the history of its acceptance. For religious belief, epidemiology is the root cause.

5 Epilogue

Happily, viruses don't win every time. Many children emerge unscathed from the worst that nuns and mullahs can throw at them. Anthony Kenny's own story has a happy ending. He eventually renounced his orders because he could no longer tolerate the obvious contradictions within Catholic belief, and he is now a highly respected scholar. But one cannot help remarking that it must be a powerful infection indeed that took a man of his wisdom and intelligence – now President of the British Academy, no less – three decades to fight off. Am I unduly alarmist to fear for the soul of my six-year-old innocent?

References

Browne, Sir T. (1635) *Religio Medici*, I, 9, p. 11.
Dawkins, R. (1976) *The Selfish Gene*, Oxford: Oxford University Press.
Dawkins, R. (1982) *The Extended Phenotype*, Oxford: W. H. Freeman.
Dawkins, R. (1989) *The Selfish Gene*, 2nd edn, Oxford: Oxford University Press.
Dennett, D. C. (1983) 'Intentional systems in cognitive ethology: the "Panglossian paradigm" defended,' *Behavioral and Brain Sciences* 6, pp. 343–90.
Dennett, D. C. (1984) *Elbow Room: The Varieties of Free Will Worth Wanting*, Oxford: Oxford University Press.
Grafen, A. (1990a) 'Sexual selection unhandicapped by the Fisher process,' *Journal of Theoretical Biology* 144, pp. 473–516.

Grafen, A. (1990b) 'Biological signals as handicaps,' *Journal of Theoretical Biology* 144, pp. 517–46.

Hofstadter, D. R. (1985) *Metamagical Themas*, Harmondsworth: Penguin Books.

Kenny, A. (1986) *A Path from Rome*, Oxford: Oxford University Press.

Kilduff, M. and Javers, R. (1978) *The Suicide Cult*, New York: Bantam.

Zahavi, A. (1975) 'Mate selection – a selection for a handicap,' *Journal of Theoretical Biology* 53, pp. 205–14.

Right and wrong

11

The Categorical Imperative
Immanuel Kant

Some philosophers have argued that actions are right or wrong regardless of the consequences and that the motive from which an action is performed is crucial to our assessment of its moral worth. Immanuel Kant (1724–1804) is the most important and the most influential of these philosophers. In this extract from *The Moral Law* (1785) he examines the question of whether it is ever morally permissible to make a promise whilst intending to break it. Application of his principle of universalizability shows that it can never be permissible: a universal law advocating promise-breaking would undermine the whole institution of promising. Kant believes that his Categorical Imperative is not only what reason demands, but also conforms with ordinary moral thinking. This book's title has been translated in a number of ways; its full literal translation is *Groundwork of the Metaphysic of Morals*.

From Immanuel Kant, *The Moral Law*

But what kind of law can this be the thought of which, even without regard to the results expected from it, has to determine the will if this is to be called good absolutely and without qualification? Since I have robbed the will of every inducement that might arise for it as a consequence of obeying any particular law, nothing is left but the conformity of actions to universal law as such, and this alone must serve the will as its principle. That is to say, I ought never to act except in such a way *that I can also will that my maxim should become a universal law*. Here bare conformity to universal law as such (without having as its base any law prescribing particular actions) is what serves the will as its principle, and must so serve it if duty is not to be everywhere an empty delusion and a chimerical concept. The ordinary reason of mankind also agrees with this completely in its practical judgements and always has the aforesaid principle before its eyes.

Take this question, for example. May I not, when I am hard pressed, make a promise with the intention of not keeping it? Here I readily distinguish the two senses which the question can have – Is it prudent, or is it right, to make a false promise? The first no doubt can often be the case. I do indeed see that it is not enough for me to extricate myself from present embarrassment by this subterfuge: I have to consider whether from this lie there may not subsequently accrue to me much greater inconvenience than that from which I now escape, and also – since, with all my supposed *astuteness*, to foresee the consequences is not so easy that I can be sure there is no chance, once confidence in me is lost, of this proving far more disadvantageous than all the ills I now think to avoid – whether it may not be a *more prudent* action to proceed here on a general maxim and make it my habit not to give a promise except with the intention of keeping it. Yet it becomes clear to me at once that such a maxim is always founded solely on fear of consequences. To tell the truth for the sake of duty is something entirely different from doing so out of concern for inconvenient results; for in the first case the concept of the action already contains in itself a law for me, while in the second case I have first of all to look around elsewhere in order to see what effects may be bound up with it for me. When I deviate from the principle of duty, this is quite certainly bad; but if I desert my prudential maxim, this can often be greatly to my advantage, though it is admittedly safer to stick to it. Suppose I seek, however, to learn in the quickest way and yet unerringly how to solve the problem 'Does a lying promise accord with duty?' I have then to ask myself 'Should I really be content that my maxim (the maxim of getting out of a difficulty by a false promise) should hold as a universal law (one valid both for myself and others)? And could I really say to myself that every one may make a false promise if he finds himself in a difficulty from which he can extricate himself in no other way?' I then become aware at once that I can indeed will to lie, but I can by no means will a universal law of lying; for by such a law there could properly be no promises at all, since it would be futile to profess a will for future action to others who would not believe my profession or who, if they did so over-hastily, would pay me back in like coin; and consequently my maxim, as soon as it was made a universal law, would be bound to annul itself.

Thus I need no far-reaching ingenuity to find out what I have to do in order to possess a good will. Inexperienced in the course of world affairs and incapable of being prepared for all the chances that happen in it, I ask myself only 'Can you also will that your maxim should become a universal law?' Where you cannot, it is to be rejected, and that not because of a prospective loss to you or even to others, but because it cannot fit as a principle into a possible enactment of universal law. For such an enactment reason compels my immediate reverence, into whose grounds (which the philosopher may investigate) I have as yet no *insight*, although I do at least understand this much: reverence is the assessment of a worth which far outweighs all the worth of what is commended by inclination, and the necessity for me to act out of *pure* reverence for the practical law is what constitutes duty, to which every other motive must give way because it is the condition of a will good *in itself*, whose value is above all else.

12

The experience machine
Robert Nozick

If you think that all that matters in life is your own felt experience then read this brief piece by Robert Nozick (1938–). His thought experiment of the Experience Machine demonstrates that most of us want more than the illusion of fulfilled desires: we want to be in touch with reality in a particular sort of way. This line of thought can be used to undermine the notion that all that matters from a moral point of view is that we achieve pleasurable states of mind: for many of us such pleasure is not the only or the ultimate worthwhile goal in life. Any philosophical theory based on the assumption that it is, is flawed.

From Robert Nozick, *Anarchy, State and Utopia*

Suppose there were an experience machine that would give you any experience you desired. Superduper neuropsychologists could stimulate your brain so that you would think and feel you were writing a great novel, or making a friend, or reading an interesting book. All the time you would be floating in a tank, with electrodes attached to your brain. Should you plug into this machine for life, preprogramming your life's experiences? If you are worried about missing out on desirable experiences, we can suppose that business enterprises have researched thoroughly the lives of many others. You can pick and choose from their large library or smorgasbord of such experiences, selecting your life's experiences for, say, the next two years. After two years have passed, you will have ten minutes or ten hours out of the tank, to select the experiences of your *next* two years. Of course, while in the tank you won't know that you're there; you'll think it's all actually happening. Others can also plug in to have the experiences they want, so there's no need to stay unplugged to serve them. (Ignore problems such as who will service the machines if everyone plugs in.) Would you plug in? *What else can matter to us, other than how our lives feel from the inside?* Nor should you refrain because of the few moments of distress between the moment you've decided and the moment you're plugged. What's a few moments of distress compared to a lifetime of bliss (if that's what you choose), and why feel any distress at all if your decision *is* the best one?

What does matter to us in addition to our experiences? First, we want to *do* certain things, and not just have the experience of doing them. In the case of certain experiences, it is only because first we want to do the actions that we want the experiences of doing them or thinking we've done them. (But *why* do we want to do the activities rather than merely to experience them?) A second reason for not plugging in is that we want to *be* a certain way, to be a certain sort of person. Someone floating in a tank is an indeterminate blob. There is no answer to the question of what a person is like who has long been in the tank. Is he courageous, kind, intelligent, witty, loving? It's not merely that it's difficult to tell; there's no way he is. Plugging into the machine is a kind of suicide. It will seem to some, trapped by a picture, that nothing about what we are like can matter except as it gets reflected in our experiences. But should it be surprising that what *we are* is important to us? Why should we be concerned only with how our time is filled, but not with what we are?

Thirdly, plugging into an experience machine limits us to a man-made reality, to a world no deeper or more important than that which people can construct. There is no *actual* contact with any deeper reality, though the experience of it can be stimulated. Many persons desire to leave themselves open to such contact and to a plumbing of deeper significance.[1] This clarifies the intensity of the conflict over psychoactive drugs, which some view as mere local experience machines, and others view as avenues to a deeper reality; what some view as equivalent to surrender to the experience machine, others view as following one of the reasons *not* to surrender!

We learn that something matters to us in addition to experience by imagining an experience machine and then realizing that we would not use it. We can continue to imagine a sequence of machines each designed to fill lacks suggested for the earlier machines. For example, since the experience machine doesn't meet our desire to *be* a certain way, imagine a transformation machine which transforms us into whatever sort of person we'd like to be (compatible with our staying us). Surely one would not use the transformation machine to become as one would wish, and thereupon plug into the experience machine![2] So something matters in addition to one's experiences *and* what one is like. Nor is the reason merely that one's experiences are unconnected with what one is like. For the experience machine might be limited to provide only experiences possible to the sort of person plugged in. Is it that we want to make a difference in the world? Consider then the result machine, which produces in the world any result you would produce and injects your vector input into any joint activity. We shall not pursue here the fascinating details of these or other machines. What is most disturbing about them is their living of our lives for us. Is it misguided to search for *particular* additional functions beyond the competence of machines to do for us? Perhaps what we desire is to live (an active verb) ourselves, in contact with reality. (And this, machines cannot do *for* us.) Without elaborating on the implications of this, which I believe connect surprisingly with issues about free will and causal accounts of knowledge, we need merely note the intricacy of the question of what matters *for people* other than their experiences. Until one finds a satisfactory answer, and determines that this answer does not *also* apply to animals, one cannot reasonably claim that only the felt experiences of animals limit what we may do to them.

Notes

1   Traditional religious views differ on the *point* of contact with a transcendent reality. Some say that contact yields eternal bliss or Nirvana, but they have not distinguished this sufficiently from merely a *very* long run on the experience machine. Others think it is intrinsically desirable to do the will of a higher being which created us all, though presumably no one would think this if we discovered we had been created as an object of amusement by some superpowerful child from another galaxy or dimension. Still others imagine an eventual merging with a higher reality, leaving unclear its desirability, or where that merging leaves *us*.

2   Some wouldn't use the transformation machine at all; it seems like *cheating*. But the one-time use of the transformation machine would not remove all challenges; there would still be obstacles for the new us to overcome, a new plateau from which to strive even higher. And is this plateau any the less earned or deserved than that provided by genetic endowment and early childhood environment? But if the transformation machine could be used indefinitely often, so that we could accomplish anything by pushing a button to transform ourselves into someone who could do it easily, there would remain no limits we *need* to strain against or try to transcend. Would there be anything left *to do*? Do some theological views place God outside of time because an omniscient omnipotent being couldn't fill up his days?

13

Higher and lower pleasures
John Stuart Mill

In this famous passage from his book *Utilitarianism* (1861), John Stuart Mill (1806–73) argues that there can be differences of quality as well as of quantity in our pleasures. Some utilitarians, such as Mill's mentor Jeremy Bentham (1748–1832), had assumed that all pleasures could be measured on the same scale. In contrast, Mill outlines his view that the position of a less than satisfied Socrates is preferable to that of a satisfied fool, which is in turn preferable to that of a satisfied pig. The kinds of pleasures available to each have to be taken into account: those who have experienced the higher, predominantly intellectual pleasures, recognize their superiority over mere animal pleasures.

From John Stuart Mill, *Utilitarianism*

The creed which accepts as the foundation of morals, Utility, or the Greatest Happiness Principle, holds that actions are right in proportion as they tend to promote happiness, wrong as they tend to produce the reverse of happiness. By happiness is intended pleasure, and the absence of pain; by unhappiness, pain, and the privation of pleasure. To give a clear view of the moral standard set up by the theory, much more requires to be said; in particular, what things it includes in the ideas of pain and pleasure; and to what extent this is left an open question. But these supplementary explanations do not affect the theory of life on which this theory of morality is grounded – namely, that pleasure, and freedom from pain, are the only things desirable as ends; and that all desirable things (which are as numerous in the utilitarian as in any other scheme) are desirable either for the pleasure inherent in themselves, or as means to the promotion of pleasure and the prevention of pain.

Now, such a theory of life excites in many minds, and among them in some of the most estimable in feeling and purpose, inveterate dislike. To suppose that life has (as they express it) no higher end than pleasure – no better and nobler object of desire and pursuit – they designate as

99

utterly mean and grovelling; as a doctrine worthy only of swine, to whom the followers of Epicurus were, at a very early period, contemptuously likened; and modern holders of the doctrine are occasionally made the subject of equally polite comparisons by its German, French, and English assailants.

When thus attacked, the Epicureans have always answered, that it is not they, but their accusers, who represent human nature in a degrading light; since the accusation supposes human beings to be capable of no pleasures except those of which swine are capable. If this supposition were true, the charge could not be gainsaid, but would then be no longer an imputation; for if the sources of pleasure were precisely the same to human beings and to swine, the rule of life which is good enough for the one would be good enough for the other. The comparison of the Epicurean life to that of beasts is felt as degrading, precisely because a beast's pleasures do not satisfy a human being's conception of happiness. Human beings have faculties more elevated than the animal appetites, and when once made conscious of them, do not regard anything as happiness, which does not include their gratification. I do not, indeed, consider the Epicureans to have been by any means faultless in drawing out their scheme of consequences from the utilitarian principle. To do this in any sufficient manner, many Stoic, as well as Christian elements require to be included. But there is no known Epicurean theory of life which does not assign to the pleasures of the intellect, of the feelings and imagination, and of the moral sentiments, a much higher value as pleasures than to those of mere sensation. It must be admitted, however, that utilitarian writers in general have placed the superiority of mental over bodily pleasures chiefly in the greater permanency, safety, uncostliness, etc., of the former – that is, in their circumstantial advantages rather than in their intrinsic nature. And on all these points utilitarians have fully proved their case; but they might have taken the other, and, as it may be called, higher ground, with entire consistency. It is quite compatible with the principle of utility to recognise the fact, that some *kinds* of pleasure are more desirable and more valuable than others. It would be absurd that while, in estimating all other things, quality is considered as well as quantity, the estimation of pleasures should be supposed to depend on quantity alone.

If I am asked, what I mean by difference of quality in pleasures, or what makes one pleasure more valuable than another, merely as a pleasure, except its being greater in amount, there is but one possible answer. Of two pleasures, if there be one to which all or almost all who have experience of both give a decided preference, irrespective of any feeling of moral obligation to prefer it, that is the more desirable pleasure. If one of the two is, by those who are competently acquainted with both, placed so far above the other that they prefer it, even though knowing it to be attended with a greater amount of discontent, and would not resign it for any quantity of the other pleasure which their nature is capable of, we are justified in ascribing to the preferred enjoyment a superiority in quality, so far out-weighing quantity as to render it, in comparison, of small account.

Now it is an unquestionable fact that those who are equally acquainted with, and equally capable of appreciating and enjoying, both, do give a most marked preference to the manner of existence which employs their higher faculties. Few human creatures would consent to be changed into any of the lower animals, for a promise of the fullest allowance of a beast's pleasures; no intelligent human being would consent to be a fool, no instructed person would be an ignoramus, no person of feeling and conscience would be selfish and base, even though they should be persuaded that the fool, the dunce, or the rascal is better satisfied with his lot than they are with theirs. They would not resign what they possess more than he for the most complete satisfaction of all the desires which they have in common with him. If they ever fancy they would, it is only in cases of unhappiness so extreme, that to escape from it they would exchange their lot for almost any other, however undesirable in their own eyes. A being of higher faculties requires more to make him happy, is capable probably of more acute suffering, and certainly accessible to it at more points, than one of an inferior type; but in spite of these liabilities, he can never really wish to sink into what he feels to be a lower grade of existence. We may give what explanation we please of this unwillingness; we may attribute it to pride, a name which is given indiscriminately to some of the most and to some of the least estimable feelings of which mankind are capable: we may refer it to the love of liberty and personal independence, an appeal to which was with the Stoics one of the most effective means for the inculcation of it; to the love of power, or to the love of excitement, both of which do really enter into and contribute to it: but its most appropriate appellation is a sense of dignity, which all human beings possess in one form or another, and in some, though by no means in exact, proportion to their higher faculties, and which is so essential a part of the happiness of those in whom it is strong, that nothing which conflicts with it could be, otherwise than momentarily, an object of desire to them. Whoever supposes that this preference takes place at a sacrifice of happiness – that the superior being, in anything like equal circumstances, is not happier than the inferior – confounds the two very different ideas, of happiness, and content. It is indisputable that the being whose capacities of enjoyment are low, has the greatest chance of having them fully satisfied; and a highly endowed being will always feel that any happiness which he can look for, as the world is constituted, is imperfect. But he can learn to bear its imperfections, if they are at all bearable; and they will not make him envy the being who is indeed unconscious of the imperfections, but only because he feels not at all the good which those imperfections qualify. It is better to be a human being dissatisfied than a pig satisfied; better to be Socrates dissatisfied than a fool satisfied. And if the fool, or the pig, are of a different opinion, it is because they only know their own side of the question. The other party to the comparison knows both sides.

It may be objected, that many who are capable of the higher pleasures, occasionally, under the influence of temptation, postpone them to the lower. But this is quite compatible with a full appreciation of the intrinsic superiority of the higher. Men often, from infirmity of character, make their election for the nearer good, though they know it to be the less valuable; and this no less when the choice is between two bodily pleasures, than when it is between bodily and mental. They pursue sensual indulgences to the injury of health, though perfectly aware that health is the greater good. It may be further objected, that many who begin with youthful enthusiasm for everything noble, as they advance in years sink into indolence and selfishness. But I do not believe that those who undergo this very common change, voluntarily choose the lower description of pleasures in preference to the higher. I believe that before they devote themselves exclusively to the one, they have already become incapable of the other. Capacity for the nobler feelings is in most natures a very tender plant, easily killed, not only by hostile influences, but by mere want of sustenance; and in the majority of young persons it speedily dies away if the occupations to which their position in life has devoted them, and the society into which it has thrown them, are not favourable to keeping that higher capacity in exercise. Men lose their high aspirations as they lose their intellectual tastes, because they have not time or opportunity for indulging them; and they addict themselves to inferior pleasures, not because they deliberately prefer them, but because they are either the only ones to which they have access, or the only ones which they are any longer capable of enjoying. It may be questioned whether any one who has remained equally susceptible to both classes of pleasure, ever knowingly and calmly preferred the lower; though many, in all ages, have broken down in an ineffectual attempt to combine both.

From this verdict of the only competent judges, I apprehend there can be no appeal. On a question which is the best worth having of two pleasures, or which of two modes of existence is the most grateful to the feelings, apart from its moral attributes and from its consequences, the judgment of those who are qualified by knowledge of both, or, if they differ, that of the majority among them, must be admitted as final. And there needs be the less hesitation to accept this judgment respecting the quality of pleasures, since there is no other tribunal to be referred to even on the question of quantity. What means are there of determining which is the acutest of two pains, or the intensest of two pleasurable sensations, except the general suffrage of those who are familiar with both? Neither pains nor pleasures are homogeneous, and pain is always heterogeneous with pleasure. What is there to decide whether a particular pleasure is worth purchasing at the cost of a particular pain, except the feelings and judgment of the experienced? When, therefore, those feelings and judgment declare the pleasures derived from the higher faculties to be preferable *in kind*, apart from the question of intensity, to those of which the animal nature, disjoined from the higher faculties, is susceptible, they are entitled on this subject to the same regard.

I have dwelt on this point, as being a necessary part of a perfectly just conception of Utility or Happiness, considered as the directive rule of human conduct. But it is by no means an indispensable condition to the acceptance of the utilitarian standard; for that standard is not the agent's own greatest happiness, but the greatest amount of happiness altogether; and if it may possibly be doubted whether a noble character is always the happier for its nobleness, there can be no doubt that it makes other people happier, and that the world in general is immensely a gainer by it. Utilitarianism, therefore, could only attain its end by the general cultivation of nobleness of character, even if each individual were only benefited by the nobleness of others, and his own, so far as happiness is concerned, were a sheer deduction from the benefit. But the bare enunciation of such an absurdity as this last, renders refutation superfluous.

14

A critique of utilitarianism
Bernard Williams

In this classic critique of the most straightforward versions of utilitarianism, Bernard Williams (1929–) presents and analyses two case studies: the cases of George and Jim. George, who is opposed to chemical and biological warfare, is faced with a situation in which it seems that as a utilitarian he should take part in research into conducting such warfare. Jim finds himself in a situation in which a utilitarian analysis suggests he should kill a man. In neither case, Williams argues, does utilitarianism leave room for personal integrity. So much the worse for utilitarianism, he thinks. For a response to this, see the reading after this: Jonathan Glover, 'The Solzhenitsyn principle'.

From J. J. C. Smart and Bernard Williams, *Utilitarianism: For and against*

Let us look . . . at two examples, to see what utilitarianism might say about them, what we might say about utilitarianism and, most importantly of all, what would be implied by certain ways of thinking about the situations. The examples are inevitably schematized, and they are open to the objection that they beg as many questions as they illuminate. There are two ways in particular in which examples in moral philosophy tend to beg important questions. One is that, as presented, they arbitrarily cut off and restrict the range of alternative courses of action – this objection might particularly be made against the first of my two examples. The second is that they inevitably present one with the situation as a going concern, and cut off questions about how the agent got into it, and correspondingly about moral considerations which might flow from that: this objection might perhaps specially arise with regard to the second of my two situations. These difficulties, however, just have to be accepted, and if anyone finds these examples cripplingly defective in this sort of respect, then he must in his own thought rework them in richer and less question-begging form. If he feels that no presentation of any imagined situation can ever be other than misleading in morality, and that there can never be any substitute for the concrete experienced complexity of actual moral situations, then this discussion, with him, must certainly grind to a halt: but then one may legitimately wonder whether every discussion with him about conduct will not grind to a halt, including any discussion about the actual situations, since discussion about how one would think and feel about situations somewhat different from the actual (that is to say, situations to that extent imaginary) plays an important role in discussion of the actual.

(1) George, who has just taken his Ph.D. in chemistry, finds it extremely difficult to get a job. He is not very robust in health, which cuts down the number of jobs he might be able to do satisfactorily. His wife has to go out to work to keep them, which itself causes a great deal of strain, since they have small children and there are severe problems about looking after them. The results of this, especially on the children, are damaging. An older chemist, who knows about this situation, says that he can get George a decently paid job in a certain laboratory, which pursues research into chemical and biological warfare. George says that he cannot accept this, since he is opposed to chemical and biological warfare. The older man replies that he is not too keen on it himself, come to that, but after all George's refusal is not going to make the job or the laboratory go away; what is more, he happens to know that if George refuses the job, it will certainly go to a contemporary of George's who is not inhibited by any such scruples and is likely if appointed to push along the research with greater zeal than George would. Indeed, it is not merely concern for George and his family, but (to speak frankly and in confidence) some alarm about this other man's excess of zeal, which has led the older man to offer to use his influence to get George the job ... George's wife, to whom he is deeply attached, has views (the details of which need not concern us) from which it follows that at least there is nothing particularly wrong with research into CBW. What should he do?

(2) Jim finds himself in the central square of a small South American town. Tied up against the wall are a row of twenty Indians, most terrified, a few defiant, in front of them several armed men in uniform. A heavy man in a sweat-stained khaki shirt turns out to be the captain in charge and, after a good deal of questioning of Jim which establishes that he got there by accident while on a botanical expedition, explains that the Indians are a random group of the inhabitants who, after recent acts of protest against the government, are just about to be killed to remind other possible protestors of the advantages of not protesting. However, since Jim is an honoured visitor from another land, the captain is happy to offer him a guest's privilege of killing one of the Indians himself. If Jim accepts, then as a special mark of the occasion, the other Indians will be let off. Of course, if Jim refuses, then there is no special occasion, and Pedro here will do what he was about to do when Jim arrived, and kill them all. Jim, with some desperate recollection of schoolboy fiction, wonders whether if

he got hold of a gun, he could hold the captain, Pedro and the rest of the soldiers to threat, but it is quite clear from the set-up that nothing of that kind is going to work: any attempt at that sort of thing will mean that all the Indians will be killed, and himself. The men against the wall, and the other villagers, understand the situation, and are obviously begging him to accept. What should he do?

To these dilemmas, it seems to me that utilitarianism replies, in the first case, that George should accept the job, and in the second, that Jim should kill the Indian. Not only does utilitarianism give these answers but, if the situations are essentially as described and there are no further special factors, it regards them, it seems to me, as *obviously* the right answers. But many of us would certainly wonder whether, in (1), that could possibly be the right answer at all; and in the case of (2), even one who came to think that perhaps that was the answer, might well wonder whether it was obviously the answer. Nor is it just a question of the rightness or obviousness of these answers. It is also a question of what sort of considerations come into finding the answer. A feature of utilitarianism is that it cuts out a kind of consideration which for some others makes a difference to what they feel about such cases: a consideration involving the idea, as we might first and very simply put it, that each of us is specially responsible for what *he* does, rather than for what other people do. This is an idea closely connected with the value of integrity. It is often suspected that utilitarianism, at least in its direct forms, makes integrity as a value more or less unintelligible. I shall try to show that this suspicion is correct. Of course, even if that is correct, it would not necessarily follow that we should reject utilitarianism; perhaps, as utilitarians sometimes suggest, we should just forget about integrity, in favour of such things as a concern for the general good. However, if I am right, we cannot merely do that, since the reason why utilitarianism cannot understand integrity is that it cannot coherently describe the relations between a man's projects and his actions.

Two kinds of remoter effect

A lot of what we have to say about this question will be about the relations between my projects and other people's projects. But before we get on to that, we should first ask whether we are assuming too hastily what the utilitarian answers to the dilemmas will be. In terms of more direct effects of the possible decisions, there does not indeed seem much doubt about the answer in either case; but it might be said that in terms of more remote or less evident effects counterweights might be found to enter the utilitarian scales. Thus the effect on George of a decision to take the job might be invoked, or its effect on others who might know of his decision. The possibility of there being more beneficent labours in the future from which he might be barred or disqualified, might be mentioned; and so forth. Such effects – in particular, possible effects on the agent's character, and effects on the public at large – are often invoked by utilitarian writers dealing with problems about lying or promise-breaking, and some similar considerations might be invoked here.

There is one very general remark that is worth making about arguments of this sort. The certainty that attaches to these hypotheses about possible effects is usually pretty low; in some cases, indeed, the hypothesis invoked is so implausible that it would scarcely pass if it were not being used to deliver the respectable moral answer, as in the standard fantasy that one of the effects of one's telling a particular lie is to weaken the disposition of the world at large to tell the truth. The demands on the certainty or probability of these beliefs as beliefs about particular actions are much milder than they would be on beliefs favouring the unconventional course. It may be said that this is as it should be, since the presumption must be in favour of the conventional course: but that scarcely seems a *utilitarian* answer, unless utilitarianism has already taken off in the direction of not applying the consequences to the particular act at all.

Leaving aside that very general point, I want to consider now two types of effect that are often invoked by utilitarians, and which might be invoked in connexion with these imaginary cases. The attitude or tone involved in invoking these effects may sometimes seem peculiar; but that sort of peculiarity soon becomes familiar in utilitarian discussions, and indeed it can be something of an achievement to retain a sense of it.

First, there is the psychological effect on the agent. Our descriptions of these situations have not so far taken account of how George or Jim will be after they have taken the one course or the other; and it might be said that if they take the course which seemed at first the utilitarian one, the effects on them will be in fact bad enough and extensive enough to cancel out the initial utilitarian advantages of that course. Now there is one version of this effect in which, for a utilitarian, some confusion must be involved, namely that in which the agent feels bad, his subsequent conduct and relations are crippled and so on, *because he thinks that he has done the wrong thing* – for if the balance of outcomes was as it appeared to be *before* invoking this effect, then he has not (from the utilitarian point of view) done the wrong thing. So that version of the effect, for a rational and utilitarian agent, could not possibly make any difference to the assessment of right and wrong. However, perhaps he is not a thoroughly rational agent, and is disposed to have bad feelings, whichever he decided to do. Now such feelings, which are from a strictly utilitarian point of view irrational – nothing, a utilitarian can point out, is advanced by having them – cannot, consistently, have any great weight in a utilitarian calculation. I shall consider in a moment an argument

107

to suggest that they should have no weight at all in it. But short of that, the utilitarian could reasonably say that such feelings should not be encouraged, even if we accept their existence, and that to give them a lot of weight is to encourage them. Or, at the very best, even if they are straightforwardly and without any discount to be put into the calculation, their weight must be small: they are after all (and at best) one man's feelings.

That consideration might seem to have particular force in Jim's case. In George's case, his feelings represent a larger proportion of what is to be weighed, and are more commensurate in character with other items in the calculation. In Jim's case, however, his feelings might seem to be of very little weight compared with other things that are at stake. There is a powerful and recognizable appeal that can be made on this point: as that a refusal by Jim to do what he has been invited to do would be a kind of self-indulgent squeamishness. That is an appeal which can be made by other than utilitarians – indeed, there are some uses of it which cannot be consistently made by utilitarians, as when it essentially involves the idea that there is something dishonourable about such self-indulgence. But in some versions it is a familiar, and it must be said a powerful, weapon of utilitarianism. One must be clear, though, about what it can and cannot accomplish. The most it can do, so far as I can see, is to invite one to consider how seriously, and for what reasons, one feels that what one is invited to do is (in these circumstances) wrong, and in particular, to consider that question from the utilitarian point of view. When the agent is not seeing the situation from a utilitarian point of view, the appeal cannot force him to do so; and if he does come round to seeing it from a utilitarian point of view, there is virtually nothing left for the appeal to do. If he does not see it from a utilitarian point of view, he will not see his resistance to the invitation, and the unpleasant feelings he associates with accepting it, *just* as disagreeable experiences of his; they figure rather as emotional expressions of a thought that to accept would be wrong. He may be asked, as by the appeal, to consider whether he is right, and indeed whether he is fully serious, in thinking that. But the assertion of the appeal, that he is being self-indulgently squeamish, will not itself answer that question, or even help to answer it, since it essentially tells him to regard his feelings just as unpleasant experiences of his, and he cannot, by doing that, answer the question they pose when they are precisely not so regarded, but are regarded as indications[1] of what he thinks is right and wrong. If he does come round fully to the utilitarian point of view then of course he will regard these feelings just as unpleasant experiences of his. And once Jim – at least – has come to see them in that light, there is nothing left for the appeal to do, since *of course* his feelings, so regarded, are of virtually no weight at all in relation to the other things at stake. The 'squeamishness' appeal is not an argument which adds in a hitherto neglected consideration. Rather, it is an invitation to consider the situation, and one's own feelings, from a utilitarian point of view.

The reason why the squeamishness appeal can be very unsettling, and one can be unnerved by the suggestion of self-indulgence in going against utilitarian considerations, is not that we are utilitarians who are uncertain what utilitarian value to attach to our moral feelings, but that we are partially at least not utilitarians, and cannot regard our moral feelings merely as objects of utilitarian value. Because our moral relation to the world is partly given by such feelings, and by a sense of what we can or cannot 'live with', to come to regard those feelings from a purely utilitarian point of view, that is to say, as happenings outside one's moral self, is to lose a sense of one's moral identity; to lose, in the most literal way, one's integrity. At this point utilitarianism alienates one from one's moral feelings; we shall see a little later how, more basically, it alienates one from one's actions as well.

If, then, one is really going to regard one's feelings from a strictly utilitarian point of view, Jim should give very little weight at all to his; it seems almost indecent, in fact, once one has taken that point of view, to suppose that he should give any at all. In George's case one might feel that things were slightly different. It is interesting, though, that one reason why one might think that – namely that one person principally affected is his wife – is very dubiously available to a utilitarian. George's wife has some reason to be interested in George's integrity and his sense of it; the Indians, quite properly, have no interest in Jim's. But it is not at all clear how utilitarianism would describe that difference.

There is an argument, and a strong one, that a strict utilitarian should give not merely small extra weight, in calculations of right and wrong, to feelings of this kind, but that he should give absolutely no weight to them at all. This is based on the point, which we have already seen, that if a course of action is, before taking these sorts of feelings into account, utilitarianly preferable, then bad feelings about that kind of action will be from a utilitarian point of view irrational. Now it might be thought that even if that is so, it would not mean that in a utilitarian calculation such feelings should not be taken into account; it is after all a well-known boast of utilitarianism that it is a realistic outlook which seeks the best in the world as it is, and takes any form of happiness or unhappiness into account. While a utilitarian will no doubt seek to diminish the incidence of feelings which are utilitarianly irrational – or at least of disagreeable feelings which are so – he might be expected to take them into account while they exist. This is without doubt classical utilitarian doctrine, but there is good reason to think that utilitarianism cannot stick to it without embracing results which are startlingly unacceptable and perhaps self-defeating.

Suppose that there is in a certain society a racial minority. Considering merely the ordinary interests of the other citizens, as opposed to their sentiments, this minority does no particular harm; we may suppose that it does not confer any very great benefits either. Its presence is in those terms neutral or mildly beneficial. However, the other citizens have such prejudices that they find the sight of this group, even the knowledge of its presence, very disagreeable. Proposals are made for removing in some way this minority. If we assume various quite plausible things (as that programmes to change the majority sentiment are likely to be protracted and ineffective) then even if the removal would be unpleasant for the minority, a utilitarian calculation might well end up favouring this step, especially if the minority were a rather small minority and the majority were very severely prejudiced, that is to say, were made very severely uncomfortable by the presence of the minority.

A utilitarian might find that conclusion embarrassing; and not merely because of its nature, but because of the grounds on which it is reached. While a utilitarian might be expected to take into account certain other sorts of consequences of the prejudice, as that a majority prejudice is likely to be displayed in conduct disagreeable to the minority, and so forth, he might be made to wonder whether the unpleasant experiences of the prejudiced people should be allowed, *merely as such*, to count. If he does count them, merely as such, then he has once more separated himself from a body of ordinary moral thought which he might have hoped to accommodate; he may also have started on the path of defeating his own view of things. For one feature of these sentiments is that they are from the utilitarian point of view itself irrational, and a thoroughly utilitarian person would either not have them, or if he found that he did tend to have them, would himself seek to discount them. Since the sentiments in question are such that a rational utilitarian would discount them in himself, it is reasonable to suppose that he should discount them in his calculations about society; it does seem quite unreasonable for him to give just as much weight to feelings – considered just in themselves, one must recall, as experiences of those that have them – which are essentially based on views which are from a utilitarian point of view irrational, as to those which accord with utilitarian principles. Granted this idea, it seems reasonable for him to rejoin a body of moral thought in other respects congenial to him, and discount those sentiments, just considered in themselves, totally, on the principle that no pains or discomforts are to count in the utilitarian sum which their subjects have just because they hold views which are by utilitarian standards irrational. But if he accepts that, then in the cases we are at present considering no extra weight at all can be put in for bad feelings of George or Jim about their choices, if those choices are, leaving out those feelings, on the first round utilitarianly rational.

The psychological effect on the agent was the first of two general effects considered by utilitarians, which had to be discussed. The second is in general a more substantial item, but it need not take so long, since it is both clearer and has little application to the present cases. This is the *precedent effect*. As Burke rightly emphasized, this effect can be important: that one morally *can* do what someone has actually done, is a psychologically effective principle, if not a deontically valid one. For the effect to operate, obviously some conditions must hold on the publicity of the act and on such things as the status of the agent (such considerations weighed importantly with Sir Thomas More); what these may be will vary evidently with circumstances.

In order for the precedent effect to make a difference to a utilitarian calculation, it must be based upon a confusion. For suppose that there is an act which would be the best in the circumstances, except that doing it will encourage by precedent other people to do things which will not be the best things to do. Then the situation of those other people must be relevantly different from that of the original agent; if it were not, then in doing the same as what would be the best course for the original agent, they would necessarily do the best thing themselves. But if the situations, are in this way relevantly different, it must be a confused perception which takes the first situation, and the agent's course in it, as an adequate precedent for the second.

However, the fact that the precedent effect, if it really makes a difference, is in this sense based on a confusion, does not mean that it is not perfectly real, nor that it is to be discounted: social effects are by their nature confused in this sort of way. What it does emphasize is that calculations of the precedent effect have got to be realistic, involving considerations of how people are actually likely to be influenced. In the present examples, however, it is very implausible to think that the precedent effect could be invoked to make any difference to the calculation. Jim's case is extraordinary enough, and it is hard to imagine who the recipients of the effect might be supposed to be; while George is not in a sufficiently public situation or role for the question to arise in that form, and in any case one might suppose that the motivations of others on such an issue were quite likely to be fixed one way or another already.

No appeal, then, to these other effects is going to make a difference to what the utilitarian will decide about our examples. Let us now look more closely at the structure of those decisions.

Integrity

The situations have in common that if the agent does not do a certain disagreeable thing, someone else will, and in Jim's situation at least the result, the state of affairs after the other man has acted, if he does, will be worse than after Jim has acted, if Jim does. The same, on a smaller scale, is true of George's case. I have already suggested that

111

it is inherent in consequentialism that it offers a strong doctrine of negative responsibility: if I know that if I do X, O_1 will eventuate, and if I refrain from doing X, O_2 will, and that O_2 is worse than O_1, then I am responsible for O_2 if I refrain voluntarily from doing X. 'You could have prevented it', as will be said, and truly, to Jim, if he refuses, by the relatives of the other Indians. (I shall leave the important question, which is to the side of the present issue, of the obligations, if any, that nest round the word 'know': how far does one, under utilitarianism, have to research into the possibilities of maximally beneficent action, including prevention?)

In the present cases, the situation of O_2 includes another agent bringing about results worse than O_1. So far as O_2 has been identified up to this point – merely as the worse outcome which will eventuate if I refrain from doing X – we might equally have said that what that other brings about is O_2; but that would be to underdescribe the situation. For what occurs if Jim refrains from action is not solely twenty Indians dead, but *Pedro's killing twenty Indians*, and that is not a result which Pedro brings about, though the death of the Indians is. We can say: what one does is not included in the outcome of what one does, while what another does can be included in the outcome of what one does. For that to be so, as the terms are now being used, only a very weak condition has to be satisfied: for Pedro's killing the Indians to be the outcome of Jim's refusal, it only has to be causally true that if Jim had not refused, Pedro would not have done it.

That may be enough for us to speak, in some sense, of Jim's responsibility for that outcome, if it occurs; but it is certainly not enough, it is worth noticing, for us to speak of Jim's *making* those things happen. For granted this way of their coming about, he could have made them happen only by making Pedro shoot, and there is no acceptable sense in which his refusal makes Pedro shoot. If the captain had said on Jim's refusal, 'you leave me with no alternative', he would have been lying, like most who use that phrase. While the deaths, and the killing, may be the outcome of Jim's refusal, it is misleading to think, in such a case, of Jim having an *effect* on the world through the medium (as it happens) of Pedro's acts; for this is to leave Pedro out of the picture in his essential role of one who has intentions and projects, projects for realizing which Jim's refusal would leave an opportunity. Instead of thinking in terms of supposed effects of Jim's projects on Pedro, it is more revealing to think in terms of the effects of Pedro's projects on Jim's decision. This is the direction from which I want to criticize the notion of negative responsibility.

There are of course other ways in which this notion can be criticized. Many have hoped to discredit it by insisting on the basic moral relevance of the distinction between action and inaction, between intervening and letting things take their course. The distinction is certainly of great moral significance, and indeed it is not easy to think of any moral outlook which could get along without making some use of it. But it is unclear, both in itself and in its moral applications, and the unclarities are of a kind which precisely cause it to give way when, in very difficult cases, weight has to be put on it. There is much to be said in this area, but I doubt whether the sort of dilemma we are considering is going to be resolved by a simple use of this distinction. Again, the issue of negative responsibility can be pressed on the question of how limits are to be placed on one's apparently boundless obligation, implied by utilitarianism, to improve the world. Some answers are needed to that, too – and answers which stop short of relapsing into the bad faith of supposing that one's responsibilities could be adequately characterized just by appeal to one's roles.[2] But, once again, while that is a real question, it cannot be brought to bear directly on the present kind of case, since it is hard to think of anyone supposing that in Jim's case it would be an adequate response for him to say that it was none of his business.

What projects does a utilitarian agent have? As a utilitarian, he has the general project of bringing about maximally desirable outcomes; how he is to do this at any given moment is a question of what causal levers, so to speak, are at that moment within reach. The desirable outcomes, however, do not just consist of agents carrying out *that* project; there must be other more basic or lower-order projects which he and other agents have, and the desirable outcomes are going to consist, in part, of the maximally harmonious realization of those projects ('in part', because one component of a utilitarianly desirable outcome may be the occurrence of agreeable experiences which are not the satisfaction of anybody's projects). Unless there were first-order projects, the general utilitarian project would have nothing to work on, and would be vacuous. What do the more basic or lower-order projects comprise? Many will be the obvious kinds of desires for things for oneself, one's family, one's friends, including basic necessities of life, and in more relaxed circumstances, objects of taste. Or there may be pursuits and interests of an intellectual, cultural or creative character. I introduce those as a separate class not because the objects of them lie in a separate class, and provide – as some utilitarians, in their churchy way, are fond of saying – 'higher' pleasures. I introduce them separately because the agent's identification with them may be of a different order. It does not have to be: cultural and aesthetic interests just belong, for many, along with any other taste; but some people's commitment to these kinds of interests just is at once more thoroughgoing and serious than their pursuit of various objects of taste, while it is more individual and permeated with character than the desire for the necessities of life.

Beyond these, someone may have projects connected with his support of some cause: Zionism, for instance, or the abolition of chemical and biological warfare. Or there may be projects which flow from some more general disposition towards human conduct and character, such as a hatred of injustice, or of cruelty, or of killing.

It may be said that this last sort of disposition and its associated project do not count as (logically) 'lower-order' relative to the higher-order project of maximizing desirable outcomes; rather, it may be said, it is itself a 'higher-order' project. The vital question is not, however, how it is to be classified, but whether it and similar projects are to count among the projects whose satisfaction is to be included in the maximizing sum, and, correspondingly, as contributing to the agent's happiness. If the utilitarian says 'no' to that, then he is almost certainly committed to a version of utililarianism as absurdly superficial and shallow as Benthamite versions have often been accused of being. For this project will be discounted, presumably, on the ground that it involves, in the specification of its object, the mention of other people's happiness or interests: thus it is the kind of project which (unlike the pursuit of food for myself) presupposes a reference to other people's projects. But that criterion would eliminate any desire at all which was not blankly and in the most straightforward sense egoistic.[3] Thus we should be reduced to frankly egoistic first-order projects, and – for all essential purposes – the one second-order utilitarian project of maximally satisfying first-order projects. Utilitarianism has a tendency to slide in this direction, and to leave a vast hole in the range of human desires, between egoistic inclinations and necessities at one end, and impersonally benevolent happiness-management at the other. But the utilitarianism which has to leave this hole is the most primitive form, which offers a quite rudimentary account of desire. Modern versions of the theory are supposed to be neutral with regard to what sorts of things make people happy or what their projects are. Utilitarianism would do well then to acknowledge the evident fact that among the things that make people happy is not only making other people happy, but being taken up or involved in any of a vast range of projects, or – if we waive the evangelical and moralizing associations of the word – commitments. One can be committed to such things as a person, a cause, an institution, a career, one's own genius, or the pursuit of danger.

Now none of these is itself the *pursuit of happiness*: by an exceedingly ancient platitude, it is not at all clear that there could be anything which was just that, or at least anything that had the slightest chance of being successful. Happiness, rather, requires being involved in, or at least content with, something else.[4] It is not impossible for utilitarianism to accept that point: it does not have to be saddled with a naïve and absurd philosophy of mind about the relation between desire and happiness. What it does have to say is that if such commitments are worthwhile, then pursuing the projects that flow from them, and realizing some of those projects, will make the person for whom they are worthwhile, happy. It may be that to claim that is still wrong: it may well be that a commitment can make sense to a man (can make sense of his life) without his supposing that it will make him *happy*.[5] But that is not the present point; let us grant to utilitarianism that all worthwhile human projects must conduce, one way or another, to happiness. The point is that even if that is true, it does not follow, nor could it possibly be true, that those projects are themselves projects of pursuing happiness. One has to believe in, or at least want, or quite minimally, be content with, other things, for there to be anywhere that happiness can come from.

Utilitarianism, then, should be willing to agree that its general aim of maximizing happiness does not imply that what everyone is doing is just pursuing happiness. On the contrary, people have to be pursuing other things. What those other things may be, utilitarianism, sticking to its professed empirical stance, should be prepared just to find out. No doubt some possible projects it will want to discourage, on the grounds that their being pursued involves a negative balance of happiness to others: though even there, the unblinking accountant's eye of the strict utilitarian will have something to put in the positive column, the satisfactions of the destructive agent. Beyond that, there will be a vast variety of generally beneficent or at least harmless projects; and some no doubt, will take the form not just of tastes or fancies, but of what I have called 'commitments'. It may even be that the utilitarian researcher will find that many of those with commitments, who have really identified themselves with objects outside themselves, who are thoroughly involved with other persons, or institutions, or activities or causes, are actually happier than those whose projects and wants are not like that. If so, that is an important piece of utilitarian empirical lore.

When I say 'happier' here, I have in mind the sort of consideration which any utilitarian would be committed to accepting: as for instance that such people are less likely to have a break-down or commit suicide. Of course that is not all that is actually involved, but the point in this argument is to use to the maximum degree utilitarian notions, in order to locate a breaking point in utilitarian thought. In appealing to this strictly utilitarian notion, I am being more consistent with utilitarianism than Smart is. In his struggles with the problem of the brain-electrode man, Smart commends the idea that 'happy' is a partly evaluative term, in the sense that we call 'happiness' those kinds of satisfaction which, as things are, we approve of. But *by what standard* is this surplus element of approval supposed, from a utilitarian point of view, to be allocated? There is no source for it, on a strictly utilitarian view, except further degrees of satisfaction, but there are none of those available, or the problem would not arise. Nor does it help to appeal to the fact that we dislike in prospect things which we like when we get there, for from a utilitarian point of view it would seem that the original dislike was merely

115

irrational or based on an error. Smart's argument at this point seems to be embarrassed by a well-known utilitarian uneasiness, which comes from a feeling that it is not respectable to ignore the 'deep', while not having anywhere left in human life to locate it.[6]

Let us now go back to the agent as utilitarian, and his higher-order project of maximizing desirable outcomes. At this level, he is committed only to that: what the outcome will actually consist of will depend entirely on the facts, on what persons with what projects and what potential satisfactions there are within calculable reach of the causal levers near which he finds himself. His own substantial projects and commitments come into it, but only as one lot among others – they potentially provide one set of satisfactions among those which he may be able to assist from where he happens to be. He is the agent of the satisfaction system who happens to be at a particular point at a particular time: in Jim's case, our man in South America. His own decisions as a utilitarian agent are a function of all the satisfactions which he can affect from where he is: and this means that the projects of others, to an indeterminately great extent, determine his decision.

This may be so either positively or negatively. It will be so positively if agents within the causal field of his decision have projects which are at any rate harmless, and so should be assisted. It will equally be so, but negatively, if there is an agent within the causal field whose projects are harmful, and have to be frustrated to maximize desirable outcomes. So it is with Jim and the soldier Pedro. On the utilitarian view, the undesirable projects of other people as much determine, in this negative way, one's decisions as the desirable ones do positively: if those people were not there, or had different projects, the causal nexus would be different, and it is the actual state of the causal nexus which determines the decision. The determination to an indefinite degree of my decisions by other people's projects is just another aspect of my unlimited responsibility to act for the best in a causal framework formed to a considerable extent by their projects.

The decision so determined is, for utilitarianism, the right decision. But what if it conflicts with some project of mine? This, the utilitarian will say, has already been dealt with: the satisfaction to you of fulfilling your project, and any satisfactions to others of your so doing, have already been through the calculating device and have been found inadequate. Now in the case of many sorts of projects, that is a perfectly reasonable sort of answer. But in the case of projects of the sort I have called 'commitments', those with which one is more deeply and extensively involved and identified, this cannot just by itself be an adequate answer, and there may be no adequate answer at all. For, to take the extreme sort of case, how can a man, as a utilitarian agent, come to regard as one satisfaction among others, and a dispensable one, a project or attitude round which he has built his life, just because someone else's projects have so structured the causal scene that that is how the utilitarian sum comes out?

The point here is not, as utilitarians may hasten to say, that if the project or attitude is that central to his life, then to abandon it will be very disagreeable to him and great loss of utility will be involved. I have already argued . . . that it is not like that; on the contrary, once he is prepared to look at it like that, the argument in any serious case is over anyway. The point is that he is identified with his actions as flowing from projects and attitudes which in some cases he takes seriously at the deepest level, as what his life is about (or, in some cases, this section of his life – seriousness is not necessarily the same as persistence). It is absurd to demand of such a man, when the sums come in from the utility network which the projects of others have in part determined, that he should just step aside from his own project and decision and acknowledge the decision which utilitarian calculation requires. It is to alienate him in a real sense from his actions and the source of his action in his own convictions. It is to make him into a channel between the input of everyone's projects, including his own, and an output of optimific decision; but this is to neglect the extent to which *his* actions and *his* decisions have to be seen as the actions and decisions which flow from the projects and attitudes with which he is most closely identified. It is thus, in the most literal sense, an attack on his integrity.[7]

These sorts of considerations do not in themselves give solutions to practical dilemmas such as those provided by our examples; but I hope they help to provide other ways of thinking about them. In fact, it is not hard to see that in George's case, viewed from this perspective, the utilitarian solution would be wrong. Jim's case is different, and harder. But if (as I suppose) the utilitarian is probably right in this case, that is not to be found out just by asking the utilitarian's questions. Discussions of it – and I am not going to try to carry it further here – will have to take seriously the distinction between my killing someone, and its coming about because of what I do that someone else kills them: a distinction based, not so much on the distinction between action and inaction, as on the distinction between my projects and someone else's projects. At least it will have to start by taking that seriously, as utilitarianism does not; but then it will have to build out from there by asking why that distinction seems to have less, or a different, force in this case than it has in George's. One question here would be how far one's powerful objection to killing people just is, in fact, an application of a powerful objection to their being killed. Another dimension of that is the issue of how much it matters that the people at risk are actual, and there, as opposed to hypothetical, or future, or merely elsewhere.[8]

There are many other considerations that could come into such a question, but the immediate point of all this is to draw one particular contrast with utilitarianism: that to reach a grounded decision in such a case should not be regarded as a matter of just discounting one's reactions, impulses and deeply held projects in the face of the pattern of utilities, nor yet merely adding them in – but in the first instance of trying to understand them.

Of course, time and circumstances are unlikely to make a grounded decision, in Jim's case at least, possible. It might not even be decent. Instead of thinking in a rational and systematic way either about utilities or about the value of human life, the relevance of the people at risk being present, and so forth, the presence of the people at risk may just have its effect. The significance of the immediate should not be underestimated. Philosophers, not only utilitarian ones, repeatedly urge one to view the world *sub specie aeternitatis*,[9] but for most human purposes that is not a good *species* to view it under. If we are not agents of the universal satisfaction system, we are not primarily janitors of any system of values, even our own: very often, we just act, as a possibly confused result of the situation in which we are engaged. That, I suspect, is very often an exceedingly good thing. To what extent utilitarians regard it as a good thing is an obscure question.

Notes

1   On the non-cognitivist meta-ethic in terms of which Smart presents his utilitarianism, the term 'indications' here would represent an understatement.
2   For some remarks bearing on this, see [Bernard Williams] *Morality: An Introduction to Ethics* (Harmondsworth: Penguin Books, 1973), the section on 'Goodness and roles', and Cohen's article there cited.
3   On the subject of egoistic and non-egoistic desires, see [Williams] 'Egoism and altruism', in *Problems of the Self* (London: Cambridge University Press, 1973).
4   This does not imply that there is no such thing as the project of pursuing pleasure. Some writers who have correctly resisted the view that all desires are desires for pleasure, have given an account of pleasure so thoroughly adverbial as to leave it quite unclear how there could be a distinctively hedonist way of life at all. Some room has to be left for that, though there are important difficulties both in defining it and living it. Thus (particularly in the case of the very rich) it often has highly ritual aspects, apparently part of a strategy to counter boredom.
5   For some remarks on this possibility, see *Morality*, section on 'What is morality about?'
6   One of many resemblances in spirit between utilitarianism and high-minded evangelical Christianity. [The philosopher J. J. C. Smart wrote the first part of the book from which this reading is extracted. Smart gave a spirited defence of utilitarianism (p. 22). Ed.]

7   Interestingly related to these notions is the Socratic idea that courage is a virtue particularly connected with keeping a clear sense of what one regards as most important. They also centrally raise questions about the value of pride. Humility, as something beyond the real demand of correct self-appraisal, was specially a Christian virtue because it involved subservience to God. In a secular context it can only represent subservience to other men and their projects.

8   For a more general discussion of this issue see Charles Fried, *An Anatomy of Values* (Cambridge, Mass.: Harvard University Press, 1970), Part Three.

9   Cf. Smart, in *Utilitarianism: For and Against*, p. 63.

15

The Solzhenitsyn principle
Jonathan Glover

Here Jonathan Glover responds to the claim made by Bernard Williams in the previous reading that utilitarianism (or consequentialism as Glover tends to call it) does not leave enough room for personal integrity. Glover examines a view he labels 'the Solzhenitsyn principle', after the Russian dissident who was unwilling to be the person who brought a lie into the world. For people who adhere to such a view, what matters is keeping their hands clean at any cost, even if the overall outcome is worse than it would have been if they had sacrificed some of their own personal purity (clearly not a utilitarian position). Glover questions whether Williams's critique of utilitarianism achieves as much as he claims it does.

From Jonathan Glover, 'It makes no difference whether or not I do it', *Proceedings of the Aristotelian Society*, suppl. vol. XLIX

The Solzhenitsyn principle

Bernard Williams has recently argued that it is desirable to find some middle way between a morality of absolute prohibitions and a morality where total outcome is decisive. Such a morality would have to leave more room, he argues, than a consequentialist morality can, for considerations of personal integrity. In such a morality, outcome is not all that matters. It is also important what role my decision or action plays in bringing it about.

Considerations of this sort seem central to people's resistance to consequentialist morality. In Solzhenitsyn's Nobel lecture, he says (echoing one of his own characters in *The First Circle*) 'And the simple step of a simple courageous man is not to take part in the lie, not to support deceit. Let the lie come into the world, even dominate the world, but not through me.'

The Solzhenitsyn principle does not commit people who hold it to the view that some acts are wrong for reasons entirely independent of outcome. It is open to us to incorporate this principle in a kind of tempered consequentialism. I may think that a certain outcome is bad, and then invoke the Solzhenitsyn principle to say that *I* must not be the person who brings it about. But this is obviously a departure from the strictest consequentialism, which is concerned with total outcomes, rather than with what would ordinarily be described as the consequences of *my* act.

How can we choose between the strictest consequentialism and the Solzhenitsyn principle? If they always generated the same answer, there would be no need to choose. But clearly they do not. In the chemical warfare problem, if there are cases where side effects give overall support to taking the job, this leads to a clash with the Solzhenitsyn principle. In those cases, to obey the principle is to do so at the cost of the total outcome being worse. The strict consequentialist will say that the principle tells us to keep our hands clean, at a cost which will probably be paid by other people. It is excessively self-regarding, placing considerations either of my own feelings or purity of character far too high on the scale of factors to be considered.

Williams has considered an argument of this kind, which he calls the 'squeamishness appeal' in the context of an example of his own. A man, arriving in a small South American town, finds that soldiers are about to shoot twenty captive Indians as a reprisal for recent anti-government protests there. The man, as a foreign visitor, is offered the privilege of shooting one Indian. If he does this, the others will be let off. There is no escape from the dilemma of accepting or refusing the offer.

Williams plausibly says that the utilitarian would think that he obviously ought to accept the offer. Williams does not himself say that the offer should be refused, but that it is not *obvious* that it should be accepted. He then refers to the criticism that a refusal might be 'self-indulgent squeamishness'. But he suggests a reply to this squeamishness appeal. He says that this appeal can only carry weight with someone already seeing the situation in terms of strict consequentialism. He says that, for anyone not seeing things from that point of view, 'he will not see his resistance to the invitation, and the unpleasant feelings he associates with accepting it, *just* as disagreeable experiences of his; they figure rather as emotional expressions of a thought that to accept would be wrong'. Williams goes on to say, 'Because our moral relation to the world is partly given by such feelings, and by a sense of what we can or cannot 'live with', to come to regard those feelings, from a purely utilitarian point of view, that is to say, as happenings outside one's moral self, is to lose a sense of one's moral identity; to lose, in the most literal way, one's integrity.'

This reply does have some force, but also severe limitations. In the first place, it does not show that the *utilitarian* who regards certain of his own feelings in this way has lost his integrity. He can agree that his morality is partly based on such feelings, but say that when he reflects on

121

his feelings he finds that they cannot all be combined into anything coherent. It then seems legitimate to disregard some of them as anomalies. When I hear of some medical experiments on an animal, I may feel a revulsion against all vivisection, but this may conflict with my feelings when I reflect on the implications of this for medical research. I do not lose my integrity by deciding that my first response was exaggerated.

The second limitation of the Williams reply is that it seems to presuppose that we can readily distinguish feelings that have moral import from other feelings. But this is not clear. The atheist . . . is surely right to attach no moral significance to his guilt feelings when he does not go to church. But his guilt feelings may not be phenomenologically distinct from those of a man whose whole morality centres round his religion.

The final doubt about the Solzhenitsyn principle is that it appears to presuppose a conventional but questionable doctrine about the moral difference between acts and omissions. According to this doctrine, I have made a worse moral choice if something bad foreseeably comes about as the result of my deliberate act than I have if something equally bad foreseeably comes about as the result of my deliberate omission. If we eliminate a complication by removing the difference of numbers, the Solzhenitsyn principle seems to suggest that it would be worse for me to shoot an Indian than for me deliberately to refuse an invitation with the foreseen and inevitable consequence that a soldier would shoot the same Indian. To look closely at arguments normally offered for this conventional view might increase our scepticism about the principle so closely related to it.

(The criticism of a possessive attitude to one's own virtue seems to be the point of the story of the old woman and the onion in *The Brothers Karamazov*. After a wicked life, an old woman was in the lake of fire. But God heard about her only good deed: she had once given an onion from her garden to a beggar. He told her guardian angel to hold out the onion for her to catch hold of it, and to try to pull her up from the lake to paradise. She was being pulled out when other sinners in the lake caught hold of her to be pulled out. The woman kicked them, saying, 'It's me who is being pulled out, not you. It's my onion, not yours.' When she said this, the onion broke and she fell back into the lake.)

Judging actions and judging people

Our inclination to make the choice I am arguing against (to prefer the Solzhenitsyn principle to strict consequentialism) is perhaps partly caused by a tendency to confuse judging actions with judging people. We ought in our thinking to keep separate the standpoints of the agent deciding between different courses of action and of the moral critic or judge, who comments on the moral quality of people's character.

The moralities of other people may lead them to perform acts that arouse our admiration, whether they are obeying absolute prohibitions or the Solzhenitsyn principle. Solzhenitsyn's own conduct while in Russia is a case in point. A more calculating, strict consequentialist morality might not have generated such a fine display of independence and bravery. (*Might* not: for the paradox here is that Solzhenitsyn's own example has done good in Russia that we cannot calculate, and has probably, in consequentialist terms, been well worth the risks taken. And even in our society, where the penalties are so much less, acts of moral independence help to create a climate where social pressures are less, and where the views of the powerful and the orthodox are treated with appropriate lack of reverence.)

Because we often admire the moral character of people following the Solzhenitsyn principle, we easily slide over into thinking their action right. But there is no equivalence here. Unless we are narrow-minded bigots, we will often admire the moral qualities of people following many different sets of beliefs: it does not follow that we are justified in following all or any of them when we have to act ourselves. The corollary of this is the platitude that we can sometimes disagree with a moral view while respecting those who act on it. Sometimes the reluctance to reject the Solzhenitsyn principle rests on neglect of this platitude.

Is there an oddity in saying that we can admire the character of those who accept the Solzhenitsyn principle just after quoting the story of the old woman and the onion?

We should distinguish here between admirable character traits on the one hand and a policy which gives exaggerated weight to preserving them on the other. Someone acting on the Solzhenitsyn principle can display such traits as honesty, loyalty, or a revulsion against killing or hurting people. These are all traits whose existence is in overall effect immensely beneficial. A consequentialist has every reason to encourage them. (This is the point sometimes exaggerated by crude consequentialists when they wrongly suggest that we admire these traits *because* of their contribution to social welfare.) We can admire these traits while thinking that they sometimes lead to the wrong decision, as happens if, in the Williams case, the man refuses to shoot an Indian. If, in explaining this, he says 'I just could not bring myself to do it', we see an admirable character trait that has too strong a grip on him. But if he says 'Before coming to South America I read an interesting article by Bernard Williams, and so I understood that I must preserve my integrity, even at the cost of nineteen lives', the onion criticism then applies.

16

Neo-Aristotelianism
Rosalind Hursthouse

In recent years virtue theory, which is derived from Aristotle's moral philosophy, has become increasingly popular as an alternative both to deontological theories such as Kant's and to consequentialism such as Mill's utilitarianism. Here Rosalind Hursthouse (1943–) sketches the main features of such virtue theory or neo-Aristotelianism, bringing out its distinctive approach. Neo-Aristotelians are interested not just in particular actions, but in the flourishing of individuals over a lifetime; they are concerned with character traits rather than duties. The essential question for a neo-Aristotelian is not 'Which actions are right or wrong?' but rather 'How am I to live well?'

From Rosalind Hursthouse, *Beginning Lives*

We have . . . an enormous vocabulary with which to describe people and their actions in ways relevant to morality. We may describe them, for instance, as courageous, honest, public-spirited, kind, fair, loyal, responsible . . . and conversely as cowardly, dishonest, mean, anti-social, cruel, disloyal, feckless and so on. There is a particular way of doing moral philosophy which exploits this rich vocabulary and our familiarity with it, namely an approach that takes as basic the idea of *the virtues* (courage, honesty, generosity, justice, public-spiritedness, kindness, etc.), the agent who has some or all of the virtues (*the virtuous person* who is courageous, honest, generous, etc.), and the way she acts (*virtuously*, i.e. courageously, honestly, etc.). It also uses, unselfconsciously and without special inverted commas, the concept of *the worthwhile*, assuming – as any of us do when we use it in serious moral conversation – that, difficult as it may be to define, it has at least some straightforward applications.

This way of doing moral philosophy derives from the ancient Greek philosophers Plato and Aristotle, most particularly from the latter. It might seem incredible that ancient Greek moral philosophy could have any useful application to our modern age; must it not be even more remote from us, even more outdated, than ancient Greek science? But, surprising as it may be, this is not so. It is true that one needs to adapt, to supplement, and to depart from, what Aristotle says to a certain extent; hence the 'neo-' in the title of this chapter. It is also true that the ancient Greek view of ethics differs in certain important respects from our modern one, and contains at least one concept which it is very difficult to translate. So understanding neo-Aristotelian theory requires a slight shift of focus and a little patience.

. . . .

We are accustomed to thinking about ethics or moral philosophy as concerned with the rightness and wrongness of actions. Is (all) abortion wrong? Would it be right to abort a fœtus that was going to become a baby who suffered very greatly? Is (all) infanticide wrong? These are the sorts of questions to which ethics or moral philosophy is supposed to provide answers. But the ancient Greeks start with a totally different sort of question; ethics is supposed to answer, for each one of us, the question 'How am I to live well?' What this question means and does not mean calls for some discussion.

'How am I to live well?'

This question can be expressed in a variety of ways; none is perfect, but one comes to understand it in grasping the variety.

> How should/ought/must I live in order to live the best life/flourish/be successful?

The first comment that needs to be made is that one should not be misled by the presence of so-called 'value' words ('well', 'should', 'best', 'must', 'ought') into thinking that these are specifically *moral* words. For then one will understand the question as 'How am I to live *morally* well?' 'What is the *morally* best life?' 'How should I live from the *moral* point of view?' And although, as we shall see, one would not be entirely wrong to do so, it is not the proper understanding of the question. We should/must/ought not read in a 'morally' qualification, any more than we would at the beginning of this sentence, or in such questions as 'How am I to do well in the exam?' 'How should/must/ought I get to the station from here?' We would not take the latter, for instance, to mean 'How should I get to the station from here from the moral point of view?' or 'What is the moral way of getting to the station from here?' Similarly, we should not take any of the given versions of the ancient Greek question as having this sort

125

of qualification either. This point shows up particularly clearly in any versions involving 'flourish' and 'be successful' – compare 'How should . . . etc. this plant be treated in order that it will flourish?' and 'How ought I to study if I am to be a successful student?' where once again we would not think for a moment that these were moral 'shoulds' or 'oughts'.

The next comment that needs to be made is also about these versions, about what is meant by 'flourish' and 'successful'. 'Flourishing' is one of the standard translations of the Greek word *eudaimonia*, and this is the concept that I said was very difficult to translate. It is used in ways which lead us to translate it (when it is an abstract noun) as 'good fortune' 'happiness', 'prosperity', 'flourishing', 'success', 'the best/good life'; where it is an adjective applied to a person it is translated as 'fortunate', 'happy', 'prospering', 'flourishing', 'successful', 'living well'.[1] The extent to which any one of these is and is not an adequate translation can be seen by comparing what we say about them and what Aristotle says about *eudaimonia*. For a start, he tells us that it is what we all want to get in life (or get out of it); what we are all aiming at, ultimately; the way we all want to be. And, he says, we all agree in one sense about what it consists in, namely, living well or faring well. But another truth about it is that we can disagree about what it consists in too, to the point where some of us can say it consists in wealth, others that it consists in pleasure or enjoyment and others that it consists of honour or virtue.

What do we say about success and prospering? Well, 'successful' and 'prosperous' have a materialistic sense in which they connote wealth and power; when we use them in this way it is obvious to us (a) that one can be happy and count oneself as fortunate without them and (b) that they do not necessarily bring with them happiness and the good fortune of loyal friends, loving relationships, the joys of art and learning and so on. So many of us will say that (material) success and prosperity are not what we want; that having them does not amount to faring well. But 'success' has a non-materialistic sense as well. Someone who possesses wealth and power may yet count her life to be not a success but a failure, perhaps because she finds herself to be unhappy and lonely and lacking the conviction that anything she does is worthwhile. Similarly, someone who lacks wealth and power may still count their lives to be a success – 'I am rich in the things that matter', one says, 'My children, my friends, my books, my memories, my job . . .' And it is the possibility of this non-material sense of 'success' which makes it a suitable translation of '*eudaimonia*'. Perhaps nowadays 'prosperous' can have only the materialistic sense, but the non-materialistic one still lurks in 'May you prosper', the wishes for a prosperous New Year, and indeed in the non-materialistic use of 'rich' I just exploited above.

My discussion here of two different senses should not be taken to imply that the word 'success' is literally ambiguous. In describing the lives of many people as successful one will not necessarily be meaning 'successful in one sense rather than another'. For it is no accident that the word has these different senses, since so many people believe that wealth and power are things that matter, are things one is fortunate in having, because they bring happiness. Hence too, the materialistic interpretation that can be given to 'the good life' or 'being well (or better) off'. This was as true of the ancient Greeks as it is of us; which is why some people say that *eudaimonia* consists in having wealth.

I said above that one of the truths that determines the concept of *eudaimonia* is that it is something everyone wants, the way everyone wants to be. Someone who said that she did not want to be *eudaimon* would be incomprehensible. Some philosophers, for instance John Stuart Mill, have maintained that this is true of happiness, and 'happiness' is certainly the most common translation that has been given. 'True (or real) happiness' would be better, since we tend to say that someone may be happy (though not truly happy) if they are living in a fool's paradise, or engaged in what we know is a fruitless activity, or brain-damaged and leading the life of a happy child; whereas such people are not flourishing or leading successful lives and none of us would want to be that way.

But even 'true (or real) happiness' is not obviously something everyone wants – unless, as I am sure was true of Mill, one is already thinking of 'true happiness' as *eudaimonia*. For, thinking of (true) happiness as something like (well-founded) contentment or satisfaction or enjoyment, one might intelligibly deny that one wanted to be happy. For surely one can think that happiness is not the most important thing in life; 'We're not put on this earth to enjoy ourselves' people say. I might want not just to be happy, but to do great deeds, discover great truths, change the world for the better, no matter what it cost me in terms of happiness.

Of course, rather than saying, 'No matter what it cost me in terms of happiness', I might say instead, 'Then I would die happy' or 'Then I would count myself as happy or content, no matter what it cost me'. This, I think, shows that 'happiness' does not have to connote bovine contentment or a life full of pleasure and free from striving and suffering; and as above, it is the possibility of this second sense – happiness despite a lot of striving, effort and suffering – which makes it a suitable translation of '*eudaimonia*'. Once again, as with 'success', the word 'happiness' is not ambiguous. It is no accident that it has these different senses since so many people do want contentment and a life that is pleasurable and enjoyment without cost.

Bearing all these points in mind, let us return to our question 'How am I to live well?' and its various versions 'How should/ought/must I live in order to flourish/be happy/successful?' We have seen that when 'success', etc. are construed in the intended way, this is a question that any one of us is bound to be interested in because we all want to flourish/be happy/successful; the very idea that someone interested in life should not want to 'make a go of it' in this way is deeply puzzling.[2] This, one might say, contrasts with wanting to be *morally* successful or wanting to lead a *morally* good life – there is nothing puzzling about someone who does not want to do that. As we noted above, the 'should/ought/must' in the various versions of the question should not be given a particularly moral reading; any more than they would be in 'How should/ought/must I live in order to be healthy?'

So much for the discussion of what the question means. But now we are clear about that, a new difficulty arises. How can the question, understood in the right way, possibly have anything to do with ethics or moral philosophy? If we understand it as asking 'How am I to live morally well?' we can see why it counts as a question for ethics to (try to) answer. But this interpretation is the one that has just been carefully ruled out. It now seems to be an entirely self-seeking or egoistic question which has nothing to do with ethics.

Another obstacle we have in understanding the ancient Greek view of ethics is that it does not embody the contrast, between the moral on the one hand and the self-seeking or egoistic on the other, which this new difficulty relies on. But the obstacle may be surmounted by looking carefully at the answer Aristotle gives to this question that apparently has nothing to do with ethics.

His answer is: 'If you want to flourish/be happy/successful you should acquire and practise the virtues – courage, justice, benevolence or charity, honesty, fidelity (in the sense of being true to one's word or promise), generosity, kindness, compassion, friendship . . .', i.e. as we might say 'You should be a morally virtuous person'.[3]

'Be a morally virtuous person'

With this answer we are clearly back in the business of doing ethics, but how could this have come about when we started with the self-seeking or egoistic question?

The claim that is basic to this Aristotelian view is that it comes about because, as human beings, we naturally have certain emotions and tendencies, and that it is simply a brute fact (made up of a vastly complex set of other facts) that *given* that we are as we naturally are, we can only flourish/be happy/successful by developing those character traits that are called the virtues – courage, justice, benevolence and so on. This has to be argued for each character trait that is said to be a virtue and all I can do here is illustrate briefly and roughly how the argument goes and what sorts of facts are appealed to.

Consider one of the simplest cases – generosity. Here are some of the relevant facts. We are naturally sociable creatures who like to have friends and want to be loved by friends and family. We also like and love people who do things for us rather than always putting themselves first. We also (and this is important) are not merely sympathetic but empathetic; the distress of others may distress us and their pleasure may be pleasurable to us. Given that this is how we are, someone who is mean and selfish is unlikely to be liked and loved and hence likely to be lonely and unhappy; someone who is generous is likely to enjoy the benefits of being liked and loved and moreover, in the exercise of their generosity will derive much added enjoyment, for the pleasures of those they benefit will be pleasures to them.

Consider another case – honesty. Amongst the relevant facts here are some that are similar to the preceding ones – that we want friends, want them to be trustworthy, want them to trust us – and some that are rather different, for instance, that there are likely to be occasions in our lives when we need to be believed (as the many fables on the theme of too often crying 'wolf!' illustrate). Folk wisdom also contains the adage that 'honesty is the best policy' and the conviction that 'the truth will come out' to the discomfort of those who have lied. The exercise of this virtue is not as immediately enjoyable as the exercise of generosity so often is, but the honest person has the advantage of not having to keep a constant guard on her tongue and has peace of mind thereby. One should also note that the honest person can tell the truth effortlessly in circumstances where it would be embarrassing, frightening, unpleasant or unfortunately impossible for the person who does not have the virtue. Literature abounds with scenes in which a character desperately needs to tell the truth, for if she does not, a profound relationship in her life is going to be destroyed – she will lose her lover, or her closest friend will feel betrayed, or her son will turn in bitterness from her, or she will put herself in the hands of the blackmailer or . . . to her subsequent irremediable regret and misery. But the truth in question is one of those truths it is hard to own up to – and she cannot bring herself to do so. But had she armed herself with the virtue of honesty she would have been able to. Much more could be said here too about the harm one does oneself through self-deception and how difficult it is to be simultaneously ruthlessly honest with oneself but dishonest to other people.

Even more than honesty, courage is a character trait one needs to arm oneself with, given that we are as we are – subject to death and pain and frightened of them. It is not so much that we need courage to endure pain and face death as ends in themselves, but that we are likely to have to face the threat of pain or danger for the sake of some good which we shall otherwise lose. One might imagine that someone in the position of the person I mentioned in the last chapter, who had the opportunity to save someone's life by donating their bone marrow and did not do it, was someone who saw this as a wonderful opportunity to do good but lacked the courage to do it. This might well be a source of deep regret, and how much more bitter the regret would be if one's cowardice led to the death of someone one loved. If I have managed to make myself courageous I am ready to save my child from the burning house or car at whatever risk to myself, to stand up to the terrorists who threaten my friends' lives and to my racist neighbours who are trying to hound me and my family from our home. In a society in which cancer has become one of the commonest ways to die we also need courage to enable us to die well, not only so that we may not waste the last years or months of our lives but also for the sake of the people we love who love us.

Now all the above is schematic. I do not pretend to have shown conclusively that generosity, honesty and courage are necessary if one is to flourish/be (truly) happy/successful, and of course much of what I have said, is open to detailed disagreement. I cannot go through many of the details here, but I will discuss one pair of objections that spring very naturally to mind, since the responses to them form part of the further exposition.

Two objections

The two objections one might want to make are that, contrary to what has been claimed, the virtues are surely neither (a) necessary nor (b) sufficient for flourishing/being (truly) happy or successful. Not necessary because, as we all know, the wicked may flourish like the green bay tree; not sufficient because my generosity, honesty and courage, for example, might, any one of them, lead to my being harmed or indeed to my whole life being ruined or ended.

How, to take the latter objection first, do we envisage that my virtue might lead to my downfall? It is not quite right to say that it is obviously the case that, having the virtue of generosity, I might fall foul of a lot of people who exploit me and rip me off, or find myself poverty-stricken. For built into each concept of a virtue is the idea of getting things *right*: in the case of generosity giving the *right* amount of things for the *right* reasons on the *right* occasions to the *right* people. 'The right amount' in many cases is 'the amount I can afford' or 'the amount I can give without depriving someone else'. So, for instance, I do not count as mean, nor even as ungenerous when, being relatively poor, or fairly well off but with a large and demanding family, I do not give lavish presents to richer friends at Christmas. Nor do I count as mean or even ungenerous if I refuse to let people exploit me; generosity does not require me to help support someone who is simply bone idle, nor to finance the self-indulgence of a spendthrift. Any virtue may contrast with several vices or failings and generosity is to be contrasted not only with meanness or selfishness but also with being prodigal, too open-handed, a sucker.

Once this point is borne in mind, examples in which I may suffer because of my virtue are considerably less easy to find. Nevertheless, there are some; sudden financial disaster might befall many of us, leaving the generous in dire straits where the mean do much better. Just as, in the past, people have been burnt at the stake for refusing to lie about what they believed, so now, under some regimes people are shut in asylums, and subjected to enforced drugging for the same reason, while the hypocrites remain free. My courage may lead me to go to the defence of someone being attacked in the street but to no avail and with the result that I am killed or maimed for life while the coward goes through her life unscathed. Given these possibilities, how can anyone claim that the question 'How am I to flourish?' is to be honestly answered by saying 'Be virtuous'?

There are two possible responses to this. One response is to grit one's teeth and deny that the virtuous person can be harmed by her possession of virtue. To be virtuous *is* to flourish, to be (truly) happy or successful; nothing counts as being harmed except doing evil and nothing counts as a genuine advantage, or being better off, than doing what is right. There is more than a grain of truth in this view, to which I shall return in a minute, but, on the face of it, it is, as a response to the sorts of examples we have envisaged, simply absurd. As Aristotle says, 'Those who maintain that, provided he is good, a man is happy (*eudaimon*) on the rack or when fallen among great misfortunes are talking nonsense . . .' (The point of these examples is that I become unable to exercise virtue either because I am dead, or because I have become physically, mentally or materially incapable of doing so.)

The second response is to deny that the answer to the question was ever supposed to offer a guarantee. If I ask my doctor 'How am I to flourish physically/be healthy?' she gives me the right answer when she says 'Give up smoking, don't work with asbestos, lose weight, take some exercise . . .' Even if, despite following her advice, I subsequently develop lung cancer or heart disease, this does not impugn its correctness; I cannot go back to her and say 'You were wrong to tell me I should give up smoking, etc.' She and I both know that doing as she says does not guarantee perfect health; nevertheless, if perfect health is what I want, the only thing I can do to achieve it is follow her advice. Continuing to smoke, work with asbestos, etc. is asking for trouble – even though, it is agreed, I may be lucky and live to be ninety.

Similarly, the claim is not that being virtuous guarantees that one will flourish. It is, rather, probabilistic – 'true for the most part', as Aristotle says. Virtue is the only reliable bet; it will probably bring flourishing –

131

though, it is agreed, I might be very unlucky and because of my virtue, wind up on the rack. So virtue is not being made out to be guaranteed sufficient for flourishing.

But now we return to the first objection. Is virtue not being made out to be necessary? It was just said to be the *only* reliable bet, as if, as in the medical case, making no effort to acquire the virtues was asking for trouble. But don't the wicked, as we said above flourish? In which case virtue cannot be necessary.

The two possible responses to this objection are elaborations on the two that were given to the other. The first denies that the wicked ever do flourish, for nothing counts as having an advantage or being well off or ... except doing what is right. The second, continuing to pursue the medical analogy, still insists that virtue is the only reliable bet and, agreeing that *sometimes* the non-virtuous flourish, maintains that this is, like fat smokers living to be ninety, rare and a matter of luck. So, for instance, it is usually true that people who are entirely selfish and inconsiderate miss out on being loved, but such a person might be lucky enough to be blessed with particular beauty or charm of manner, or by lucky chance come across someone else very loving who fell for them completely in the mysterious way that sometimes happens. But, the claim is, we can all recognize that this *is* a matter of luck – one could never rely on it.

However, many people may feel that this response is implausible. 'It is not simply by pure chance and luck that non-virtuous people flourish', it might be said. 'Power is just as good a bet as virtue, if not a better one, for flourishing. If you have power, people will, as a matter of fact, love you for that; you will be respected and honoured – and all despite the fact that in order to get and maintain power you will undoubtedly have to be selfish, dishonest, unjust, callous ... to a certain extent. So the answer to "How am I to flourish?" should not be "Acquire virtue" but "Acquire power".'

This objection can be seen as a form of one of the oldest, and still current, debates in moral philosophy. In Plato's *Republic* it takes on a form specifically related to the virtue of justice: if injustice is more profitable than justice to the man of strength, then practising injustice is surely the best way of life for the strong. Its most modern version is entirely general: 'What reason have I to be moral?' One very important question it raises is whether morality, or moral judgements, provide reasons for everyone for acting. If some action is wrong, ought not to be done (because, say, it is dishonest or unjust), does this mean that everyone has a reason not to do it, or is it open to the powerful to say truly that there is no reason for them to refrain?

What, then, should be said about this old, but still hotly debated issue? When we were considering how 'success' could work as a translation of '*eudaimonia*' we noted that one could be successful in a material sense – wealthy and powerful – while still counting one's life not a success but a failure, because, say, one felt lonely and unfulfilled. Now consider someone who is (a) successful in the materialistic sense, (b) non-virtuous – they have acquired their power by cheating and lying, ruthlessly sacrificing people when it suited them, but (c) perfectly happy – they do not feel guilty, or lonely, or unfulfilled or that their life is a failure in any way. The question we then ask ourselves is: do we find this person's life enviable or desirable? And the 'grain of truth' I said was contained in the view that nothing counts as a genuine advantage or being better off than doing what is right is that many of us are going to say 'No'. We may be hard put to explain *why* we say 'No'; perhaps we cannot say anything more than that we could not live like that, or that we would not want to have cheated our friends or to have let our parents or children down. But our inability to say more than this does not matter; all that matters is that we can view a life containing every apparent benefit and advantage as one that we do not want because it contains having acted wrongly in various ways.

To anyone who thinks this way, Aristotle's answer to 'How am I to flourish?' is going to emerge as the only possible answer. 'Acquire power' was, in any case, an answer that could only recommend itself to the minority who thought they could achieve this, and it now appears that even if I count myself as part of this minority, I may still not regard the acquisition of power as something that will give me the life I want.

The limitations of the answer

Aristotle's view allows that his answer will not work for everyone. It fails for two different sorts of people. One is the sort of person who has been sufficiently corrupted by their upbringing not to be able to see anything amiss in the life of the person who is 'successfully' non-virtuous. It is an important part of his view, and of neo-Aristotelianism generally, that there really is something amiss to be seen; it is not just that those of us who find the life unenviable see things one way and those who find it enviable see things differently. And I should mention here that this is one area of neo-Aristotelianism which is well-known to be problematic. Opponents of the theory insist that the admission that the answer fails in this way is fatal, and commits neo-Aristotelianism to denying that there is any truth or objectivity in claims about what counts as a flourishing or successful human life. Once it is admitted that people who are not intellectually lacking may see things differently from the upholders of virtue, and admitted further that no process of rational argument will get them to see things any other way, once these two points are admitted, it is clear that there can be no truth about the matter. It is not that the upholders of virtue are seeing things correctly, as they really are, while the corrupted are making mistakes. There is no question here of 'correctness' or 'mistakes' or 'how things really are', just two different attitudes, or sets of reactions or preferences, or ways of seeing the world, neither of which can lay claim to being the correct one.

Supporters of the theory maintain that this objection relies on an inappropriate conception of truth, objectivity and reality, a conception which works well enough when applied to physics but won't work when applied to either morals or human psychology. To say even that much is, I hope, to show that there is no point in my pretending to settle this issue here. It is currently one of the major disputes in philosophy, with ramifications in the philosophy of language and of mind as well as in moral philosophy. I believe that 'our side' is going to win; but I would not want to conceal the fact that there is a large question mark here.

The other sort of person for whom Aristotle's answer may not work would be an 'unnatural' human being, an exception that brings us back to the beginning of the discussion of how 'You should acquire and practise the virtues' could be an answer to 'How should I live in order to flourish?'

I said that this came about because, *qua* human beings, we naturally have certain emotions and tendencies such that, as a matter of brute fact, we can only flourish by developing those character traits that are called the virtues. We are, for example, naturally sociable creatures who . . . and so on. But facts about what is natural to a species are only ever facts about what is true of most of their members. As a species we are sighted, but some people are born blind; as a species we are five-fingered and five-toed, but some people are born with extra (or fewer) fingers or toes. As a species we are sociable, but this does not rule out the possibility that some of us may be born solitary types – 'natural' hermits, and thereby 'unnatural' human beings. If there are people who by nature do not enjoy the company of others and feel out of place sharing our communal life (it is thought possible that (some) psychopaths are such people) then the Aristotelian answer may fail in such a case, precisely because it fails to connect with what such a person wants. However, it is worth noting that, even in this case, it may well be that the Aristotelian answer is better than any other for such a person, for it may be that he wants other things that necessitate his associating with other people. Suppose, for instance, that he prefers solitude to company but also desires knowledge. Well, we do not live long enough to acquire much knowledge on our own; if he wants knowledge this person needs teachers, advisers and eventually intellectual peers to learn from. He will need justice to govern his dealings with them, and also honesty and generosity at least in respect of the sharing of discoveries. Someone for whom the Aristotelian answer failed completely would be someone very odd indeed.

Nevertheless, he exists as a possibility, and this is another area that some people find unsatisfactory about neo-Aristotelianism. It is deeply embedded in our thinking about ethics that in *some* sense it 'applies' to everyone. *If* people take that sense to involve ethics providing reasons for action for everyone then they may want to reject neo-Aristotelianism on the grounds that it does not yield such a result. This too is a debate that I cannot begin to settle here; however, in relation to it I should mention the very important senses in which neo-Aristotelianism does have general application to nearly all, albeit not quite all, human beings. For they are, I suspect, essential to the very possibility of ethics or morality as a subject-matter. If they were not true, morality would not exist, or would be unimaginably different.

According to neo-Aristotelianism, in brief, human beings are 'for the most part' (a) the sorts of creatures that can flourish, and (b) do so in the same way as each other, and (c) flourish side by side, all together, not at each other's expense. The significance of these three points emerges most clearly when we see under what conditions each would be false.

For instance, (a) would be false if we were characteristically neurotic, bent on misery and self-destruction and in some sense genuinely not interested in flourishing. It would also be false if we characteristically had bad emotional tendencies which were uncontrollable. (It is certainly part of Aristotelian theory that we are subject to bad emotional tendencies, but also part of it that they can all be trained to accord harmoniously with each other and with reason.) It would also be false if certain racist or sexist claims were true. Some of these have indeed amounted to claiming that to be a black or a female human being is to be subject to uncontrollable emotional tendencies which make it impossible that one should flourish – at least in this life. But according to neo-Aristotelianism, (nearly) all of us can flourish. We can make our lives successful in the fullest sense.

(b) would be false if another sort of sexist claim were true; if, for instance, men and women really were so different that different virtues and vices were appropriate to them. It is implicit in what some people have said that courage is a male virtue and compassion a female one, as if women did not need courage, and cowardice was no vice in them, and men did not need compassion, and callousness was no vice in them. But according to neo-Aristotelianism, the same answer to 'How should I live?' works for each of us in (nearly) every case.

(c) would be false if, facetiously, we were vampires. More seriously, it would be false if something like Mother Teresa's life, a life devoted to the relief of human suffering, really were the best life for a human being. For, without in any way decrying her, it must be said that her life is predicated on, not only the suffering, but also the evil actions, of others. If her life were paradigm, ideal, human flourishing then we couldn't all flourish. A less surprising way for (c) to be false would be the answer we were considering earlier, 'Acquire power'. *If* exercising power were the best life for a human being then, once again, not every human being can lead the best life. If there are to be flourishing human beings who get their own way by pushing other people around, there must be some non-flourishing ones who get pushed.

Closely related to this answer would be (something like) the Homeric one, that the best life is the one of military endeavour and glory. Centuries of literature have represented this life as noble and honourable and perhaps indeed it can be. But it does require that the condition of human life be war, not peace, and in war many people's lives are the reverse of flourishing. But it is built into the answer given by neo-Aristotelianism that, in theory, it can work not only for (nearly) each one of us but also for (nearly) all of us.

It is a contingent fact that we are one of the sorts of creatures who can only flourish living together, and another contingent fact that in theory, ideally, we can *all* flourish living together. If the latter were not true – if it were part of the concept of a flourishing human life that not everyone could lead it, even ideally and in theory – then, I suspect, the whole history of Western moral philosophy would have been different.

Notoriously, Aristotle himself did not, in fact, believe that we could all flourish. Embarrassingly for his supporters (particularly his female ones) he not only believed that some people were 'naturally' slaves, but also that women were, as such, defective human beings. But his lamentable parochialism in these matters does not infect the theory; his (and Plato's) concept of a flourishing human life as something that, ideally and in theory, we could all lead together, persisted through the moral philosophy of the Romans and became part of Christianity. Subsequent generations of Western moral philosophers have been students of the ancient Greek and Roman moral philosophy, or been Christian; indeed, until very recently, most have been both. Some aspects of Judæo-Christian morality do not mesh well with ancient Greek ethics, but others have meshed so well that it is now extremely difficult to be clear about which aspects of our moral thinking are genuinely secular and which require a theological backing to make sense. The rather general idea that morality 'applies' to everyone, or that everyone 'ought' to be moral, or has reason to be moral no matter how 'unnatural' or atypical a human being they are, is doubtless connected (whether one realizes it or not) with the Judæo-Christian idea that no human being can escape God's commands, and with the Christian idea that any human being, no matter how psychologically odd, has an immortal soul which can be saved or lost by acting as virtue requires. But it also, I suspect, is connected (once again, whether one realizes it or not) with the Aristotelian idea that the best life for (nearly) all human beings is the life we live together, practising the virtues to our mutual benefit and enjoyment.

Notes

1   Etymologically it means 'well (*eu*)-demoned/geniused', i.e. blessed with a
    good genius or attendant spirit (*daimon*).
2   Though perhaps not incomprehensible, if we can understand a certain sort
    of neuroticism in which the person seems bent on misery and self-destruc-
    tion. Aristotle appears not to recognize the existence of such people.
3   This is not strictly Aristotle's answer, since his list of the virtues is not the
    same as ours, though having much in common with it. Moreover, the Greek
    term that we translate as 'virtue' (*arete*) has no specifically moral overtones
    and, if we were concentrating on what Aristotle said, would be better trans-
    lated as 'excellence'. This is the neo-Aristotelian answer.

17

A defence of abortion
Judith Jarvis Thomson

It might seem obvious that if you could establish that a foetus is a person then you would have an excellent argument against abortion. However, in this article Judith Jarvis Thomson (1929–) makes a strong case for the conclusion that in at least some cases it would not be morally wrong to have an abortion even if the foetus involved was clearly a person. She builds her case by means of a thought experiment designed to show what is at issue. Imagine that you woke one morning to find that you had had a famous violinist plugged into your kidneys and that if you were to unplug him he would die. Would it be wrong to unplug him? What does this show about cases of abortion?

From Judith Jarvis Thomson, 'A defence of abortion', *Philosophy and Public Affairs*, vol. 1, no. 1

Most opposition to abortion relies on the premiss that the foetus is a human being, a person, from the moment of conception. The premiss is argued for, but, as I think, not well. Take, for example, the most common argument. We are asked to notice that the development of a human being from conception through birth into childhood is continuous; then it is said that to draw a line, to choose a point in this development and say 'before this point the thing is not a person, after this point it is a person' is to make an arbitrary choice, a choice for which in the nature of things no good reason can be given. It is concluded that the foetus is, or anyway that we had better say it is, a person from the moment of conception. But this conclusion does not follow. Similar things might be said about the development of an acorn into an oak tree, and it does not follow that acorns are oak trees, or that we had better say they are. Arguments of this form are sometimes called 'slippery slope arguments' – the phrase is perhaps self-explanatory – and it is dismaying that opponents of abortion rely on them so heavily and uncritically.

I am inclined to agree, however, that the prospects for 'drawing a line' in the development of the foetus look dim. I am inclined to think also that we shall probably have to agree that the foetus has already become a human person well before birth. Indeed, it comes as a surprise when one first learns how early in its life it begins to acquire human characteristics. By the tenth week, for example, it already has a face, arms and legs, fingers and toes; it has internal organs, and brain activity is detectable.[1] On the other hand, I think that the premiss is false, that the foetus is not a person from the moment of conception. A newly fertilized ovum, a newly implanted clump of cells, is no more a person than an acorn is an oak tree. But I shall not discuss any of this. For it seems to me to be of great interest to ask what happens if, for the sake of argument, we allow the premiss. How, precisely, are we supposed to get from there to the conclusion that abortion is morally impermissible? Opponents of abortion commonly spend most of their time establishing that the foetus is a person, and hardly any time explaining the step from there to the impermissibility of abortion. Perhaps they think the step too simple and obvious to require much comment. Or perhaps instead they are simply being economical in argument. Many of those who defend abortion rely on the premiss that the foetus is not a person, but only a bit of tissue that will become a person at birth; and why pay out more arguments than you have to? Whatever the explanation, I suggest that the step they take is neither easy nor obvious, that it calls for closer examination than it is commonly given, and that when we do give it this closer examination we shall feel inclined to reject it.

I propose, then, that we grant that the foetus is a person from the moment of conception. How does the argument go from here? Something like this, I take it. Every person has a right to life. So the foetus has a right to life. No doubt the mother has a right to decide what shall happen in and to her body; everyone would grant that. But surely a person's right to life is stronger and more stringent than the mother's right to decide what happens in and to her body, and so outweighs it. So the foetus may not be killed; an abortion may not be performed.

It sounds plausible. But now let me ask you to imagine this. You wake up in the morning and find yourself back to back in bed with an unconscious violinist. A famous unconscious violinist. He has been found to have a fatal kidney ailment, and the Society of Music Lovers has canvassed all the available medical records and found that you alone have the right blood type to help. They have therefore kidnapped you, and last night the violinist's circulatory system was plugged into yours, so that your kidneys can be used to extract poisons from his blood as well as your own. The director of the hospital now tells you, 'Look, we're sorry the Society of Music Lovers did this to you – we would never have permitted it if we had known. But still, they did it, and the violinist now is plugged into you. To unplug you would be to kill him. But never mind, it's only for nine months. By then he will have recovered from his ailment, and can safely be unplugged from you.' Is it morally incumbent on you to accede to this situation? No doubt it would be very nice of you if you did, a great kindness. But do you *have* to accede to it? What if it were not nine months, but nine years? or longer still? What if the director of the hospital says, 'Tough luck, I agree, but you've now got to stay in bed, with the violinist plugged into you, for the rest of your life. Because remember this. All persons have a right to life, and violinists are persons. Granted you have a right to decide what happens in and to your body, but a person's right to life outweighs your right to decide what happens in and to your body. So you cannot ever be unplugged from him.' I imagine you would regard this as outrageous, which suggests that something really is wrong with that plausible-sounding argument I mentioned a moment ago.

In this case, of course, you were kidnapped; you didn't volunteer for the operation that plugged the violinist into your kidneys. Can those who oppose abortion on the ground I mentioned make an exception for a pregnancy due to rape? Certainly. They can say that persons have a right to life only if they didn't come into existence because of rape; or they can say that all persons have a right to life, but that some have less of a right to life than others, in particular, that those who came into existence because of rape have less. But these statements have a rather unpleasant sound. Surely the question of whether you have a right to life at all, or how much of it you have, shouldn't turn on the question of whether or not you are the product of a rape. And in fact the people who oppose abortion on the ground I mentioned do not make this distinction, and hence do not make an exception in the case of rape.

Nor do they make an exception for a case in which the mother has to spend the nine months of her pregnancy in bed. They would agree that would be a great pity, and hard on the mother; but all the same, all persons have a right to life, the foetus is a person, and so on. I suspect, in fact, that they would not make an exception for a case in which, miraculously enough, the pregnancy went on for nine years, or even the rest of the mother's life.

Some won't even make an exception for a case in which continuation of the pregnancy is likely to shorten the mother's life; they regard abortion as impermissible even to save the mother's life. Such cases are nowadays very rare, and many opponents of abortion do not accept this extreme view. All the same, it is a good place to begin: a number of points of interest come out in respect to it.

1. Let us call the view that abortion is impermissible even to save the mother's life 'the extreme view'. I want to suggest first that it does not issue from the argument I mentioned earlier without the addition of some fairly powerful premises. Suppose a woman has become pregnant, and now learns that she has a cardiac condition such that she will die if she

carries the baby to term. What may be done for her? The foetus, being a person, has a right to life, but as the mother is a person too, so has she a right to life. Presumably they have an equal right to life. How is it supposed to come out that an abortion may not be performed? If mother and child have an equal right to life, shouldn't we perhaps flip a coin? Or should we add to the mother's right to life her right to decide what happens in and to her body, which everybody seems to be ready to grant – the sum of her rights now outweighing the foetus's right to life?

The most familiar argument here is the following. We are told that performing the abortion would be directly killing[2] the child, whereas doing nothing would not be killing the mother, but only letting her die. Moreover, in killing the child, one would be killing an innocent person, for the child has committed no crime, and is not aiming at his mother's death. And then there are a variety of ways in which this might be continued. (1) But as directly killing an innocent person is always and absolutely impermissible, an abortion may not be performed. Or, (2) as directly killing an innocent person is murder, and murder is always and absolutely impermissible, an abortion may not be performed.[3] Or, (3) as one's duty to refrain from directly killing an innocent person is more stringent than one's duty to keep a person from dying, an abortion may not be performed. Or, (4) if one's only options are directly killing an innocent person or letting a person die, one must prefer letting the person die, and thus an abortion may not be performed.[4]

Some people seem to have thought that these are not further premises which must be added if the conclusion is to be reached but that they follow from the very fact that an innocent person has a right to life.[5] But this seems to me to be a mistake, and perhaps the simplest way to show this is to bring out that while we must certainly grant that innocent persons have a right to life, the theses in (1) to (4) are all false. Take (2), for example. If directly killing an innocent person is murder, and thus is impermissible, then the mother's directly killing the innocent person inside her is murder, and thus is impermissible. But it cannot seriously be thought to be murder if the mother performs an abortion on herself to save her life. It cannot seriously be said that she *must* refrain, that she *must* sit passively by and wait for her death. Let us look again at the case of you and the violinist. There you are, in bed with the violinist, and the director of the hospital says to you, 'It's all most distressing, and I deeply sympathize, but you see this is putting an additional strain on your kidneys, and you'll be dead within the month. But you *have* to stay where you are all the same. Because unplugging you would be directly killing an innocent violinist, and that's murder, and that's impermissible.' If anything in the world is true, it is that you do not commit murder, you do not do what is impermissible, if you reach around to your back and unplug yourself from that violinist to save your life.

The main focus of attention in writings on abortion has been on what a third party may or may not do in answer to a request from a woman for an abortion. This is in a way understandable. Things being as they are, there isn't much a woman can safely do to abort herself. So the question asked is what a third party may do, and what the mother may do, if it is mentioned at all, is deduced, almost as an afterthought, from what it is concluded that third parties may do. But it seems to me that to treat the matter in this way is to refuse to grant to the mother that very status of person which is so firmly insisted on for the foetus. For we cannot simply read off what a person may do from what a third party may do. Suppose you find yourself trapped in a tiny house with a growing child. I mean a very tiny house, and a rapidly growing child – you are already up against the wall of the house and in a few minutes you'll be crushed to death. The child on the other hand won't be crushed to death; if nothing is done to stop him from growing he'll be hurt, but in the end he'll simply burst open the house and walk out a free man. Now I could well understand it if a bystander were to say, 'There's nothing we can do for you. We cannot choose between your life and his, we cannot be the ones to decide who is to live, we cannot intervene.' But it cannot be concluded that you too can do nothing, that you cannot attack it to save your life. However innocent the child may be, you do not have to wait passively while it crushes you to death. Perhaps a pregnant woman is vaguely felt to have the status of house, to which we don't allow the right of self-defence. But if the woman houses the child, it should be remembered that she is a person who houses it.

I should perhaps stop to say explicitly that I am not claiming that people have a right to do anything whatever to save their lives. I think, rather, that there are drastic limits to the right of self-defence. If someone threatens you with death unless you torture someone else to death, I think you have not the right, even to save your life, to do so. But the case under consideration here is very different. In our case there are only two people involved, one whose life is threatened, and one who threatens it. Both are innocent: the one who is threatened is not threatened because of any fault, the one who threatens does not threaten because of any fault. For this reason we may feel that we bystanders cannot intervene. But the person threatened can.

In sum, a woman surely can defend her life against the threat to it posed by the unborn child, even if doing so involves its death. And this shows not merely that the theses in (1) to (4) are false; it shows also that the extreme view of abortion is false, and so we need not canvass any other possible ways of arriving at it from the argument I mentioned at the outset.

2.   The extreme view could of course be weakened to say that while abortion is permissible to save the mother's life, it may not be performed by

a third party, but only by the mother herself. But this cannot be right either. For what we have to keep in mind is that the mother and the unborn child are not like two tenants in a small house which has, by an unfortunate mistake, been rented to both; the mother *owns* the house. The fact that she does adds to the offensiveness of deducing that the mother can do nothing from the supposition that third parties can do nothing. But it does more than this: it casts a bright light on the supposition that third parties can do nothing. Certainly it lets us see that a third party who says 'I cannot choose between you' is fooling himself if he thinks this is impartiality. If Jones has found and fastened on a certain coat, which he needs to keep him from freezing, then it is not impartiality that says 'I cannot choose between you' when Smith owns the coat. Woman have said again and again 'This body is *my* body!' and they have reason to feel angry, reason to feel that it has been like shouting into the wind. Smith, after all, is hardly likely to bless us if we say to him, 'Of course it's your coat, anybody would grant that it is. But no one may choose between you and Jones who is to have it.'

We should really ask what it is that says 'no one may choose' in the face of the fact that the body that houses the child is the mother's body. It may be simply a failure to appreciate this fact. But it may be something more interesting, namely the sense that one has a right to refuse to lay hands on people, even where it would be just and fair to do so, even where justice seems to require that somebody do so. Thus justice might call for somebody to get Smith's coat back from Jones, and yet you have a right to refuse to be the one to lay hands on Jones, a right to refuse to do physical violence to him. This, I think, must be granted. But then what should be said is not 'no one may choose' but only '*I* cannot choose', and indeed not even this, but '*I* will not *act*', leaving it open that somebody else can or should, and in particular that anyone in a position of authority, with the job of securing people's rights, both can and should. So this is no difficulty. I have not been arguing that any given third party must accede to the mother's request that he perform an abortion to save her life, but only that he may.

I suppose that in some views of human life the mother's body is only on loan to her, the loan not being one which gives her any prior claim to it. One who held this view might well think it impartiality to say 'I cannot choose'. But I shall simply ignore this possibility. My own view is that if a human being has any just, prior claim to anything at all, he has a just, prior claim to his own body. And perhaps this needn't be argued for here anyway, since, as I mentioned, the arguments against abortion we are looking at do grant that the woman has a right to decide what happens in and to her body.

But although they do grant it, I have tried to show that they do not take seriously what is done in granting it. I suggest the same thing will reappear even more clearly when we turn away from cases in which the mother's life is at stake, and attend, as I propose we now do, to the vastly more common cases in which a woman wants an abortion for some less weighty reason than preserving her own life.

3.   Where the mother's life is not at stake, the argument I mentioned at the outset seems to have a much stronger pull. 'Everyone has a right to life, so the unborn person has a right to life.' And isn't the child's right to life weightier than anything other than the mother's own right to life, which she might put forward as ground for an abortion?

This argument treats the right to life as if it were unproblematic. It is not, and this seems to me to be precisely the source of the mistake.

For we should now, at long last, ask what it comes to, to have a right to life. In some views having a right to life includes having a right to be given at least the bare minimum one needs for continued life. But suppose that what in fact *is* the bare minimum a man needs for continued life is something he has no right at all to be given? If I am sick unto death, and the only thing that will save my life is the touch of Henry Fonda's cool hand on my fevered brow, then all the same, I have no right to be given the touch of Henry Fonda's cool hand on my fevered brow. It would be frightfully nice of him to fly in from the West Coast to provide it. It would be less nice, though no doubt well meant, if my friends flew out to the West Coast and carried Henry Fonda back with them. But I have no right at all against anybody that he should do this for me. Or again, to return to the story I told earlier, the fact that for continued life that violinist needs the continued use of your kidneys does not establish that he has a right to be given the continued use of your kidneys. He certainly has no right against you that *you* should give him continued use of your kidneys. For nobody has any right to use your kidneys unless you give him such a right; and nobody has the right against you that you shall give him this right – if you do allow him to go on using your kidneys, this is a kindness on your part, and not something he can claim from you as his due. Nor has he any right against anybody else that *they* should give him continued use of your kidneys. Certainly he had no right against the Society of Music Lovers that they should plug him into you in the first place. And if you now start to unplug yourself, having learned that you will otherwise have to spend nine years in bed with him, there is nobody in the world who must try to prevent you, in order to see to it that he is given something he has a right to be given.

Some people are rather stricter about the right to life. In their view, it does not include the right to be given anything, but amounts to, and only to, the right not to be killed by anybody. But here a related difficulty arises. If everybody is to refrain from killing that violinist, then everybody must refrain from doing a great many different sorts of things.

Everybody must refrain from slitting his throat, everybody must refrain from shooting him – and everybody must refrain from unplugging you from him. But does he have a right against everybody that they shall refrain from unplugging you from him? To refrain from doing this is to allow him to continue to use your kidneys. It could be argued that he has a right against us that *we* should allow him to continue to use your kidneys. That is, while he had no right against us that we should give him the use of your kidneys, it might be argued that he anyway has a right against us that we shall not now intervene and deprive him of the use of your kidneys. I shall come back to third-party interventions later. But certainly the violinist has no right against you that *you* shall allow him to continue to use your kidneys. As I said, if you do allow him to use them, it is a kindness on your part, and not something you owe him.

The difficulty I point to here is not peculiar to the right to life. It reappears in connection with all the other natural rights; and it is something which an adequate account of rights must deal with. For present purposes it is enough just to draw attention to it. But I would stress that I am not arguing that people do not have a right to life – quite to the contrary, it seems to me that the primary control we must place on the acceptability of an account of rights is that it should turn out in that account to be a truth that all persons have a right to life. I am arguing only that having a right to life does not guarantee having either a right to be given the use of or a right to be allowed continued use of another person's body – even if one needs it for life itself. So the right to life will not serve the opponents of abortion in the very simple and clear way in which they seem to have thought it would.

4.   There is another way to bring out the difficulty. In the most ordinary sort of case, to deprive someone of what he has a right to is to treat him unjustly. Suppose a boy and his small brother are jointly given a box of chocolates for Christmas. If the older boy takes the box and refuses to give his brother any of the chocolates, he is unjust to him, for the brother has been given a right to half of them. But suppose that, having learned that otherwise it means nine years in bed with that violinist, you unplug yourself from him. You surely are not being unjust to him, for you gave him no right to use your kidneys, and no one else can have given him any such right. But we have to notice that in unplugging yourself, you are killing him; and violinists, like everybody else, have a right to life, and thus in the view we were considering just now, the right not to be killed. So here you do what he supposedly has a right you shall not do, but you do not act unjustly to him in doing it.

The emendation which may be made at this point is this: the right to life consists not in the right not to be killed, but rather in the right not to be killed unjustly. This runs a risk of circularity, but never mind: it would enable us to square the fact that the violinist has a right to life with the fact that you do not act unjustly toward him in unplugging yourself, thereby killing him. For if you do not kill him unjustly, you do not violate his right to life, and so it is no wonder you do him no injustice.

But if this emendation is accepted, the gap in the argument against abortion stares us plainly in the face: it is by no means enough to show that the foetus is a person, and to remind us that all persons have a right to life – we need to be shown also that killing the foetus violates its right to life, i.e. that abortion is unjust killing. And is it?

I suppose we may take it as a datum that in a case of pregnancy due to rape the mother has not given the unborn person a right to the use of her body for food and shelter. Indeed, in what pregnancy could it be supposed that the mother has given the unborn person such a right? It is not as if there were unborn persons drifting about the world, to whom a woman who wants a child says 'I invite you in'.

But it might be argued that there are other ways one can have acquired a right to the use of another person's body than by having been invited to use it by that person. Suppose a woman voluntarily indulges in intercourse, knowing of the chance it will issue in pregnancy, and then she does become pregnant; is she not in part responsible for the presence, in fact the very existence of the unborn person inside her? No doubt she did not invite it in. But doesn't her partial responsibility for its being there itself give it a right to the use of her body?[6] If so, then her aborting it would be more like the boy's taking away the chocolates, and less like your unplugging yourself from the violinist – doing so would be depriving it of what it does have a right to, and thus would be doing it an injustice.

And then, too, it might be asked whether or not she can kill it even to save her own life: If she voluntarily called it into existence, how can she now kill it, even in self-defence?

The first thing to be said about this is that it is something new. Opponents of abortion have been so concerned to make out the independence of the foetus, in order to establish that it has a right to life, just as its mother does, that they have tended to overlook the possible support they might gain from making out that the foetus is *dependent* on the mother, in order to establish that she has a special kind of responsibility for it, a responsibility that gives it rights against her which are not possessed by any independent person – such as an ailing violinist who is a stranger to her.

On the other hand, this argument would give the unborn person a right to its mother's body only if her pregnancy resulted from a voluntary act, undertaken in full knowledge of the chance a pregnancy might result from it. It would leave out entirely the unborn person whose existence is due to rape. Pending the availability of some further argument, then we would be left with the conclusion that unborn persons whose existence is due to rape have no right to the use of their mother's bodies, and thus that aborting them is not depriving them of anything they have a right to and hence is not unjust killing.

And we should also notice that it is not at all plain that this argument really does go even as far as it purports to. For there are cases and cases, and the details make a difference. If the room is stuffy, and I therefore open a window to air it, and a burglar climbs in, it would be absurd to say, 'Ah, now he can stay, she's given him the right to the use of her house – for she is partially responsible for his presence there, having voluntarily done what enabled him to get in, in full knowledge that there are such things as burglars, and that burglars burgle.' It would be still more absurd to say this if I had had bars installed outside my windows, precisely to prevent burglars from getting in, and a burglar got in only because of a defect in the bars. It remains equally absurd if we imagine it is not a burglar who climbs in, but an innocent person who blunders or falls in. Again, suppose it were like this: people-seeds drift about in the air like pollen, and if you open your windows, one may drift in and take root in your carpets or upholstery. You don't want children, so you fix up your windows with fine mesh screens, the very best you can buy. As can happen, however, and on very, very rare occasions does happen, one of the screens is defective; and a seed drifts in and takes root. Does the person-plant who now develops have a right to the use of your house? Surely not – despite the fact that you voluntarily opened your windows, you knowingly kept carpets and upholstered furniture, and you knew that screens were sometimes defective. Someone may argue that you are responsible for its rooting, that it does have a right to your house, because after all you *could* have lived out your life with bare floors and furniture, or with sealed windows and doors. But this won't do – for by the same token anyone can avoid a pregnancy due to rape by having a hysterectomy, or anyway by never leaving home without a (reliable!) army.

It seems to me that the argument we are looking at can establish at most that there are *some* cases in which the unborn person has a right to the use of its mother's body, and therefore *some* cases in which abortion is unjust killing. There is room for much discussion and argument as to precisely which, if any. But I think we should side-step this issue and leave it open, for at any rate the argument certainly does not establish that all abortion is unjust killing.

5.   There is room for yet another argument here, however. We surely must all grant that there may be cases in which it would be morally indecent to detach a person from your body at the cost of his life. Suppose you learn that what the violinist needs is not nine years of your life, but only one hour: all you need to do to save his life is to spend one hour in that bed

with him. Suppose also that letting him use your kidneys for that one hour would not affect your health in the slightest. Admittedly you were kidnapped. Admittedly you did not give anyone permission to plug him into you. Nevertheless it seems to me plain you *ought* to allow him to use your kidneys for that hour – it would be indecent to refuse.

Again, suppose pregnancy lasted only an hour, and constituted no threat to life or health. And suppose that a woman becomes pregnant as a result of rape. Admittedly she did not voluntarily do anything to bring about the existence of a child. Admittedly she did nothing at all which would give the unborn person a right to the use of her body. All the same it might well be said, as in the newly emended violinist story, that she *ought* to allow it to remain for that hour – that it would be indecent in her to refuse.

Now some people are inclined to use the term 'right' in such a way that it follows from the fact that you ought to allow a person to use your body for the hour he needs, that he has a right to use your body for the hour he needs, even though he has not been given that right by any person or act. They may say that it follows also that if you refuse, you act unjustly toward him. This use of the term is perhaps so common that it cannot be called wrong; nevertheless it seems to me to be an unfortunate loosening of what we would do better to keep a tight rein on. Suppose that box of chocolates I mentioned earlier had not been given to both boys jointly, but was given only to the older boy. There he sits, stolidly eating his way through the box, his small brother watching enviously. Here we are likely to say 'You ought not to be so mean. You ought to give your brother some of those chocolates.' My own view is that it just does not follow from the truth of this that the brother has any right to any of the chocolates. If the boy refuses to give his brother any, he is greedy, stingy, callous – but not unjust. I suppose that the people I have in mind will say it does follow that the brother has a right to some of the chocolates, and thus that the boy does act unjustly if he refuses to give his brother any. But the effect of saying this is to obscure what we should keep distinct, namely the difference between the boy's refusal in this case and the boy's refusal in the earlier case, in which the box was given to both boys jointly, and in which the small brother thus had what was from any point of view clear title to half.

A further objection to so using the term 'right' that from the fact that A ought to do a thing for B, it follows that B has a right against A that A do it for him, is that it is going to make the question of whether or not a man has a right to a thing turn on how easy it is to provide him with it; and this seems not merely unfortunate, but morally unacceptable. Take the case of Henry Fonda again. I said earlier that I had no right to the touch of his cool hand on my fevered brow, even though I needed it to save my life. I said it would be frightfully nice of him to fly in from the West Coast to provide me with it, but that I had no right against him that he should do so. But suppose he isn't on the West Coast. Suppose he has only to walk across the room, place a hand briefly on my brow – and lo, my life is saved. Then surely he ought to do it, it would be indecent to refuse. Is it to be said 'Ah, well, it follows that in this case she has a right to the touch of his hand on her brow, and so it would be an injustice in him to refuse?' So that I have a right to it when it is easy for him to provide it, though no right when it's hard? It's rather a shocking idea that anyone's rights should fade away and disappear as it gets harder and harder to accord them to him.

So my own view is that even though you ought to let the violinist use your kidneys for the one hour he needs, we should not conclude that he has a right to do so – we should say that if you refuse, you are, like the boy who owns all the chocolates and will give none away, self-centred and callous, indecent in fact, but not unjust. And similarly, that even supposing a case in which a woman pregnant due to rape ought to allow the unborn person to use her body for the hour he needs, we should not conclude that he has a right to do so; we should conclude that she is self-centred, callous, indecent, but not unjust, if she refuses. The complaints are no less grave; they are just different. However, there is no need to insist on this point. If anyone does wish to deduce 'he has a right' from 'you ought', then all the same he must surely grant that there are cases in which it is not morally required of you that you allow that violinist to use your kidneys, and in which he does not have a right to use them, and so also for mother and unborn child. Except in such cases as the unborn person has a right to demand it – and we were leaving open the possibility that there may be such cases – nobody is morally *required* to make large sacrifices, of health, of all other interests and concerns, of all other duties and commitments, for nine years, or even for nine months, in order to keep another person alive.

6.   We have in fact to distinguish between two kinds of Samaritan: the Good Samaritan and what we might call the Minimally Decent Samaritan. The story of the Good Samaritan, you will remember, goes like this:

> A certain man went down from Jerusalem to Jericho, and fell among thieves, which stripped him of his raiment, and wounded him, and departed, leaving him half dead.
>
> And by chance there came down a certain priest that way; and when he saw him, he passed by on the other side.
>
> And likewise a Levite, when he was at the place, came and looked on him, and passed by on the other side.
>
> But a certain Samaritan, as he journeyed, came where he was; and when he saw him he had compassion on him.

And went to him, and bound up his wounds, pouring in oil and wine, and set him on his own beast, and brought him to an inn, and took care of him.

And on the morrow, when he departed, he took out two pence, and gave them to the host, and said unto him, 'Take care of him; and whatsoever thou spendest more, when I come again, I will repay thee.'

(Luke 10: 30–5)

The Good Samaritan went out of his way, at some cost to himself, to help one in need of it. We are not told what the options were, that is, whether or not the priest and the Levite could have helped by doing less than the Good Samaritan did, but assuming they could have, then the fact they did nothing at all assuming they were not even Minimally Decent Samaritans, not because they were not Samaritans, but because they were not even minimally decent.

These things are a matter of degree, of course, but there is a difference, and it comes out perhaps most clearly in the story of Kitty Genovese, who, as you will remember, was murdered while thirty-eight people watched or listened, and did nothing at all to help her. A Good Samaritan would have rushed out to give direct assistance against the murderer. Or perhaps we had better allow that it would have been a Splendid Samaritan who did this, on the ground that it would have involved a risk of death for himself. But the thirty-eight not only did not do this, they did not even trouble to pick up a phone to call the police. Minimally Decent Samaritanism would call for doing at least that, and their not having done it was monstrous.

After telling the story of the Good Samaritan, Jesus said 'Go, and do thou likewise.' Perhaps he meant that we are morally required to act as the Good Samaritan did. Perhaps he was urging people to do more than is morally required of them. At all events it seems plain that it was not morally required of any of the thirty-eight that he rush out to give direct assistance at the risk of his own life, and that it is not morally required of anyone that he give long stretches of his life – nine years or nine months – to sustaining the life of a person who has no special right (we were leaving open the possibility of this) to demand it.

Indeed, with one rather striking class of exceptions, no one in any country in the world is *legally* required to do anywhere near as much as this for anyone else. The class of exceptions is obvious. My main concern here is not the state of the law in respect to abortion, but it is worth drawing attention to the fact that in no state in this country is any man compelled by law to be even a Minimally Decent Samaritan to any person; there is no law under which charges could be brought against the thirty-eight who stood by while Kitty Genovese died. By contrast, in most states in this country women are compelled by law to be not merely Minimally Decent Samaritans, but Good Samaritans to unborn persons inside them. This doesn't by itself settle anything one way or the other, because it may well be argued that there should be laws in this country – as there are in many European countries – compelling at least Minimally Decent Samaritanism.[7] But it does show that there is a gross injustice in the existing state of the law. And it shows also that the groups currently working against liberalization of abortion laws, in fact working toward having it declared unconstitutional for a state to permit abortion, had better start working for the adoption of Good Samaritan laws generally, or earn the charge that they are acting in bad faith.

I should think, myself, that Minimally Decent Samaritan laws would be one thing, Good Samaritan laws quite another, and in fact highly improper. But we are not here concerned with the law. What we should ask is not whether anybody should be compelled by law to be a Good Samaritan, but whether we must accede to a situation in which somebody is being compelled – by nature, perhaps – to be a Good Samaritan. We have, in other words, to look now at third-party interventions. I have been arguing that no person is morally required to make large sacrifices to sustain the life of another who has no right to demand them, and this even where the sacrifices do not include life itself; we are not morally required to be Good Samaritans or anyway Very Good Samaritans to one another. But what if a man cannot extricate himself from such a situation? What if he appeals to us to extricate him? It seems to me plain that there are cases in which we can, cases in which a Good Samaritan would extricate him. There you are, you were kidnapped, and nine years in bed with that violinist lie ahead of you. You have your own life to lead. You are sorry, but you simply cannot see giving up so much of your life to the sustaining of his. You cannot extricate yourself, and ask us to do so. I should have thought that – in light of his having no right to the use of your body – it was obvious that we do not have to accede to your being forced to give up so much. We can do what you ask. There is no injustice to the violinist in our doing so.

7. Following the lead of the opponents of abortion. I have throughout been speaking of the foetus merely as a person, and what I have been asking is whether or not the argument we began with, which proceeds only from the foetus's being a person, really does establish its conclusion. I have argued that it does not.

But of course there are arguments and arguments, and it may be said that I have simply fastened on the wrong one. It may be said that what is important is not merely the fact that the foetus is a person, but that it is a person for whom the woman has a special kind of responsibility issuing from the fact that she is its mother. And it might be argued that all my analogies are therefore irrelevant – for you do not have that

151

special kind of responsibility for that violinist. Henry Fonda does not have that special kind of responsibility for me. And our attention might be drawn to the fact that men and women both *are* compelled by law to provide support for their children.

I have in effect dealt (briefly) with this argument in section 4 above; but a (still briefer) recapitulation now may be in order. Surely we do not have any such 'special responsibility' for a person unless we have assumed it, explicitly or implicitly. If a set of parents do not try to prevent pregnancy, do not obtain an abortion, and then at the time of birth of the child do not put it out for adoption, but rather take it home with them, then they have assumed responsibility for it, they have given it rights, and they cannot *now* withdraw support from it at the cost of its life because they now find it difficult to go on providing for it. But if they have taken all reasonable precautions against having a child, they do not simply by virtue of their biological relationship to the child who comes into existence have a special responsibility for it. They may wish to assume responsibility for it, or they may not wish to. And I am suggesting that if assuming responsibility for it would require large sacrifices, then they may refuse. A Good Samaritan would not refuse – or anyway, a Splendid Samaritan, if the sacrifices that had to be made were enormous. But then so would a Good Samaritan assume responsibility for that violinist; so would Henry Fonda, if he is a Good Samaritan, fly in from the West Coast and assume responsibility for me.

8. My argument will be found unsatisfactory on two counts by many of those who want to regard abortion as morally permissible. First, while I argue that abortion is not impermissible, I do not argue that it is always permissible. There may well be cases in which carrying the child to term requires only Minimally Decent Samaritanism of the mother, and this is a standard we must not fall below. I am inclined to think it a merit of my account precisely that it does *not* give a general yes or a general no. It allows for and supports our sense that, for example, a sick and desperately frightened fourteen-year-old schoolgirl, pregnant due to rape, may *of course* choose abortion, and that any law which rules this out is an insane law. And it also allows for and supports our sense that in other cases resort to abortion is even positively indecent. It would be indecent in the woman to request an abortion, and indecent in a doctor to perform it, if she is in her seventh month, and wants the abortion just to avoid the nuisance of postponing a trip abroad. The very fact that the arguments I have been drawing attention to treat all cases of abortion, or even all cases of abortion in which the mother's life is not at stake, as morally on a par, ought to have made them suspect at the outset.

Secondly, while I am arguing for the permissibility of abortion in some cases, I am not arguing for the right to secure the death of the unborn child. It is easy to confuse these two things in that up to a certain point in the life of the foetus it is not able to survive outside the mother's body; hence removing it from her body guarantees its death. But they are importantly different. I have argued that you are not morally required to spend nine months in bed, sustaining the life of that violinist; but to say this is by no means to say that if, when you unplug yourself, there is a miracle and he survives, you then have a right to turn round and slit his throat. You may detach yourself even if this costs him his life; you have no right to be guaranteed his death, by some other means, if unplugging yourself does not kill him. There are some people who will feel dissatisfied by this feature of my argument. A woman may be utterly devastated by the thought of a child, a bit of herself, put out for adoption and never seen or heard of again. She may therefore want not merely that the child be detached from her, but more, that it die. Some opponents of abortion are inclined to regard this as beneath contempt – thereby showing insensitivity to what is surely a powerful source of despair. All the same, I agree that the desire for the child's death is not one which anybody may gratify, should it turn out to be possible to detach the child alive.

At this place, however, it should be remembered that we have only been pretending throughout that the foetus is a human being from the moment of conception. A very early abortion is surely not the killing of a person, and so is not dealt with by anything I have said here.

Notes

I am very much indebted to James Thomson for discussion, criticism, and many helpful suggestions.

1   Daniel Callahan, *Abortion: Law, Choice and Morality* (New York, 1970), p. 373. This book gives a fascinating survey of the available information on abortion. The Jewish tradition is surveyed in David M. Feldman, *Birth Control in Jewish Law* (New York, 1968), Part 5, the Catholic tradition in John T. Noonan, Jr., 'An almost absolute value in history', in John T. Noonan, Jr. (ed.) *The Morality of Abortion* (Cambridge, Mass., 1970).
2   The term 'direct' in the arguments I refer to is a technical one. Roughly, what is meant by 'direct killing' is either killing as an end in itself, or killing as a means to some end, for example, the end of saving someone else's life. See note 5, below, for an example of its use.
3   Cf. *Encyclical Letter of Pope Pius XI on Christian Marriage*, St Paul Editions (Boston, n.d.), p. 32: 'however much we may pity the mother whose health and even life is gravely imperiled in the performance of the duty allotted to her by nature, nevertheless what could ever be a sufficient reason for excusing in any way the direct murder of the innocent? This is precisely

what we are dealing with here.' Noonan (*The Morality of Abortion*, p. 43) reads this as follows: 'What cause can ever avail to excuse in any way the direct killing of the innocent? For it is a question of that.'

4   The thesis in (4) is in an interesting way weaker than those in (1), (2) and (3): they rule out abortion even in cases in which both mother *and* child will die if the abortion is not performed. By contrast, one who held the view expressed in (4) could consistently say that one needn't prefer letting two persons die to killing one.

5   Cf. the following passage from Pius XII, *Address to the Italian Catholic Society of Midwives*: 'The baby in the maternal breast has the right to life immediately from God. – Hence there is no man, no human authority, no science, no medical, eugenic, social, economic or moral "indication" which can establish or grant a valid juridical ground for a direct deliberate disposition of an innocent human life, that is a disposition which looks to its destruction either as an end or as a means to another end perhaps in itself not illicit. – The baby, still not born, is a man in the same degree and for the same reason as the mother' (quoted in Noonan, *The Morality of Abortion*, p. 45).

6   The need for a discussion of this argument was brought home to me by members of the Society for Ethical and Legal Philosophy, to whom this paper was originally presented.

7   For a discussion of the difficulties involved, and a survey of the European experience with such laws, see James M. Ratcliffe (ed.) *The Good Samaritan and the Law* (New York, 1966).

18

Moral luck
Thomas Nagel

Kant thought that luck should not come into ethics. Every action which can be assessed in moral terms must be freely performed: you should not be held morally responsible for anything outside your conscious control. This view seems plausible: our notions of moral praise and blame are focused on what is and is not avoidable, on what is within the agent's control. However, as Thomas Nagel (1937–) shows in this article, the situation is more complex. If we take Kant's notion of responsibility seriously we find that it leads to apparently paradoxical conclusions. Nagel does not claim to have any solution to the difficulties he lays bare, but his analysis suggests that our common notions of moral responsibility need to be refined.

From Thomas Nagel, 'Moral luck', *Proceedings of the Aristotelian Society*, supp. vol. L

Kant believed that good or bad luck should influence neither our moral judgment of a person and his actions, nor his moral assessment of himself.

> The good will is not good because of what it effects or accomplishes or because of its adequacy to achieve some proposed end; it is good only because of its willing, i.e., it is good of itself. And, regarded for itself, it is to be esteemed incomparably higher than anything which could be brought about by it in favor of any inclination or even of the sum total of all inclinations. Even if it should happen that, by a particularly unfortunate fate or by the niggardly provision of a stepmotherly nature, this will should be wholly lacking in power to accomplish its purpose, and if even the greatest effort should not avail it to achieve anything of its end, and if there remained only the good will (not as a mere wish but as the summoning of all the means in our power), it would sparkle like a jewel in its own right, as something that had its full worth in itself. Usefulness or fruitlessness can neither diminish nor augment this worth.[1]

He would presumably have said the same about a bad will: whether it accomplishes its evil purposes is morally irrelevant. And a course of action that would be condemned if it had a bad outcome cannot be vindicated if by luck it turns out well. There cannot be moral risk. This view seems to be wrong, but it arises in response to a fundamental problem about moral responsibility to which we possess no satisfactory solution.

The problem develops out of the ordinary conditions of moral judgment. Prior to reflection it is intuitively plausible that people cannot be morally assessed for what is not their fault, or for what is due to factors beyond their control. Such judgment is different from the evaluation of something as a good or bad thing, or state of affairs. The latter may be present in addition to moral judgment, but when we blame someone for his actions we are not merely saying it is bad that they happened, or bad that he exists: we are judging *him*, saying he is bad, which is different from his being a bad thing. This kind of judgment takes only a certain kind of object. Without being able to explain exactly why, we feel that the appropriateness of moral assessment is easily undermined by the discovery that the act or attribute, no matter how good or bad, is not under the person's control. While other evaluations remain, this one seems to lose its footing. So a clear absence of control, produced by involuntary movement, physical force, or ignorance of the circumstances, excuses what is done from moral judgment. But what we do depends in many more ways than these on what is not under our control – what is not produced by a good or bad will, in Kant's phrase. And external influences in this broader range are not usually thought to excuse what is done from moral judgment, positive or negative.

Let me give a few examples, beginning with the type of case Kant has in mind. Whether we succeed or fail in what we try to do nearly always depends to some extent on factors beyond our control. This is true of murder, altruism, revolution, the sacrifice of certain interests for the sake of others – almost any morally important act. What has been done, and what is morally judged, is partly determined by external factors. However jewel-like the good will may be in its own right, there is a morally significant difference between rescuing someone from a burning building and dropping him from a twelfth-storey window while trying to rescue him. Similarly, there is a morally significant difference between reckless driving and manslaughter. But whether a reckless driver hits a pedestrian depends on the presence of the pedestrian at the point where he recklessly passes a red light. What we do is also limited by the opportunities and choices with which we are faced, and these are largely determined by factors beyond our control. Someone who was an officer in a concentration camp might have led a quiet and harmless life if the Nazis had never come to power in Germany. And someone who led a quiet and harmless life in Argentina might have become an officer in a concentration camp if he had not left Germany for business reasons in 1930.

I shall say more later about these and other examples. I introduce them here to illustrate a general point. Where a significant aspect of what someone does depends on factors beyond his control, yet we continue to treat him in that respect as an object of moral judgment, it can be called moral luck. Such luck can be good or bad. And the problem posed by this phenomenon, which led Kant to deny its possibility, is that the broad range of external influences here identified seems on close examination to undermine moral assessment as surely as does the narrower range of familiar excusing conditions. If the condition of control is consistently applied, it threatens to erode most of the moral assessments we find it natural to make. The things for which people are morally judged are determined in more ways than we at first realize by what is beyond their control. And when the seemingly natural requirement of fault or responsibility is applied in light of these facts, it leaves few pre-reflective moral judgments intact. Ultimately, nothing or almost nothing about what a person does seems to be under his control.

Why not conclude, then, that the condition of control is false – that it is an initially plausible hypothesis refuted by clear counter-examples? One could in that case look instead for a more refined condition which picked out the *kinds* of lack of control that really undermine certain moral judgments, without yielding the unacceptable conclusion derived from the broader condition, that most or all ordinary moral judgments are illegitimate.

What rules out this escape is that we are dealing not with a theoretical conjecture but with a philosophical problem. The condition of control does not suggest itself merely as a generalization from certain clear cases. It seems *correct* in the further cases to which it is extended beyond the original set. When we undermine moral assessment by considering new ways in which control is absent, we are not just discovering what *would* follow given the general hypothesis, but are actually being persuaded that in itself the absence of control is relevant in these cases too. The erosion of moral judgment emerges not as the absurd consequence of an over-simple theory, but as a natural consequence of the ordinary idea of moral assessment, when it is applied in view of a more complete and precise account of the facts. It would therefore be a mistake to argue from the unacceptability of the conclusions to the need for a different account of the conditions of moral responsibility. The view that moral luck is paradoxical is not a *mistake*, ethical or logical, but a perception of one of the ways in which the intuitively acceptable conditions of moral judgment threaten to undermine it all.

It resembles the situation in another area of philosophy, the theory of knowledge. There too, conditions which seem perfectly natural, and which grow out of the ordinary procedures for challenging and defending claims to knowledge, threaten to undermine all such claims if consistently applied. Most skeptical arguments have this quality: they do not depend on the imposition of arbitrarily stringent standards of knowledge, arrived at by misunderstanding, but appear to grow inevitably from the consistent application of ordinary standards.[2] There is a substantive parallel as well, for epistemological skepticism arises from consideration of the respects in which our beliefs and their relation to reality depend on factors beyond our control. External and internal causes produce our beliefs. We may subject these processes to scrutiny in an effort to avoid error, but our conclusions at this next level also result, in part, from influences which we do not control directly. The same will be true no matter how far we carry the investigation. Our beliefs are always, ultimately, due to factors outside our control, and the impossibility of encompassing those factors without being at the mercy of others leads us to doubt whether we know anything. It looks as though, if any of our beliefs are true, it is pure biological luck rather than knowledge.

Moral luck is like this because while there are various respects in which the natural objects of moral assessment are out of our control or influenced by what is out of our control, we cannot reflect on these facts without losing our grip on the judgments.

There are roughly four ways in which the natural objects of moral assessment are disturbingly subject to luck. One is the phenomenon of constitutive luck – the kind of person you are, where this is not just a question of what you deliberately do, but of your inclinations, capacities, and temperament. Another category is luck in one's circumstances – the kind of problems and situations one faces. The other two have to do with the causes and effects of action: luck in how one is determined by antecedent circumstances, and luck in the way one's actions and projects turn out. All of them present a common problem. They are all opposed by the idea that one cannot be more culpable or estimable for anything than one is for that fraction of it which is under one's control. It seems irrational to take or dispense credit or blame for matters over which a person has no control, or for their influence on results over which he has partial control. Such things may create the conditions for action, but action can be judged only to the extent that it goes beyond these conditions and does not just result from them.

Let us first consider luck, good and bad, in the way things turn out. Kant, in the above-quoted passage, has one example of this in mind, but the category covers a wide range. It includes the truck driver who accidentally runs over a child, the artist who abandons his wife and five children to devote himself to painting,[3] and other cases in which the possibilities of success and failure are even greater. The driver, if he is entirely without fault, will feel terrible about his role in the event, but will not have to reproach himself. Therefore this example of agent-regret[4] is not yet a case of *moral* bad luck. However, if the driver was guilty of even a minor degree of negligence – failing to have his brakes checked recently, for example – then if that negligence contributes to the death of the child, he will not merely feel terrible. He will blame himself for the death. And what makes this an example of moral luck is that he would have to blame himself only slightly for the negligence itself if no situation arose which required him to brake suddenly and violently to avoid hitting a child. Yet the *negligence* is the same in both cases, and the driver has no control over whether a child will run into his path.

The same is true at higher levels of negligence. If someone has had too much to drink and his car swerves on to the sidewalk, he can count himself morally lucky if there are no pedestrians in its path. If there were, he would be to blame for their deaths, and would probably be prosecuted for manslaughter. But if he hurts no one, although his recklessness is exactly the same, he is guilty of a far less serious legal offence and will certainly reproach himself and be reproached by others much less severely. To take another legal example, the penalty for attempted murder is less than that for successful murder – however similar the intentions and motives of the assailant may be in the two cases. His degree of culpability can depend, it would seem, on whether the victim happened to be wearing a bullet-proof vest, or whether a bird flew into the path of the bullet – matters beyond his control.

Finally, there are cases of decision under uncertainty – common in public and private life. Anna Karenina goes off with Vronsky, Gaugin leaves his family, Chamberlain signs the Munich agreement, the Decembrists persuade the troops under their command to revolt against the czar, the American colonies declare their independence from Britain, you introduce two people in an attempt at match-making. It is tempting in all such cases to feel that some decision must be possible, in the light of what is known at the time, which will make reproach unsuitable no matter how things turn out. But this is not true; when someone acts in such ways he takes his life, or his moral position, into his hands, because how things turn out determines what he has done. It is possible *also* to assess the decision from the point of view of what could be known at the time, but this is not the end of the story. If the Decembrists had succeeded in overthrowing Nicholas I in 1825 and establishing a constitutional regime, they would be heroes. As it is, not only did they fail and pay for it, but they bore some responsibility for the terrible punishments meted out to the troops who had been persuaded to follow them. If the American Revolution had been a bloody failure resulting in greater repression, then Jefferson, Franklin and Washington would still have made a noble attempt, and might not even have regretted it on their way to the scaffold, but they would also have had to blame themselves for what they had helped to bring on their

159

compatriots. (Perhaps peaceful efforts at reform would eventually have succeeded.) If Hitler had not overrun Europe and exterminated millions, but instead had died of a heart attack after occupying the Sudetenland, Chamberlain's action at Munich would still have utterly betrayed the Czechs, but it would not be the great moral disaster that has made his name a household word.[5]

In many cases of difficult choice the outcome cannot be foreseen with certainty. One kind of assessment of the choice is possible in advance, but another kind must await the outcome, because the outcome determines what has been done. The same degree of culpability of estimability in intention, motive, or concern is compatible with a wide range of judgments, positive or negative, depending on what happened beyond the point of decision. The *mens rea* which could have existed in the absence of any consequences does not exhaust the grounds of moral judgment. Actual results influence culpability or esteem in a large class of unquestionably ethical cases ranging from negligence through political choice.

That these are genuine moral judgments rather than expressions of temporary attitude is evident from the fact that one can say *in advance* how the moral verdict will depend on the results. If one negligently leaves the bath running with the baby in it, one will realize, as one bounds up the stairs towards the bathroom, that if the baby has drowned one has done something awful, whereas if it has not one has merely been careless. Someone who launches a violent revolution against an authoritarian regime knows that if he fails he will be responsible for much suffering that is in vain, but if he succeeds he will be justified by the outcome. I do not mean that *any* action can be retroactively justified by history. Certain things are so bad in themselves, or so risky, that no results can make them all right. Nevertheless, when moral judgment does depend on the outcome, it is objective and timeless and not dependent on a change of standpoint produced by success or failure. The judgment after the fact follows from an hypothetical judgment that can be made beforehand, and it can be made as easily by someone else as by the agent.

From the point of view which makes responsibility dependent on control, all this seems absurd. How is it possible to be more or less culpable depending on whether a child gets into the path of one's car, or a bird into the path of one's bullet? Perhaps it is true that what is done depends on more than the agent's state of mind or intention. The problem then is, why is it not irrational to base moral assessment on what people do, in this broad sense? It amounts to holding them responsible for the contributions of fate as well as for their own – provided they have made some contribution to begin with. If we look at cases of negligence or attempt, the pattern seems to be that overall culpability corresponds to the product of mental or intentional fault and the seriousness of the outcome. Cases of decision under uncertainty are less easily explained in this way, for it seems that the overall judgment can even shift from positive to negative depending on the outcome. But here too it seems rational to subtract the effects of occurrences subsequent to the choice, that were merely possible at the time, and concentrate moral assessment on the actual decision in light of the probabilities. If the object of moral judgment is the *person*, then to hold him accountable for what he has done in the broader sense is akin to strict liability, which may have its legal uses but seems irrational as a moral position.

The result of such a line of thought is to pare down each act to its morally essential core, an inner act of pure will assessed by motive and intention. Adam Smith advocates such a position in *The Theory of Moral Sentiments*, but notes that it runs contrary to our actual judgments.

> But how well soever we may seem to be persuaded of the truth of this equitable maxim, when we consider it after this manner, in abstract, yet when we come to particular cases, the actual consequences which happen to proceed from any action, have a very great effect upon our sentiments concerning its merit or demerit, and almost always either enhance or diminish our sense of both. Scarce, in any one instance, perhaps, will our sentiments be found, after examination, to be entirely regulated by this rule, which we all acknowledge ought entirely to regulate them.[6]

Joel Feinberg points out further that restricting the domain of moral responsibility to the inner world will not immunize it to luck. Factors beyond the agent's control, like a coughing fit, can interfere with his decisions as surely as they can with the path of a bullet from his gun.[7] Nevertheless the tendency to cut down the scope of moral assessment is pervasive, and does not limit itself to the influence of effects. It attempts to isolate the will from the other direction, so to speak, by separating out constitutive luck. Let us consider that next.

Kant was particularly insistent on the moral irrelevance of qualities of temperament and personality that are not under the control of the will. Such qualities as sympathy or coldness might provide the background against which obedience to moral requirements is more or less difficult, but they could not be objects of moral assessment themselves, and might well interfere with confident assessment of its proper object – the determination of the will by the motive of duty. This rules out moral judgment of many of the virtues and vices, which are states of character that influence choice but are certainly not exhausted by dispositions to act deliberately in certain ways. A person may be greedy, envious, cowardly, cold, ungenerous, unkind, vain, or conceited, but *behave* perfectly by a monumental effort of will. To possess these vices is to be unable to help having certain feelings under certain circumstances, and to have strong spontaneous impulses to act badly. Even if one controls the impulses one still has the vice. An envious person hates the greater success of others. He can be morally condemned as envious even if he congratulates them cordially and does nothing to denigrate or spoil their success. Conceit, likewise, need not be displayed. It is fully present in someone who cannot help dwelling with secret satisfaction on the superiority of his own achievements, talents, beauty, intelligence, or virtue. To some extent such a quality may be the product of earlier choices; to some extent it may be amenable to change by current actions. But it is largely a matter of constitutive bad fortune. Yet people are morally condemned for such qualities, and esteemed for others equally beyond control of the will: they are assessed for what they are *like*.

To Kant this seems incoherent because virtue is enjoined on everyone and therefore must in principle be possible for everyone. It may be easier for some than for others, but it must be possible to achieve it by making the right choices, against whatever temperamental background.[8] One may want to have a generous spirit, or regret not having one, but it makes no sense to condemn oneself or anyone else for a quality which is not within the control of the will. Condemnation implies that you should not be like that, not that it is unfortunate that you are.

Nevertheless, Kant's conclusion remains intuitively unacceptable. We may be persuaded that these moral judgments are irrational, but they reappear involuntarily as soon as the argument is over. This is the pattern throughout the subject.

The third category to consider is luck in one's circumstances, and I shall mention it briefly. The things we are called upon to do, the moral tests we face, are importantly determined by factors beyond our control. It may be true of someone that in a dangerous situation he would behave in a cowardly or heroic fashion, but if the situation never arises, he will never have the chance to distinguish or disgrace himself in this way, and his moral record will be different.[9]

A conspicuous example of this is political. Ordinary citizens of Nazi Germany had an opportunity to behave heroically by opposing the regime. They also had an opportunity to behave badly, and most of them are culpable for having failed this test. But it is a test to which the citizens of other countries were not subjected, with the result that even if they, or some of them, would have behaved as badly as the Germans in like circumstances, they simply did not and therefore are not similarly culpable. Here again one is morally at the mercy of fate, and it may seem irrational upon reflection, but our ordinary moral attitudes would be unrecognizable without it. We judge people for what they actually do or fail to do, not just for what they would have done if circumstances had been different.[10]

This form of moral determination by the actual is also paradoxical, but we can begin to see how deep in the concept of responsibility the paradox is embedded. A person can be morally responsible only for what he does; but what he does results from a great deal that he does not do; therefore he is not morally responsible for what he is and is not responsible for. (This is not a contradiction, but it is a paradox.)

It should be obvious that there is a connection between these problems about responsibility and control and an even more familiar problem, that of freedom of the will. This is the last type of moral luck I want to take up, though I can do no more within the scope of this essay than indicate its connection with the other types.

If one cannot be responsible for consequences of one's acts due to factors beyond one's control, or for antecedents of one's acts that are properties of temperament not subject to one's will, or for the circumstances that pose one's moral choices, then how can one be responsible even for the stripped-down acts of the will itself, if *they* are the product of antecedent circumstances outside of the will's control?

The area of genuine agency, and therefore of legitimate moral judgment, seems to shrink under this scrutiny to an extensionless point. Everything seems to result from the combined influence of factors, antecedent and posterior to action, that are not within the agent's control. Since he cannot be responsible for them, he cannot be responsible for their results – though it may remain possible to take up the aesthetic or other evaluative analogues of the moral attitudes that are thus displaced.

It is also possible, of course, to brazen it out and refuse to accept the results, which indeed seem unacceptable as soon as we stop thinking about the arguments. Admittedly, if certain surrounding circumstances had been different, then no unfortunate consequences would have followed from a wicked intention, and no seriously culpable act would have been performed; but since the circumstances were *not* different, and the agent *in fact* succeeded in perpetrating a particularly cruel murder, *that* is what he did, and that is what he is responsible for. Similarly, we may admit that if certain antecedent circumstances had been different, the agent would never have developed into the sort of person who would do such a thing; but since he *did* develop (as the inevitable result of those antecedent circumstances) into the sort of swine he is, and into the person who committed such a murder, *that* is what he is blameable for. In both cases one is responsible for what one actually does – even if what one actually does depends in important ways on what is not within one's control. This compatibilist account of our moral judgments would leave room for the ordinary conditions of responsibility – the absence of coercion, ignorance, or involuntary movement – as part of the determination of what someone has done – but it is understood not to exclude the influence of a great deal that he has not done.[11]

The only thing wrong with this solution is its failure to explain how skeptical problems arise. For they arise not from the imposition of an arbitrary external requirement, but from the nature of moral judgment itself. Something in the ordinary idea of what someone does must explain how it can seem necessary to subtract from it anything that merely happens – even though the ultimate consequence of such subtraction is that nothing remains. And something in the ordinary idea of knowledge must explain why it seems to be undermined by any influences on belief not within the control of the subject – so that knowledge seems impossible without an impossible foundation in autonomous reason. But let us leave epistemology aside and concentrate on action, character, and moral assessment.

The problem arises, I believe, because the self which acts and is the object of moral judgment is threatened with dissolution by the absorption of its acts and impulses into the class of events. Moral judgment of a person is judgment not of what happens to him, but of him. It does not say merely that a certain event or state of affairs is fortunate or unfortunate or even terrible. It is not an evaluation of a state of the world, or of an individual as part of the world. We are not thinking just that it would be better if he were different, or did not exist, or had not done some of the things he has done. We are judging *him*, rather than his existence or characteristics. The effect of concentrating on the influence of what is not under his control is to make this responsible self seem to disappear, swallowed up by the order of mere events.

What, however, do we have in mind that a person must *be* to be the object of these moral attitudes? While the concept of agency is easily undermined, it is very difficult to give it a positive characterization. That is familiar from the literature on Free Will.

I believe that in a sense the problem has no solution, because something in the idea of agency is incompatible with actions being events, or people being things. But as the external determinants of what someone has done are gradually exposed, in their effect on consequences, character, and choice itself, it becomes gradually clear that actions are events and people things. Eventually nothing remains which can be ascribed to the responsible self, and we are left with nothing but a portion of the larger sequence of events, which can be deplored or celebrated, but not blamed or praised.

Though I cannot define the idea of the active self that is thus undermined, it is possible to say something about its sources. There is a close connexion between our feelings about ourselves and our feelings about others. Guilt and indignation, shame and contempt, pride and admiration are internal and external sides of the same moral attitudes. We are unable to view ourselves simply as portions of the world, and from inside we have a rough idea of the boundary between what is us and what is not, what we do and what happens to us, what is our personality and what is an accidental handicap. We apply the same essentially internal conception of the self to others. About ourselves we feel pride, shame, guilt, remorse

– and agent-regret. We do not regard our actions and our characters merely as fortunate or unfortunate episodes – though they may also be that. We cannot *simply* take an external evaluative view of ourselves – of what we most essentially are and what we do. And this remains true even when we have seen that we are not responsible for our own existence, or our nature, or the choices we have to make, or the circumstances that give our acts the consequences they have. Those acts remain ours and we remain ourselves, despite the persuasiveness of the reasons that seem to argue us out of existence.

It is this internal view that we extend to others in moral judgment – when we judge *them* rather than their desirability or utility. We extend to others the refusal to limit ourselves to external evaluation, and we accord to them selves like our own. But in both cases this comes up against the brutal inclusion of humans and everything about them in a world from which they cannot be separated and of which they are nothing but contents. The external view forces itself on us at the same time that we resist it. One way this occurs is through the gradual erosion of what we do by the subtraction of what happens.[12]

The inclusion of consequences in the conception of what we have done is an acknowledgement that we are parts of the world, but the paradoxical character of moral luck which emerges from this acknowledgment shows that we are unable to operate with such a view, for it leaves us with no one to be. The same thing is revealed in the appearance that determinism obliterates responsibility. Once we see an aspect of what we or someone else does as something that happens, we lose our grip on the idea that it has been done and that we can judge the doer and not just the happening. This explains why the absence of determinism is no more hospitable to the concept of agency than is its presence – a point that has been noticed often. Either way the act is viewed externally, as part of the course of events.

The problem of moral luck cannot be understood without an account of the internal conception of agency and its special connection with the moral attitudes as opposed to other types of value. I do not have such an account. The degree to which the problem has a solution can be determined only by seeing whether in some degree the incompatibility between this conception and the various ways in which we do not control what we do is only apparent. I have nothing to offer on that topic either. But it is not enough to say merely that our basic moral attitudes toward ourselves and others are determined by what is actual; for they are also threatened by the sources of that actuality, and by the external view of action which forces itself on us when we see how everything we do belongs to a world that we have not created.

Notes

1   *Foundations of the Metaphysics of Morals*, first section, third paragraph.
2   See Thompson Clarke, 'The legacy of skepticism', *Journal of Philosophy* IXIX 20 (November 9, 1972), pp. 754–69.
3   Such a case, modelled on the life of Gauguin, is discussed by Bernard Williams in 'Moral luck', *Proceedings of the Aristotelian Society*, suppl. vol. I (1976), pp 115–35 (to which the original version of this essay was a reply). He points out that though success or failure cannot be predicted in advance, Gauguin's most basic retrospective feelings about the decision will be determined by the development of his talent. My disagreement with Williams is that his account fails to explain why such retrospective attitudes can be called moral. If success does not permit Gauguin to justify himself to others, but still determines his most basic feelings, that shows only that his most basic feelings need not be moral. It does not show that morality is subject to luck. If the retrospective judgment were moral, it would imply the truth of a hypothetical judgment made in advance, of the form 'If I leave my family and become a great painter, I will be justified by success; if I don't become a great painter, the act will be unforgivable.'
4   Williams's term (ibid.).
5   For a fascinating but morally repellent discussion of the topic of justification by history, see Maurice Merleau-Ponty, *Humanisme et Terreur* (Paris: Gallimard, 1947), translated as *Humanism and Terror* (Boston: Beacon Press, 1969).
6.   Pt II, sect. 3, Introduction, para. 5.
7   'Problematic responsibility in law and morals', in Joel Feinberg. *Doing and Deserving* (Princeton, NJ: Princeton University Press, 1970).
8   'if nature has put little sympathy in the heart of a man, and if he, though an honest man, is by temperament cold and indifferent to the sufferings of others, perhaps because he is provided with special gifts of patience and fortitude and expects or even requires that others should have the same – and such a man would certainly not be the meanest product of nature – would not he find in himself a source from which to give himself a far higher worth than he could have got by having a good-natured temperament?' (*Foundations of the Metaphysics of Morals*, first section, eleventh paragraph).
9   Cf. Thomas Gray, 'Elegy Written in Country Churchyard':
      Some mute inglorious Milton here may rest,
      Some Cromwell, guiltless of his country's blood.
   An unusual example of circumstantial moral luck is provided by the kind of moral dilemma with which someone can be faced through no fault of his own, but which leaves him with nothing to do which is not wrong. See chapter 5 [in *Mortal Questions*], and Bernard Williams, 'Ethical consistency', *Proceedings of the Aristotelian Society*, suppl. vol. XXXIX (1965), reprinted in *Problems of the Self* (Cambridge: Cambridge University Press, 1973), pp. 166–86.
10   Circumstantial luck can extend to aspects of the situation other than individual behavior. For example, during the Vietnam War even U.S. citizens

who had opposed their country's actions vigorously from the start often felt compromised by its crimes. Here they were not even responsible; there was probably nothing they could do to stop what was happening, so the feeling of being implicated may seem unintelligible. But it is nearly impossible to view the crimes of one's own country in the same way that one views the crimes of another country, no matter how equal one's lack of power to stop them in the two cases. One *is* a citizen of one of them, and has a connexion with its actions (even if only through taxes that cannot be withheld) – that one does not have with the other's. This makes it possible to be ashamed of one's country, and to feel a victim of moral bad luck that one was an American in the 1960s.

11　The corresponding position in epistemology would be that knowledge consists of true beliefs formed in certain ways, and that it does not require all aspects of the process to be under the knower's control, actually or potentially. Both the correctness of these beliefs and the process by which they are arrived at would therefore be importantly subject to luck. The Nobel Prize is not awarded to people who turn out to be wrong, no matter how brilliant their reasoning.

12　See P. F. Strawson's discussion of the conflict between the objective attitude and personal reactive attitudes in 'Freedom and resentment', *Proceedings of the British Academy*, 1962, repr. in P. F. Strawson (ed.) *Studies in the Philosophy of Thought and Action* (London: Oxford University Press, 1968), and in P. F. Strawson, *Freedom and Resentment and Other Essays* (London: Methuen, 1974).

19

Relativism

Bernard Williams

Moral relativism is, in its simplest form, the view that since there are no objective values in the world right and wrong are to be decided entirely by reference to local custom. What is accepted within one society just *is* morally right for its members even if it conflicts with our own deepest held views. There is no vantage point from which competing moral approaches can be judged. All intervention in other societies on moral grounds is wrong. In this reading Bernard Williams (1929–) reveals the inconsistencies inherent in such a position.

From Bernard Williams, *Morality*

Let us ... look round a special view or assemblage of views which has been built on the site of moral disagreements between societies. This is *relativism*, the anthropologist's heresy, possibly the most absurd view to have been advanced even in moral philosophy. In its vulgar and unregenerate form (which I shall consider, since it is both the most distinctive and the most influential form) it consists of three propositions: that 'right' means (can only be coherently understood as meaning) 'right for a given society'; that 'right for a given society' is to be understood in a functionalist sense; and that (therefore) it is wrong for people in one society to condemn, interfere with, etc., the values of another society. A view with a long history, it was popular with some liberal colonialists, notably British administrators in places (such as West Africa) in which white men held no land. In that historical role, it may have had, like some other muddled doctrines, a beneficent influence, though modern African nationalism may well deplore its tribalist and conservative implications.

Whatever its results, the view is clearly inconsistent, since it makes a claim in its third proposition, about what is right and wrong in one's dealings with other societies, which uses a *nonrelative* sense of 'right' not allowed for in the first proposition. The claim that human sacrifice, for instance, was 'right for' the Ashanti comes to be taken as saying that human sacrifice was right among the Ashanti, and this in turn as saying that human sacrifice among the Ashanti was right; i.e., we had no business to interfere with it. But this last is certainly not the sort of claim allowed by the theory. The most the theory can allow is the claim that it was right for (i.e., functionally valuable for) our society not to interfere with Ashanti society, and, first, this is certainly not all that was meant, and, second, is very dubiously true.

Apart from its logically unhappy attachment of a nonrelative morality of toleration or non-interference to a view of morality as relative, the theory suffers in its functionalist aspects from some notorious weaknesses of functionalism in general, notably difficulties that surround the identification of 'a society'. If 'society' is regarded as a cultural unit, identified in part through its values, then many of the functionalist propositions will cease to be empirical propositions and become bare tautologies: it is tediously a necessary condition of the survival of a group-with-certain-values that the group should retain those values. At the other extreme, the survival of a society could be understood as the survival of certain persons and their having descendants, in which case many functionalist propositions about the necessity of cultural survival will be false. When in Great Britain some Welsh nationalists speak of the survival of the Welsh language as a condition of the survival of Welsh society, they manage sometimes to convey an impression that it is a condition of the survival of Welsh people, as though the forgetting of Welsh were literally lethal.

In between these two extremes is the genuinely interesting territory, a province of informative social science, where there is room for such claims as that a given practice or belief is integrally connected with much more of a society's fabric than may appear on the surface, that it is not an excrescence, so that discouragement or modification of this may lead to much larger social change than might have been expected; or, again, that a certain set of values or institutions may be such that if they are lost, or seriously changed, the people in the society, while they may physically survive, will do so only in a deracinated and hopeless condition. Such propositions, if established, would of course be of first importance in deciding what to do; but they cannot take over the work of deciding what to do.

Here, and throughout the questions of conflict of values between societies, we need (and rarely get) some mildly realistic picture of what decisions might be being made by whom, of situations to which the considerations might be practically relevant. Of various paradigms that come to mind, one is that of conflict, such as the confrontation of other societies with Nazi Germany. Another is that of control, where (to eliminate further complications of the most obvious case, colonialism) one might take such a case as that of the relations of the central government of Ghana to residual elements of traditional Ashanti society. In neither case would functionalist propositions in themselves provide any answers at all. Still less will they where a major issue is whether a given group should be realistically or desirably regarded as 'a society' in a relevant sense, or whether its values and its future are to be integrally related to those of a larger group – as with the case of blacks in the United States.

The central confusion of relativism is to try to conjure out of the fact that societies have differing attitudes and values an *a priori* nonrelative principle to determine the attitude of one society to another; this is impossible. If we are going to say that there are ultimate moral disagreements between societies, we must include, in the matters they can disagree about, their attitudes to other moral outlooks. It is also true, however, that there are inherent features of morality that tend to make it difficult to regard a morality as applying only to a group. The element of universalization which is present in any morality, but which applies under tribal morality perhaps only to members of the tribe, progressively comes to range over persons as such. Less formally, it is essential ... to morality and its role in any society that certain sorts of reactions and motivations should be strongly internalized, and these cannot merely evaporate because one is confronted with human beings in another society. Just as *de gustibus non disputandum* is not a maxim which applies to morality, neither is 'when in Rome do as the Romans do', which is at best a principle of etiquette.

Nor is it just a case of doing as the Romans do, but of putting up with it. Here it would be a platitude to point out that of course someone who against wider experience of the world may rightly come to regard some moral reaction of his to unfamiliar conduct as parochial and will seek to modify or discount it. There are many important distinctions to be made here between the kinds of thoughts appropriate to such a process in different cases: sometimes he may cease to regard a certain issue as a moral matter at all, sometimes he may come to see that what abroad looked the same as something he would have deplored at home was actually, in morally relevant respects, a very different thing. (Perhaps – though one can scarcely believe it – there were some missionaries or others who saw the men in a polygamous society in the light of seedy bigamists at home.) But it would be a particular moral view, and one both psychologically and morally implausible, to insist that these adaptive reactions were the only correct ones, that confronted with practices which are found and felt as inhuman, for instance, there is an *a priori* demand of acceptance. In the fascinating book by Bernal de Diaz, who went with Cortez to Mexico, there is an account of what they all felt when they came upon the sacrificial temples. This morally unpretentious collection of bravos was genuinely horrified by the Aztec practices. It would surely be absurd to regard this reaction as merely parochial or self-righteous. It rather indicated something which their conduct did not always indicate, that they regarded the Indians as men rather than as wild animals.

It is fair to press this sort of case, and in general the cases of actual confrontation. 'Every society has its own standards' may be, even if confused, a sometimes useful maxim of social study; as a maxim of social study it is also painless. But what, after all, is one supposed to do if confronted with a human sacrifice? – not a real question for many of us, perhaps, but a real question for Cortez. 'It wasn't their business,' it may be said; 'they had no right to be there anyway.' Perhaps – though this, once more, is necessarily a nonrelative moral judgement itself. But even if they had no right to be there, it is a matter for real moral argument what would *follow* from that. For if a burglar comes across the owner of the house trying to murder somebody, is he morally obliged not to interfere because he is trespassing?

None of this is to deny the obvious facts that many have interfered with other societies when they should not have done; have interfered without understanding; and have interfered often with a brutality greater than that of anything they were trying to stop. I am saying only that it cannot be a consequence of the nature of morality itself that no society ought ever to interfere with another, or that individuals from one society confronted with the practices of another ought, if rational, to react with acceptance. To draw these consequences is the characteristic (and inconsistent) step of vulgar relativism.

Politics

20

Of the natural condition of mankind
Thomas Hobbes

Imagine human life outside of society without any overall authority or power keeping anyone in check. What would life be like in such a world? This is the question that Thomas Hobbes (1588–1679) asked himself in *Leviathan* (1651). His interest was not so much in the history of humanity but in the elements from which society was built and the reasons for particular practices and laws. In the brief extract from *Leviathan* included here, Hobbes sketches his bleak picture of life in what he calls a State of Nature. Given the grim life possible under such circumstances it is not surprising that people group together under a common authority for protection and the possibility of a better way of living.

From Thomas Hobbes, *Leviathan*

1.   Nature hath made men so equal, in the faculties of the body, and mind; as that though there be found one man sometimes manifestly stronger in body, or of quicker mind than another; yet when all is reckoned together, the difference between man, and man, is not so considerable, as that one man can thereupon claim to himself any benefit, to which another may not pretend, as well as he. For as to the strength of body, the weakest has strength enough to kill the strongest, either by secret machination, or by confederacy with others, that are in the same danger with himself.

2.   And so to the faculties of the mind, (setting aside the arts grounded upon words, and especially that skill of proceeding upon general, and infallible rules, called science; which very few have, and but in few things; as being not a native faculty, born with us; nor attained (as prudence,) while we look after somewhat else,) I find yet a greater equality amongst men, than that of strength. For prudence, is but experience; which equal time, equally bestows on all men, in those things they equally apply themselves unto. That which may perhaps make such equality incredible, is but a vain

175

conceit of one's own wisdom, which almost all men think they have in a greater degree, than the vulgar; that is, than all men but themselves, and a few others, whom by fame, or for concurring with themselves, they approve. For such is the nature of men, that howsoever they may acknowledge many others to be more witty, or more eloquent, or more learned; yet they will hardly believe there be many so wise as themselves; for they see their own wit at hand, and other men's at a distance. But this proveth rather that men are in that point equal, than unequal. For there is not ordinarily a greater sign of the equal distribution of any thing, than that every man is contented with his share.

3.   From this equality of ability, ariseth equality of hope in the attaining of our ends. And therefore if any two men desire the same thing, which nevertheless they cannot both enjoy, they become enemies; and in the way to their end, (which is principally their own conservation, and sometimes their delectation only,) endeavour to destroy, or subdue one another. And from hence it comes to pass, that where an invader hath no more to fear, than another man's single power; if one plant, sow, build, or possess a convenient seat, others may probably be expected to come prepared with forces united, to dispossess, and deprive him, not only of the fruit of his labour, but also of his life, or liberty. And the invader again is in the like danger of another.

4.   And from this diffidence of one another, there is no way for any man to secure himself, so reasonable, as anticipation; that is, by force, or wiles, to master the persons of all men he can, so long, till he see no other power great enough to endanger him: and this is no more than his own conservation requireth, and is generally allowed. Also because there be some, that taking pleasure in contemplating their own power in the acts of conquest, which they pursue farther than their security requires; if others, that otherwise would be glad to be at ease within modest bounds, should not by invasion increase their power, they would not be able, long time, by standing only on their defence, to subsist. And by consequence, such augmentation of dominion over men, being necessary to a man's conservation, it ought to be allowed him.

5.   Again, men have no pleasure, (but on the contrary a great deal of grief) in keeping company, where there is no power able to over-awe them all. For every man looketh that his companion should value him, at the same rate he sets upon himself: and upon all signs of contempt, or undervaluing, naturally endeavours, as far as he dares (which amongst them that have no common power to keep them in quiet, is far enough to make them destroy each other,) to extort a greater value from his contemners, by damage; and from others, by the example.

6.   So that in the nature of man, we find three principal causes of quarrel. First, competition; secondly, diffidence; thirdly, glory.

7.   The first, maketh men invade for gain; the second, for safety; and the third, for reputation. The first use violence, to make themselves masters of other men's persons, wives, children, and cattle; the second, to defend them; the third, for trifles, as a word, a smile, a different opinion, and any other sign of undervalue, either direct in their persons, or by reflection in their kindred, their friends, their nation, their profession, or their name.

8.   Hereby it is manifest, that during the time men live without a common power to keep them all in awe, they are in that condition which is called war; and such a war, as is of every man, against every man. For WAR, consisteth not in battle only, or the act of fighting; but in a tract of time, wherein the will to contend by battle is sufficiently known: and therefore the notion of *time*, is to be considered in the nature of war; as it is in the nature of weather. For as the nature of foul weather, lieth not in a shower or two of rain; but in an inclination thereto of many days together: so the nature of war, consisteth not in actual fighting; but in the known disposition thereto, during all the time there is no assurance to the contrary. All other time is PEACE.

9.   Whatsoever therefore is consequent to a time of war, where every man is enemy to every man; the same is consequent to the time, wherein men live without other security, than what their own strength, and their own invention shall furnish them withal. In such condition, there is no place for industry; because the fruit thereof is uncertain: and consequently no culture of the earth; no navigation, nor use of the commodities that may be imported by sea; no commodious building; no instruments of moving, and removing such things as require much force; no knowledge of the face of the earth; no account of time; no arts; no letters; no society; and which is worst of all, continual fear, and danger of violent death; and the life of man, solitary, poor, nasty, brutish, and short.

10.   It may seem strength to some man, that has not well weighed these things; that nature should thus dissociate, and render men apt to invade, and destroy one another: and he may therefore, not trusting to this infer- ence, made from the passions, desire perhaps to have the same con- firmed by experience. Let him therefore consider with himself, when taking a journey, he arms himself, and seeks to go well accompanied; when going to sleep, he locks his doors; when even in his house he locks his chests; and this when he knows there be laws, and public officers, armed, to revenge all injuries shall be done him; what opinion he has of

his fellow-subjects, when he rides armed; of his fellow citizens, when he locks his doors; and of his children, and servants, when he locks his chests. Does he not there as much accuse mankind by his actions, as I do by my words? But neither of us accuse man's nature in it. The desires, and other passions of man, are in themselves no sin. No more are the actions, that proceed from those passions, till they know a law that forbids them: which till laws be made they cannot know: nor can any law be made, till they have agreed upon the person that shall make it.

11.   It may peradventure be thought, there was never such a time, nor condition of war as this; and I believe it was never generally so, over all the world: but there are many places, where they live so now. For the savage people in many places of America, except the government of small families, the concord whereof dependeth on natural lust, have no government at all; and live at this day in that brutish manner, as I said before. Howsoever, it may be perceived what manner of life there would be, where there were no common power to fear; by the manner of life, which men that have formerly lived under a peaceful government, use to degenerate into, in a civil war.

12.   But though there had never been any time, wherein particular men were in a condition of war one against another; yet in all times, kings, and persons of sovereign authority, because of their independency, are in continual jealousies, and in the state and posture of gladiators; having their weapons pointing, and their eyes fixed on one another; that is, their forts, garrisons, and guns upon the frontiers of their kingdoms; and continual spies upon their neighbours; which is a posture of war. But because they uphold thereby, the industry of their subjects; there does not follow from it, that misery, which accompanies the liberty of particular men.

13.   To this war of every man against every man, this also is consequent; that nothing can be unjust. The notions of right and wrong, justice and injustice have there no place. Where there is no common power, there is no law: where no law, no injustice. Force, and fraud, are in war the two cardinal virtues. Justice, and injustice are none of the faculties neither of the body, nor mind. If they were, they might be in a man that were alone in the world, as well as his senses, and passions. They are qualities, that relate to men in society, not in solitude. It is consequent also to the same condition, that there be no propriety, no dominion, no *mine* and *thine* distinct; but only that to be every man's, that he can get; and for so long, as he can keep it. And thus much for the ill condition, which man by mere nature is actually placed in; though with a possibility to come out of it, consisting partly in the passions, partly in his reason.

14.   The passions that incline men to peace, are fear of death; desire of such things as are necessary to commodious living; and a hope by their industry to obtain them. And reason suggesteth convenient articles of peace, upon which men may be drawn to agreement. These articles, are they, which otherwise are called the Laws of Nature.

21

Two concepts of liberty
Isaiah Berlin

What is freedom? Historically, Isaiah Berlin (1909–97) argues, two different concepts of liberty have arisen: the negative and the positive. Negative liberty, familiar from the liberal tradition, is the kind of liberty described by John Stuart Mill in *On Liberty* (1859), namely freedom from constraint or interference. You are free, in this sense, to the extent that no one is preventing you doing what you might want to do. Positive freedom, on the other hand, is a matter of the doors that you can actually pass through, not just of those that lie open: it is what you can actually do. The notion of positive liberty derives from the wish to be one's own master. Berlin's main claim in this important article (first delivered as a lecture in 1958) is that the notion of positive liberty has frequently been distorted and used to suppress dissidents on the grounds that they are being forced to do what at some level they really desire and that this makes them more free than they would otherwise have been. It is not that Berlin is opposed to positive freedom in itself; it is only abuses of the concept that he objects to.

From Isaiah Berlin, *Four Essays on Liberty*

I

To coerce a man is to deprive him of freedom – freedom from what? Almost every moralist in human history has praised freedom. Like happiness and goodness, like nature and reality, the meaning of this term is so porous that there is little interpretation that it seems able to resist. I do not propose to discuss either the history of this protean word or the more than two hundred senses of it recorded by historians of ideas. I propose to examine no more than two of these senses – but they are central ones, with a great deal of human history behind them, and, I dare say, still to come. The first of these political senses of freedom or liberty (I shall use both words to mean the same), which (following much precedent) I shall call the 'negative' sense, is involved in the answer to the question 'What is the area within which the subject – a person or group of persons – is or should be left to do or be what he is able to do or be, without interference by other persons?' The second, which I shall call the 'positive' sense, is involved in the answer to the question 'What, or who, is the source of control or interference that can determine someone to do, or be, this rather than that?' The two questions are clearly different, even though the answers to them may overlap.

The notion of 'negative' freedom

I am normally said to be free to the degree to which no man or body of men interferes with my activity. Political liberty in this sense is simply the area within which a man can act unobstructed by others. If I am prevented by others from doing what I could otherwise do, I am to that degree unfree; and if this area is contracted by other men beyond a certain minimum, I can be described as being coerced, or, it may be, enslaved. Coercion is not, however, a term that covers every form of inability. If I say that I am unable to jump more than ten feet in the air, or cannot read because I am blind, or cannot understand the darker pages of Hegel, it would be eccentric to say that I am to that degree enslaved or coerced. Coercion implies the deliberate interference of other human beings within the area in which I could otherwise act. You lack political liberty or freedom only if you are prevented from attaining a goal by human beings.[1] Mere incapacity to attain a goal is not lack of political freedom.[2] This is brought out by the use of such modern expressions as 'economic freedom' and its counterpart, 'economic slavery'. It is argued, very plausibly, that if a man is too poor to afford something on which there is no legal ban – a loaf of bread, a journey round the world recourse to the law courts – he is as little free to have it as he would be if it were forbidden him by law. If my poverty were a kind of disease, which prevented me from buying bread, or paying for the journey round the world or getting my case heard, as lameness prevents me from running, this inability would not naturally be described as a lack of freedom, least of all political freedom. It is only because I believe that my inability to get a given thing is due to the fact that other human beings have made arrangements whereby I am, whereas others are not, prevented from having enough money with which to pay for it, that I think myself a victim of coercion or slavery. In other words, this use of the term depends on a particular social and economic theory about the causes of my poverty or weakness. If my lack of material means is due to my lack of mental or physical capacity, then I begin to speak of being deprived of freedom (and not simply about poverty) only if I accept the theory.[3] If, in addition, I believe that I am being kept in want by a specific arrangement which I consider unjust or unfair, I speak of economic slavery or oppression. The nature of things does not madden us, only ill

181

will does, said Rousseau.[4] The criterion of oppression is the part that I believe to be played by other human beings, directly or indirectly, with or without the intention of doing so, in frustrating my wishes. By being free in this sense I mean not being interfered with by others. The wider the area of non-interference the wider my freedom.

This is what the classical English political philosophers meant when they used this word.[5] They disagreed about how wide the area could or should be. They supposed that it could not, as things were, be unlimited, because if it were, it would entail a state in which all men could boundlessly interfere with all other men; and this kind of 'natural' freedom would lead to social chaos in which men's minimum needs would not be satisfied; or else the liberties of the weak would be suppressed by the strong. Because they perceived that human purposes and activities do not automatically harmonise with one another, and because (whatever their official doctrines) they put high value on other goals, such as justice, or happiness, or culture, or security, or varying degrees of equality, they were prepared to curtail freedom in the interests of other values and, indeed, of freedom itself. For, without this, it was impossible to create the kind of association that they thought desirable. Consequently, it is assumed by these thinkers that the area of men's free action must be limited by law. But equally it is assumed, especially by such libertarians as Locke and Mill in England, and Constant and Tocqueville in France, that there ought to exist a certain minimum area of personal freedom which must on no account be violated; for if it is overstepped, the individual will find himself in an area too narrow for even that minimum development of his natural faculties which alone makes it possible to pursue, and even to conceive, the various ends which men hold good or right or sacred. It follows that a frontier must be drawn between the area of private life and that of public authority. Where it is to be drawn is a matter of argument, indeed of haggling. Men are largely interdependent, and no man's activity is so completely private as never to obstruct the lives of others in any way. 'Freedom for the pike is death for the minnows';[6] the liberty of some must depend on the restraint of others. Freedom for an Oxford don, others have been known to add, is a very different thing from freedom for an Egyptian peasant.

This proposition derives its force from something that is both true and important, but the phrase itself remains a piece of political claptrap. It is true that to offer political rights, or safeguards against intervention by the State, to men who are half-naked, illiterate, underfed and diseased is to mock their condition; they need medical help or education before they can understand, or make use of, an increase in their freedom. What is freedom to those who cannot make use of it? Without adequate conditions for the use of freedom, what is the value of freedom? First things come first: there are situations in which – to use a saying satirically attributed to the nihilists by Dostoevsky – boots are superior to Pushkin; individual freedom is not everyone's primary need. For freedom is not the mere absence of frustration of whatever kind; this would inflate the meaning of the word until it meant too much or too little. The Egyptian peasant needs clothes or medicine before, and more than, personal liberty, but the minimum freedom that he needs today, and the greater degree of freedom that he may need tomorrow, is not some species of freedom peculiar to him, but identical with that of professors, artists, and millionaires.

What troubles the consciences of Western liberals is, I think, the belief, not that the freedom that men seek differs according to their social or economic conditions, but that the minority who possess it have gained it by exploiting, or, at least, averting their gaze from, the vast majority who do not. They believe, with good reason, that if individual liberty is an ultimate end for human beings, none should be deprived of it by others; least of all that some should enjoy it at the expense of others. Equality of liberty; not to treat others as I should not wish them to treat me; repayment of my debt to those who alone have made possible my liberty or prosperity or enlightenment; justice, in its simplest and most universal sense – these are the foundations of liberal morality. Liberty is not the only goal of men. I can, like the Russian critic Belinsky, say that if others are to be deprived of it – if my brothers are to remain in poverty, squalor, and chains – then I do not want it for myself. I reject it with both hands and infinitely prefer to share their fate. But nothing is gained by a confusion of terms. To avoid glaring inequality or widespread misery I am ready to sacrifice some, or all, of my freedom: I may do so willingly and freely; but it is freedom that I am giving up for the sake of justice or equality or the love of my fellow men. I should be guilt-stricken, and rightly so, if I were not, in some circumstances, ready to make this sacrifice. But a sacrifice is not an increase in what is being sacrificed, namely freedom, however great the moral need or the compensation for it. Everything is what it is: liberty is liberty, not equality or fairness or justice or culture or human happiness or a quiet conscience. If the liberty of myself or my class or nation depends on the misery of a number of other human beings, the system which promotes this is unjust and immoral. But if I curtail or lose my freedom in order to lessen the shame of such inequality, and do not thereby materially increase the individual liberty of others, an absolute loss of liberty occurs. This may be compensated for by a gain in justice or in happiness or in peace, but the loss remains, and it is a confusion of values to say that although my 'liberal', individual freedom may go by the board, some other kind of freedom – 'social' or 'economic' – is increased. Yet it remains true that the freedom of some must at times be curtailed to secure the freedom of others. Upon what principle should this be done? If freedom is a sacred, untouchable value, there can be no such principle. One or other of these conflicting rules or principles must, at any rate in practice, yield: not always for reasons which can be clearly stated, let alone generalised into rules or universal maxims. Still, a practical compromise has to be found.

Philosophers with an optimistic view of human nature, and a belief in the possibility of harmonising human interests, such as Locke or Adam Smith and, in some moods, Mill, believed that social harmony and progress were compatible with reserving a large area for private life over which neither the State nor any other authority must be allowed to trespass. Hobbes, and those who agreed with him, especially conservative or reactionary thinkers, argued that if men were to be prevented from destroying one another, and making social life a jungle or a wilderness, greater safeguards must be instituted to keep them in their places; he wished correspondingly to increase the area of centralized control and decrease that of the individual. But both sides agreed that some portion of human existence must remain independent of the sphere of social control. To invade that preserve, however small, would be despotism. The most eloquent of all defenders of freedom and privacy, Benjamin Constant, who had not forgotten the Jacobin dictatorship, declared that at the very least the liberty of religion, opinion, expression, property must be guaranteed against arbitrary invasion. Jefferson, Burke, Paine, Mill, compiled different catalogues of individual liberties, but the argument for keeping authority at bay is always substantially the same. We must preserve a minimum area of personal freedom if we are not to 'degrade or deny our nature'.[7] We cannot remain absolutely free, and must give up some of our liberty to preserve the rest. But total self-surrender is self-defeating. What then must the minimum be? That which a man cannot give up without offending against the essence of his human nature. What is this essence? What are the standards which it entails? This has been, and perhaps always will be, a matter of infinite debate. But whatever the principle in terms of which the area of non-interference is to be drawn, whether it is that of natural law or natural rights, or of utility, or the pronouncements of a categorical imperative, or the sanctity of the social contract, or any other concept with which men have sought to clarify and justify their convictions, liberty in this sense means liberty *from*: absence of interference beyond the shifting, but always recognisable, frontier. 'The only freedom which deserves the name, is that of pursuing our own good in our own way', said the most celebrated of its champions.[8] If this is so, is compulsion ever justified? Mill had no doubt that it was. Since justice demands that all individuals be entitled to a minimum of freedom, all other individuals were of necessity to be restrained, if need be by force, from depriving anyone of it. Indeed, the whole function of law was the prevention of just such collisions: the State was reduced to what Lassalle contemptuously described as the functions of a night-watchman or traffic policeman.

What made the protection of individual liberty so sacred to Mill? In his famous essay he declares that unless the individual is left to live as he wishes in 'the part [of his conduct] which merely concerns himself',[9] civilisation cannot advance; the truth will not, for lack of a free market in ideas, come to light; there will be no scope for spontaneity, originality, genius, for mental energy, for moral courage. Society will be crushed by the weight of 'collective mediocrity'.[10] Whatever is rich and diversified will be crushed by the weight of custom, by men's constant tendency to conformity, which breeds only 'withered capacities', 'pinched and hidebound', 'cramped and warped' human beings. 'Pagan self-assertion' is as worthy as 'Christian self-denial'.[11] 'All errors which a man is likely to commit against advice and warning, are far outweighed by the evil of allowing others to constrain him to what they deem his good.'[12] The defence of liberty consists in the 'negative' goal of warding off interference. To threaten a man with persecution unless he submits to a life in which he exercises no choices of his goals; to block before him every door but one, no matter how noble the prospect upon which it opens, or how benevolent the motives of those who arrange this, is to sin against the truth that he is a man, a being with a life of his own to live. This is liberty as it has been conceived by liberals in the modern world from the days of Erasmus (some would say of Occam) to our own. Every plea for civil liberties and individual rights, every protest against exploitation and humiliation, against the encroachment of public authority, or the mass hypnosis of custom or organised propaganda, springs from this individualistic, and much disputed, conception of man.

Three facts about this position may be noted. In the first place Mill confuses two distinct notions. One is that all coercion is, in so far as it frustrates human desires, bad as such, although it may have to be applied to prevent other, greater evils; while non-interference, which is the opposite of coercion, is good as such, although it is not the only good. This is the 'negative' conception of liberty in its classical form. The other is that men should seek to discover the truth, or to develop a certain type of character of which Mill approved – critical, original, imaginative, independent, non-conforming to the point of eccentricity, and so on – and that truth can be found, and such character can be bred, only in conditions of freedom. Both these are liberal views, but they are not identical, and the connection between them is, at best, empirical. No one would argue that truth or freedom of self-expression could flourish where dogma crushes all thought. But the evidence of history tends to show (as, indeed, was argued by James Stephen in his formidable attack on Mill in his *Liberty, Equality, Fraternity*) that integrity, love of truth and fiery individualism grow at least as often in severely disciplined communities among, for example, the puritan Calvinists of Scotland or New England, or under military discipline, as in more tolerant or indifferent societies; and if this is so, Mill's argument for liberty as a necessary condition for the growth of human genius falls to the ground. If his two goals proved incompatible, Mill would be faced with a cruel dilemma, quite apart from the further difficulties created by the inconsistency of his doctrines with strict utilitarianism, even in his own humane version of it.[13]

In the second place, the doctrine is comparatively modern. There seems to be scarcely any discussion of individual liberty as a conscious political ideal (as opposed to its actual existence) in the ancient world. Condorcet has already remarked that the notion of individual rights was absent from the legal conceptions of the Romans and Greeks; this seems to hold equally of the Jewish, Chinese and all other ancient civilisations that have since come to light.[14] The domination of this ideal has been the exception rather than the rule, even in the recent history of the West. Nor has liberty in this sense often formed a rallying cry for the great masses of mankind. The desire not to be impinged upon, to be left to oneself, has been a mark of high civilisation on the part of both individuals and communities. The sense of privacy itself, of the area of personal relationships as something sacred in its own right, derives from a conception of freedom which, for all its religious roots, is scarcely older, in its developed state, than the Renaissance or the Reformation.[15] Yet its decline would mark the death of a civilisation, of an entire moral outlook.

The third characteristic of this notion of liberty is of greater importance. It is that liberty in this sense is not incompatible with some kinds of autocracy, or at any rate with the absence of self-government. Liberty in this sense is principally concerned with the area of control, not with its source. Just as a democracy may, in fact, deprive the individual citizen of a great many liberties which he might have in some other form of society, so it is perfectly conceivable that a liberal-minded despot would allow his subjects a large measure of personal freedom. The despot who leaves his subjects a wide area of liberty may be unjust, or encourage the wildest inequalities, care little for order, or virtue, or knowledge; but provided he does not curb their liberty, or at least curbs it less than many other regimes, he meets with Mill's specification.[16] Freedom in this sense is not, at any rate logically, connected with democracy or self-government. Self-government may, on the whole, provide a better guarantee of the preservation of civil liberties than other regimes, and has been defended as such by libertarians. But there is no necessary connection between individual liberty and democratic rule. The answer to the question 'Who governs me?' is logically distinct from the question 'How far does government interfere with me?' It is in this difference that the great contrast between the two concepts of negative and positive liberty, in the end, consists.[17] For the 'positive' sense of liberty comes to light if we try to answer the question, not 'What am I free to do or be?', but 'By whom am I ruled?' or 'Who is to say what I am, and what I am not, to be or do?' The connection between democracy and individual liberty is a good deal more tenuous than it seemed to many advocates of both. The desire to be governed by myself, or at any rate to participate in the process by which my life is to be controlled, may be as deep a wish as that of a free area for action, and perhaps historically older. But it is not a desire for the same thing. So different is it, indeed, as to have led in the end to the great clash of ideologies that dominates our world. For it is this, the 'positive' conception of liberty, not freedom from, but freedom to – to lead one prescribed form of life – which the adherents of the 'negative' notion represent as being, at times, no better than a specious disguise for brutal tyranny.

II

The notion of positive freedom

The 'positive' sense of the word 'liberty' derives from the wish on the part of the individual to be his own master. I wish my life and decisions to depend on myself, not on external forces of whatever kind. I wish to be the instrument of my own, not of other men's, acts of will. I wish to be a subject, not an object; to be moved by reasons, by conscious purposes, which are my own, not by causes which affect me, as it were, from outside. I wish to be somebody, not nobody; a doer – deciding, not being decided for, self-directed and not acted upon by external nature or by other men as if I were a thing, or an animal, or a slave incapable of playing a human role, that is, of conceiving goals and policies of my own and realising them. This is at least part of what I mean when I say that I am rational, and that it is my reason that distinguishes me as a human being from the rest of the world. I wish, above all, to be conscious of myself as a thinking, willing, active being, bearing responsibility for my choices and able to explain them by reference to my own ideas and purposes. I feel free to the degree that I believe this to be true, and enslaved to the degree that I am made to realise that it is not.

The freedom which consists in being one's own master, and the freedom which consists in not being prevented from choosing as I do by other men, may, on the face of it, seem concepts at no great logical distance from each other – no more than negative and positive ways of saying much the same thing. Yet the 'positive' and 'negative' notions of freedom historically developed in divergent directions not always by logically reputable steps, until, in the end, they came into direct conflict with each other.

One way of making this clear is in terms of the independent momentum which the, initially perhaps quite harmless, metaphor of self-mastery acquired. 'I am my own master'; 'I am slave to no man'; but may I not (as Platonists or Hegelians tend to say) be a slave to nature? Or to my own 'unbridled' passions? Are these not so many species of the identical genus 'slave' – some political or legal, others moral or spiritual? Have not men had the experience of liberating themselves from spiritual

187

slavery, or slavery to nature, and do they not in the course of it become aware, on the one hand, of a self which dominates, and, on the other, of something in them which is brought to heel? This dominant self is then variously identified with reason, with my 'higher nature', with the self which calculates and aims at what will satisfy it in the long run, with my 'real', or 'ideal', or 'autonomous' self, or with my self 'at its best'; which is then contrasted with irrational impulse, uncontrolled desires, my 'lower' nature, the pursuit of immediate pleasures, my 'empirical' or 'heteronomous' self, swept by every gust of desire and passion, needing to be rigidly disciplined if it is ever to rise to the full height of its 'real' nature. Presently the two selves may be represented as divided by an even larger gap: the real self may be conceived as something wider than the individual (as the term is normally understood), as a social 'whole' of which the individual is an element or aspect: a tribe, a race, a Church, a State, the great society of the living and the dead and the yet unborn. This entity is then identified as being the 'true' self which, by imposing its collective, or 'organic', single will upon its recalcitrant 'members', achieves its own, and, therefore, their, 'higher' freedom. The perils of using organic metaphors to justify the coercion of some men by others in order to raise them to a 'higher' level of freedom have often been pointed out. But what gives such plausibility as it has to this kind of language is that we recognise that it is possible, and at times justifiable, to coerce men in the name of some goal (let us say, justice or public health) which they would, if they were more enlightened, themselves pursue, but do not, because they are blind or ignorant or corrupt. This renders it easy for me to conceive of myself as coercing others for their own sake, in their, not my, interest. I am then claiming that I know what they truly need better than they know it themselves. What, at most, this entails is that they would not resist me if they were rational and as wise as I, and understood their interests as I do. But I may go on to claim a good deal more than this. I may declare that they are actually aiming at what in their benighted state they consciously resist, because there exists within them an occult entity – their latent rational will, or their 'true' purpose – and that this entity, although it is belied by all that they overtly feel and do and say, is their 'real' self, of which the poor empirical self in space and time may know nothing or little; and that this inner spirit is the only self that deserves to have its wishes taken into account.[18] Once I take this view, I am in a position to ignore the actual wishes of men or societies, to bully, oppress, torture them in the name, and on behalf, of their 'real' selves, in the secure knowledge that whatever is the true goal of man (happiness, performance of duty, wisdom, a just society, self-fulfilment) must be identical with his freedom – the free choice of his 'true', albeit submerged and inarticulate, self.

This paradox has been often exposed. It is one thing to say that I know what is good for X, while he himself does not; and even to ignore his wishes for its – and his – sake; and a very different one to say that he has *eo ipso* chosen it, not indeed consciously, not as he seems in everyday life, but in his role as a rational self which his empirical self may not know – the 'real' self which discerns the good, and cannot help choosing it once it is revealed. This monstrous impersonation, which consists in equating what X would choose if he were something he is not, or at least not yet, with what X actually seeks and chooses, is at the heart of all political theories of self-realisation. It is one thing to say that I may be coerced for my own good, which I am too blind to see: this may, on occasion, be for my benefit; indeed it may enlarge the scope of my liberty; it is another to say that if it is my good, then I am not being coerced, for I have willed it, whether I know this or not, and am free – or 'truly' free – even while my poor earthly body and foolish mind bitterly reject it, and struggle with the greatest desperation against those who seek, however benevolently, to impose it.

This magical transformation, or sleight of hand (for which William James so justly mocked the Hegelians), can no doubt be perpetrated just as easily with the 'negative' concept of freedom, where the self that should not be interfered with is no longer the individual with his actual wishes and needs as they are normally conceived, but the 'real' man within, identified with the pursuit of some ideal purpose not dreamed of by his empirical self. And, as in the case of the 'positively' free self, this entity may be inflated into some super-personal entity – a State, a class, a nation, or the march of history itself, regarded as a more 'real' subject of attributes than the empirical self. But the 'positive' conception of freedom as self-mastery, with its suggestion of a man divided against himself, has, in fact, and as a matter of history, of doctrine and of practice, lent itself more easily to this splitting of personality into two: the transcendent, dominant controller, and the empirical bundle of desires and passions to be disciplined and brought to heel. It is this historical fact that has been influential. This demonstrates (if demonstration of so obvious a truth is needed) that conceptions of freedom directly derive from views of what constitutes a self, a person, a man. Enough manipulation of the definition of man, and freedom can be made to mean whatever the manipulator wishes. Recent history has made it only too clear that the issue is not merely academic.

Notes

1 I do not, of course, mean to imply the truth of the converse.
2 Helvétius made this point very clearly: 'The free man is the man who is not in irons, nor imprisoned in a gaol, nor terrorised like a slave by the fear of punishment.' It is not lack of freedom not to fly like an eagle or swim like a whale. *De l'ésprit*, first discourse, chapter 4.

3   'The Marxist conception of social laws is, of course, the best-known version of this theory, but it forms a large element in some Christian and utilitarian, and all socialist, doctrines.

4   *Émile*, book 2: p. 320 in *Oeuvres complètes*, ed. Bernard Gagnebin and others (Paris, 1959–), vol. 4.

5   'A free man', said Hobbes, 'is he that . . . is not hindered to do what he has a will to.' *Leviathan*, chapter 21: p. 146 in Richard Tuck's edition (Cambridge, 1991). Law is always a fetter, even if it protects you from being bound in chains that are heavier than those of the law, say some more repressive law or custom, or arbitrary despotism or chaos. Bentham says much the same.

6   R. H. Tawney, *Equality* (1931), 3rd edn (London, 1938), chapter 5, section 2, 'Equality and liberty', p. 208 (not in previous editions).

7   Constant, *Principes de politique*, chapter 1: p. 275 in Benjamin Constant, *De la liberté chez les modernes: écrits politiques*, ed. Marcel Gauchet ([Paris], 1980).

8   J. S. Mill, *On Liberty*, chapter 1: p. 226 in *Collected Works of John Stuart Mill*, ed. J. M. Robson (Toronto/London, 1981–), vol. 18.

9   ibid., p. 224.

10   ibid., chapter 3, p. 268.

11   ibid., pp. 265–6.

12   ibid., chapter 4, p. 277.

13   This is but another illustration of the natural tendency of all but a very few thinkers to believe that all the things they hold good must be intimately connected, or at least compatible, with one another. The history of thought, like the history of nations, is strewn with examples of inconsistent, or at least disparate, elements artificially yoked together in a despotic system, or held together by the danger of some common enemy. In due course the danger passes, and conflicts between the allies arise, which often disrupt the system, sometimes to the great benefit of mankind.

14   See the valuable discussion of this in Michel Villey, *Leçons d'histoire de la philosophie du droit* (Paris, 1957), which traces the embryo of the notion of subjective rights to Occam.

15   'Christian (and Jewish or Muslim) belief in the absolute authority of divine or natural laws, or in the equality of all men in the sight of God, is very different from belief in freedom to live as one prefers.

16   Indeed, it is arguable that in the Prussia of Frederick the Great or in the Austria of Joseph II men of imagination, originality and creative genius, and, indeed, minorities of all kinds, were less persecuted and felt the pressure, both of institutions and custom, less heavy upon them than in many an earlier or later democracy.

17   'Negative liberty' is something the extent of which, in a given case, it is difficult to estimate. It might, prima facie, seem to depend simply on the power to choose between at any rate two alternatives. Nevertheless, not all choices are equally free, or free at all. If in a totalitarian State I betray my friend under threat of torture, perhaps even if I act from fear of losing my job, I can reasonably say that I did not act freely. Nevertheless, I did, of course, make a choice, and could, at any rate in theory, have chosen to be

killed or tortured or imprisoned. The mere existence of alternatives is not, therefore, enough to make my action free (although it may be voluntary) in the normal sense of the word. The extent of my freedom seems to depend on (a) how many possibilities are open to me (although the method of counting these can never be more than impressionistic; possibilities of action are not discrete entities like apples, which can be exhaustively enumerated); (b) how easy or difficult each of these possibilities is to actualise; (c) how important in my plan of life, given my character and circumstances, these possibilities are when compared with each other; (d) how far they are closed and opened by deliberate human acts; (e) what value not merely the agent, but the general sentiment of the society in which he lives, puts on the various possibilities. All these magnitudes must be 'integrated', and a conclusion, necessarily never precise, or indisputable, drawn from this process. It may well be that there are many incommensurable degrees of freedom, and that they cannot be drawn up on a single scale of magnitude. Moreover, in the case of societies, we are faced by such (logically absurd) questions as 'Would arrangement X increase the liberty of Mr. A more than it would that of Messrs, B, C, and D between them, added together?' The same difficulties arise in applying utilitarian criteria. Nevertheless, provided we do not demand precise measurement, we can give valid reasons for saying that the average subject of the King of Sweden is, on the whole, a good deal freer today [1958] than the average citizen of Spain or Albania. Total patterns of life must be compared directly as wholes, although the method by which we make the comparison, and the truth of the conclusions, are difficult or impossible to demonstrate. But the vagueness of the concepts, and the multiplicity of the criteria involved, are attributes of the subject-matter itself, not of our imperfect methods of measurement, or incapacity for precise thought.

18   'The ideal of true freedom is the maximum of power for all the members of human society alive to make the best of themselves', said T. H. Green in 1881. *Lecture on Liberal Legislation and Freedom of Contract*: p. 200 in T.H. Green, *Lectures on the Principles of Political Obligation and Other Writings*, ed. Paul Harris and John Morrow (Cambridge, 1986). Apart from the confusion of freedom with equality, this entails that if a man chose some immediate pleasure – which (in whose view?) would not enable him to make the best of himself (what self?) – what he was exercising was not 'true' freedom; and, if deprived of it, he would not lose anything that mattered. Green was a genuine liberal, but many a tyrant could use this formula to justify his worst acts of oppression.

22

Freedom to box
Nigel Warburton

Many groups try to curb freedom in various respects, some with justification, others not. In this article I criticize the attempt by the British Medical Association to criminalize the sport of boxing. The article examines the particular arguments used against boxing, setting them in the wider context of liberalism, paternalism and legal moralism.

From Nigel Warburton, 'Freedom to box', *Journal of Medical Ethics*, vol. 24

Introduction

The British Medical Association (BMA) has, in recent years, been a driving force in the campaign to outlaw all boxing, amateur and professional alike. Here I shall examine its arguments, as laid out in its most recent statement, *The Boxing Debate*, 1993,[1] and bring out their philosophical assumptions and implications. This will involve critical thinking about the structure of the arguments and a discussion of the wider issues of the limits of individual freedom in a civilised society.

The BMA's case

There are two sorts of brain damage that result from boxing: acute and chronic. Acute damage is severe and usually immediate: it may result in anything from concussion to debilitating brain dysfunction or even death. Chronic damage is more subtle and only becomes apparent over a number of years, often some time after a boxer has given up fighting. It is the long term cumulative effect of repeated blows to the head, and usually takes the form of *dementia pugilistica* also known as 'punch drunk syndrome'. Symptoms may range from mild loss of co-ordination to complete cognitive decline and parkinsonism. There have been suggestions too that a career in boxing can trigger Alzheimer's disease in later life.

192

Acute brain damage, particularly where it has resulted in death, paralysis or severe loss of cognitive faculties has been the focus of media attention, and the BMA has exploited a crop of recent boxing deaths to draw attention to its campaign. However, in *The Boxing Debate*, the authors declare that chronic damage is the issue of most concern to the BMA.[2] The empirical evidence about the risks of chronic and acute damage is controversial, not least because the structure of a career in professional boxing has changed significantly in recent years, and most of the longitudinal studies were based on a situation in which a boxer might fight many hundreds of competitive bouts with short recovery periods in between. Today's professionals may only fight two or three times a year. Nevertheless, unsurprisingly, there is a weight of medical evidence suggesting that a career in boxing, whether amateur or professional (but especially professional) carries with it *some* risk of brain damage.

Let us then accept, for the purposes of this analysis, that boxing is a dangerous sport in this respect. What, then, is the structure of the BMA's argument which leads from this relatively uncontroversial fact to the conclusion that boxing of all kinds should be criminalised? So far we have this:

Premise one: boxing is a very risky activity for participants.
Conclusion: therefore boxing should be banned.

As it stands, the conclusion is an obvious non sequitur. What we need is a further premise. The BMA has presented us with an enthymeme, an argument with a missing premise. The missing premise is implicit rather than explicitly stated. This is unfortunate as it leaves a certain latitude of interpretation about which general principle is being instantiated in this case. One plausible candidate is as follows:

Implicit premise: all very risky activities should be banned.

This implicit premise turns the above into a valid argument, though its premises need be shown to be true. One obvious area which needs clarification is that of the threshold of riskiness which justifies banning any activity. How dangerous does an activity have to be before we are justified in using the cudgel of the criminal law to suppress it? Again, unfortunately, the BMA's report is unforthcoming on this matter.

However, let us assume that the yardstick in such cases is the riskiness of boxing. This surely must be an acceptable assumption as far as the BMA is concerned. Yet if we make this move, the BMA is faced with the unattractive situation of having to condemn a number of other obvious 'companions in guilt'. Take the straightforward case of acute injuries which result in death. According to coroners' reports to the Office of Population

Censuses and Surveys for the years 1986–1992, there were only three deaths in England and Wales attributed to boxing. In the same period there were 77 deaths in motor sports; 69 in air sports; 54 in mountaineering; 40 in ball games; and 28 in horse riding.[3] The Isle of Man's TT motorcycle race has a death toll of 167 since its inception in 1907; the total number of deaths from motorcycle racing in Britain in that period must be considerably higher. Clearly then, consistency demands that the BMA take a similarly hard line on all these other sports, perhaps with a rigour proportional to the death rate in each one. If it isn't prepared to do this, then we certainly need an explanation as to why boxing deserves to be singled out for this treatment.

Chronic damage

As far as chronic damage is concerned, the paucity of reliable statistical information even for a single sport makes comparisons between sports extremely difficult. However, if we move away from sport to other health-affecting activities, then it is clear that from a social point of view heavy drinking and heavy smoking pose a far greater risk to long term wellbeing than does a career in boxing. Yet, whilst the BMA is concerned about the effects of heavy drinking and smoking, there is no indication that it is prepared to bite the bullet and call for the *criminalisation* of these practices. In that realm education seems to be its prime goal. Yet the BMA doesn't consider itself inconsistent in this area. It has addressed the issue of the companions-in-guilt move. It holds to the line that boxing stands apart from other activities as being *particularly* dangerous, and as having as an intrinsic element of the sport the aim of injuring your opponent. The three main responses the BMA gives to the companions-in-guilt move are as follows.

1. *The move is usually made in terms of acute injuries or deaths rather than chronic injuries*. The BMA apparently concedes that as far as risk of acute injuries is concerned boxing may not be the most dangerous sport; however, it is the high risk of chronic brain damage that most worries the BMA.

This response is not adequate to rebuff the companions-in-guilt move. The move can just as easily be made in terms of chronic injuries by pointing to the dangers of heavy drinking and heavy smoking and the extremely high risks of chronic damage to users' health that is associated with them. Yet, as we have seen, there is no question of the BMA biting the bullet and calling for a legal ban on these activities. The BMA could, perhaps, strengthen its case by focussing on the fact that the sort of chronic damage which boxers risk is brain damage, which puts an individual's whole personality at risk. However, precisely the same point could be made about the chronic damage caused by heavy drinking.

2. *Relatively few people participate in boxing.* This supposedly skews the statistics, making boxing seem safer than it really is.

An obvious response to this point is that if relatively few people are injured or killed as a result of boxing then from a pragmatic angle the BMA would do well to focus its energies elsewhere, in areas where there is an opportunity to save many lives rather than just a few.

3. *The level of exposure to risk per second is high in boxing.* On this point the BMA's argument is worth quoting in full:

> A professional boxer may only compete in a few fights a year with each fight lasting on average less than half an hour. Compare this to the exposure of rugby players to injury, with each player taking part in a far greater number of matches, each lasting for an hour and twenty minutes. If the number of deaths and injuries are viewed in relation to the numbers taking part and to the level of exposure it can be seen that the boxer faces a far greater chance of death or debilitating injury each time they enter the ring than does the rugby player (or any other sports person for that matter) when they step onto the pitch.[4]

This smacks of sophistry. The BMA seems here to have retreated to the position that because boxing is more dangerous per second than other sports then it must be classified as the most dangerous sport. But this is not comparing like with like: we need to look at the relative dangers for a typical participant rather than the absolute risk per second. We should consider such things as the level of exposure within a calendar year for a typical boxer (which is quite different from considering the risk level per second of competitive activity).

None of the BMA's three responses to the companions-in-guilt move is, then, adequate. The charge of inconsistency still holds. However, it has one further argument, the intent argument.

The intent argument

Conceding that the rate of acute injuries incurred in boxing is relatively low, the authors of *The Boxing Debate* comment:

> It should be noted that all the injuries sustained were intentional and a legitimate part of boxing, unlike similar injuries occurring in sporting activities which are primarily accidental.[5]

In other words, there is something special about the way in which the injuries were brought about in boxing, something which supposedly singles

195

out boxing from all other sports. Boxers intend to injure their opponents because they know that that is the best way of being sure of winning a fight. The possibility of a win by knockout implies, according to the BMA, that 'extra points are given for brain damage'.[6] However, even if we accept this description of boxing and the intentions of participants, this does not explain why it should matter that the damage was caused intentionally. If a rugby player tackles another to stop him or her scoring a try, knowing that there is a significant risk of injuring his or her opponent, it is not instantly clear how this is different from a boxer deliberately punching an opponent hard because this is the best way of winning a fight. In the first, the risk of injury is foreseeable, but not the point of the sport; in the second, the risk of injury is foreseeable, and causing injury is one way of winning a bout. However, if a typical career in rugby tends to put you at greater risk of serious injury than a typical career in boxing, then that is, from a medical point of view, the most important factor. It is, surely, the consequences of the sport which matter, not how the injuries happen to have been caused. Besides, although the rules of rugby don't force you to hurt your opponent any more than do the rules of boxing, it is clear that it is possible to injure your opponent in rugby by acting within the rules and this can certainly be to your team's advantage. The England Rugby Union winger Jon Sleightholme interviewed before a recent match against the New Zealand Barbarians made the following comments about what it would take to beat their opponents:

> It's all about tackling. To beat any New Zealand team, you have to put them down from first minute to last. And I'm not talking about any old tackle, either; it has to be aggressive, offensive tackling, the sort that hurts people.[7]

There is one possible interpretation of the intent argument that would make sense from a view which concentrates on the consequences of actions rather than just their motivation. This is the suggestion that because boxers intend to injure each other they are more likely to succeed in doing so. Mike Tyson, for example, has commented

> I try to catch my opponent on the tip of the nose because I try to punch the bone into his brain.[3]

Yet the fact remains that, despite these terrifyingly violent intentions, boxing does not put its participants at greater risk than many other socially acceptable activities. This version of the intent argument, then, does nothing to explain why boxing should be given such singular treatment. However, the BMA doesn't appear to be suggesting that violent intent makes boxing more dangerous than it would otherwise be; rather it is the existence of the violent intent itself which damns the sport. This is straight-forwardly a moral argument, one that stands or falls independently of medical evidence. The sentiment implicit in the comments in the BMA report quoted above is brought out more explicitly in an editorial in the *Journal of the American Medical Association*:

> It is morally wrong for one human being to attempt intentionally to harm the brain of another. The major purpose of a sport event is to win. When the surest way to win is by damaging the opponent's brain, and this becomes standard procedure, the sport is morally wrong. Many say that it is often the intent of American football players to harm their opponents, thereby removing them from the game, especially defensive linemen and linebackers going after the quarterback. This may be true, but such harm is not the intent of the game.[9]

Most boxers would dispute the claim that they intentionally harm the brains of their opponents: what they intend to do is win, not cause brain damage. And often they intend to win on points. But even if we concede that causing brain damage is the surest way to win, and that this is immoral, it does not follow logically that the sport should be made illegal. There are numerous activities which are on the whole considered immoral which are not the appropriate concern of the law. Further argument is still needed to make the move from establishing that a practice is immoral to concluding that therefore it should be criminalised.

Before following up this last point, I want to review my conclusions so far. First, the BMA's medical arguments seem vulnerable to various forms of the companions-in-guilt move. Secondly, the intent argument is an argument about the moral status of boxing, and even if it is established that boxing is intrinsically immoral, it doesn't follow that it should necessarily be banned. Further justification is needed.

Changing the criminal law

Three basic approaches to the justification of criminalisation stand out: liberalism, paternalism and legal moralism.[10]

Liberalism

At the heart of liberalism is some version of the Harm Principle. This is the view that changes to criminal law can only be justified in cases in which a significant risk of harm to others occurs. Coercion of adults is never acceptable when it is done purely for the good of the individuals concerned rather than to avert the risk of harm to others. The law should not be used to force people to become good or happy or healthy. If we think people are harming themselves we can remonstrate with them, attempt to educate them, entreat them or persuade them; but we shouldn't use the law against them. This sort of principle was famously endorsed by John Stuart Mill in *On Liberty*, and is the mainstay of liberal arguments about changes to the criminal law.

Roman law

Some university teachers explain the Harm Principle by standing in front of the class swinging their fists and saying 'My freedom to swing my fist ends where your nose begins'. Yet this is slightly misleading for the present case, since there is a further aspect of the Harm Principle which this neglects, namely that if someone consents to be hit, then, provided that the consent is informed consent and freely given, that person is not considered to have been harmed in the appropriate sense when the fist connects. This notion was instantiated in Roman law in the principle known as *volenti non fit injuria* (to one who has consented no harm is done). It is not instantiated in British law, as was made apparent in the 1991 'Spanner' case in which 15 consenting sadomasochists were charged with assault, despite the fact that they had all consented to their injuries, and that the injuries were less serious than many incurred on a rugby field (though incurred on different parts of their anatomy).[11] Boxers consent to be hit hard within the rules of the sport, and with the safeguard of a referee instructed to intervene to prevent, wherever possible, serious injury to either participant. So boxers should be free from legal interference with their activities.

It is important that consent is both freely given and informed. It could plausibly be argued that some boxers are more or less forced into the sport by family or peer group pressure, or perhaps through poverty. In some cases the pressure to become a professional boxer may be so intense that it would be fair to say that the individual had not freely chosen to put him- or herself at such risk. Where this is the case, the liberal would argue that a harm had been done to the boxer. In some cases boxers are ignorant of the levels of risk involved in their sport: in such cases consent, no matter how freely given, is not informed. It would be relatively straightforward for the BMA to produce some kind of exam which any would-be boxer had to pass before he or she could be said to have given informed consent to participate in the sport. This exam could test a boxer's knowledge of recent medical research on the effect of repeated blows to the head.

There is one area relating to consent in which the BMA's activities would be supported by liberals, namely with regard to young people boxing. Liberals typically only allow that adequately informed adults can consent to participate in extremely harmful activities. Serious brain damage so clearly undermines the possibility of a full and happy life, that young people should not be allowed to consent to any activity that has a high risk of this sort of injury. So paternalism would be justified towards young people, even though we respect adults' autonomy by allowing them to participate in activities which carry great risks. Even if adults choose badly for themselves, this is better than removing choice altogether. With children, though, it is different: we are justified in preventing them voluntarily putting themselves in great danger, since they aren't in a position to give genuine consent to actions with such far-reaching consequences. The only problem with this position is that, if we are to prevent young boxers from hitting each other, consistency seems to demand that we should also prevent them engaging in a variety of other activities which are as dangerous in the long term as boxing. We should, then, prevent them from smoking, from drinking heavily, and from playing rugby, not just be discouraging them, but by force where necessary.[12] Again, if the BMA wants to single out boxing for special treatment, it needs to indicate why: the only argument offered in *The Boxing Debate* which is immune from the companions-in-guilt move is the intent argument. And, as we have seen, that is a moral argument which needs independent justification and is not the particular province of an association of doctors. Nor does it alone logically entail that the law should be changed.

Paternalism

Paternalists argue that the criminal law should sometimes be used to protect individuals against themselves and from making bad choices for themselves. Coercion is sometimes justified in order to protect an individual from what would otherwise harm him or her. The coercion is for the individual's sake, not because harm will otherwise be done to society or to non-consenting bystanders. It is clear from this that the BMA's arguments are, for the most part, paternalistic. Boxers put themselves at risk of acute brain damage, and, just as worryingly, of *dementia pugilistica*. Both types of brain damage are harmful to the person concerned so the criminal law should be brought in to prevent individuals putting themselves at such levels of risk. Yet, as we have seen, the BMA's paternalism falls foul of the companions-in-guilt move: to be consistent in their paternalism, the BMA would have to admit that smoking, rugby union, most motor sports, mountaineering, heavy drinking, and a whole range of popular activities should also be banned.

Legal moralism

Legal moralism describes the belief that some activities are simply immoral, whether or not they cause harm to anyone, and that the law should

199

sometimes be used to curb such activities. When the BMA resorts to the intent argument, it seems to rely on an implicit appeal to a form of legal moralism. Boxing involves violent intent; having violent intent is immoral; therefore boxing should be banned. That is the most plausible interpretation of the passing comments in *The Boxing Debate* on this topic. As we have seen, however, this is based on a simplistic assessment of boxers' intentions. However, even if the BMA could show that boxing involved an immoral intent of some kind, it would be extremely difficult to move from this to a justification of a legal ban for this reason alone. As it is, the BMA's comments about the intent argument are so sketchy that they certainly could not provide a justification for a ban; nor do they amount to a plausible defence of the claim that boxing is distinctively and importantly different from most other dangerous sports.

Conclusion

The position advocated by the BMA in *The Boxing Debate* is a form of inconsistent paternalism propped up with legal moralism. The arguments are too weak to justify any change to the criminal law covering the activities of consenting adults. At best they might justify a campaign to educate young people about the relative dangers of boxing and the serious consequences of chronic damage to the brain, however it is caused. There is, too, an important consideration which the BMA failed to investigate. Any change in the criminal law should surely produce a state of affairs preferable to the one before the law was changed. Yet most people associated with boxing are convinced that the effect of criminalising boxing would be to force it underground where the medical controls would be negligible or non-existent, and there would be a much higher risk of boxers sustaining debilitating injuries. If the BMA is principally concerned to minimise harmful injuries, then it must at least address the possibility that the proposed ban on the sport, if implemented, could make matters considerably worse than they now are.

References and notes

1   British Medical Association, *The Boxing Debate* (London: British Medical Association, June 1993).
2   Ibid.
3   Cited in House of Lords debate about boxing. See *Hansard* 563 (5 April 1995), p. 308.
4   BMA, *Boxing Debate*, p. 67.
5   Ibid., p. 56.

6   Ibid., p. 10.
7   Hewett C. Lomu's absence may not be a blessing. *The Independent* 30 November 1996, p. 28.
8   J. C. Oates *On Boxing*, Hopewell, N J: Ecco Press, 1994, p.12.
9   [Editorial: Boxing should be banned in civilised countries – round 3. *Journal of the American Medical Association* 255 (1986), pp. 2483–4.
10   In using this tripartite distinction I am following the author of Consent and the criminal law: philosophical foundations. Appendix C of *Consent in the Criminal Law,* Law Commission Consultation Paper 139 (London: HMSO Publications, 1995) pp. 245–82.
11   For an interesting discussion of this case and the social, legal and moral issues raised by it see B. Thompson *Sadomasochism* (London: Cassell, 1994).
12   There are, of course, legal limits on the purchase of tobacco and alcohol by young people, but at present the law permits the consumption of these substances in private.

23

Discrimination and sexual justice
Janet Radcliffe Richards

In this extract from her book *The Sceptical Feminist* (1980, 2nd edn 1994), Janet Radcliffe Richards examines a range of arguments about sexual discrimination. She shows that discrimination against women where sex is not relevant is always unfair. She goes on to examine arguments for and against reverse or positive discrimination – the kind of discrimination that is designed to redress previous unfairness.

From Janet Radcliffe Richards, *The Sceptical Feminist*

Selection discrimination

The question to be settled is this. Can we prove quite generally that it is always unfair to choose a man rather than a woman for something they would both like to do, when the woman could do it better than the man?

It is very important to get this question properly focused. We are considering at the moment only the rejection of women who are *actually* more suitable for the position in question than the competing men. If woman are rejected because of poor education that may show discrimination against them at an earlier point, but not at this one. If they are unsuitable because they will work badly with a prejudiced work force, or because someone is wanted who will not be away to have children, that may show unfairness in the structure of society, but does not involve the rejection of *actually suitable women* at this point. The selectors cannot be accused of selection discrimination as long as they choose the best candidate for the purpose in question. *Discrimination on grounds of sex is counting sex as relevant in contexts where it is not*, and leads to the rejection of *suitable* women. It is not discrimination on grounds of sex to reject women who are not suitable, even if their unsuitability is *caused* by their being women. When that happens it is their unsuitability, and not their sex, which has caused their rejection. The question at issue now is specifically whether discrimination against women who really are suitable for a position could ever be defended according to the principles of social justice which have been outlined here.

There is, of course, one perfectly obvious selection rule, applicable in any situation where people are competing for something they want. It is 'choose the candidate most suited to the position'. The question we are dealing with, therefore, is that of what possible reason there could be for adding to this eminently sensible rule, either openly or surreptitiously, the proviso 'but no women', or 'but make it harder for women'. There are various justifications around.

One which can be dismissed straight away is the suggestion which appears from time to time that the whole situation stems from kindness on the part of men, who want to protect women from all the hard things of life. It has already been argued that paternalism is not to be tolerated. Even if men did really think they were doing what was good for women in spite of themselves (which puts rather a strain on one's credulity) it would still not be justified. And while many women may still be perfectly willing to be grateful for any male chivalry which offers to take from them any chore they find burdensome, they can hardly be expected to respond with the same appreciation when men use their stranglehold on the running of everything to prevent women's doing the things they *want* to do. Feminists will believe men's good intentions when they make offers, not rules which they assure everyone are purely in women's interest.

However, although the kindness-to-women argument does appear, it is not the usual justification for discriminatory practices. By far the commonest argument takes the line that women are to be excluded because they are not equal to the task in question. They cannot be dockers or bus drivers because they are not strong enough,[1] they cannot go into the professions or business because they are not clever enough, or can't concentrate, or are prone to hysteria, or will leave to have children or follow their husbands. The usual feminist response to this line is an indignant denial of the whole thing: either the accusations are false, or if women are in some ways inferior to men it is because men have deprived women of proper education. There is of course much truth in this. However, this is one clear case in which feminists would do better to forget about factual arguments for a while and concentrate on the logic. This reasoning is absolutely absurd for two reasons (both, incidentally, clearly pointed out by Mill[2]).

In the first place, nearly all the differences claimed to exist between men and women are differences of *average*. No one with the slightest claim to sense could argue that *all* men were stronger or more intellectual or more forceful than *all* women. But the fact (when it is one) that the average woman cannot do something or other which the average man can do provides not a shred of justification for a rule or practice which also excludes all the exceptional ones who can do it, or demands that the women should perform better than the men to be admitted. You might as well try to argue that if black men were stronger on average than white ones, white men should not be allowed to lift heavy loads, or if Yorkshire people were cleverer than Lancashire ones, no one from Lancashire should be allowed to go to university. Average differences between men and women would account for different success rates in various activities, but they could not possibly account for selection policies which differentiated between them.

Second, even if there were cases where it looked as though all women actually might be worse at something than all men, that *still* would not account for a rule specifically excluding them or saying they should do better than men to be admitted, because, as Mill said, 'What women by nature cannot do, it is quite superfluous to forbid them from doing. What they can do, but not so well as the men who are their competitors, competition suffices to exclude them from . . .'[3] If men really think, for instance, that a certain level of strength is needed for driving buses, why not just say what that level is and test all applicants for strength? If they really think that all women will fail, why *add* 'but no women'? If the presumption were true no women would get in anyway. It is ridiculous to say that a rule specifically excluding women is needed *because* the work calls for a certain level of strength which women are presumed never to reach. If this is an example of the wonders of male logic, perhaps it is hardly surprising if women feel that they cannot aspire to it.

Some people try to escape this conclusion by saying that if women are inferior to men on average in certain respects it is a waste of time to look at women applicants, because there is so little likelihood of their succeeding. Certainly if such average differences did exist it would account for advising people who were making selections not to spend too much time interviewing women: it is not possible to interview everyone, and some principles of simplification have to be followed. But still, that would not in the least account for general rules excluding all women, which would apply even to the ones who happened to be so strikingly good at their work that they could not be overlooked, and the ones who produced good evidence that they did not suffer from the usual defects of their sex. Maxims for the guidance of selectors, giving some indication of where to look for what is wanted, are quite different from the lists of characteristics needed for the job. If most women are unsuitable for something, it is understandable that a selector should miss by accident some of the ones who are suitable. It is quite different, and not acceptable, to refuse to consider any women, even the ones whose excellence cannot be missed.

In fact there is no escape from the obvious conclusion, which is this. If a general rule is made saying what characteristics are needed for a certain position, and to the list of these characteristics is added the proviso 'but exclude women' or 'make it harder for women', it is *not* added because it is thought that all or most women do not reach the required standards. You do not make additional rules to prevent what would not happen anyway under the existing ones. *The only conceivable reason for a rule or practice excluding women is its perpetrators' thinking that without such a rule women would have to be let in:* that on grounds of strict suitability, women, or more women, would have to be admitted. And since the rule against women cannot be justified by saying that women are not generally suitable, it must follow that they are being kept out on other grounds, unspecified.

Since they are unspecified, and since it appears to be necessary to hide them under specious arguments about women's unsuitability, it must be presumed that the real reasons are not of a sort people want exposed to the light of day. It is not, however, difficult to work out what they must be. What, for instance, must be happening if an employer passes over a competent woman in favour of a less competent man? It means that the job will be less well done, and therefore (to put it schematically) that he will be losing money by appointing the man. Why should he do that? He is actually willing to *pay* for something or other, and it is hard to see what it could possibly be other than the simple cause of male supremacy. In other words, individual women are apparently *suffering in the cause of male supremacy*, and individual men are gaining in the same cause. What could possibly be more unfair than that?

However, perhaps it will be said that that conclusion has been reached far too quickly. To give the opposition a fuller opportunity, therefore, let us consider a much more ingenious defence of selection discrimination.

We can start with the fact that when we select someone for any purpose we are rarely looking for a single characteristic, because the position to be filled is always in some way complex. For instance, in looking for a doctor most of us do not want someone who just happens to be skilled in medical science. We also want someone who is kind and considerate and good at explaining things, and who treats patients with respect. Most of us would not be at all sorry if medical schools took such things more into consideration when planning their intake. We certainly do not think that they would be discriminating against nasty, inept or uncommunicative people in making this requirement, even though of course it would make life more difficult for nasty people who wanted to study medicine. All we should be doing would be making a fair selection for our requirements.

Now a sufficiently ingenious plotter against the well-being of women might argue in a similar way, as follows. He could say that when he kept women out of various positions, or allowed in only a few women, this was not because he had anything against women or wanted to advance the position of men; it was just that he, too, had a complex purpose. He thought it important for the good of all that there should be a lot of children, brought up at home by their mothers (just as it would be good for society as a whole to have kind and communicative doctors). When he made his selection for doctors, lawyers, miners or anything else, therefore, he had this complex purpose in mind. He did not choose women for the work, even though they could undoubtedly do it, because in that way they would be encouraged to leave home, and the results would be detrimental to the whole of society.

Forget for the moment that we may consider it bad to want to have more children, or unnecessary that children should be brought up at home. If we can show that the argument does not work even while accepting the opposition's dubious premises the victory will be twice itself. For now let us accept the legitimacy of the aim, and see whether the accusation that women are unfairly treated in being excluded from various activities can be escaped by these means.

To find this out, consider what method would be adopted by someone who wanted to increase the population, but was also motivated by the principle that everyone's well-being was to be maximized; that all people were to be given as much of what they wanted as possible. We are assuming that a higher population is for the benefit of everyone, but still the required children have to be produced by individual women, and women differ considerably in their interest in children. Some want them very much, and others not at all. A benevolent social planner would obviously like the children to be provided as far as possible by women who actually wanted to care for children, because in that way society would be getting what it wanted by means of individuals' getting more of what *they* wanted; obviously an ideal arrangement.

The first thing to do, therefore, is concentrate on the women who want children more than anything else, and make sure by means of marriage bureaux (if we are keeping marriage), fertility clinics, family allowances and domestic help that every woman who wants children can have as many as she likes. If after that there are still not enough children, we go on to women who like the idea of having children but are not willing to sacrifice other things like careers for them, and we find that by means of flexible working arrangements, part-time work, special arrangements to preserve increments and status during periods of absence, and so on, we can make it possible for these women to have both of the things they want (children and career). We make them happier than they would have been with only one, and at the same time produce the children which are wanted for the good of everyone. If even this does not produce enough children we move on to the women who have no special interest in children but who could easily be persuaded to have them, and make having children a thing which brings with it positive rewards, such as a higher income or social prestige. And once more we make everyone happy: the state gets the children it wants through giving individual women what they want. This is the method which must always be adopted by the ideal social planner. Maximizing the good means as far as possible producing the public good *through* what is good for individuals.

That is the socially just way of going about things, but it could hardly present a greater contrast with the method described before, where the supposed social good is achieved by closing other opportunities to women. It is true that in both situations society gets the children it wants, but there the similarities end. Social effort in this case is put not into allowing women who positively want children to have as many of them as possible, but into systematically closing other options until child-rearing becomes the most attractive one left, even for women who do not like the idea at all. And it is important to point out that *society as a whole loses by this method: the coercion of women into child care is carried out at cost to society as well as to individual women.* In the first place, if women are excluded from work other than child rearing, that work is less well done; women would not be specifically excluded unless it were thought that without that exclusion they would have to be admitted, as was argued before. There is what might be called a lower social product: less is produced for the good of all. Second, one may presume that women forced into child rearing will do it far less happily, and less well, than women who do it willingly, so both mothers and children will suffer. That is another social loss. And finally, the greatest loss of all comes with the women who despite all the restrictions still decide to work outside the home because of poverty, or because they will not choose home and family at any price. Because all the attractive things have been closed to force women into their homes there is now nothing left for them but boring and underpaid work, which they take on to their own extreme dissatisfaction and the benefit of absolutely nobody. They work, but are excluded from work which would have allowed them to contribute fully to society. Both individuals *and* society suffer. That is a total loss.

The situation is therefore this. If society wants more children there are two possible sets of procedures it can adopt. One encourages women to have children by removing obstacles and offering rewards; the other attempts to coerce them into having children by taking away all acceptable options. In the coercing situation there is a smaller social product than in the persuading one (that is, there is a lower total of well-being in the society), because some of the most competent people are excluded from what they would otherwise have done well for the benefit of all. And in addition to that, they themselves are made unhappy in the process.

Why then should anyone want such a situation? Why should men (who presumably must have made the original arrangements) settle for a lower total level of satisfaction than might be achieved? Whether they are aware of the answer or not, it is clear what it must be. The men must at some level of consciousness think that they themselves get more as a result of the coercion arrangement than they would by the other one. But if men get more when the total well-being is small than they would if the total were larger, women lose on two counts: *they get an unfairly small share of an unfairly small whole.* That is grossly unfair. Men are being kept in their position of advantage by the extreme general disadvantage of women, and individual women themselves lose additionally in the process. Women therefore do not do better, or anything like as well, as they would in a situation where they were in fair competition with men.

It should be noted, incidentally, that this conclusion cannot be escaped by arguing that the cost of producing children by the supposedly just method would be too high, and that society would suffer as a result of that. If the cost of inducing women to stay at home and have children is too high for society to bear, it means that women are demanding high rewards for doing the work, and that in turn implies that they cannot want to do it very much. If women do not want to have children without high rewards, and society as a whole is not willing to pay the necessary price, on what grounds can it be said that large numbers of children are for the benefit of everyone, or that society in general wants them? It looks as though the only way to come to this conclusion is by not counting women as part of society as a whole.

The conclusion of all this is that in a just society the way to make individuals produce what is for the general good is not to exclude some people from parts of the competition in order to force them to do something else. That way other work is less well done, and individuals are made unhappy in the process. The way to proceed is to make the work to be done attractive to the people we want to do it, that way getting the work done well and increasing the satisfaction of individuals in the process.

The conclusion is a pleasingly neat one from the point of view of selection discrimination. It is that it is never fair to eliminate a group from an area of activity (or to make admission harder for them than for other groups) on grounds which are unconnected with the purpose for which the selection is being made. *It is always unfair to practise selection discrimination against women* or against any other group.[4]

The really important part of this conclusion is that it still stands *whether or not the underlying structures, within which the selection is being made, are themselves just.* This is most important, because as has already been said it would be humanly impossible to recognize a state of justice once it had been reached: we should always go on trying to get something better. We may not know when we have the best possible organization from the point of view of social justice, but as long as we are *aiming* to produce what is of the greatest benefit to everyone, we must be wrong in eliminating any group from the competition, since that will not only lower the well-being of the members of that group; but also lessen what is produced for the satisfaction of others.

It is interesting to note, incidentally, that this conclusion is much like the second part of Rawls's difference principle, which states that there is to be fair competition for the most desirable positions in society.[5] It shows that the second part of the principle is deducible from the first, and not a separate thing.

The problem of reverse discrimination

We have, then, established that discrimination against women, treating their sex as a reason for putting them at a disadvantage in competitions where sex is not relevant, is always substantially unfair.

Clear and neat as that conclusion is, however, and useful in allowing us to pin down demonstrable injustice and charge individual culprits instead of having to rail in general about the unfair structures of society (for which it is hard to blame anyone in particular), it does raise problems for feminists in the context of the issue of reverse discrimination. The usual form recommended for reverse discrimination is that women of a lower calibre than men should be chosen for certain work in preference to them. It is a thing which many feminists think ought to happen, but the last section seemed to show that this would be absolutely unfair; that reverse discrimination would be open to exactly the same conclusive objections as ordinary discrimination.

More specifically, the argument seems to show that several explicit provisions of the Sex Discrimination Act must be unfair. For instance, the Act states that when appointments are made to various positions there are certain things which are not to be allowed to count against women applicants, the most striking of which, perhaps, is that they are not to be rejected on the grounds that they will meet a prejudiced public and work force. There is no doubt that when people are prejudiced against women a man would often do the required work better; if the public have no confidence in a female door-to-door seller of insurance or encyclopaedias a man will sell more. To insist that this sort of thing should not be allowed to count against women is actually to say that women should be appointed even when they are less good than men. In other words, it provides for a certain amount of positive discrimination.

It will not do to say in a vague way that sometimes it must be all right to discriminate in favour of women. The argument of the last section showed that *whenever* consideration of sex entered into selections for whose purpose sex was not relevant that was unfair, and the whole point is to try to achieve fairness. We cannot simply assert that unfairness sometimes has to be tolerated. Of course it has already been argued that sometimes *formal* unfairness has to be tolerated in the interests of substantial fairness, but since the necessity of selecting the best candidate is *part of the account of what it is to be substantially fair* there is nothing higher which can override it. You cannot say that some substantial unfairness must be tolerated in the interests of greater substantial fairness, in the way that some bad must be tolerated to achieve a great deal of good, because fairness is not a thing to be shared out; it is a principle according to which other things are shared out. Anyone who is treated with substantial unfairness gets the wrong amount of good and bad.

If positive discrimination is to be justified, something much stronger is needed. Some of the usual defences of it which appear should be assessed.

Probably the commonest defence is the argument that since women have been badly treated in the past, what they should now be given is *compensation* for what they have missed. Compensation is a method of making up for past deprivations. It is not (to avoid confusion later on) a way of putting things right for the future, or improving matters generally; it is a means to give women the level of satisfaction they ought to have had anyway, by giving them enough now to fill the gap left by their previous deprivation. It is the sort of thing which would happen if an employer were to make up for employees' having been underpaid in the past by giving them all their back pay, with an allowance for interest and inflation, and perhaps damages.

If women have indeed been treated unfairly in the past, it does seem proper that they should be given compensation now. If men have had more than their fair share, they should give some of their ill-gotten gains to women, since they got them at women's expense in the first place. However, the question now is not of whether women should be compensated, but of whether the way to go about that is by means of positive discrimination. And there seems little doubt that it is not a proper means of compensation, for several reasons.

In the first place, you cannot actually compensate women in general for their past suffering by changing the rules now and allowing some women to achieve advantages for which they are not really qualified. Even if that would do as a compensation for the women chosen, it would be no compensation whatever for the others. It might perhaps improve things for the future, but that is not compensation. It would do nothing for the women who had been passed over earlier, and their unhappiness might even be increased by seeing other women being given advantages far beyond anything they had ever had. Reverse discrimination fails as a means of compensating women for their sufferings, both because you cannot compensate a group by giving benefits to some of its members (people need compensating individually or collectively, not by some method of representation), and anyway, the women who are individually compensated by discrimination are usually already the most privileged among women. Reverse discrimination is no compensation for women in general.

Perhaps then the idea is to compensate some individuals, rather than the whole group, for their past injustice. That looks more promising. However it still does not work as a justification of a general policy of reverse discrimination in favour of women. If the concern is really with underprivilege and its redress, why should it matter whether the person being helped is a woman rather than a man? Why should one discriminate generally in favour of women, when it might involve benefiting an already well off woman at the expense of a badly off man? If compensation is all that is at issue, why not have the rule that the worst off (of either sex) are to be compensated? To say that women's grievances should be redressed in preference to men's is to be unfair to men: it gives women the privilege of having their lack of privilege take precedence over men's lack of privilege, and when this is looked at from the point of view of deprived individuals there seems to be nothing to be said for it at all. Many men are less privileged than many women. The fact that women are on average less well off than men might justify someone's deciding to take particular care when assessing women candidates for anything, because there was a higher probability that they would need compensating than men would, but it would not justify a general rule.

Suppose, then, we argued that reverse discrimination should not be specifically in favour of women, but in favour of any underprivileged person. (That would still in practice tend to favour women, but would escape the charge that the practice was systematically unfair to men.) Even then it would not be justified.

This can be illustrated rather schematically. Suppose a benevolent man who runs a business is sympathetic to the problems of women, and is willing to do without some of his profit to benefit them. He has two positions to fill, one responsible and interesting, and one rather dull. In competition for them are a well qualified man and a less qualified woman. He has two options: to give the better job to the woman or to give it to the man. Suppose first he gives it to the woman. She then has a high degree of satisfaction (we are to suppose that she is not so hopelessly incompetent as to be unhappy, only less good than the man would have been). Her inefficiency loses money for the firm, but the employer does not mind that because he is willing to make sacrifices to benefit women. The man, on the other hand, has a low degree of satisfaction in the lesser job. Suppose, however, that the employer takes the other option, and appoints the man to the better job. The man then has a high degree of satisfaction, and the firm makes the usual profit. The employer is willing to forgo this in the interests of the woman, as before, and so gives her a high salary for her work in the lesser job. She therefore has also a high degree of satisfaction, though of course of a different sort. There seems, therefore, to be no doubt about which arrangement the employer should make. He should not make an arrangement which would benefit the woman only, if he could make one which would benefit the man as well.

Of course that example is very artificial, and no doubt objections could be brought against it in its present form, but it does illustrate a general point. To have a general policy of appointing women to positions for which they are not well qualified is not the best way to compensate them for past injustice. We should do much better to allow the best qualified people to do the work, because if work is worth doing it is in the interests of all that it should be done well. If we make such arrangements it will mean that we have a greater social product with which to compensate women, and others, for their past injustices, and that is what we should do. Compensation should come not in the form of unmerited advancement, but in the form of other primary social goods (to use Rawls's term[6]).

The general conclusion of all these arguments is that although no doubt some compensation is due to women for their unjust treatment, the idea of compensation does not justify reverse discrimination in their favour.

Still, the defenders of reverse discrimination have no reason to retreat yet. All this talk of compensation, they can argue, is beside the point. If we are going to be fussy about the precise meaning of 'compensation', then let us concede that compensation is not what justifies reverse discrimination. What we want to achieve is not compensation but *an improvement of the position of women until society is fair to them*, and as a matter of fact probably the best way to achieve this is to appoint to positions of importance women who are rather less good at the work than the men who are in competition with them. As long as they are not such hopeless failures as to confirm everyone's ideas that women are not capable of any serious work, their holding those positions will be enough to make other women set their sights higher, and make people in general more used to seeing women in former male preserves and expecting more of them. High expectations make an important contribution to high performance. That is quite a different point from the compensation argument, though the two are very often confused. Furthermore it escapes all the objections to which the other is open, including, most importantly, the general argument, that it is always unfair to select people for work on the basis of anything other than their suitability for it.

The point is this. If our present society is unfair to women, it is obviously fair that it should be changed; it is fair that we should set in motion social programmes to turn society into one which is better for women. We also think that when things are fairer to women society as a whole will benefit, because it will no longer waste their skills. Admittedly women now may not have the skills they should have had, and since it is prob- ably too late for the women of this generation to acquire them we should perhaps think of compensating them for their disadvantage by other means, rather than giving them positions of responsibility. But that would be to take a short term view. We have to plan not only for the people who are alive now, but for the world our great-granddaughters will have to contend with. It would be unfair to them to let things go on as they are now, and unfair to their contemporaries to have potential skill wasted. Our social aims, therefore, become more complicated. We have to maintain our concern with high standards in the various professions, but we have also to think of the need to advance women. We want good doctors, certainly, but at the same time we want to encourage people to think of women as doctors. *If, as a matter of fact*, we think that the best way to achieve this is to have a good many successful women doctors, we may consider making rules which allow a woman to become a doctor with slightly lower medical qualifications than a man. *But this does not offend against the principle that there should be no discrimination in selection procedures, because we are still concerned to choose the best people for the job which needs doing*. It is just that the nature of the work to be done has changed, so that different people become suitable for it. We now want, for example, good doctors, who *also* advance the positions of women. As long as lowering the medical qualifications for women was causally relevant to the end to be achieved, it would be justified.

This way of looking at the matter does seem to remove the *prima facie* objections to reverse discrimination. Or perhaps a better way of putting it would be to say that reverse discrimination is not well named, because discrimination on grounds of sex involves counting sex as rele- vant in contexts where it is not, and the argument being put forward now is that in some unexpected contexts it *may* be relevant. In these contexts what appears to be discrimination in favour of women is not discrimina- tion at all.

Notes

1 See Sheila Rowbotham, *Woman's Consciousness, Man's World* (Harmonds- worth, 1973), p. 95.
2 John Stuart Mill, 'The subjection of women', in Alice Rossi (ed.) *The Feminist Papers* (New York, 1974), pp. 214ff. and *passim*.
3. Ibid., pp. 205–6.
4. This point needs one qualification. The point is that no society can ever, in justice, have a policy of irrelevantly leaving out any group from the com- petition for desirable places in society: to do so is tantamount to declaring that the social structures are unjust. However, an individual who thinks that the structures of society are unfair to one sex or the other may decide to go

against the rules; that is, may decide to practise (say) some surreptitious reverse discrimination. That may be all right, in the way that overt reverse discrimination may be all right. What is not all right is to build selection discrimination into any rules, or to practise it surreptitiously if you think the rules are just.

5   John Rawls, *A Theory of Justice* (Oxford, 1972), p. 60 and *passim*.
6   Defined as the things people may reasonably be presumed to want whatever else they want (Rawls, *A Theory of Justice*, pp. 62, 92 and *passim*).

24

Letter from Birmingham City Jail

Martin Luther King Jr

In this extract from his letter from jail, the great civil rights campaigner Martin Luther King Jr sets out the case for civil disobedience, what he calls 'direct action': non-violent law-breaking to draw attention to and protest against unjust laws or practices. In this case the unjust laws were racist ones. King's letter provides a case study in civil disobedience. In recent history acts of civil disobedience have led to a wide range of unjust laws being abandoned. This fact challenges the notion that it is always morally wrong to break the law. Yet the spirit in which the law is broken is crucial to the question of whether it is an act of dignified civil disobedience or self-serving criminality.

From Martin Luther King Jr, *Why We Can't Wait*

My dear Fellow Clergymen,

While confined here in the Birmingham City Jail, I came across your recent statement calling our present activities 'unwise and untimely'. Seldom, if ever, do I pause to answer criticism of my work and ideas. If I sought to answer all of the criticisms that cross my desk, my secretaries would be engaged in little else in the course of the day, and I would have no time for constructive work. But since I feel that you are men of genuine goodwill and your criticisms are sincerely set forth, I would like to answer your statement in what I hope will be patient and reasonable terms.

I think I should give the reason for my being in Birmingham, since you have been influenced by the argument of 'outsiders coming in.' I have the honor of serving as president of the Southern Christian Leadership Conference, an organization operating in every Southern state, with headquarters in Atlanta, Georgia. We have some eighty-five affiliate organizations all across the South – one being the Alabama Christian

Movement for Human Rights. Whenever necessary and possible we share staff, educational and financial resources with our affiliates. Several months ago our local affiliate here in Birmingham invited us to be on call to engage in a nonviolent direct action program if such were deemed necessary. We readily consented and when the hour came we lived up to our promises. So I am here, along with several members of my staff, because we were invited here. I am here because I have basic organizational ties here.

Beyond this, I am in Birmingham because injustice is here. Just as the eighth-century prophets left their little villages and carried their 'thus saith the Lord' far beyond the boundaries of their home towns; and just as the Apostle Paul left his little village of Tarsus and carried the gospel of Jesus Christ to practically every hamlet and city of the Graeco-Roman world, I too am compelled to carry the gospel of freedom beyond my particular home town. Like Paul, I must constantly respond to the Macedonian call for aid.

Moreover, I am cognizant of the interrelatedness of all communities and states. I cannot sit idly by in Atlanta and not be concerned about what happens in Birmingham. Injustice anywhere is a threat to justice everywhere. We are caught in an inescapable network of mutuality, tied in a single garment of destiny. Whatever affects one directly affects all indirectly. Never again can we afford to live with the narrow, provincial 'outside agitator' idea. Anyone who lives inside the United States can never be considered an outsider anywhere in this country.

You deplore the demonstrations that are presently taking place in Birmingham. But I am sorry that your statement did not express a similar concern for the conditions that brought the demonstrations into being. I am sure that each of you would want to go beyond the superficial social analyst who looks merely at effects, and does not grapple with underlying causes. I would not hesitate to say that it is unfortunate that so-called demonstrations are taking place in Birmingham at this time, but I would say in more emphatic terms that it is even more unfortunate that the white power structure of this city left the Negro community with no other alternative.

In any nonviolent campaign there are four basic steps: (1) Collection of the facts to determine whether injustices are alive. (2) Negotiation, (3) Self-purification and (4) Direct Action. We have gone through all of these steps in Birmingham. There can be no gainsaying of the fact that racial injustice engulfs this community.

Birmingham is probably the most thoroughly segregated city in the United States. Its ugly record of police brutality is known in every section of this country. Its unjust treatment of Negroes in the courts is a notorious reality. There have been more unsolved bombings of Negro homes and churches in Birmingham than in any city in this nation. These are the hard, brutal and unbelievable facts. On the basis of these conditions Negro leaders sought to negotiate with the city fathers. But the political leaders consistently refused to engage in good faith negotiation.

Then came the opportunity last September to talk with some of the leaders of the economic community. In these negotiating sessions certain promises were made by the merchants – such as the promise to remove the humiliating racial signs from the stores. On the basis of these promises Rev. Shuttlesworth and the leaders of the Alabama Christian Movement for Human Rights agreed to call a moratorium on any type of demonstrations. As the weeks and months unfolded we realized that we were the victims of a broken promise. The signs remained. Like so many experiences of the past we were confronted with blasted hopes, and the dark shadow of a deep disappointment settled upon us. So we had no alternative except that of preparing for direct action, whereby we would present our very bodies as a means of laying our case before the conscience of the local and national community. We were not unmindful of the difficulties involved. So we decided to go through a process of self-purification. We started having workshops on nonviolence and repeatedly asking ourselves the questions, 'Are you able to accept blows without retaliating?' 'Are you able to endure the ordeals of jail?' We decided to set our direct action program around the Easter season, realizing that with the exception of Christmas, this was the largest shopping period of the year. Knowing that a strong economic withdrawal program would be the by-product of direct action, we felt that this was the best time to bring pressure on the merchants for the needed changes. Then it occurred to us that the March election was ahead and so we speedily decided to postpone action until after election day. When we discovered that Mr Connor was in the run-off, we decided again to postpone action so that the demonstrations could not be used to cloud the issues. At this time we agreed to begin our nonviolent witness the day after the run-off.

This reveals that we did not move irresponsibly into direct action. We too wanted to see Mr. Connor defeated; so we went through postponement after postponement to aid in this community need. After this we felt that direct action could be delayed no longer.

You may well ask, 'Why direct action? Why sit-ins, marches, etc.? Isn't negotiation a better path?' You are exactly right in your call for negotiation. Indeed, this is the purpose of direct action. Nonviolent direct action seeks to create such a crisis and establish such creative tension that a community that has constantly refused to negotiate is forced to confront the issue. It seeks so to dramatize the issue that it can no longer be ignored. I just referred to the creation of tension as a part of the work of the nonviolent resister. This may sound rather shocking. But I must confess that I am not afraid of the word tension. I have earnestly worked and preached against violent tension, but there is a type of constructive nonviolent tension that is necessary for growth. Just as Socrates felt that it was necessary to create a tension in the mind so that individuals could rise from the bondage of myths and half-truths to the unfettered realm of creative analysis and objective appraisal, we must see the need of having nonviolent gadflies to create the kind of tension in society that will help men to rise from the dark depths of prejudice and racism to the majestic heights of understanding and brotherhood. So the purpose of the direct action is to create a situation so crisis-packed that it will inevitably open the door to negotiation. We, therefore, concur with you in your call for negotiation. Too long has our beloved Southland been bogged down in the tragic attempt to live in monologue rather than dialogue.

One of the basic points in your statement is that our acts are untimely. Some have asked, 'Why didn't you give the new administration time to act?' The only answer that I can give to this inquiry is that the new administration must be prodded about as much as the outgoing one before it acts. We will be sadly mistaken if we feel that the election of Mr Boutwell will bring the milennium to Birmingham. While Mr Boutwell is much more articulate and gentle than Mr Connor, they are both segregationists, dedicated to the task of maintaining the status quo. The hope I see in Mr Boutwell is that he will be reasonable enough to see the futility of massive resistance to desegregation. But he will not see this without pressure from the devotees of civil rights. My friends, I must say to you that we have not made a single gain in civil rights without determined legal and nonviolent pressure. History is the long and tragic story of the fact that privileged groups seldom give up their privileges voluntarily. Individuals may see the moral light and voluntarily give up their unjust posture; but as Reinhold Niebuhr has reminded us, groups are more immoral than individuals.

We know through painful experience that freedom is never voluntarily given by the oppressor; it must be demanded by the oppressed. Frankly, I have never yet engaged in a direct action movement that was 'well timed', according to the timetable of those who have not suffered unduly from the disease of segregation. For years now I have heard the words 'Wait!' It rings in the ear of every Negro with a piercing familiarity. This 'Wait' has almost always meant 'Never'. It has been a tranquilizing thalidomide, relieving the emotional stress for a moment, only to give birth to an ill-formed infant of frustration. We must come to see with the distinguished jurist of yesterday that 'justice too long delayed is justice denied'. We have waited for more than three hundred and forty years for our constitutional and God-given rights. The nations of Asia and Africa are moving with jet-like speed toward the goal of political independence, and we still creep at horse-and-buggy pace toward the gaining of a cup of coffee at a lunch counter. I guess it is easy for those who have never felt the stinging darts of segregation to say, 'Wait'. But when you have seen vicious mobs lynch your mothers and fathers at will and drown your sisters and brothers at whim; when you have seen hate-filled policemen curse, kick, brutalize and even kill your black brothers and sisters with impunity; when you see the vast majority of your twenty million Negro brothers smothering in an air-tight cage of poverty in the midst of an affluent society; when you suddenly find your tongue twisted and your speech stammering as you seek to explain to your six-year-old daughter why she can't go to the public amusement park that has just been advertised on television, and see tears welling up in her little eyes when she is told that Funtown is closed to colored children, and see the depressing clouds of inferiority begin to form in her little mental sky, and see her begin to distort her little personality by unconsciously developing a bitterness toward white people; when you have to concoct an answer for a five-year-old son asking in agonizing pathos: 'Daddy, why do white people treat colored people so mean?'; when you take a cross-country drive and find it necessary to sleep night after night in the uncomfortable corners of your automobile because no motel will accept you; when you are humiliated day in and day out by nagging signs reading 'white' and 'colored'; when your first name becomes 'nigger' and your middle name becomes 'boy' (however old you are) and your last name becomes 'John', and when your wife and mother are never given the respected title 'Mrs'; when you are harried by day and haunted at night by the fact that you are a Negro, living constantly at tip-toe stance never quite knowing what to expect next, and plagued with inner fears and outer resentments; when you are forever righting a degenerating sense of 'nobod-iness'; then you will understand why we find it difficult to wait. There comes a time when the cup of endurance runs over, and men are no longer willing to be plunged into an abyss of injustice where they experience the blackness of corroding despair. I hope, sirs, you can understand our legit-imate and unavoidable impatience.

You express a great deal of anxiety over our willingness to break laws. This is certainly a legitimate concern. Since we so diligently urge people to obey the Supreme Court's decision of 1954 outlawing segrega-tion in the public schools, it is rather strange and paradoxical to find us consciously breaking laws. One may well ask, 'How can you advocate breaking some laws and obeying others?' The answer is found in the fact that there are two types of laws: There are *just* and there are *unjust* laws. I would agree with Saint Augustine that 'An unjust law is no law at all.'

Now what is the difference between the two? How does one deter-mine when a law is just or unjust? A just law is a man-made code that squares with the moral law or the law of God. An unjust law is a code that is out of harmony with the moral law. To put it in the terms of Saint Thomas Aquinas, an unjust law is a human law that is not rooted in eternal and natural law. Any law that uplifts human personality is just. Any law that degrades human personality is unjust. All segregation statutes are unjust because segregation distorts the soul and damages the personality. It gives the segregator a false sense of superiority, and the segregated a false sense of inferiority. To use the words of Martin Buber, the great Jewish philosopher, segregation substitutes an 'I-it' relationship for the 'I-thou' relationship, and ends up relegating persons to the status of things. So segregation is not only politically, economically and sociologically unsound, but it is morally wrong and sinful. Paul Tillich has said that sin is separation. Isn't segregation an existential expression of man's tragic separation, an expression of his awful estrangement, his terrible sinfulness? So I can urge men to disobey segregation ordinances because they are morally wrong.

Let us turn to a more concrete example of just and unjust laws. An unjust law is a code that a majority inflicts on a minority that is not binding on itself. This is difference made legal. On the other hand a just law is a code that a majority compels a minority to follow that it is willing to follow itself. This is sameness made legal.

Let me give another explanation. An unjust law is a code inflicted upon a minority which that minority had no part in enacting or creating because they did not have the unhampered right to vote. Who can say that the legislature of Alabama which set up the segregation laws was democratically elected? Throughout the state of Alabama all types of conniving methods are used to prevent Negroes from becoming registered voters and there are some counties without a single Negro registered to vote despite the fact that the Negro constitutes a majority of the population. Can any law set up in such a state be considered democratically structured?

These are just a few examples of unjust and just laws. There are some instances when a law is just on its face and unjust in its application. For instance, I was arrested Friday on a charge of parading without a permit. Now there is nothing wrong with an ordinance which requires a permit for a parade, but when the ordinance is used to preserve segregation and to deny citizens the First Amendment privilege of peaceful assembly and peaceful protest, then it becomes unjust.

I hope you can see the distinction I am trying to point out. In no sense do I advocate evading or defying the law as the rabid segregationist would do. This would lead to anarchy. One who breaks an unjust law must do it *openly, lovingly* (not hatefully as the white mothers did in New Orleans when they were seen on television screaming 'nigger, nigger, nigger'), and with a willingness to accept the penalty. I submit that an individual who breaks a law that conscience tells him is unjust, and willingly accepts the penalty by staying in jail to arouse the conscience of the community over its injustice, is in reality expressing the very highest respect for law.

Of course, there is nothing new about this kind of civil disobedience. It was seen sublimely in the refusal of Shadrach, Meshach and Abednego to obey the laws of Nebuchadnezzar because a higher moral law was involved. It was practiced superbly by the early Christians who were willing to face hungry lions and the excruciating pain of chopping blocks, before submitting to certain unjust laws of the Roman empire. To a degree academic freedom is a reality today because Socrates practiced civil disobedience.

We can never forget that everything Hitler did in Germany was 'legal' and everything the Hungarian freedom fighters did in Hungary was 'illegal'. It was 'illegal' to aid and comfort a Jew in Hitler's Germany. But I am sure that if I had lived in Germany during that time I would have aided and comforted my Jewish brothers even though it was illegal. If I lived in a Communist country today where certain principles dear to the Christian faith are suppressed, I believe I would openly advocate disobeying these anti-religious laws. I must make two honest confessions to you, my Christian and Jewish brothers. First, I must confess that over the last few years I have been gravely disappointed with the white moderate. I have almost reached the regrettable conclusion that the Negro's great stumbling-block in the stride toward freedom is not the White Citizen's Council-er or the Ku Klux Klanner, but the white moderate who is more devoted to 'order' than to justice; who prefers a negative peace which is the absence of tension to a positive peace which is the presence of justice; who constantly says, 'I agree with you in the goal you seek, but I can't agree with your methods of direct action'; who paternalistically feels that he can set the timetable for another man's freedom; who lives by the myth of time and who constantly advises the Negro to wait until a 'more convenient season'. Shallow understanding from people of goodwill is more frustrating than absolute misunderstanding from people of ill will. Lukewarm acceptance is much more bewildering than outright rejection.

I had hoped that the white moderate would understand that law and order exist for the purpose of establishing justice, and that when they fail to do this they become dangerously structured dams that block the flow of social progress. I had hoped that the white moderate would understand that the present tension of the South is merely a necessary phase of the transition from an obnoxious negative peace, where the Negro passively accepted his unjust plight, to a substance-filled positive peace, where all men will respect the dignity and worth of human personality. Actually, we who engage in nonviolent direct action are not the creators of tension. We merely bring to the surface the hidden tension that is already alive. We bring it out in the open where it can be seen and dealt with. Like a boil that can never be cured as long as it is covered up but must be opened with all its pus-flowing ugliness to the natural medicines of air and light, injustice must likewise be exposed, with all of the tension its exposing creates, to the light of human conscience and the air of national opinion before it can be cured.

25

All animals are equal
Peter Singer

Peter Singer (1946–) makes an impassioned case for revising our moral and political horizons to include non-human animals. To treat animals capable of suffering as if they were not sentient is a serious form of speciesism that we should oppose. The two forms of speciesism which Singer objects to most strongly are experimenting on animals and eating their flesh. However, beyond these he claims that philosophy has a duty to challenge the assumptions of the age, and that in this case, philosophy should be challenging our preconceptions about our relations with other animals. The philosophical problem of equality should not just be formulated in terms of human equality, but should investigate the issue of equality for animals.

From Peter Singer, 'All animals are equal', *Philosophic Exchange*, vol. 1, no. 5

In recent years a number of oppressed groups have campaigned vigorously for equality. The classic instance is the Black Liberation movement, which demands an end to the prejudice and discrimination that has made blacks second-class citizens. The immediate appeal of the Black Liberation movement and its initial, if limited, success made it a model for other oppressed groups to follow. We became familiar with liberation movements for Spanish-Americans, gay people, and a variety of other minorities. When a majority group – women – began their campaign, some thought we had come to the end of the road. Discrimination on the basis of sex, it has been said, is the last universally accepted form of discrimination, practised without secrecy or pretence even in those liberal circles that have long prided themselves on their freedom from prejudice against racial minorities.

One should always be wary of talking of 'the last remaining form of discrimination'. If we have learnt anything from the liberation movements, we should have learnt how difficult it is to be aware of latent prejudice in our attitudes to particular groups until this prejudice is forcefully pointed out.

A liberation movement demands an expansion of our moral horizons and an extension or reinterpretation of the basic moral principle of equality. Practices that were previously regarded as natural and inevitable come to be seen as the result of an unjustifiable prejudice. Who can say with confidence that all his or her attitudes and practices are beyond criticism? If we wish to avoid being numbered amongst the oppressors, we must be prepared to re-think even our most fundamental attitudes. We need to consider them from the point of view of those most disadvantaged by our attitudes, and the practices that follow from these attitudes. If we can make this unaccustomed mental switch we may discover a pattern in our attitudes and practices that consistently operates so as to benefit one group – usually the one to which we ourselves belong – at the expense of another. In this way we may come to see that there is a case for a new liberation movement. My aim is to advocate that we make this mental switch in respect of our attitudes and practices towards a very large group of beings: members of species other than our own – or, as we popularly though misleadingly call them, animals. In other words, I am urging that we extend to other species the basic principle of equality that most of us recognize should be extended to all members of our own species.

All this may sound a little far-fetched, more like a parody of other liberation movements than a serious objective. In fact, in the past the idea of 'The Rights of Animals' really has been used to parody the case for women's rights. When Mary Wollstonecraft, a forerunner of later feminists, published her *Vindication of the Rights of Women* in 1792, her ideas were widely regarded as absurd, and they were satirized in an anonymous publication entitled *A Vindication of the Rights of Brutes*. The author of this satire (actually Thomas Taylor, a distinguished Cambridge philosopher) tried to refute Wollstonecroft's reasonings by showing that they could be carried one stage further. If sound when applied to women, why should the arguments not be applied to dogs, cats, and horses? They seemed to hold equally well for these 'brutes'; yet to hold that brutes had rights was manifestly absurd; therefore the reasoning by which this conclusion had been reached must be unsound, and if unsound when applied to brutes, it must also be unsound when applied to women, since the very same arguments had been used in each case.

One way in which we might reply to this argument is by saying that the case for equality between men and women cannot validly be extended to non-human animals. Women have a right to vote, for instance, because they are just as capable of making rational decisions as men are; dogs, on the other hand, are incapable of understanding the significance of voting, so they cannot have the right to vote. There are many other obvious ways in which men and women resemble each other closely, while humans and other animals differ greatly. So, it might be said, men and women are similar beings, and should have equal rights, while humans and non-humans are different and should not have equal rights.

The thought behind this reply to Taylor's analogy is correct up to a point, but it does not go far enough. There *are* important differences between humans and other animals, and these differences must give rise to *some* differences, in the rights that each have. Recognizing this obvious fact, however, is no barrier to the case for extending the basic principle of equality to non-human animals. The differences that exist between men and women are equally undeniable, and the supporters of Women's Liberation are aware that these differences may give rise to different rights. Many feminists hold that women have the right to an abortion on request. It does not follow that since these same people are campaigning for equality between men and women they must support the right of men to have abortions too. Since a man cannot have an abortion, it is meaningless to talk of his right to have one. Since a pig can't vote it is meaningless to talk of its right to vote. There is no reason why either Women's Liberation or Animal Liberation should get involved in such nonsense. The extension of the basic principle of equality from one group to another does not imply that we must treat both groups in exactly the same way, or grant exactly the same rights to both groups. Whether we should do so will depend on the nature of the members of the two groups. The basic principle of equality, I shall argue, is equality of consideration; and equal consideration for different beings may lead to different treatment and different rights.

So there is a different way of replying to Taylor's attempt to parody Wollstonecraft's arguments, a way which does not deny the differences between humans and non-humans, but goes more deeply into the question of equality, and concludes by finding nothing absurd in the idea that the basic principle of equality applies to so-called 'brutes'. I believe that we reach this conclusion if we examine the basis on which our opposition to discrimination on grounds of race or sex ultimately rests. We will then see that we would be on shaky ground if we were to demand equality for blacks, women, and other groups of oppressed humans while denying equal consideration to non-humans.

When we say that all human beings, whatever their race, creed, or sex, are equal, what is it that we are asserting? Those who wish to defend a hierarchical, inegalitarian society have often pointed out that by whatever test we choose, it simply is not true that all humans are equal. Like it or not, we must face the fact that humans come in different shapes and sizes; they come with differing moral capacities, differing intellectual abilities, differing amounts of benevolent feeling and sensitivity to the needs of others, differing abilities to communicate effectively, and differing capacities to experience pleasure and pain. In short, if the demand for equality were based on the actual equality of all human beings, we would have to stop demanding equality. It would be an unjustifiable demand.

Still, one might cling to the view that the demand for equality among human beings is based on the actual equality of the different races and sexes. Although humans differ as individuals in various ways, there are no differences between the races and sexes *as such*. From the mere fact that a person is black, or a woman, we cannot infer anything else about that person. This, it may be said, is what is wrong with racism and sexism. The white racist claims that whites are superior to blacks, but this is false – although there are differences between individuals, some blacks are superior to some whites in all of the capacities and abilities that could conceivably be relevant. The opponent of sexism would say the same: a person's sex is no guide to his or her abilities, and this is why it is unjustifiable to discriminate on the basis of sex.

This is a possible line of objection to racial and sexual discrimination. It is not, however, the way someone really concerned about equality would choose, because taking this line could, in some circumstances, force one to accept a most inegalitarian society. The fact that humans differ as individuals, rather than as races or sexes, is a valid reply to someone who defends a hierarchical society like, say, South Africa, in which all whites are superior in status to all blacks. The existence of individual variations that cut across the lines of race or sex, however, provides us with no defence at all against a more sophisticated opponent of equality, one who proposes that, say, the interests of those with IQ ratings above 100 be preferred to the interests of those with IQs below 100. Would a hierarchical society of this sort really be so much better than one based on race or sex? I think not. But if we tie the moral principle of equality to the factual equality of the different races or sexes, taken as a whole, our opposition to racism and sexism does not provide us with any basis for objecting to this kind of inegalitarianism.

There is a second important reason why we ought not to base our opposition to racism and sexism on any kind of factual equality, even the limited kind which asserts that variations in capacities and abilities are spread evenly between the different races and sexes: we can have no absolute guarantee that these abilities and capacities really are distributed evenly, without regard to race or sex, among human beings. So far as actual abilities are concerned, there do seem to be certain measurable differences between both races and sexes. These differences do not, of course, appear in each case, but only when averages are taken. More important still, we do not yet know how much of these differences is really due to the different genetic endowments of the various races and sexes, and how much is due to environmental differences that are the result of past and continuing discrimination. Perhaps all of the important differences will eventually prove to be environmental rather than genetic. Anyone opposed to racism and sexism will certainly hope that this will be so, for it will make the task of ending discrimination a lot easier; nevertheless it would be dangerous to rest the case against racism and sexism on the belief that all significant differences are environmental in origin. The opponent of, say, racism who takes this line will be unable to avoid conceding that if differences in ability did after all prove to have some genetic connection with race, racism would in some way be defensible.

It would be folly for the opponent of racism to stake his whole case on a dogmatic commitment to one particular outcome of a difficult scientific issue which is still a long way from being settled. While attempts to prove that differences in certain selected abilities between races and sexes are primarily genetic in origin have certainly not been conclusive, the same must be said of attempts to prove that these differences are largely the result of environment. At this stage of the investigation we cannot be certain which view is correct, however much we may hope it is the latter.

Fortunately, there is no need to pin the case for equality to one particular outcome of this scientific investigation. The appropriate response to those who claim to have found evidence of genetically-based differences in ability between the races or sexes is not to stick to the belief that the genetic explanation must be wrong, whatever evidence to the contrary may turn up: instead we should make it quite clear that the claim to equality does not depend on intelligence, moral capacity, physical strength, or similar matters of fact. Equality is a moral ideal, not a simple assertion of fact. There is no logically compelling reason for assuming that a factual difference in ability between two people justifies any difference in the amount of consideration we give to satisfying their needs and interests. The principle of the equality of human beings is not a description of an alleged actual equality among humans: it is a prescription of how we should treat humans.

Jeremy Bentham incorporated the essential basis of moral equality into his utilitarian system of ethics in the formula: 'Each to count for one and none for more than one.' In other words, the interests of every being affected by an action are to be taken into account and given the same weight as the like interests of any other being. A later utilitarian, Henry Sidgwick, put the point in this way: 'The good of any one individual is of no more importance, from the point of view (if I may say so) of the Universe, than the good of any other.'[1] More recently, the leading figures in modern moral philosophy have shown a great deal of agreement in specifying as a fundamental presupposition of their moral theories some similar requirement which operates so as to give everyone's interests equal consideration – although they cannot agree on how this requirement is best formulated.[2]

It is an implication of this principle of equality that our concern for others ought not to depend on what they are like, or what abilities they possess – although precisely what this concern requires us to do may vary according to the characteristics of those affected by what we do. It is on this basis that the case against racism and the case against sexism must both ultimately rest; and it is in accordance with this principle that speciesism is also to be condemned. If possessing a higher degree of intelligence does not entitle one human to use another for his own ends, how can it entitle humans to exploit non-humans?

Many philosophers have proposed the principle of equal consideration of interests, in some form or other, as a basic moral principle; but, as we shall see in more detail shortly, not many of them have recognized that this principle applies to members of other species as well as to our own. Bentham was one of the few who did realize this. In a forward-looking passage, written at a time when black slaves in the British dominions were still being treated much as we now treat non-human animals, Bentham wrote:

> The day *may* come when the rest of the animal creation may acquire those rights which never could have been witholden from them but by the hand of tyranny. The French have already discovered that the blackness of the skin is no reason why a human being should be abandoned without redress to the caprice of a tormentor. It may one day come to be recognized that the number of the legs, the villosity of the skin, or the termination of the *os sacrum*, are reasons equally insufficient for abandoning a sensitive being to the same fate. What else is it that should trace the insuperable line? Is it the faculty of reason, or perhaps the faculty of discourse? But a full-grown horse or dog is beyond comparison a more rational, as well as a more conversable animal, than an infant of a day, or a week, or even a month, old. But suppose they were otherwise, what would it avail? The question is not, Can they reason? nor Can they *talk*? but, *Can they suffer*?[3]

In this passage Bentham points to the capacity for suffering as the vital characteristic that gives a being the right to equal consideration. The capacity for suffering – or more strictly, for suffering and/or enjoyment or happiness – is not just another characteristic like the capacity for language, or for higher mathematics. Bentham is not saying that those who try to mark 'the insuperable line' that determines whether the interests of a being should be considered happen to have selected the wrong characteristic. The capacity for suffering and enjoying things is a pre-requisite for having interests at all, a condition that must be satisfied before we can speak of interests in any meaningful way. It would be nonsense to say that it was

227

not in the interests of a stone to be kicked along the road by a schoolboy. A stone does not have interests because it cannot suffer. Nothing that we can do to it could possibly make any difference to its welfare. A mouse, on the other hand, does have an interest in not being tormented, because it will suffer if it is.

If a being suffers, there can be no moral justification for refusing to take that suffering into consideration. No matter what the nature of the being, the principle of equality requires that its suffering be counted equally with the like suffering – in so far as rough comparisons can be made – of any other being. If a being is not capable of suffering, or of experiencing enjoyment or happiness, there is nothing to be taken into account. This is why the limit of sentience (using the term as a convenient, if not strictly accurate, shorthand for the capacity to suffer or experience enjoyment or happiness) is the only defensible boundary of concern for the interests of others. To make this boundary by some characteristic like intelligence or rationality would be to mark it in an arbitrary way. Why not choose some other characteristic, like skin colour?

The racist violates the principle of equality by giving greater weight to the interests of members of his own race, when there is a clash between their interests and the interests of those of another race. Similarly the speciesist allows the interests of his own species to override the greater interests of members of other species.[4] The pattern is the same in each case. Most human beings are speciesists. I shall now very briefly describe some of the practices that show this.

For the great majority of human beings, especially in urban, industrialized societies, the most direct form of contact with members of other species is at meal-times: we eat them. In doing so we treat them purely as means to our ends. We regard their life and well-being as subordinate to our taste for a particular kind of dish. I say 'taste' deliberately – this is purely a matter of pleasing our palate. There can be no defence of eating flesh in terms of satisfying nutritional needs, since it has been established beyond doubt that we could satisfy our need for protein and other essential nutrients far more efficiently with a diet that replaced animal flesh by soy beans, or products derived from soy beans, and other high-protein vegetable products.[5]

It is not merely the act of killing that indicates what we are ready to do to other species in order to gratify our tastes. The suffering we inflict on the animals while they are alive is perhaps an even clearer indication of our speciesism than the fact that we are prepared to kill them.[6] In order to have meat on the table at a price that people can afford, our society tolerates methods of meat production that confine sentient animals in cramped, unsuitable conditions for the entire durations of their lives. Animals are treated like machines that convert fodder into flesh, and any innovation that results in a higher 'conversion ratio' is liable to be adopted.

As one authority on the subject has said, 'cruelty is acknowledged only when profitability ceases'.[7]

Since, as I have said, none of these practices cater for anything more than our pleasures of taste, our practice of rearing and killing other animals in order to eat them is a clear instance of the sacrifice of the most important interests of other beings in order to satisfy trivial interests of our own. To avoid speciesism we must stop this practice, and each of us has a moral obligation to cease supporting the practice. Our custom is all the support that the meat industry needs. The decision to cease giving it that support may be difficult, but it is no more difficult than it would have been for a white Southerner to go against the traditions of his society and free his slaves: if we do not change our dietary habits, how can we censure those slave-holders who would not change their own way of living?

The same form of discrimination may be observed in the widespread practice of experimenting on other species in order to see if certain substances are safe for human beings, or to test some psychological theory about the effect of severe punishment on learning, or to try out various new compounds just in case something turns up . . .

In the past, argument about vivisection has often missed this point, because it has been put in absolutist terms: Would the abolitionist be prepared to let thousands die if they could be saved by experimenting on a single animal? The way to reply to this purely hypothetical question is to pose another: Would the experimenter be prepared to perform his experiment on an orphaned human infant, if that were the only way to save many lives? (I say 'orphan' to avoid the complication of parental feelings, although in doing so I am being over-fair to the experimenter, since the non-human subjects of experiments are not orphans.) If the experimenter is not prepared to use an orphaned human infant, then his readiness to use non-humans is simple discrimination, since adults apes, cats, mice, and other mammals are more aware of what is happening to them, more self-directing and, so far as we can tell, at least as sensitive to pain, as any human infant. There seems to be no relevant characteristic that human infants possess that adult mammals do not have to the same or a higher degree. (Someone might try to argue that what makes it wrong to experiment on a human infant is that the infant will, in time and if left alone, develop into more than the non-human, but one would then, to be consistent, have to oppose abortion, since the foetus has the same potential as the infant – indeed, even contraception and abstinence might be wrong on this ground, since the egg and sperm, considered jointly, also have the same potential. In any case, this argument still gives us no reason for selecting a non-human, rather than a human with severe and irreversible brain damage, as the subject for our experiments.)

The experimenter, then, shows a bias in favour of his own species whenever he carries out an experiment on a non-human for a purpose that he would not think justified him in using a human being at an equal or lower level of sentience, awareness, ability to be self-directing, etc. No one familiar with the kind of results yielded by most experiments on animals can have the slightest doubt that if this bias were eliminated the number of experiments performed would be a minute fraction of the number performed today.

Experimenting on animals, and eating their flesh, are perhaps the two major forms of speciesism in our society. By comparison, the third and last form of speciesism is so minor as to be insignificant but it is perhaps of some special interest to those for whom this article was written. I am referring to speciesism in modern philosophy.

Philosophy ought to question the basic assumptions of the age. Thinking through, critically and carefully, what most people take for granted is, I believe, the chief task of philosophy, and it is this task that makes philosophy a worthwhile activity. Regrettably, philosophy does not always live up to its historic role. Philosophers are human beings and they are subject to all the preconceptions of the society to which they belong. Sometimes they succeed in breaking free of the prevailing ideology: more often they become its most sophisticated defenders. So, in this case, philosophy as practised in the universities today does not challenge anyone's preconceptions about our relations with other species. By their writings, those philosophers who tackle problems that touch upon the issue reveal that they make the same unquestioned assumptions as most other humans, and what they say tends to confirm the reader in his or her comfortable speciesist habits.

I could illustrate this claim by referring to the writings of philosophers in various fields – for instance, the attempts that have been made by those interested in rights to draw the boundary of the sphere of rights so that it runs parallel to the biological boundaries of the species *Homo sapiens*, including infants and even mental defectives, but excluding those other beings of equal or greater capacity who are so useful to us at mealtimes and in our laboratories. I think it would be a more appropriate conclusion to this chapter, however, if I concentrated on the problem with which we have been centrally concerned, the problem of equality.

It is significant that the problem of equality, in moral and political philosophy, is invariably formulated in terms of human equality. The effect of this is that the question of the equality of other animals does not confront the philosopher, or student, as an issue itself – and this is already an indication of the failure of philosophy to challenge accepted beliefs. Still, philosophers have found it difficult to discuss the issue of human equality without raising, in a paragraph or two, the question of the status of other animals. The reason for this, which should be apparent from what I have said already, is that if humans are to be regarded as equal to one another, we need some sense of 'equal' that does not require any actual, descriptive equality of capacities, talents, or other qualities. If equality is to be related to any actual characteristics of humans, these characteristics must be some lowest common denominator, pitched so low that no human lacks them – but then the philosopher comes up against the catch that any such set of characteristics which covers *all* humans will not be possessed *only by humans*. In other words, it turns out that in the only sense in which we can truly say, as an assertion of fact, that all humans are equal, at least some members of other species are also equal – equal, that is, to each other and to humans. If, on the other hand, we regard the statement 'All humans are equal' in some non-factual way, perhaps as a prescription, then, as I have already argued, it is even more difficult to exclude non-humans from the sphere of equality.

This result is not what the egalitarian philosopher originally intended to assert. Instead of accepting the radical outcome to which their own reasonings naturally point, however, most philosophers try to reconcile their beliefs in human equality and animal inequality by arguments that can only be described as devious.

As an example, I take William Frankena's well-known article, 'The concept of social justice'. Frankena opposes the idea of basing justice on merit, because he sees that this could lead to highly inegalitarian results. Instead he proposes the principle that '... all men are to be treated as equals, not because they are equal, in any respect, but simply because they are human. They are human because they have emotions and desires, and are able to think, and hence are capable of enjoying a good life in a sense in which other animals are not.'[8]

But what is this capacity to enjoy the good life which all humans have, but no other animals? Other animals have emotions and desires, and appear to be capable of enjoying a good life. We may doubt that they can think – although the behaviour of some apes, dolphins, and even dogs suggests that some of them can – but what is the relevance of thinking? Frankena goes on to admit that by 'the good life' he means 'not so much the morally good life as the happy or satisfactory life', so thought would appear to be unnecessary for enjoying the good life; in fact to emphasize the need for thought would make difficulties for the egalitarian since only some people are capable of leading intellectually satisfying lives, or morally good lives. This makes it difficult to see what Frankena's principle of equality has to do with simply being *human*. Surely every sentient being is capable of leading a life that is happier or less miserable than some alternative life, and hence has a claim to be taken into account. In this respect the distinction between humans and non-humans is not a sharp division, but rather a continuum along which we move gradually, and with overlaps between the species, from simple capacities for enjoyment and satisfaction, or pain and suffering, to more complex ones.

Faced with a situation in which they see a need for some basis for the moral gulf that is commonly thought to separate humans and animals, but can find no concrete difference that will do the job without undermining the equality of humans, philosophers tend to waffle. They resort to high-sounding phrases like 'the intrinsic dignity of the human individual'.[9] They talk of the 'intrinsic worth of all men' as if men (humans?) had some worth that other beings did not,[10] or they say that humans, and only humans, are 'ends in themselves' while 'everything other than a person can only have value for a person'.[11]

This idea of a distinctive human dignity and worth has a long history; it can be traced back directly to the Renaissance humanists, for instance to Pico della Mirandola's *Oration on the Dignity of Man*. Pico and other humanists based their estimate of human dignity on the idea that man possessed the central, pivotal position in the 'Great Chain of Being' that led from the lowliest forms of matter to God himself; this view of the universe, in turn, goes back to both classical and Judaeo-Christian doctrines. Modern philosophers have cast off these metaphysical and religious shackles and freely invoke the dignity of mankind without needing to justify the idea at all. Why should we not attribute 'intrinsic dignity' or 'intrinsic worth' to ourselves? Fellow humans are unlikely to reject the accolades we so generously bestow on them, and those to whom we deny the honour are unable to object. Indeed, when one thinks only of humans, it can be very liberal, very progressive, to talk of the dignity of all human beings. In so doing, we implicitly condemn slavery, racism, and other violations of human rights. We admit that we ourselves are in some fundamental sense on a par with the poorest, most ignorant members of our own species. It is only when we think of humans as no more than a small subgroup of all the beings that inhabit our planet that we may realize that in elevating our own species we are at the same time lowering the relative status of all other species.

The truth is that the appeal to the intrinsic dignity of human beings appears to solve the egalitarian's problems only as long as it goes unchallenged. Once we ask *why* it should be that all humans – including infants, mental defectives, psychopaths, Hitler, Stalin, and the rest – have some kind of dignity or worth that no elephant, pig, or chimpanzee can ever achieve, we see that this question is as difficult to answer as our original request for some relevant fact that justifies the inequality of humans and other animals. In fact, these two questions are really one: talk of intrinsic dignity or moral worth only takes the problem back one step, because any satisfactory defence of the claim that all and only humans have intrinsic dignity would need to refer to some relevant capacities or characteristics that all and only humans possess. Philosophers frequently introduce ideas of dignity, respect, and worth at the point at which other reasons appear to be lacking, but this is hardly good enough. Fine phrases are the last resource of those who have run out of arguments.

232

Notes

1   *The Methods of Ethics* (7th edn.), p. 382.
2   For example, R. M. Hare, *Freedom and Reason* (Oxford: Clarendon Press, 1963) and J. Rawls, *A Theory of Justice* (Cambridge, Mass.: Harvard University Press, 1972); for a brief account of the essential agreement on this issue between these and other positions, see R. M. Hare, 'Rules of war and moral reasoning', *Philosophy and Public Affairs* 1 (1972).
3   *Introduction to the Principles of Morals and Legislation*, ch. XVII.
4   I owe the term 'speciesism' to Richard Ryder.
5   In order to product 1 lb. of protein in the form of beef or veal, we must feed 21 lb. of protein to the animal. Other forms of livestock are slightly less inefficient, but the average ratio in the US is still 1 : 8. It has been estimated that the amount of protein lost to humans in this way is equivalent to 90 per cent of the annual world protein deficit. For a brief account, see Frances Moor Lappé, *Diet for a Small Planet* (New York: Friends of The Earth/Ballantine, 1971), pp. 4–11.
6   Although one might think that killing a being is obviously the ultimate wrong one can do to it, I think that the infliction of suffering is a clearer indication of speciesism because it might be argued that at least part of what is wrong with killing a human is that most humans are conscious of their existence over time, and have desires and purposes that extend into the future – see, for instance, M. Tooley, 'Abortion and infanticide', *Philosophy and Public Affairs* 1 (1972). Of course, if one took this view one would have to hold – as Tooley does – that killing a human infant or mental defective is not in itself wrong, and is less serious than killing certain higher mammals that probably do have a sense of their own existence over time.
7   Ruth Harrison, *Animal Machines* (London 1964). For an account of farming conditions, see my *Animal Liberation* (New York: Cape, 1975).
8   In R. Brandt (ed.) *Social Justice* (Englewood Cliffs, NJ: Prentice Hall, 1962), p. 19.
9   Frankena, in Brandt, *Social Justice*, p. 23.
10   H. A. Bedau, 'Egalitarianism and the idea of equality' in J. R. Pennock and J. W. Chapman (eds) *Nomos IX: Equality*, New York, 1967.
11   G. Vlastos, 'Justice and equality' in Brandt, *Social Justice*, p. 48.

The external world

26
About the things we may doubt
René Descartes

You may feel sure that you are sitting reading these words now. But couldn't even this basic belief be mistaken? Perhaps an evil demon is deliberately and cunningly manipulating your sensory input; perhaps you are really just wired up to a sophisticated virtual reality machine and what looks like a book in front of you is really nothing more than a series of electrical impulses sent directly into your brain. How do you even know that you have a body at all? These questions and ideas might seem far-fetched, but they force you to think about the limits of what you know. They are the sorts of questions that René Descartes asked himself in his *Meditations* (1642), an extract from which is printed here (the whole of the First Meditation and part of the Second is included). He pushed sceptical doubts to the limit, but claimed to have discovered one kind of thought that was immune from all doubt. For an interesting discussion of the nature and importance of Descartes's work, see reading after this one, 'Descartes'.

From René Descartes, *Meditations*

First Meditation

About the things we may doubt

It is some time ago now since I perceived that, from my earliest years, I had accepted many false opinions as being true, and that what I had since based on such insecure principles could only be most doubtful and uncertain; so that I had to undertake seriously once in my life to rid myself of all the opinions I had adopted up to then, and to begin afresh from the foundations, if I wished to establish something firm and constant in the sciences. But as this undertaking seemed to me very great, I waited until

I had attained an age sufficiently mature that I could not hope, at a later stage in life, to be more fit to execute my plan; and this has made me delay so long that I should henceforth consider that I was committing a fault if I were still to use in deliberation the time which remains to me for action.

Now therefore, that my mind is free from all cares, and that I have obtained for myself assured leisure in peaceful solitude, I shall apply myself seriously and freely to the general destruction of all my former opinions. Now it will not be necessary, in order to accomplish this aim, to prove that they are all false, a point which perhaps I would never reach; but inasmuch as reason persuades me already that I must avoid believing things which are not entirely certain and indubitable, no less carefully than those things which seem manifestly false, the slightest ground for doubt that I find in any, will suffice for me to reject all of them. And to this end there will be no need for me to examine each one individually, which would be an endless task; but because the destruction of the foundations necessarily brings down with it the rest of the edifice, I shall make an assault first on the principles on which all my former opinions were based.

Everything I have accepted up to now as being absolutely true and assured, I have learned from or through the senses. But I have sometimes found that these senses played me false, and it is prudent never to trust entirely those who have once deceived us.

But, although the senses sometimes deceive us, concerning things which are barely perceptible or at a great distance, there are perhaps many other things about which one cannot reasonably doubt, although we know them through the medium of the senses, for example, that I am here, sitting by the fire, wearing a dressing-gown, with this paper in my hands, and other things of this nature. And how could I deny that these hands and this body belong to me, unless perhaps I were to assimilate myself to those insane persons whose minds are so troubled and clouded by the black vapours of the bile that they constantly assert that they are kings, when they are very poor; that they are wearing gold and purple, when they are quite naked; or who imagine that they are pitchers or that they have a body of glass? But these are madmen, and I would not be less extravagant if I were to follow their example.

However, I must here consider that I am a man, and consequently that I am in the habit of sleeping and of representing to myself in my dreams those same things, or sometimes even less likely things, which insane people do when they are awake. How many times have I dreamt at night that I was in this place, dressed by the fire, although I was quite naked in my bed? It certainly seems to me at the moment that I am not looking at this paper with my eyes closed; that this head that I shake is not asleep; that I hold out this hand intentionally and deliberately, and that I am aware of it. What happens in sleep does not seem as clear and distinct as all this. But in thinking about it carefully, I recall having often been deceived in sleep by similar illusions, and, reflecting on this circumstance more closely, I see so clearly that there are no conclusive signs by means of which one can distinguish clearly between being awake and being asleep, that I am quite astonished by it; and my astonishment is such that it is almost capable of persuading me that I am asleep now.

Let us suppose, then, that we are now asleep, and that all these particulars, namely, that we open our eyes, move our heads, hold out our hands, and such like actions, are only false illusions; and let us think that perhaps our hands and all our body are not as we see them. Nevertheless, we must at least admit that the things which appear to us in sleep are, as it were, pictures and paintings which can only be formed in the likeness of something real and true; and that therefore these general things at least, namely, eyes, head, hands and all the rest of the body are not imaginary things but are real and existent. For indeed painters, even when they study with the utmost skill to represent Sirens and Satyrs by strange and extraordinary shapes, cannot attribute to them entirely new forms and natures, but only make a certain mixture and compound of the limbs of various animals; or if perhaps their imagination is extravagant enough to invent something so new that we have never seen the like of it, and that, in this way, their work presents us with something purely fictitious and absolutely false, at least the colours of which they have composed it are real. And by the same reasoning, although these general things, viz. eyes, head, hands and the like, may be imaginary, we have to admit that there are even simpler and more universal things which are true and exist, from the mixture of which, no more or less than from the mixture of certain real colours, all the images of things, whether true and real or fictitious and fantastic, which dwell in our thoughts, are formed. Corporeal nature in general, and its extension, are of this class of things: together with the figure of extended things, their quantity or size, and their number, as also the place where they are, the time during which they exist, and such like.

This is why perhaps that, from this, we shall not be wrong in concluding that physics, astronomy, medicine, and all the other sciences which depend on the consideration of composite things, are most doubtful and uncertain, but that arithmetic, geometry and the other sciences of this nature, which deal only with very simple and general things, without bothering about their existence or non-existence, contain something certain and indubitable. For whether I am awake or sleeping, two and three added together always make five, and a square never has more than four sides; and it does not seem possible that truths so apparent can be suspected of any falsity or uncertainty.

Nevertheless, I have for a long time had in my mind the belief that there is a God who is all-powerful and by whom I was created and made as I am. And who can give me the assurance that this God has not arranged that there should be no earth, no heaven, no extended body, no figure, no magnitude, or place, and that nevertheless I should have the perception of all these things, and the persuasion that they do not exist other than as I see them? And, further, as I sometimes think that others are mistaken, even in the things they think they know most certainly, it is possible that God has wished that I should be deceived every time I add two and three or count the sides of a square, or form some judgement even simpler, if anything simpler than that can be imagined. But perhaps God has not wished me to be deceived in this way, for he is said to be supremely good. However, if it were in contradiction to his goodness to have made me in such a way that I always deceived myself, it would seem also to be contrary to his goodness to allow me to be wrong sometimes, and nevertheless it is beyond doubt that he permits it.

There will be some perhaps who would prefer to deny the existence of a God so powerful than to believe that all other things are uncertain. But let us not oppose them for the moment, and let us suppose in their favour that everything said here about a God is a fable. Nevertheless, however they suppose that I reached the state and being which I possess, whether they attribute it to some destiny or fate, or to chance or to a continuous sequence and conjunction of events, it is certain that, because fallibility and error are a kind of imperfection, the less powerful the author to whom they attribute my origin, the more probable it will be that I am so imperfect as to be deceived all the time. I have certainly nothing to say in reply to such reasonings, but am constrained to avow that, of all the opinions that I once accepted as true, there is not one which is not now legitimately open to doubt, not through any lack of reflection or lightness of judgement, but for very strong and deeply considered reasons; so that if I wish to find anything certain and assured in the sciences, I must from now on check and suspend judgement on these opinions and refrain from giving them more credence than I would do to things which appeared to me manifestly false.

But it is not enough to have made these observations; I must also take care to remember them; for those old and customary opinions still recur often in my mind, long and familiar usage giving them the right to occupy my mind against my will and, as it were, to dominate my mind. And I shall never rid myself of the habit of acquiescing in them and of having confidence in them so long as I look upon them as what in fact they are, that is to say, in some degree doubtful, as I have just shown, and yet highly probable, so that it is more reasonable to believe than to deny them. This is why I think I shall proceed more prudently if, taking an opposite course, I endeavour to deceive myself, pretending that all these opinions are false and imaginary, until, having so balanced my prejudices that they may not make my judgement incline more to one side than to another, my judgement may no longer be overpowered as hitherto by bad usage and turned from the right path which can lead it to the knowledge of truth. For I am assured that, meanwhile, there can be no danger or error in this course, and that, for the present, it would be impossible to press my distrust too far, for it is not now action I seek as my end but simply meditation and knowledge.

I shall suppose, therefore, that there is, not a true God, who is the sovereign source of truth, but some evil demon, no less cunning and deceiving than powerful, who has used all his artifice to deceive me. I will suppose that the heavens, the air, the earth, colours, shapes, sounds and all external things that we see, are only illusions and deceptions which he uses to take me in. I will consider myself as having no hands, eyes, flesh, blood or senses, but as believing wrongly that I have all these things. I shall cling obstinately to this notion; and if, by this means, it is not in my power to arrive at the knowledge of any truth, at the very least it is in my power to suspend my judgement. This is why I shall take great care not to accept into my belief anything false, and shall so well prepare my mind against all the tricks of this great deceiver that, however powerful and cunning he may be, he will never be able to impose on me.

But this undertaking is arduous, and a certain indolence leads me back imperceptibly into the ordinary course of life. And just as a slave who was enjoying in his sleep an imaginary freedom, fears to be awakened when he begins to suspect that his liberty is only a dream, and conspires with these pleasant illusions to be deceived by them longer, so I fall back of my own accord into my former opinions, and fear to awake from this slumber lest the laborious wakeful hours which would follow this peaceful rest, instead of bringing me any light of day into the knowledge of truth, would not be sufficient to disperse the shadows caused by the difficulties which have just been raised.

Second Meditation

Of the nature of the human mind; and that it is easier to know than the body

The Meditation of yesterday has filled my mind with so many doubts that it is no longer in my power to forget them. And yet I do not see how I shall be able to resolve them; and, as though I had suddenly fallen into very deep water, I am so taken unawares that I can neither put my feet firmly down on the bottom nor swim to keep myself on the surface. I make an effort, nevertheless, and follow afresh the same path upon which I entered yesterday, in keeping away from everything of which I can conceive the slightest doubt, just as if I knew that it was absolutely false;

and I shall continue always in this path until I have encountered something which is certain, or at least, if I can do nothing else, until I have learned with certainty that there is nothing certain in the world.

Archimedes, in order to take the terrestrial globe from its place and move it to another, asked only for a point which was fixed and assured. So also, I shall have the right to entertain high hopes, if I am fortunate enough to find only one thing which is certain and indubitable.

I suppose therefore that all the things I see are false; I persuade myself that none of those things ever existed that my deceptive memory represents to me; I suppose I have no senses; I believe that body, figure, extension, movement and place are only fictions of my mind. What then, shall be considered true? Perhaps only this, that there is nothing certain in the world.

But how do I know there is not some other thing, different from those I have just judged to be uncertain, about which one could not have the slightest doubt? Is there not a God, or some other power, which puts these thoughts into my mind? But that is unnecessary, for perhaps I am capable of producing them myself. Myself, then, at least am I not something? But I have already denied that I have any senses or any body. I hesitate however, for what follows from that? Am I so dependent on body and senses that I cannot exist without them? But I had persuaded myself that there was nothing at all in the world: no sky, no earth, no minds or bodies; was I not, therefore, also persuaded that I did not exist? No indeed; I existed without doubt, by the fact that I was persuaded, or indeed by the mere fact that I thought at all. But there is some deceiver both very powerful and very cunning, who constantly uses all his wiles to deceive me. There is therefore no doubt that I exist, if he deceives me; and let him deceive me as much as he likes, he can never cause me to be nothing, so long as I think I am something. So that, after having thought carefully about it, and having scrupulously examined everything, one must then, in conclusion, take as assured that the proposition: *I am, I exist*, is necessarily true, every time I express it or conceive of it in my mind.

But I, who am certain that I am, do not yet know clearly enough what I am; so that henceforth I must take great care not imprudently to take some other object for myself, and thus avoid going astray in this knowledge which I maintain to be more certain and evident than all I have had hitherto.

For this reason, I shall now consider afresh what I thought I was before I entered into these last thoughts; and I shall retrench from my former opinions everything that can be invalidated by the reasons I have already put forward, so that absolutely nothing remains except that which is entirely indubitable. What, then, did I formerly think I was? I thought I was a man. But what is a man? Shall I say rational animal?

No indeed: for it would be necessary next to inquire what is meant by animal, and what by rational, and, in this way, from one single question, we would fall unwittingly into an infinite number of others, more difficult and awkward than the first, and I would not wish to waste the little time and leisure remaining to me by using it to unravel subtleties of this kind. But I shall rather stop to consider here the thoughts which sprang up hitherto spontaneously in my mind, and which were inspired by my own nature alone, when I applied myself to the consideration of my being. I considered myself, firstly, as having a face, hands, arms, and the whole machine made up of flesh and bones, such as it appears in a corpse and which I designated by the name of body. I thought, furthermore, that I ate, walked, had feelings and thought, and I referred all these actions to the soul; but I did not stop to consider what this soul was, or at least, if I did, I imagined it was something extremely rare and subtle, like a wind, flame or vapour, which permeated and spread through my most substantial parts. As far as the body was concerned, I was in no doubt as to its nature, for I thought I knew it quite distinctly, and, if I had wished to explain it according to the notions I had of it, I would have described it in this way: by body, I understand all that can be terminated by some figure; that can be contained in some place and fill a space in such a way that any other body is excluded from it; that can be perceived, either by touch, sight, hearing, taste or smell; that can be moved in many ways, not of itself, but by something foreign to it by which it is touched and from which it receives the impulse. For as to having in itself the power to move, to feel and to think, I did not believe in any way that these advantages might be attributed to corporeal nature; on the contrary, I was somewhat astonished to see that such faculties were to be found in certain bodies.

But as to myself, who am I, now that I suppose there is someone who is extremely powerful and, if I may so say, malicious and cunning, who employs all his efforts and industry to deceive me? Can I be sure of having the least of all the characteristics that I have attributed above to the nature of bodies? I pause to think about it carefully, I turn over all these things in my mind, and I cannot find one of which I can say that it is in me. There is no need for me to stop and enumerate them. Let us pass, then, to the attributes of the soul, and see if there are any of these in me. The first are eating and walking; but if it is true that I have no body, it is true also that I cannot walk or eat. Sensing is another attribute, but again this is impossible without the body; besides, I have frequently believed that I perceived in my sleep many things which I observed, on awakening, I had not in reality perceived. Another attribute is thinking, and I here discover an attribute which does belong to me; this alone cannot be detached from me. *I am, I exist*: this is certain; but for how long? For as long as I think, for it might perhaps happen, if I ceased to think, that I would at the same time cease to be or to exist. I now admit nothing which is not necessarily true: I am therefore, precisely speaking, only a thing which thinks, that is to say, a mind, understanding, or reason, terms whose significance was hitherto unknown to me.

27

Descartes

Bernard Williams and

Bryan Magee

This is a transcript from the BBC television series *The Great Philosophers*. Here Bernard Williams (1929–) in conversation with Bryan Magee (1930–) gives a clear and illuminating account of Descartes's thought, its context and its relevance.

From *The Great Philosophers*, edited by Bryan Magee

Introduction

Magee When the term 'Modern Philosophy' is used in universities it is normally to make the distinction from Ancient and Medieval Philosophy. So it does not mean the philosophy of the twentieth century; it means philosophy since the Reformation. In fact, there is one man who is generally, and I think rightly, regarded as the inaugurator of modern philosophy: Descartes. In clearer terms, then, what the term 'Modern Philosophy' means is 'philosophy from Descartes onwards'.

René Descartes was born in France in 1596. He received an unusually good education, but he also had unusual independence of mind, and while still a student he perceived that the various authorities he was studying often put forward arguments that were invalid. As a young man he became a soldier, and travelled widely in Europe, though without seeing any fighting; and he was struck by the fact that the world of practical life was as full of contradictions as the world of books. He became fascinated by the question whether there was any way at all in which we human beings could get to know anything for certain, and if so how. He stopped travelling, and went into seclusion in Holland, the country in which intellectual life in those days was at its freest. And there, during the twenty years from 1629 to 1649, he produced work of the profoundest originality in mathematics and philosophy and also did a great deal of work in science. (Philosophy and science had not yet been clearly demarcated, and were not to be so until the eighteenth century.) He invented the branch of mathematics known as co-ordinate geometry. It was his idea to measure the position of a point by its distance from two fixed lines – so every time we look at a graph we are looking at something invented by Descartes. In fact, those two familiar lines on a graph are known by his name: 'Cartesian axes', 'Cartesian' being the adjective from 'Descartes'. His most famous works of philosophy are *Discourse on the Method*, which was published in 1637, and *Meditations*, published in 1642.

Descartes never married, though he had an illegitimate daughter who died at the age of five: her death was the greatest emotional blow of his life. He always had an eye to dress, was proud of being an officer, and on the whole preferred the company of men of affairs to that of scholars. However, during the years of his creative work he lived a very solitary life. But when he was fifty-three he was prevailed on by Queen Christina of Sweden, against his will, to go to Stockholm and become her tutor in philosophy. It was a deadly mistake. In the bitter Swedish winter he succumbed to pneumonia, and he died in the following year, 1650.

With me to discuss the first of modern philosophers is Bernard Williams, Professor of Philosophy at the University of California, Berkeley, and author of one of the best-known books on Descartes.

Discussion

Magee I think the best way for us to begin is to get our minds clear about the position from which Descartes started. What, when he began, did he see as his main problem?

Williams Because of the education you referred to, and his experience of the life around him, he had been impressed with the idea that there was no certain way of acquiring knowledge. It looked as though there were some sorts of knowledge around, but there was no reliable method by which people could advance knowledge. To put the situation in a historical context, it is important to realise that science in our sense really didn't exist: there was no science as an organised international enterprise, with research methods and laboratories and so on. Moreover, there was room for a great range of opinions about what chances there might be of there being a science. On the one hand there were people, perfectly sensible people, who thought that if you found the right method you could solve all the fundamental problems of understanding nature in a short while. For instance, Francis Bacon, the English statesman, thought that it should be possible to get science on the right road in a very brief period. On the other hand there were people, sceptical people, who thought that there wasn't going to be any knowledge, that there could be no rational way of organising inquiry.

One important reason why there was so much scepticism around stemmed from the religious Reformation. After the Reformation, all sorts of claims were made about how religious truth might be found. These claims conflicted with one another, and there was no way of deciding between them. This gave rise to a great deal of controversy, and one thing that was said, particularly by enemies of religion, was that there was no way of solving any of these questions: there were all these disagreements, and no way of resolving them. Religious people, reacting against that, said in turn that religion was no different in this from any-thing else. There was no way of putting *anything* on a firm foundation. Scepticism was thus an important current in the intellectual climate of Descartes's time, coexisting in an odd way with very extravagant hopes of what science might be able to do, in particular through what we would now call technology. For instance, there were great hopes that there could be a scientific medicine, and a scientific industry, and so on. But nobody knew how to do it.

Magee For so fundamental a would-be innovator as Descartes the insti-tutions of his day must also have presented severe problems. Almost every serious institution of learning or teaching was in the hands of an authori-tarian Church whose own intellectual leaders were in thrall to ancient authority.

Williams That is certainly true. Of course there were many different reli-gious influences, as I just said. One effect of the Reformation had been that some seats of learning had more of a Protestant complexion, while others such as those in Descartes's own Paris were Catholic. But of course the point you mentioned about authority is very important. Although there had been a good deal of research into what we would now call mechanics, or a kind of mathematical physics, in the Middle Ages – and we shouldn't forget that fact – a great deal of what passed for knowledge took the form of commentaries on ancient books, above all (though not exclusively) those of Aristotle. And one thing that Descartes and others of his generation knew for certain was that historical authority was not the same thing as first-order research or inquiry.

Magee Perhaps one can sum it up by saying that Descartes saw his problem as how to find a safe way *out* of this situation. The crucial ques-tion was, did a reliable method exist, at least in principle, for getting knowledge and for accumulating knowledge? If it did, what was it? In modern parlance one could say that his quest was for a research programme – and prior to that, a research method.

Williams Yes, I think that's a correct description of the situation. However, there is one further fact that conditions all of his work and is very important – that science was not conceived as a shared or joint or organised enterprise as it is now. For us it's just taken for granted that science means scientists, a lot of people who communicate with one another, and among whom there's a division of intellectual labour. At that time, the first half of the seventeenth century, it was still a reasonable project for one man to have the idea that he could lay the foundations of all future science. Descartes did really believe that, and it was not a piece of megalomaniac insanity on his part, as it would be in the modern world for anybody to have that idea.

Magee In my introduction to this discussion I said that Descartes became fascinated by the question of whether there was anything we could know for certain. He was clear from the outset that certainty and truth are not the same thing. To put it crudely, certainty is a state of mind, whereas truth is a property of statements which usually relates to the way things are out there in the external world. But Descartes believed that only if you had grounds for certainty could you know you had hold of the truth; and therefore that the pursuit of truth *involves* the pursuit of certainty. This meant that he thought from the beginning that the method he was looking for would have to be one which not only delivered the goods in the form of worthwhile conclusions but could also defend itself successfully against the arguments of sceptics. Now how did he go about meeting that double-barrelled requirement?

Williams Descartes had a set of conditions on inquiry. Some of them were just sensible rules about dividing questions up into manageable parts, trying to get your ideas clear, and things like that. But he had also a rule, very characteristic of his thought, that you shouldn't accept as true anything about which you could entertain the slightest doubt. Now, on the face of it that isn't a sensible rule, because in ordinary life we're constantly seeking true beliefs about things, but we don't necessarily want to make those beliefs as certain as we could make them. But Descartes was trying to get the foundations of science: not only the foundations of *a* science, in the sense of fundamental general truths about the world, but also the foundations of inquiry. He wanted to lay the foundations of the possibility of going on to find out more things, and to establish that scientific knowledge was actually possible. To do this, he felt that it was essential that you should start the search for truth with a search for certainty.

He wanted to put the scientific enterprise (as we might call it) into a shape in which it could no longer be attacked by sceptics. So the first thing he wanted to do was to engage in what we might call *pre-emptive scepticism.* In order to put the foundations of knowledge beyond the reach of scepticism he said to himself, in effect: 'I will do everything the sceptics can do, only better. By pressing the sceptical inquiry hard enough, I hope to come out the other side with something that will be absolutely foundational and rock hard.'

It is not that Descartes confused the idea of looking for truth and the idea of looking for certainty. He saw that they were two separate things. But he thought that the right way of searching for truth and, above all, of making the search for truth into a systematic process, was to start by searching for certainty.

Magee This led to the famous 'Cartesian doubt', didn't it – *doubt as method*. This is not the method referred to in the title *Discourse on the Method*, though it is an important part of it. Can you explain how Descartes's methodological doubt worked?

Williams Since he was looking for certainty, he started by laying aside anything in which he could find the slightest doubt. As he famously put it, it's like having a barrel of apples, and some of them are bad and some of them are sound, and you want to separate out the sound ones. So you take them all out first, look at them one by one, throw away the ones that are dubious and put back only the absolutely sound ones. So he started by trying to empty his mind of all beliefs, laying aside anything in which he could see the slightest doubt.

He did that in three stages. He started by laying aside things that just on ordinary commonsensical grounds you might possibly find doubtful. For instance he reminded himself of such well-known facts as that straight sticks can look bent in water or that things may look curious colours to you if you have defects of eyesight, and so on. But he wanted to go beyond those everyday kinds of doubt or grounds of doubt that apply to some of the things we perceive. The next step was to doubt that at any given moment he was awake and perceiving anything at all. He entertained the following thought. He had often dreamt in the past that he was perceiving things, and when he was dreaming, he had thought, just as he does now, that he was seeing people, or tables, or whatever, around him. But, of course, he had woken up and found it was all illusion. Now: how can he be certain at this very instant that he is not dreaming? That is an unnerving kind of sceptical consideration. It had been used by sceptics before, but he gave it an orderly and settled place in his inquiry. Now of course the doubt based on dreaming does depend upon knowing *something*. It depends upon knowing that in the past you have sometimes woken up and found you had been dreaming; it depends on the idea that sometimes you sleep, sometimes you wake, sometimes you dream, and so on. So it does depend on knowing something about the world.

But then he took another step, to the most extreme doubt possible. He imagined a malign spirit (the *malicious demon*, as it's sometimes called in the literature) whose sole intent was to deceive him as much as it could. He then put to himself the following question: suppose there were such a spirit, is there anything he could not mislead me about? This is, of course, a pure thought-experiment. We must emphasise that Descartes never meant this philosophical doubt to be a tool for everyday living. He makes that point over and over again. The Method of Doubt, and particularly the fantasy or model of the evil spirit, is used only as a form of intellectual critique to winnow out his beliefs, and see whether some were more certain than others.

Magee   And of course the ultimate purpose – his long-range strategy in winnowing out everything that he could possibly, in any imaginable circumstances, doubt – is to find rock-hard, indubitable propositions which can then function as the premisses for arguments, thus providing unshakeable foundations on which an edifice of knowledge can be built.

Williams   That's right. There are in fact two things. He wants to find rock-hard indubitable propositions, that is to say propositions which in some sense cannot be doubted, which will resist the most extreme doubt. He wants them in part as premisses of arguments. He also wants them in a more general role, to provide a background that will validate the methods of inquiry I was referring to before, and we can perhaps say something about how that works.

Magee   But meanwhile we have left the ball in the court of the malicious demon, and we must somehow get it back. After peeling away all imaginably doubtable propositions, Descartes found there were some things that it was simply impossible not to be sure of. Will you tell us what they were?

Williams   The doubt reaches a turning point; it gets to the end, and Descartes does a U-turn and starts coming back, constructing knowledge as he goes. The point at which the doubt stops is the reflection that he is himself engaged in thinking. As he said, the malicious demon can deceive me as he will, but he can never deceive me in this respect, namely to make me believe that I am thinking when I am not. If I have a false thought that is still a thought: in order to have a deceived thought, I've got to have a thought, so it must be true that I am thinking. And from that Descartes drew another conclusion, or at least he immediately associated with that another truth, namely that he existed. And so his fundamental first certainty was 'I am thinking, therefore I exist;' or *Cogito ergo sum* in the Latin formulation, from which it is often called simply the *Cogito*.

Magee It's worth stressing the point – which Descartes himself made clear – that by 'thinking' he meant not only conceptual thought but all forms of conscious experience, including feelings, perceptions, pains and so on. This being so, it's not unfair to say that what he was really saying was: 'I am consciously aware, therefore I know that I must exist.'

Williams That's right. In the great work called *Meditations* in which this is most carefully and elaborately set out, he does actually show a great deal of finesse in pushing the boundaries of the *Cogito* forward step by step through various kinds of mental experience. But the sum of what he gets to is exactly that, yes.

Magee Now in the very process of arriving at these fundamental and indubitable propositions Descartes has shown that although we can be certain of them, any inference we may make from them is liable to error, and therefore nothing indubitable *follows* from them. For instance, I cannot doubt that I am at this moment having the experience of seeing you, Bernard Williams, as being, among other things, a material object out there in the external world, but from that it does not follow that there is a world external to myself with material objects existing in it independently of my experience. And the same argument applies right across the board. Although I can always be certain that the immediate deliverances of my consciousness are whatever they are, I can never be certain of the validity of any inference I make from them to something else.

Williams Well, it depends on what sort of inference it is. What he thought was that the mere fact that I have the experience of being confronted with this table, for instance, doesn't guarantee the existence of the table. That certainty was removed even at the dream state of the doubt, and it is made even clearer when Descartes invokes the malicious demon. Using that model, he sees that he might have just this experience and yet nothing actually be there. So one cannot immediately infer the actual world from one's experience. What Descartes tries to do now is to construct a set of considerations that will enable him to put the world back – though it must be said straight away that the form in which the world is put back is rather different from that in which it was originally conceived by common sense. Having moved all the furniture out of the attic in the course of the doubt, we don't simply stuff it all back again in a totally unreconstructed form. We have a different view of the world when we reconstitute it than we did in our original unreflective experience. It is a very important fact about the Method of Doubt that this is so. Descartes conducts the doubt for positive reasons, and when he puts the world back, it has been subtly modified by an intellectual critique of how we can know things. But the question now is how he puts it back.

251

Magee He seems, in arriving at his indubitable propositions, to have painted himself into a corner. He has his indubitable propositions all right, but in the process of reaching them he has shown that nothing can be inferred from them.

Williams Well, all he's seen at the earlier stage of the proceedings is that the most obvious way of inferring the world from his experiences isn't valid. He's now going to give you a way which he claims is valid. Having got to the point at which he recognises nothing except the contents of his consciousness, it is obvious that if he's going to put the world back he's got to do it entirely out of the contents of his consciousness – there is nothing else available to him. So he's got to find something in the contents of his consciousness that leads outside himself. He claims that what this is is the idea of God. He discovers among the contents of his consciousness the conception of God. And he argues that this is unique among all the ideas that he has; among all the things that are in his mind, this alone is such that the mere fact that he has this idea proves that there really is something corresponding to it, that is to say, there really is a God.

Magee That's a difficult argument for modern readers to swallow including those who believe in God.

Williams Yes. In fact he has two different arguments, both of which he uses in *Meditations*, for doing this. One is a medieval argument called the ontological argument; perhaps we needn't spend time on that. It presents a logical or metaphysical puzzle, but it's much less characteristic of Descartes. The other argument is more characteristic of Descartes, though it also uses scholastic or medieval materials. It relies on a supposedly necessary principle to the effect that the lesser cannot give rise to, or be the cause of, the greater. Descartes is sure that he has an idea of God, and that idea is the idea of an infinite thing. Although in itself it's only an idea, the fact that it is the idea of an infinite thing demands a very special explanation. Descartes claims that no finite creature, as he knows himself to be, could possibly have given rise to such an idea, the idea of an infinite being. It could have been implanted in him only by God himself: as Descartes memorably puts it at one point, as the mark of the maker on his work. God, as it were, signed him by leaving in him this infinite idea of God himself. When he reflects that the lesser cannot give rise to the greater, he realises that since he has this idea of God, it can be only because there actually is a God who has created him.

Magee And having derived the certainty of God's existence from the deliverances of his own consciousness, he then proceeds to derive the certainty of the existence of the external world from his certainty of God's existence.

Williams   That's right. He next considers what he knows about this God. He reflects in the following way: I know that God exists, that he's omnipotent, that he created me, and I know that he's benevolent. (These are of course all traditional Christian beliefs.) Because God created me and is benevolent, he is concerned as much with my intellectual welfare as with my moral welfare. And what that means is that if I do my bit – and that's very important – and I clarify my ideas as much as I should, and I don't assent precipitately to things I haven't thought out properly; if I do my bit in that sense, then God will validate the things which I am then very strongly disposed to believe. Now I find that however much criticism I make of my ideas, however carefully I think out what is involved in my beliefs about the physical world, although I can suspend judgment in the doubt (I wouldn't have got to this point if I couldn't), I do have a very strong tendency to believe that there is a material world there. And since I have this disposition and I have done everything in my power to make sure that my beliefs are not founded on error, then God will at the end make sure that I am not fundamentally and systematically mistaken. That is, I can rightfully believe that there is such a world.

Magee   This becomes, doesn't it, Descartes's way of refuting anyone who is radically sceptical about the possibilities of philosophy or science? But in asserting that the world with which they deal is given to us by a God whose existence and benevolence are self-evident he has not so much answered the sceptic as tried to pre-empt him.

Williams   Well, it is essential to his position that he believes that these arguments that introduce God will be assented to by any person of good faith, who concentrates on them enough. That's *absolutely* essential. It would ruin his whole position if he accepted the idea that whether you believe in God is a matter of culture or psychological upbringing, and that perfectly sensible people can disagree about whether there's a God or not however hard they think about it. For Descartes, to deny the existence of God when confronted with these arguments would be as perverse and as totally in bad faith as it would be to deny that twice two is four. The idea is that if you put these proofs before the sceptic and lead him properly through them, and if the sceptic is an honest person, and is not just mouthing words or trying to impress, he must at the end assent. Some people have not assented because they haven't thought hard enough; they have not treated these questions in an orderly manner. A lot of the sceptics are no doubt fakes, who simply go around making a rhetorical position and don't really think about it. But if you're in good faith and think hard enough about it, then you will come to see this truth and then you cannot consistently deny the existence of the external world. That's what Descartes believed.

Magee   One historically important outcome of this set of arguments was the positing of a world consisting of two different sorts of entity. There is the external world, given to me by a God on whom I can rely. But there is also me, observing the external world. Now in arriving at the *Cogito* I found it possible to think away from my conception of myself everything except this very act of thought itself – and this, said Descartes, means that I must irreducibly *be* thought. I can conceive of myself as existing without a body, but I cannot conceive of myself as existing without conscious awareness; so the material which is my body is not part of the quintessential me. This chimes, of course, with the traditional Christian view, held for quite different reasons. And it leads straight to a view of the world as split between subjects which are pure thought and objects which are pure extension. This is the famous 'Cartesian dualism', the bifurcation of nature between mind and matter, observer and observed, subject and object. It has become built into the whole of Western man's way of looking at things, including the whole of our science.

Williams   In many ways that is true. At the extreme point of the doubt, Descartes can be said to think that the external world may not exist. But the 'external world' is a phrase that has many things packed into it. The 'external world' is outside what? – outside *me*. But 'outside me' does not mean 'outside my body'. My body is part of the external world, in Descartes's sense: it is itself one of the things outside me. In the end, when through knowledge of God the external world has been restored, I indeed get my body back. It then turns out that I indeed *have* a body. But it never turns out that I *am* a body. What I ordinarily call *me*, according to Descartes, is actually two things: on the one hand, an immaterial – and he also believed immortal – soul, which, as you say, was purely intellectual, purely mental, had no physical extension at all; and, on the other, a body. It follows that when in ordinary life we talk about ourselves in the first person we happily put together statements of quite different kinds. One can say to somebody else quite cheerfully, 'I am embarrassed, I am thinking about Paris, and I weigh a hundred and fifty pounds.' For Descartes, that's just what the grammarians used to call a zeugma – I'm actually talking about two quite different things. When I say I'm thinking about Paris, that's a statement about my mind – that is to say, according to Descartes, about what is really *me*. When I say I weigh a hundred and fifty pounds, that's only a way of speaking –

Magee   – about your body, which is not *you*, really, at all.

Williams That's right. An American philosopher put it well: in Descartes's view, to say 'I weigh a hundred and fifty pounds' is much like saying 'on the way here I had a puncture'.

Magee At the beginning we said that Descartes's strategic aim was to establish the possibility of what we now call science; and you have shown us the arguments by which he arrived at his particular view of the external world. How is that a world that can be treated scientifically?

Williams I mentioned earlier that when through the help of God we put the world back again, we didn't put back the same world that we'd thrown away; it has been criticised in the process. In our reflections we come to the conclusion not only that there is an external world, but that, just as thought is my essence as a thinking thing, so the external world, too, has an essence and that is simply extension. All there is to it essentially is that it takes up space and that it is susceptible to being treated by geometry and the mathematical sciences. All its more colourful aspects – the fact that it *is* coloured, and that there are tastes and sounds – are really subjective. They're on the mental side; they are subjective phenomena that occur in consciousness, caused by this physical, extended, geometrical world.

Magee He had a striking example of the essential separateness from a continuing substance of all its sense-dependent properties, an example well worth citing. Pick up in your hand, he says, a piece of wax. It has a certain size and shape, a certain solid feel to the hand, a certain texture, temperature, colour, smell and so on; and to us it seems to be the combination of those properties. But if you put it in front of the fire every single one of them changes: it becomes liquid, falls into a different shape, gets hotter, turns dark brown, gives off a different smell, and so on and so forth. Yet we still want to say it's the same wax. What is there about it that's the same? Surely, there is now *nothing* about it that is the same? Answer: yes there is, namely one and the same continuous history of space-occupancy. And this is measurable jointly in terms of space and of time. And both forms of measurement are essentially mathematical.

Williams Yes. It is disputed what exactly Descartes thought the wax argument proved, just by itself. But he certainly used that example to illustrate, if not actually to prove, what he thought was a fundamental idea, that a material thing just is something that occupies space – indeed, in a sense, is a piece of space. He thought that a material body was itself a piece or volume of space, rather than just being *in* space, in part because he didn't believe in a vacuum. He thought that the whole physical world was one extended item, and that separate things in it, tables or whatever, were local areas of this in certain states of motion. This is a foundation for the

255

mathematical physics of the seventeenth century. In its own terms it didn't come off. Eventually it was going to be replaced by the classical dynamics of Newton which had a different conception of the physical world. But Descartes's picture did a great deal to establish the notion of a physical world which is fundamentally of a mathematical character and permits mathematical physics to be done. It is a very significant fact about the scientific revolution that started in the period we're discussing, in Descartes's lifetime and through his work, that the first of the great sciences to get going was mathematical physics. Chemistry, the science that deals with sorts of things in greater particularity, is much more a product of the eighteenth and nineteenth centuries than of the seventeenth century.

Magee Wouldn't it be fair to say that Descartes, in his day, did more to establish the possibility of science as such, and to 'sell' it to the general educated people of Western Europe, than anyone else, with the possible exception only of Bacon?

Williams I think that is probably so. There is a figure who is also enormously famous and whose actual physics is nearer to classical physics as it came out in the end, and that is Galileo. But Galileo was more notorious, perhaps, than respectable, because he was tried and condemned by the Inquisition. Descartes's intellectual influence in this respect was very great, even though the details of his physics were eventually to be, in good part, repudiated.

Magee Up to this point in our discussion, Descartes hasn't provided us with any physics: what he has done is show that a mathematically based physics is possible, that is to say intellectually within our powers and at the same time applicable to the real world. Can you expand on this distinction between doing the science and showing it to be possible?

Williams Yes. What he hopes to have shown by the manoeuvres that we have followed so far is that the world is so constructed that man is capable of knowing about it. In a sense, man and the world are made for each other, by God. For Descartes, man in his essence is not actually part of nature, because man is this immaterial intellectual substance which isn't part of the natural world, or subject to scientific laws. Man is not part of nature in that sense but nevertheless his intellectual powers are well adjusted to it. That means we can conduct a mathematical physics. Now Descartes thought that some of the fundamental principles of physics could themselves be known by what we would call philosophical reflection. He thought in particular we could know by such reflection that physics has to have a conservation law. There has to be some quantity that was conserved. Descartes actually picked on, as the quantity that was conserved, something, namely motion, which wasn't conserved, and indeed in terms of classical physics later was not even well defined. But the idea was there and it was supposed to be *a priori*; known by reflection. There were some other fundamental physical principles that he thought could be known *a priori*. But beyond that, he thought that truths of physics had to be discovered empirically.

This is quite important because Descartes is, rightly, said to be a rationalist philosopher. He thinks that fundamental properties of the world and of the mind can be discovered by reflection. He does not think that everything is derived from experience. But it's sometimes supposed that he was such a strong rationalist that he thought that the whole of science was to be deduced from metaphysics by purely mathematical or logical reasoning: that if I sat and thought hard enough about the *Cogito* and matter and God I'd arrive at the whole of science. He thought no such thing. In fact, he is absolutely consistent in saying that experiments are necessary to distinguish between some ways of explaining nature and others. You can build different models. This is a very modern aspect of his thought. You can build or construct different intellectual models of the world within his laws, and experiment is needed to discover which truly represent nature.

Magee Is experiment seen by him as designed to test our theories about nature, or as giving us the data out of which those theories are themselves constructed?

Williams It's designed for a number of different things, actually, but the basic point is the following. If you take the fundamental laws of nature, the principles on which matter moves, there are a lot of different mechanisms you could imagine which would produce superficially the same effect. You then make differential experiments, arranging a set-up in which one thing will happen if one model corresponds to reality, and something else will happen if a different model does. So you select between models. And that really is quite a good description of quite a lot of what physicists do.

Magee Essentially, it's the modern notion of the crucial experiment.

Williams Descartes was very keen on that idea. One of the things that he admirably insisted on was that it was no good blundering around the world trying out experiments simply to see what you could find out. You had to ask the right questions. This is another application of a principle we have already mentioned, that God is on your side if you do your bit. God will not allow you to be systematically deceived if you don't systematically deceive yourself. So what you have to do is to think of the right questions: God has arranged things so that nature will give you the answers.

Magee I think it's time we made the point that although God was indispensable to Descartes in arriving at 'the method' once you're in possession of the method you don't have to be a believer in God to use it.

Williams That's right. It is a very important point, that Descartes wanted to free the process of science from theological constraints, theological interference. In one way, he wanted to free it from theological foundations, if that means foundations that can be provided only by theologians. But, as we have seen, God was at the foundation of his system, and he was extremely keen to say that his inquiry did not leave us with a Godless world. His world was made by God, and our knowledge of it is guaranteed by God. Where you have to appeal to God in your intellectual life, however, is not (as you rightly say) in conducting science, but in proving to sceptics that it can be conducted. Moreover, Descartes very sensibly thought you shouldn't spend a lot of time proving to sceptics that it can be conducted. It needs to be done only once, and he thought he'd done it.

Descartes laid great emphasis on God, and it is my own belief that he was absolutely sincere in doing so. I don't think he was a faker of any kind in this respect, although he did conciliate the priests in various ways: he was not a man for getting into trouble with the Church. But although he was sincere himself, the construction he produced is one that made it easier for God to disappear from the world and from people's understanding of the world.

Magee Some people have claimed that Descartes was not a sincere believer in God at all, and they point to passages in his works which are unquestionably ironic. But I do not think their claim can be upheld, for the simple reason that Descartes's entire life's work would fall to the ground if it were true. For all I know, he may have been an insincere Christian, but that would be an entirely different matter. He certainly took an unillusioned view of the Church. But that he sincerely believed in the existence of God is something about which, in my view, there is no room for serious doubt. People who think the opposite are, I suspect, confusing disbelief in Christianity with disbelief in God – a thing which far too many Christians have been apt to do, both then and now.

But I want to turn to something else. A little while ago we touched on Cartesian dualism, the division of total reality into spirit and matter, but then somehow we failed to follow it up. Can we do that now? The most obvious problem it presented was how to explain the interaction between the two. How does Descartes account for spirit's ability to push material objects around in space?

Williams Frankly, the answer is that he never really did. Leibniz somewhat scornfully said on this subject of the interaction, 'Monsieur Descartes seems to have given up the game so far as we can see.' Just before Descartes went to Sweden, he wrote a book in which he did, curiously, try to localise the interactions between mind and body in the pineal gland, which is to be found at the base of the brain. But it barely even makes sense. The idea that this abstract non-material item, the mind, something that is almost though not quite in the same category as a number, could induce a change in the physical world by redirecting certain animal spirits, which is what he believed, is so difficult to conceive even in principle that it was a scandal for everybody. A lot of the philosophy of the seventeenth century, and indeed subsequently, addressed itself to trying to find some more adequate representation of the relation of mind and body than Descartes left us with.

Magee Even so, Cartesian dualism in some form or other got embedded in Western thought for three hundred years.

Williams Well, I think that some distinction between subject and object, knower and known, is a distinction that it is simply impossible for us to do without. There are philosophical systems that try to say that we have no conception of the known independently of the knower, that – in effect – we make up the whole world. But that sort of view, even in its more sophisticated forms, is quite difficult to believe. We use, and certainly science uses, some kind of dualism between the knower and the known, the idea of a world that is independent of our process of knowing it. What very few people now assent to is the absolute dualism between the completely pure mind and the body. The knower has to be understood as an essentially embodied creature, and not just as a pure spirit. This had been accepted in philosophy earlier than Descartes, for instance by St Thomas Aquinas or by Aristotle.

Magee Are there any other really crucial flaws in the Cartesian system?

Williams The argument for God seemed one of the weakest parts of the system as time went on, and this had an important historical result because, as you said earlier, it looked as if Descartes, in using the method of doubt, had painted himself into a corner. If he can't get out of the corner by using theological means, there was not any way of doing it, so that if you travel with him down the road of the doubt, it seems that you end up in this idealist position where you're left with nothing except the contents of consciousness.

There's another feature of Descartes's position that should be mentioned. Even in his own lifetime his system was attacked for being circular. God is supposed to validate everything. We've emphasised in the course of this discussion the role of God, particularly in validating our

259

beliefs about the external world, but Descartes also thought that God played an important role in validating our belief in argument in general. But of course it is by argument that he arrives at the belief in God itself. So even at the time his work appeared, people objected that he was involved in a circle.

Magee   Only because he 'clearly and distinctly' apprehends that God exists can he make any progress from the *Cogito* at all. But only because he knows that God exists and is no deceiver does he have any assurance that what he 'clearly and distinctly' apprehends is true.

Williams   The details of this are very much a matter of particular interest for the study of Descartes. But there is a very general problem, of which this is an example, which is the question of philosophy's relation to its own existence. The Cartesian circle, as it's called, is a particular example in this context of the difficulty that philosophy has in stating the possibility of its own existence. It has to allow for its own discovery, its own validity and so on, and it is difficult for it to avoid some sort of circle or some regress there.

Magee   This is a point of such general importance that it's worth pausing over for a moment. Every general explanatory framework claiming validity must be able to explain both its own validity and how we are able to arrive at it. To take an example a long way removed from Descartes: if a philosophy maintains that philosophical beliefs have nothing to do with truth but serve merely to promote the class interests of the people subscribing to them, then it is maintaining that it itself has nothing to do with truth but serves merely to promote the class interests of the persons subscribing to it. Thus it is self-disqualifying as a serious philosophy. Or if another approach holds as its central principle that all meaningful statements must either be tautologically true or be empirically verifiable then it itself is, again, instantly disqualified, because that statement itself is neither tautologically true nor empirically verifiable. Many belief-systems raise difficulties of this kind for themselves: if they were true we should be barred from regarding them as such, and in some cases we would not even be able to formulate them. *A theory has to make room for itself.* It has to be able to provide a non-self-contradictory legitimation of itself, and of the means whereby we have arrived at it. If it cannot do that it is self-contradictory or incoherent, and in either case untenable.

But to return to Descartes: his influence on philosophy has been simply immense, hasn't it? Can you say something about that?

Williams   If you summarise it in one thing, it was Descartes, and almost Descartes alone, who brought it about that the centre of Western philosophy for these past centuries has been the theory of knowledge. He brought it about that philosophy started from the question 'What can I know?' rather than questions such as 'What is there?' or 'How is the world?' Moreover, the question is not 'What can be known?' or even 'What can we know?' but 'What can *I* know?' That is, it starts from a first-person egocentric question. I mentioned right at the beginning that it was possible in his time to think that science could perhaps be done by one person. But even when you lay that historical context aside, it is a very important part of his enterprise that it is autobiographical. It is no accident that his two great works, *Discourse on the Method* and the *Meditations*, are written in the first person. They are works of philosophical self-inquiry. This first-person and epistemological emphasis has been the principal influence of Descartes.

Magee   After Descartes, it is not until our own century that any significant number of philosophers have disputed that 'What can I know?' is the central question of philosophy.

Williams   Well, there is a question about what you make of Hegel in that respect. There are various ways of taking Hegel, in one of which you can see Hegel as trying to get back to a kind of Aristotelian view of philosophy in which this question is less dominant. But it is certainly important that at the end of the nineteenth century, and in our own century, people have moved away from the epistemological emphasis of Descartes more to a logical and linguistic emphasis and have tried to make the philosophy of language rather than the theory of knowledge the centre of philosophy.

Magee   Given that the philosophy of Descartes has the faults we have mentioned – and others which we have not mentioned – and given that the central focus of philosophers' concern has in any case moved away from the problem of knowledge, why is the study of Descartes still so valuable? Let me express this personally. You worked, on and off, for a period of over twenty years at a book about Descartes: why did you consider it worth that enormous investment of your life?

Williams   I think for two reasons. Let us leave on one side the case for an historical understanding of the role that Descartes has played in getting us into the present situation. Just to know what he said in a little bit of detail is, I think, very important simply to understanding who we are and where we've come from. But the reason why I think that his work – when I say 'his work' I have particularly in mind the *Meditations* – is something that, if one's interested in philosophy, one wants to read now, is that the path it follows, the path of asking 'What do I know?', 'What can I doubt?' and so on, is presented in an almost irresistible way. It is not an accident that this emphasis in philosophy has been so overwhelmingly important. It isn't that Descartes, just because he was a dazzling stylist, can perform long-distance mesmerism on the mind of Europe. That isn't the reason. The reason is that he discovered something intrinsically compelling, the idea that I say to myself: I have all these beliefs, but how can I get behind them to see if they're really true? How can I stand back from my beliefs to see which of them are prejudices? How much room is there for scepticism? These are really compelling questions, and it needs a great deal of philosophical imagination and work to get oneself out of this very natural pattern of reflection; and, as Descartes said, when you have been through that process you do not merely end up where you were at the beginning. It is not just a matter of recovering from a self-inflicted philosophical illness.

Another question that is put to you dramatically by Descartes is 'What am I?' We can imagine ourselves as other than we are. We have a power of extracting ourselves imaginatively from our actual circumstances. We can imagine ourselves looking out on the world from a different body. We can imagine looking into a mirror and seeing a different face – and, what's important, looking into a mirror, seeing a different face, and not being surprised. And this gives me the idea, a powerful idea, that I am independent of the body and the past that I have. That is an experience basic to the Cartesian idea that I am somehow independent of all these material things. If you look at Cartesian dualism from the outside, as a theory, it is very difficult to believe, for the reasons that we've touched on. But at the same time there is something in it that is hard to resist, if you come to it through a certain set of reflections. The set of reflections that Descartes with unexampled clarity and force lays before you and which lead you down that path – as I think, a mistaken path – are not only very striking, but, as it were, near to the bone. Here again, you cannot return unchanged from trying to overcome Descartes's reflections. It is a prime philosophical task to try to arrive at an understanding of oneself, of one's imagination, of one's ideas of what one might be, that can free one from his dualistic model.

28

Colours
George Berkeley

In this brief extract from a dialogue by George Berkeley (1685–1753), the characters Hylas and Philonous discuss the question of whether colours are really in objects. Philonous presents vigorous arguments against the idea that they are. If colours really were in objects, how would we know the true colour of an object, since objects appear differently in different lights?

From George Berkeley, *Three Dialogues between Hylas and Philonous*

Philonous   Are the beautiful red and purple we see on yonder clouds, really in them? Or do you imagine they have in themselves any other form, than that of a dark mist or vapour?

Hylas   I must own, Philonous, those colours are not really in the clouds as they seem to be at this distance. They are only apparent colours.

Philonous   *Apparent* call you them? how shall we distinguish these apparent colours from real?

Hylas   Very easily. Those are to be thought apparent, which appearing only at a distance, vanish upon a nearer approach.

Philonous   And those I suppose are to be thought real, which are discovered by the most near and exact survey.

Hylas   Right.

Philonous   Is the nearest and exactest survey made by the help of a microscope, or by the naked eye?

Hylas   By a microscope, doubtless.

Philonous   But a microscope often discovers colours in an object different from those perceived by the unassisted sight. And in case we had microscopes magnifying to any assigned degree; it is certain, that no object whatsoever viewed through them, would appear in the same colour which it exhibits to the naked eye.

Hylas And what will you conclude from all this? You cannot argue that
there are really and naturally no colours on objects: because by artificial managements they may be altered, or made to vanish.

Philonous I think it may evidently be concluded from your own concessions, that all the colours we see with our naked eyes, are only
apparent as those on the clouds, since they vanish upon a more close
and accurate inspection, which is afforded us by a microscope. Then
as to what you say by way of prevention: I ask you, whether the real
and natural state of an object is better discovered by a very sharp
and piercing sight, or by one which is less sharp?

Hylas By the former without doubt.

Philonous Is it not plain from *dioptrics*, that microscopes make the sight
more penetrating, and represent objects as they would appear to the
eye, in case it were naturally endowed with a most exquisite sharpness?

Hylas It is.

Philonous Consequently the microscopical representation is to be thought
that which best sets forth the real nature of the thing, or what it is
in itself. The colours therefore by it perceived, are more genuine and
real, than those perceived otherwise.

Hylas I confess there is something in what you say.

Philonous Besides, it is not only possible but manifest, that there actually are animals, whose eyes are by Nature framed to perceive those
things, which by reason of their minuteness escape our sight. What
think you of those inconceivably small animals perceived by glasses?
Must we suppose they are all stark blind? Or, in case they see, can
it be imagined their sight hath not the same use in preserving their
bodies from injuries, which appears in that of all other animals? And
if it hath, is it not evident, they must see particles less than their own
bodies, which will present them with a far different view in each
object, from that which strikes our senses? Even our own eyes
do not always represent objects to us after the same manner. In the
jaundice, every one knows that all things seem yellow. Is it not therefore highly probable, those animals in whose eyes we discern a
very different texture from that of ours, and whose bodies abound
with different humours, do not see the same colours in every object
that we do? From all which, should it not seem to follow, that all
colours are equally apparent, and that none of those which we
perceive are really inherent in any outward object?

Hylas It should.

Philonous The point will be past all doubt, if you consider, that in case
colours were real properties or affections inherent in external bodies,
they could admit of no alteration, without some change wrought in
the very bodies themselves: but is it not evident from what hath been

said, that upon the use of microscopes, upon a change happening in the humours of the eye, or a variation of distance, without any manner of real alteration in the things itself, the colours of any object are either changed, or totally disappear? Nay all other circumstances remaining the same, change but the situation of some objects, and they shall present different colours to the eye. The same thing happens upon viewing an object in various degrees of light. And what is more known, than that the same bodies appear differently coloured by candle-light, from what they do in the open day? Add to these the experiment of a prism, which separating the heterogeneous rays of light, alters the colours of any object; and will cause the whitest to appear of a deep blue or red to the naked eye. And now tell me, whether you are still of opinion, that every body hath its true real colour inhering in it; and if you think it hath, I would fain know farther from you, what certain distance and position of the object, what peculiar texture and formation of the eye, what degree or kind of light is necessary for ascertaining that true colour, and distinguishing it from apparent ones.

Hylas   I own myself entirely satisfied, that they are all equally apparent; and that there is no such thing as colour really inhering in external bodies, but that it is altogether in the light.

29

Of the origin of ideas
David Hume

Where do all our thoughts originate? David Hume (1711–76) gave a clear answer to this question: in experience. He used the word 'impression' to refer to a direct sensory experience, such as what you see when you look at a cat. 'Idea', for him, like 'impression', is a technical term: it means a copy of an impression, as when you remember seeing your cat, you have an idea of the cat in his sense. His view that our thoughts originate in experience can then be rephrased as all our ideas are copies of impressions. In this extract from his *Enquiry Concerning Human Understanding* (an early version of which appeared in 1748) he explains this view and some of its consequences, including an apparent counter-example in the case of the missing shade of blue.

From David Hume, *Enquiry Concerning Human Understanding*

Of the origin of ideas

Every one will readily allow, that there is a considerable difference between the perceptions of the mind, when a man feels the pain of excessive heat, or the pleasure of moderate warmth, and when he afterwards recalls to his memory this sensation, or anticipates it by his imagination. These faculties may mimic or copy the perceptions of the senses; but they never can entirely reach the force and vivacity of the original sentiment. The utmost we say of them, even when they operate with greatest vigour, is, that they represent their object in so lively a manner, that we could *almost* say we feel or see it: But, except the mind be disordered by disease or madness, they never can arrive at such a pitch of vivacity, as to render these perceptions altogether undistinguishable. All the colours of poetry, however splendid, can never paint natural objects in such a manner as to make the description be taken for a real landskip. The most lively thought is still inferior to the dullest sensation.

We may observe a like distinction to run through all the other perceptions of the mind. A man in a fit of anger, is actuated in a very different manner from one who only thinks of that emotion. If you tell me, that any person is in love, I easily understand your meaning, and form a just conception of his situation; but never can mistake that conception for the real disorders and agitations of the passion. When we reflect on our past sentiments and affections, our thought is a faithful mirror, and copies its objects truly; but the colours which it employs are faint and dull, in comparison of those in which our original perceptions were clothed. It requires no nice discernment or metaphysical head to mark the distinction between them.

Here therefore we may divide all the perceptions of the mind into two classes or species, which are distinguished by their different degrees of force and vivacity. The less forcible and lively are commonly denominated *Thoughts* or *Ideas*. The other species want a name in our language, and in most others; I suppose, because it was not requisite for any, but philosophical purposes, to rank them under a general term or appellation. Let us, therefore, use a little freedom, and call them *Impressions*; employing that word in a sense somewhat different from the usual. By the term *impression*, then, I mean all our more lively perceptions, when we hear, or see, or feel, or love, or hate, or desire, or will. And impressions are distinguished from ideas, which are the less lively perceptions, of which we are conscious, when we reflect on any of those sensations or movements above mentioned.

Nothing, at first view, may seem more unbounded than the thought of man, which not only escapes all human power and authority, but is not even restrained within the limits of nature and reality. To form monsters, and join incongruous shapes and appearances, costs the imagination no more trouble than to conceive the most natural and familiar objects. And while the body is confined to one planet, along which it creeps with pain and difficulty; the thought can in an instant transport us into the most distant regions of the universe; or even beyond the universe, into the unbounded chaos, where nature is supposed to lie in total confusion. What never was seen, or heard of, may yet be conceived; nor in any thing beyond the power of thought, except what implies an absolute contradiction.

But though our thought seems to possess this unbounded liberty, we shall find, upon a nearer examination, that it is really confined within very narrow limits, and that all this creative power of the mind amounts to no more than the faculty of compounding, transposing, augmenting, or diminishing the materials afforded us by the senses and experience. When we think of a golden mountain, we only join two consistent ideas, *gold*, and *mountain*, with which we were formerly acquainted. A virtuous horse we can conceive; because, from our own feeling, we can conceive virtue; and this we may unite to the figure and shape of a horse, which is an animal familiar to us. In short, all the materials of thinking are derived either from our outward or inward sentiment: the mixture and compositions of these belongs alone to the mind and will. Or, to express myself in philosophical language, all our ideas or more feeble perceptions are copies of our impressions or more lively ones.

To prove this, the two following arguments will, I hope, be sufficient. First, when we analyze our thoughts or ideas, however compounded or sublime, we always find that they resolve themselves into such simple ideas as were copied from a precedent feeling or sentiment. Even those ideas, which, at first view, seem the most wide of this origin, are found, upon a nearer scrutiny, to be derived from it. The idea of God, as meaning an infinitely intelligent, wise, and good Being, arises from reflecting on the operations of our own mind, and augmenting, without limit, those qualities of goodness and wisdom. We may prosecute this enquiry to what length we please; where we shall always find, that every idea which we examine is copied from a similar impression. Those who would assert that this position is not universally true nor without exception, have only one, and that an easy method of refuting it; by producing that idea, which, in their opinion, is not derived from this source. It will then be incumbent on us, if we would maintain our doctrine, to produce the impression, or lively perception, which corresponds to it.

Secondly. If it happen, from a defect of the organ, that a man is not susceptible of any species of sensation, we always find that he is as little susceptible of the correspondent ideas. A blind man can form no notion of colours; a deaf man of sounds. Restore either of them that sense in which he is deficient; by opening this new inlet for his sensations, you also open an inlet for the ideas; and he finds no difficulty in conceiving these objects. The case is the same, if the object, proper for exciting any sensation, has never been applied to the organ. A Laplander or Negro has no notion of the relish of wine. And though there are few or no instances of a like deficiency in the mind, where a person has never felt or is wholly incapable of a sentiment or passion that belongs to his species; yet we find the same observation to take place in a less degree. A man of mild manners can form no idea of inveterate revenge or cruelty; nor can a selfish heart easily conceive the heights of friendship and generosity. It is readily allowed, that other beings may possess many senses of which we can have no conception; because the ideas of them have never been introduced to us in the only manner by which an idea can have access to the mind, to wit, by the actual feeling and sensation.

There is, however, one contradictory phenomenon, which may prove that it is not absolutely impossible for ideas to arise, independent of their correspondent impressions. I believe it will readily be allowed, that the several distinct ideas of colour, which enter by the eye, or those of sound, which are conveyed by the ear, are really different from each other; though at the same time, resembling. Now if this be true of different colours, it must be no less so of the different shades of the same colour; and each shade produces a distinct idea, independent of the rest. For if this should be denied, it is possible, by the continual gradation of shades, to run a colour insensibly into what is most remote from it; and if you will not allow any of the means to be different, you cannot, without absurdity, deny the extremes to be the same. Suppose, therefore, a person to have enjoyed his sight for thirty years, and to have become perfectly acquainted with colours of all kinds except one particular shade of blue, for instance, which it never has been his fortune to meet with. Let all the different shades of that colour, except that single one, be placed before him, descending gradually from the deepest to the lightest; it is plain that he will perceive a blank, where that shade is wanting, and will be sensible that there is a greater distance in that place between the contiguous colours than in any other. Now I ask, whether it be possible for him, from his own imagination, to supply this deficiency, and raise up to himself the idea of that particular shade, though it had never been conveyed to him by his senses? I believe there are few but will be of opinion that he can: and this may serve as a proof that the simple ideas are not always, in every instance, derived from the correspondent impressions; though this instance is so singular, that it is scarcely worth our observing, and does not merit that for it alone we should alter our general maxim.

Here, therefore, is a proposition, which not only seems, in itself, simple and intelligible; but, if a proper use were made of it, might render every dispute equally intelligible, and banish all that jargon, which has so long taken possession of metaphysical reasonings, and drawn disgrace upon them. All ideas, especially abstract ones, are naturally faint and obscure: the mind has but a slender hold of them: they are apt to be confounded with other resembling ideas; and when we have often employed any term, though without a distinct meaning, we are apt to imagine it has a determinate idea annexed to it. On the contrary, all impressions, that is, all sensations, either outward or inward, are strong and vivid: the limits between them are more exactly determined: nor is it easy to fall into any error or mistake with regard to them. When we entertain, therefore, any suspicion that a philosophical term is employed without any meaning or idea (as is but too frequent), we need but enquire, *from what impression is that supposed idea derived?* And if it be impossible to assign any, this will serve to confirm our suspicion. By bringing ideas into so clear a light we may reasonably hope to remove all dispute, which may arise, concerning their nature and reality.

30

Epistemology naturalized – nature know thyself
Alex Orenstein

Willard van Orman Quine (1908–) has given a holistic account of our knowledge, emphasizing the interrelation of the parts of our conceptual framework. No belief is in principle immune from possible revision, and this includes beliefs acquired by observation. What makes one theory preferable to another is such aspects as its explanatory power, its parsimony, and precision. Here Alex Orenstein gives a brief overview of Quine's epistemology, bringing out the originality of his approach to the question of our relation to the external world.

From *Routledge Encyclopedia of Philosophy*, edited by Edward Craig

---

The problem of our knowledge of the external world is traditionally stated as one of how a self with private mental states can come to have knowledge of the external world. Quine's restatement is strikingly more naturalistic:

> I am a physical object sitting in a physical world. Some of the forces of this physical world impinge on my surface. Light rays strike my retinas; molecules bombard my eardrums and fingertips. I strike back, emanating concentric air waves. These waves take the form of a torrent of discourse about tables, people, molecules, light rays, retinas, air waves, prime numbers, infinite classes, joy and sorrow, good and evil.
>
> (1966: 215)

In its traditional statement the problem lies in how, starting with 'experience' in the form of immediately given impressions or sense-data, we justify our claims to know objects such as tables, chairs or molecules. This vantage point was that of a first philosophy, intended as providing a foundation of certainty for the sciences by standing outside of them and legitimizing their accomplishments. Quine rejects this formulation. His naturalized epistemology rephrases the problem as one of how we learn to talk about or refer to objects (ordinary as well as scientific). What are the conditions that lead to reference? How is scientific discourse possible?

The traditional accounts of the linkage between 'experience' and our knowledge vary from mentalistic conceptions, like that of Hume, in which all our ideas are copies of sense impressions, to more neutral linguistic formulations, in which cognitive claims are to be translated into observation sentences. On Quine's holistic account, one cannot deal with the empirical content of sentences, much less of terms – the linguistic correlates of ideas – one by one, either via definition, translation or some other sort of linkage. To study the relation of knowledge and science to observation sentences is to trace the psychological and linguistic development of the knower, that is, the potential user of scientific language. Observation sentences serve as both the starting point in human language learning as well as the empirical grounds for science. The problem of knowledge now is how, starting with observation sentences, we can proceed to talk of tables, chairs, molecules, neutrinos, sets and numbers. One of the reasons for doing epistemology by studying the roots of reference is simply the failure of the traditional empiricists' programme mentioned above. Another is that it enables one to dispense with mentalistic notions such as 'experience' or 'observation'. One relies instead on two components which are already part of a naturalist's ontology: the physical happening at the nerve endings, the neural input or stimulus; and the linguistic entity, the observation sentence. These two serve as naturalistic surrogates for 'experience' and 'observation'. On Quine's empiricist and behaviourist account, observation sentences are those that can be learned purely by ostension and as such as causally most proximate to the stimulus. This account is not vulnerable to attacks on the notion of observation as dependent on the theories one holds, since observation sentences are precisely those which are learnable without any background information. Another point of difference with empiricists concerns the alleged certainty or incorrigibility of observation. Though Quine's observation sentences are assented to with a minimum of background information and are thus included among those sentences less likely to be revised, they are not in principle immune from revision.

Unlike traditional epistemology, then, Quine's epistemology is naturalistic: we cannot stand apart from our place as part of nature and make philosophical judgments. This is part of the theme that philosophy is continuous with science, science being the part of nature most suitable for knowing itself.

The naturalistic philosopher begins his reasoning within the inherited world theory as a going concern. He tentatively believes all of

271

it, but believes also that some unidentified portions are wrong. He tries to improve, clarify and understand the system from within.

(Quine 1981: 72)

References

Quine, W. V. (1966) *The Ways of Paradox and Other Essays*, New York: Random House.
—— (1981) *Theories and Things*, Cambridge, Mass. Harvard University Press.

Section five

Science

Section 5

31

The problem of demarcation
Karl Popper

How should we distinguish between science and non-science? This is the problem of demarcation. Karl Popper (1902–94) explained the progress of science in terms of bold conjectures which scientists then attempt to falsify rather than confirm. What makes a conjecture a scientific one is that it is open to be tested and perhaps refuted. Theories which are in principle immune to refutation are not scientific. In this reading Popper outlines his approach and considers possible criticisms of it. Popper's views about the nature of scientific progress have had a wide influence, not least upon practising scientists.

From Karl Popper, 'Replies to my critics', in *The Philosophy of Karl Popper*, edited by P. A. Schilpp

---

Science versus non-science

I now turn to the *problem of demarcation*, and to explaining how this problem is related to the problems of empirical content and of testability.

The great scientists, such as Galileo, Kepler, Newton, Einstein, and Bohr (to confine myself to a few of the dead) represent to me a simple but impressive idea of science. Obviously, no such list, however much extended, would *define* scientist or science *in extenso*. But it suggests for me an oversimplification, one from which we can, I think, learn a lot. It is the working of great scientists which I have in my mind as my paradigm for science. Not that I lack respect for the lesser ones; there are hundreds of great men and great scientists who come into the almost heroic category.

But with all respect for the lesser scientists, I wish to convey here a heroic and romantic idea of science and its workers: men who humbly devoted themselves to the search for truth, to the growth of our

275

knowledge; men whose life consisted in an adventure of bold ideas. I am prepared to consider with them many of their less brilliant helpers who were equally devoted to the search for truth – for great truth. But I do not count among them those for whom science is no more than a profession, a technique: those who are not deeply moved by great problems and by the oversimplifications of bold solutions.

It is science in this heroic sense that I wish to study. As a side result I find that we can throw a lot of light even on the more modest workers in applied science.

This, then, for me is science. I do not try to define it, for very good reasons. I only wish to draw a simple picture of the kind of men I have in mind, and of their activities. And the picture will be an oversimplification: these are men of bold ideas, but highly critical of their own ideas; they try to find whether their ideas are right by trying first to find whether they are not perhaps wrong. They work with bold conjectures and severe attempts at refuting their own conjectures.

My criterion of demarcation between science and non-science is a simple logical analysis of this picture. How good or bad it is will be shown by its fertility.

Bold ideas are new, daring, hypotheses or conjectures. And severe attempts at refutations are severe critical discussions and severe empirical tests.

When is a conjecture daring and when is it not daring, in the sense here proposed? Answer: it is daring if and only if it takes a great risk of being false – if matters could be otherwise, and seem at the time to be otherwise.

Let us consider a simple example. Copernicus's or Aristarchus's conjecture that the sun rather than the earth rests at the centre of the universe was an incredibly daring one. It was, incidentally, false; nobody accepts today the conjecture that the sun is (in the sense of Aristarchus and Copernicus) at rest in the centre of the universe. But this does not affect the boldness of the conjecture, nor its fertility. And one of its main consequences – that the earth does not rest at the centre of the universe but that it has (at least) a daily and an annual motion – is still fully accepted, in spite of some misunderstandings of relativity.[1]

But it is not the present acceptance of the theory which I wish to discuss, but its boldness. It was bold because it clashed with all then accepted views, *and* with the prima facie evidence of the senses. It was bold because it postulated a hitherto unknown hidden reality behind the appearances.

It was not bold in another very important sense: neither Aristarchus nor Copernicus suggested a feasible crucial experiment. In fact, they did not suggest that anything was wrong with the traditional appearances: they let the accepted appearances severely alone; they only reinterpreted them. They were not anxious to stick out their necks by predicting new observable appearances. (This is an oversimplification as far as Copernicus is concerned, but it is almost certainly true of Aristarchus.)

To the degree that this is so, Aristarchus's and Copernicus's theories may be described in my terminology as unscientific or metaphysical. To the degree that Copernicus did make a number of minor predictions, his theory is, in my terminology, scientific. But even as a metaphysical theory it was far from meaningless; and in proposing a new bold view of the universe it made a tremendous contribution to the advent of the new science.

Kepler went much further. He too had a bold metaphysical view, partly based upon the Copernican theory, of the reality of the world. But his view led him to many new detailed predictions of the appearances. At first these predictions did not tally with the observations. He tried to reinterpret the observations in the light of his theories; but his addiction to the search for truth was even greater than his enthusiasm for the metaphysical harmony of the world. Thus he felt forced to give up a number of his favoured theories, one by one, and to replace them by others which fitted the facts. It was a great and a heartrending struggle. The final outcome, his famous and immensely important three laws, he did not really like – except the third. But they stood up to his severest tests – they agreed with the detailed appearances, the observations which he had inherited from Tycho.

Kepler's laws are excellent approximations to what we think today are the true movements of the planets of our solar system. They are even excellent approximations to the movements of the distant binary star systems which have since been discovered. Yet they are merely *approximations* to what seems to be the truth; *they are not true*.

They have been tested in the light of new theories – of Newton's theory and of Einstein's – which predicted small deviations from Kepler's laws. (According to Newton, Kepler's laws are correct only for two-body systems . . . .) Thus the crucial experiments went against Kepler, very slightly, but sufficiently clearly.

Of these three theories – Kepler's, Newton's, and Einstein's – the latest and still the most successful is Einstein's; and it was this theory which led me into the philosophy of science. What impressed me so greatly about Einstein's theory of gravitation were the following points.

(1) It was a very bold theory. It greatly deviated in its fundamental outlook from Newton's theory which at that time was utterly successful. (The small deviation of the perihelion of Mercury did not seriously trouble anybody in the light of its other almost incredible successes. Whether it should have done is another matter.)

(2) From the point of view of Einstein's theory, Newton's theory was an excellent approximation, though false (just as from the point of view of Newton's theory, Kepler's and Galileo's theories were excellent

approximations, though false). Thus it is not its truth which decides the scientific character of a theory.

(3) Einstein derived from his theory three important predictions of vastly different observable effects, two of which had not been thought of by anybody before him, and all of which contradicted Newton's theory, so far as they could be said to fall within the field of application of this theory at all.

But what impressed me perhaps most were the following two points.

(4) Einstein declared that these predictions were crucial: if they did not agree with his precise theoretical calculations, he would regard his theory as refuted.

(5) But even if they were observed as predicted, Einstein declared that *his theory was false*: he said that it would be a better approximation to the truth than Newton's, but he gave reasons why he would not, even if all predictions came out right, regard it as a true theory. He sketched a number of demands which a true theory (a unified field theory) would have to satisfy, and declared that his theory was at best an approximation to this so far unattained unified field theory.

It may be remarked in passing that Einstein, like Kepler, failed to achieve his scientific dream – or his metaphysical dream: it does not matter in this context what label we use. What we call today Kepler's laws or Einstein's theory of gravitation are results which in no way satisfied their creators, who each continued to work on his dream to the end of his life. And even of Newton a similar point can be made: he never believed that a theory of action at a distance could be a finally acceptable explanation of gravity.[2]

Einstein's theory was first tested by Eddington's famous eclipse experiment of 1919. In spite of his unbelief in the truth of his theory, his belief that it was merely a new important approximation towards the truth, Einstein never doubted the outcome of this experiment; the inner coherence, the inner logic of his theory convinced him that it was a step forward even though he thought that it could not be true. It has since passed a series of further tests, all very successfully. But some people still think the agreement between Einstein's theory and the observations may be the result of (incredibly improbable) accidents. It is impossible to rule this out; yet the agreement may rather be the result of Einstein's theory's being a fantastically good approximation to the truth.[3]

The picture of science at which I have so far only hinted may be sketched as follows.

There is a reality behind the world as it appears to us, possibly a many-layered reality, of which the appearances are the outermost layers. What the great scientist does is boldly to guess, daringly to conjecture, what these inner realities are like. This is akin to myth making.

(Historically we can trace back the ideas of Newton via Anaximander to Hesiod, and the ideas of Einstein via Faraday, Boscovič, Leibniz, and Descartes to Aristotle and Parmenides.[4]) The boldness can be gauged by the distance between the world of appearance and the conjectured reality, the explanatory hypotheses.

But there is another, a special kind of boldness – *the boldness of predicting* aspects of the world of appearance which so far have been overlooked but which it must possess if the conjectured reality is (more or less) right, if the explanatory hypotheses are (approximately) true. It is this more special kind of boldness which I have usually in mind when I speak of bold scientific conjectures. It is the boldness of a conjecture which takes a real risk – the risk of being tested, and refuted; the risk of clashing with reality.

Thus my proposal was, and is, that it is this second boldness, together with the readiness to look out for tests and refutations, which distinguishes 'empirical' science from non-science, and especially from pre-scientific myths and metaphysics.

I will call this proposal (D): (D) for *'demarcation'*.

The italicized proposal (D) is what I still regard as the centre of my philosophy. But I have always been highly critical of any idea of my own; and so I tried at once to find fault with this particular idea, years before I published it. And I published it together with the main results of this criticism. My criticism led me to a sequence of refinements or improvements of the proposal (D): they were not later concessions, but they were published together with the proposal as parts of the proposal itself.[5]

Difficulties with the demarcation proposal

1. From the beginning I called my criterion of demarcation a *proposal*. This was partly because of my uneasiness about definitions and my dislike of them. Definitions are either abbreviations and therefore unnecessary, though perhaps convenient, or they are Aristotelian attempts to 'state the essence' of a word, and therefore unconscious conventional dogmas . . . . If I define 'science' by my criterion of demarcation (I admit that this is more or less what I am doing) then anybody could propose another definition, such as 'science is the sum total of true statements'. A discussion of the merits of such definitions can be pretty pointless. This is why I gave here first a description of great or heroic science and then a proposal for a criterion which allows us to demarcate – roughly – this kind of science. Any demarcation in my sense *must* be rough. (This is one of the great differences from any formal meaning criterion of any artificial 'language of science'.) For the transition between metaphysics and science is not a

sharp one: what was a metaphysical idea yesterday can become a testable scientific theory tomorrow; and this happens frequently (I gave various examples in *The Logic of Scientific Discovery* and elsewhere: atomism is perhaps the best).

Thus one of the difficulties is that our criterion must not be too sharp; and in the chapter 'Degrees of testability;' of *The Logic of Scientific Discovery* I suggested (as a kind of second improvement of the criterion (D) of the foregoing section) that a theory is scientific to the degree to which it is testable.

This, incidentally, led later to one of the most fruitful discoveries of that book: that there are degrees of testability (or of scientific character), which can be identified with degrees of empirical content (or informative content).

2.   The formula (D) of the foregoing section is expressed in somewhat psychological language. It can be considerably improved if one speaks of *theoretical systems* or *systems of statements*, as I did throughout *The Logic of Scientific Discovery*. This leads at once to the recognition of one of the problems connected with the falsifiability criterion of demarcation: even if we can apply it to *systems* of statements, it may be difficult if not impossible to say which particular statement, or which subsystem of a system of statements, has been exposed to a particular experimental test. Thus we may describe a *system* as scientific or empirically testable, while being most uncertain about its constituent parts.

An example is Newton's theory of gravitation. It has often been asked whether Newton's laws of motion, or which of them, are masked definitions rather than empirical assertions.

My answer is as follows: Newton's theory is a system. *If we falsify it, we falsify the whole system.* We may perhaps put the blame on one of its laws or on another. But this means only that we *conjecture* that a certain change in the system will free it from falsification; or in other words, that we conjecture that a certain alternative system will be an improvement, a better approximation to the truth.

But this means: attributing the blame for a falsification to a certain subsystem is a typical hypothesis, a conjecture like any other, though perhaps hardly more than a vague suspicion if no definite alternative suggestion is being made. And the same applies the other way round: the decision that a certain subsystem is not to be blamed for the falsification is likewise a typical conjecture. The attribution or non-attribution of responsibility for failure is conjectural, like everything in science; and what matters is the proposal of a new alternative and competing conjectural system that is able to pass the falsifying test.

3.   Points (1) and (2) illustrate that however correct my criterion of bold conjectures and severe refutations may be, there are difficulties which must not be overlooked. A primitive difficulty of this kind may be described as follows. A biologist offers the conjecture that all swans are white. When black swans are discovered in Australia, he says that it is not refuted. He insists that these black swans are a new kind of bird since it is *part of the defining property* of a swan that it is white. In other words, he can escape the refutation, though I think that he is likely to learn more if he admits that he was wrong.

In any case – and this is very important – the theory 'All swans are white' is refutable at least in the following clear logical sense: it must be declared refuted by anybody who accepts that there is at least one non-white swan.

4.   The principle involved in this example is a very primitive one, but it has a host of applications. For a long time chemists have been inclined to regard atomic weights, melting points, and similar properties as *defining properties* of materials: there can be no water whose freezing point differs from 0°C; it just would not be water, however similar in other respects it might be to water. But if this is so, then according to my criterion of demarcation 'Water freezes at 0°C' would not be a scientific or an empirical statement; it would be a tautology – part of a definition.

Clearly, there is a problem here: either my criterion of demarcation is refuted, or we have to admit the possibility of discovering water whose freezing point is other than 0°C.

5   I plead of course for the second possibility, and I hold that from this simple example we can learn a lot about the advantages of my proposal (D). For let us assume we have discovered water with a different freezing point. Is this still to be called 'water'? *I assert that the question is totally irrelevant.* The scientific hypothesis was that a liquid (no matter what you call it) with a considerable list of chemical and physical properties freezes at 0°C. If any of these properties which have been conjectured to be constantly conjoined should not materialize then *we were wrong*; and thus *new and interesting problems open up*. The least of them is whether or not we should continue to call the liquid in question 'water': *this* is purely arbitrary or conventional. Thus my criterion of demarcation is not only not refuted by this example: it helps us to discover what is significant for science and what is arbitrary and irrelevant.

6.   As explained in the very first chapter of *The Logic of Scientific Discovery*, we can always adopt evasive tactics in the face of refutations. For historical reasons I originally called these tactics 'conventionalist stratagems (or twists)', but now call them '*immunizing tactics or stratagems*':[6]

we can always immunize a theory against refutation. There are many such evasive immunizing tactics; and if nothing better occurs to us, we can always deny the objectivity – or even the existence – of the refuting observation. (Remember the people who *refused* to look through Galileo's telescope.) Those intellectuals who are more interested in being right than in learning something interesting but unexpected are by no means rare exceptions.

7.   None of the difficulties so far discussed is terribly serious: it may seem that a little intellectual honesty would go a long way to overcome them. By and large this is true. But how can we describe this intellectual honesty in logical terms? I described it in *The Logic of Scientific Discovery* as a *rule of method*, or a *methodological rule*: 'Do not try to evade falsification, but stick your neck out!'

8.   But I was yet a little more self-critical: I first noticed that such a rule of method is, necessarily, somewhat vague – as is the problem of demarcation altogether. Clearly, one can say that if you avoid falsification *at any price*, you give up empirical science in my sense. But I found that, in addition, supersensitivity with respect to refuting criticism was just as dangerous: there is a legitimate place for dogmatism, though a very limited place. He who gives up his theory too easily in the face of apparent refutations will never discover the possibilities inherent in his theory. *There is room in science for debate*: for attack and therefore also for defence. Only if we try to defend them can we learn all the different possibilities inherent in our theories. As always, science is conjecture. You have to conjecture when to stop defending a favourite theory, and when to try a new one.

9.   Thus I did not propose the simple rule: 'Look out for refutations, and never dogmatically defend your theory.' Still, it was much better advice than dogmatic defence at any price. The truth is that we must be constantly critical; self-critical with respect to our own theories, and self-critical with respect to our own criticism; and, of course, we must never evade an issue.

This, then, is roughly the *methodological form* of (D), of the criterion of demarcation. Propose theories which can be criticized. Think about possible decisive falsifying experiments – crucial experiments. But do not give up your theories too easily – not, at any rate, before you have critically examined your criticism.

Empirical-scientific and non-scientific theories

The difficulties connected with my criterion of demarcation (D) are important, but must not be exaggerated. It is vague, since it is a methodological rule, and since the demarcation between science and non-science is vague. But it is more than sharp enough to make a distinction between many physical theories on the one hand, and metaphysical theories, such as psychoanalysis, or Marxism (in its present form), on the other. This is, of course, one of my main theses; and nobody who has not understood it can be said to have understood my theory.

The situation with Marxism is, incidentally, very different from that with psychoanalysis. Marxism was once a scientific theory: it predicted that capitalism would lead to increasing misery and, through a more or less mild revolution, to socialism; it predicted that this would happen first in the technically highest developed countries; and it predicted that the technical evolution of the 'means of production' would lead to social, political, and ideological developments, rather than the other way round.

But the (so-called) socialist revolution came first in one of the technically backward countries. And instead of the means of production producing a new ideology, it was Lenin's and Stalin's ideology that Russia must push forward with its industrialization ('Socialism is dictatorship of the proletariat plus electrification') which promoted the new development of the means of production.

Thus one might say that Marxism was once a science, but one which was refuted by some of the facts which happened to clash with its predictions (I have here mentioned just a few of these facts).[7]

However, Marxism is no longer a science; for it broke the methodological rule that we must accept falsification, and it immunized itself against the most blatant refutations of its predictions. Ever since then, it can be described only as non-science – as a metaphysical dream, if you like, married to a cruel reality.

Psychoanalysis is a very different case. It is an interesting psychological metaphysics (and no doubt there is some truth in it, as there is so often in metaphysical ideas), but it never was a science. There may be lots of people who are Freudian or Adlerian cases: Freud himself was clearly a Freudian case, and Adler an Adlerian case. But what prevents their theories from being scientific in the sense here described is, very simply, that they do not exclude any physically possible human behaviour. Whatever anybody may do is, in principle, explicable in Freudian or Adlerian terms. (Adler's break with Freud was more Adlerian than Freudian, but Freud never looked on it as a refutation of his theory.)

The point is very clear. Neither Freud nor Adler excludes any particular person's acting in any particular way, whatever the outward circumstances. Whether a man sacrificed his life to rescue a drowning child (a case of sublimation) or whether he murdered the child by drowning him (a case of repression) could not possibly be predicted or excluded by Freud's theory; *the theory was compatible with everything that could happen – even without any special immunization treatment*.

Thus while Marxism became non-scientific by its adoption of an immunizing strategy, psychoanalysis was immune to start with, and remained so.[8] In contrast, most physical theories are pretty free of immunizing tactics and *highly falsifiable to start with*. As a rule, *they exclude an infinity of conceivable possibilities*.

The main value of my criterion of demarcation was, of course, to point out these differences. And it led me to the theory that the empirical content of a theory could be measured by the number of possibilities which it excluded (provided a reasonably non-immunizing methodology was adopted).

Ad hoc hypotheses and auxiliary hypotheses

There is one important method of avoiding or evading refutations: it is the method of auxiliary hypotheses or *ad hoc* hypotheses.

If any of our conjectures goes wrong – if, for example, the planet Uranus does not move exactly as Newton's theory demands – *then we have to change the theory*. But there are in the main two kinds of changes; *conservative and revolutionary*. And among the more conservative changes there are again two: *ad hoc hypotheses* and *auxiliary hypotheses*.

In the case of the disturbances in the motion of Uranus the adopted hypothesis was partly revolutionary: what was conjectured was the existence of a new planet, something which did not affect Newton's laws of motion, but which did affect the much older 'system of the world'. The new conjecture was auxiliary rather than *ad hoc*, for although there was only this one *ad hoc* reason for introducing it, it was *independently testable*: the position of the new planet (Neptune) was calculated, the planet was discovered optically, and it was found that it fully explained the anomalies of Uranus. Thus the auxiliary hypothesis stayed within the Newtonian theoretical framework, and the threatened refutation was transformed into a resounding success.

I call a conjecture '*ad hoc*' if it is introduced (like this one) to explain a particular difficulty, but if (in contrast to this one) *it cannot be tested independently*.

It is clear that, like everything in methodology, the distinction between an *ad hoc* hypothesis and a conservative auxiliary hypothesis is a little vague. Pauli introduced the hypothesis of the neutrino quite consciously as an *ad hoc* hypothesis. He had originally no hope that one day independent evidence would be found; at the time this seemed practically impossible. So we have an example here of an *ad hoc* hypothesis which, with the growth of knowledge, did shed its *ad hoc* character. And we have a warning here not to pronounce too severe an edict against *ad hoc* hypotheses: they may become testable after all, as may also happen to a metaphysical hypothesis. But in general, our criterion of testability warns us against *ad hoc* hypotheses; and Pauli was at first far from happy about the neutrino, which would in all likelihood have been abandoned in the end, had not new methods provided independent tests for its existence.

Ad hoc hypotheses – that is, at the time untestable auxiliary hypotheses – can save almost any theory from any *particular* refutation. But this does not mean that we can go on with an *ad hoc* hypothesis as long as we like. It may become testable; and a negative test may force us either to give it up or to introduce a new secondary *ad hoc* hypothesis, and so on, *ad infinitum*. This, in fact, is a thing we almost always avoid. (I say 'almost' because methodological rules are not hard and fast.)

Moreover, the possibility of making things up with *ad hoc* hypotheses must not be exaggerated: there are many refutations which cannot be evaded in this way, even though some kind of immunizing tactic such as ignoring the refutation is always possible.

Notes

1   See [Popper] *Conjectures and Refutations*, (London: Routledge and Kegan Paul, 1963), p. 110: 'From the point of view of general relativity, . . . the earth rotates . . . *in precisely that sense in which a bicycle wheel rotates.*'
2   See *Conjectures and Refutations*, ch. 3, n. 20–2, pp. 106f.
3   See also my paper 'The present significance of two arguments of Henri Poincaré', *Methodology and Science* 14 (1981), pp. 260–4.
4   See the index of *Conjectures and Refutations* under these names, and vol. III of *The Postscript* (London: Hutchinson, 1982), *Quantum Theory and the Schism in Physics*, [Popper] sect. 20.
5   I must stress this point, because Ayer has asserted on pp. 583f. of 'Philosophy and scientific method', *Proceedings of the XIVth International Congress of Philosophy, Vienna: 2nd to 9th September 1968*, vol. I, pp. 536–42, that 'In modern times two theses have held the field. According to one of them, what is required is that the hypothesis be verifiable: according to the other, that it be falsifiable.' And after outlining very briefly a history of the verifiability criterion, he writes: 'In its current form, all that it requires of a scientific hypothesis is that it should figure non-trivially in a theory which is open to confirmation when taken as a whole.'

'In the case of the principle of falsifiability', Ayer continues, 'the process of adaptation has been less explicit. Some of its adherents still talk as if the formulation which was given to it by Professor Popper in the opening chapters of his *Logik der Forschung* [*The Logic of Scientific Discovery*] continued to hold good. The fact is, however, that Professor Popper himself found it necessary to modify it in the course of this very book.' To this I can only reply that (1) it seems to me better to introduce the necessary modifications in 'this very book' in which the proposal was made; (2) I introduced falsifiability as a criterion of demarcation on p. 40 of *The Logic of Scientific Discovery* and I 'found it necessary' to outline all the various objections on the next page, in the same section, announcing my intention to discuss each of them more fully later; (3) the one difficulty which I postponed for later – the formal non-falsifiability of probability statements – was solved by a methodological proposal.

6   The term is due to Hans Albert.
7   For a fuller discussion see [Popper] *The Open Society and Its Enemies* (London: Routledge and Kegan Paul, 1945), vol. II, pp. 108f.
8   See *Conjectures and Refutations*, ch. 1, especially pp. 35–8.

32

Anomaly and the emergence
of scientific discoveries
Thomas Kuhn

In this brief extract from his book *The Structure of Scientific Revolutions* (1962) Thomas Kuhn (1922–) describes a psychological experiment which he thinks illuminates the nature of scientific discovery. The history of science is characterized by periods of normal science within which scientists work. Scientists working within the received paradigm will not give it up easily, even in the face of anomalous results. Indeed, such anomalous results may be difficult or impossible to discern given the scientists' background expectations and the way these colour what they observe. However at key points in history paradigm shifts – changes in the fundamental assumptions of the various sciences – occur.

From Thomas Kuhn, *The Structure of Scientific Revolutions*

In a psychological experiment that deserves to be far better known outside the trade, Bruner and Postman asked experimental subjects to identify on short and controlled exposure a series of playing cards. Many of the cards were normal, but some were made anomalous, e.g., a red six of spades and black four of hearts. Each experimental run was constituted by the display of a single card to a single subject in a series of gradually increased exposures. After each exposure the subject was asked what he had seen, and the run was terminated by two successive correct identifcations.[1]

Even on the shortest exposures many subjects identified most of the cards, and after a small increase all the subjects identified them all. For the normal cards these identifications were usually correct, but the anomalous cards were almost always identified, without apparent hesitation or puzzlement, as normal. The black four of hearts might, for example, be identified as the four of either spades or hearts. Without any awareness of trouble, it was immediately fitted to one of the conceptual categories prepared by prior experience. One would not even like to say that the subjects had seen something different from what they identified. With a further increase of exposure to the anomalous cards, subjects did begin to hesitate and to display awareness of anomaly. Exposed, for example, to the red six of spades, some would say: That's the six of spades, but there's something wrong with it – the black has a red border. Further increase of exposure resulted in still more hesitation and confusion until finally, and sometimes quite suddenly, most subjects would produce the correct identification without hesitation. Moreover, after doing this with two or three of the anomalous cards, they would have little further difficulty with the others. A few subjects, however, were never able to make the requisite adjustment of their categories. Even at forty times the average exposure required to recognize normal cards for what they were, more than 10 per cent of the anomalous cards were not correctly identified. And the subjects who then failed often experienced acute personal distress. One of them exclaimed: 'I can't make the suit out, whatever it is. It didn't even look like a card that time. I don't know what color it is now or whether it's a spade or a heart. I'm not even sure now what a spade looks like. My God!'[2] In the next section we shall occasionally see scientists behaving this way too.

Either as a metaphor or because it reflects the nature of the mind, that psychological experiment provides a wonderfully simple and cogent schema for the process of scientific discovery. In science, as in the playing card experiment, novelty emerges only with difficulty, manifested by resistance, against a background provided by expectation. Initially, only the anticipated and usual are experienced even under circumstances where anomaly is later to be observed. Further acquaintance, however, does result in awareness of something wrong or does relate the effect to something that has gone wrong before. That awareness of anomaly opens a period in which conceptual categories are adjusted until the initially anomalous has become the anticipated. At this point the discovery has been completed. I have already urged that that process or one very much like it is involved in the emergence of all fundamental scientific novelties. Let me now point out that, recognizing the process, we can at last begin to see why normal science, a pursuit not directed to novelties and tending at first to suppress them, should nevertheless be so effective in causing them to arise.

In the development of any science, the first received paradigm is usually felt to account quite successfully for most of the observations and experiments easily accessible to that science's practitioners. Further development, therefore, ordinarily calls for the construction of elaborate equipment, the development of an esoteric vocabulary and skills, and a refinement of concepts that increasingly lessens their resemblance to their usual common-sense prototypes. That professionalization leads, on the one hand, to an immense restriction of the scientist's vision and to a considerable resistance to paradigm change. The science has become increasingly rigid. On the other hand, within those areas to which the paradigm directs the attention of the group, normal science leads to a detail of information and to a precision of the observation-theory match that could be achieved in no other way. Furthermore, that detail and precision-of-match have a value that transcends their not always very high intrinsic interest. Without the special apparatus that is constructed mainly for anticipated functions, the results that lead ultimately to novelty could not occur. And even when the apparatus exists, novelty ordinarily emerges only for the man who, knowing *with precision* what he should expect, is able to recognize that something has gone wrong. Anomaly appears only against the background provided by the paradigm. The more precise and far-reaching that paradigm is, the more sensitive an indicator it provides of anomaly and hence of an occasion for paradigm change. In the normal mode of discovery, even resistance to change has a use ... By ensuring that the paradigm will not be too easily surrendered, resistance guarantees that scientists will not be lightly distracted and that the anomalies that lead to paradigm change will penetrate existing knowledge to the core. The very fact that a significant scientific novelty so often emerges simultaneously from several laboratories is an index both to the strongly traditional nature of normal science and to the completeness with which that traditional pursuit prepares the way for its own change.

Notes

1   J. S. Bruner and Leo Postman, "On the perception of incongruity: a paradigm," *Journal of Personality* XVIII (1949) pp. 206–23.
2   Ibid., p. 218. My colleague Postman tells me that, though knowing all about the apparatus and display in advance, he nevertheless found looking at the incongruous cards acutely uncomfortable.

33

How to defend society against science
Paul Feyerabend

In this reading the controversial and outspoken philosopher Paul Feyerabend (1924–94) attacks science and scientific education head on. Deliberately polemical and uncompromising, Feyerabend does what philosophers have traditionally done, but which few present-day professional philosophers dare to do: he challenges the cherished beliefs of society. His position is radical by any standards, since he claims that science is simply a form of ideology like any other ideology. For a critique of Feyerabend's position, see the following reading by Sokal and Bricmont, 'Feyerabend: anything goes'.

From Paul Feyerabend, 'How to defend society against science', *Radical Philosophy*, vol. 2

Fairytales

I want to defend society and its inhabitants from all ideologies, science included. All ideologies must be seen in perspective. One must not take them too seriously. One must read them like fairytales which have lots of interesting things to say but which also contain wicked lies, or like ethical prescriptions which may be useful rules of thumb but which are deadly when followed to the letter.

Now – is this not a strange and ridiculous attitude? Science, surely, was always in the forefront of the fight against authoritarianism and super-stition. It is to science that we owe our increased intellectual freedom *vis-à-vis* religious beliefs; it is to science that we owe the liberation of mankind from ancient and rigid forms of thought. Today these forms of thought are nothing but bad dreams – and this we learned from science. Science and enlightenment are one and the same thing – even the most radical critics of society believe this. Kropotkin wants to overthrow all traditional institutions and forms of belief, with the exception of science. Ibsen criticises the most intimate ramifications of 19th century bourgeois ideology, but he leaves science untouched. Lévi-Strauss has made us realise that Western Thought is not the lonely peak of human achievement it was once believed to be, but he excludes science from his relativization of ideologies. Marx and Engels were convinced that science would aid the workers in their quest for mental and social liberation. Are all these people deceived? Are they all mistaken about the role of science? Are they all the victims of a chimaera?

To these questions my answer is a firm *Yes and No.*

Now, let me explain my answer.

My explanation consists of two parts, one more general, one more specific.

The general explanation is simple. Any ideology that breaks the hold a comprehensive system of thought has on the minds of men contributes to the liberation of man. Any ideology that makes man question inherited beliefs is an aid to enlightenment. A truth that reigns without checks and balances is a tyrant who must be overthrown and any falsehood that can aid us in the overthrow of this tyrant is to be welcomed. It follows that 17th and 18th century science indeed *was* an instrument of liberation and enlightenment. It does not follow that science is bound to *remain* such an instrument. There is nothing inherent in science or in any other ideology that makes it *essentially* liberating. Ideologies can deteriorate and become stupid religions. Look at Marxism. And that the science of today is very different from the science of 1650 is evident at the most superficial glance.

For example, consider the role science now plays in education. Scientific 'facts' are taught at a very early age and in the very same manner in which religious 'facts' were taught only a century ago. There is no attempt to waken the critical abilities of the pupil so that he may be able to see things in perspective. At the universities the situation is even worse, for indoctrination is here carried out in a much more systematic manner. Criticism is not entirely absent. Society, for example, and its institutions, are criticised most severely and often most unfairly and this already at the elementary school level. But science is excepted from the criticism. In society at large the judgement of the scientist is received with the same reverence as the judgement of bishops and cardinals was accepted not too long ago. The move towards 'demythologization', for example, is largely motivated by the wish to avoid any clash between Christianity and scientific ideas. If such a clash occurs, then science is certainly right and Christianity wrong. Pursue this investigation further and you will see that science has now become as oppressive as the ideologies it had once to fight. Do not be misled by the fact that today hardly anyone gets killed for joining a scientific heresy. This has nothing to do with science. It has something to do with the general quality of our civilization. Heretics in science are still made to suffer from the *most severe* sanctions this relatively tolerant civilization has to offer.

But – is this description not utterly unfair? Have I not presented the matter in a very distorted light by using tendentious and distorting terminology? Must we not describe the situation in a very different way? I have said that science has become *rigid,* that it has ceased to be an instrument of *change* and *liberation* without adding that it has found the *truth*, or a large part thereof. Considering this additional fact we realise, so the objection goes, that the rigidity of science is not due to human wilfulness. It lies in the nature of things. For once we have discovered the truth – what else can we do but follow it?

This trite reply is anything but original. It is used whenever an ideology wants to reinforce the faith of its followers. 'Truth' is such a nicely neutral word. Nobody would deny that it is commendable to speak the truth and wicked to tell lies. Nobody would deny that – and yet nobody knows what such an attitude amounts to. So it is easy to twist matters and to change allegiance to truth in one's everyday affairs into allegiance to the Truth of an ideology which is nothing but the dogmatic defence of that ideology. And it is of course *not* true that we *have* to follow the truth. Human life is guided by many ideas. Truth is one of them. Freedom and mental independence are others. If Truth, as conceived by some ideologists, conflicts with freedom then we have a *choice.* We may abandon freedom. But we may also abandon Truth. (Alternatively, we may adopt a more sophisticated idea of truth that no longer contradicts freedom; that was Hegel's solution.) My criticism of modern science is that it inhibits freedom of thought. If the reason is that it has found the truth and now follows it then I would say that there are better things than first finding, and then following such a monster.

This finishes the general part of my explanation.

There exists a more specific argument to defend the exceptional position science has in society today. Put in a nutshell the argument says (1) that science has finally found the correct *method* for achieving results and (2) that there are many *results* to prove the excellence of the method. The argument is mistaken – but most attempts to show this lead into a dead end. Methodology has by now become so crowded with empty sophistication that it is extremely difficult to perceive the simple errors at the basis. It is like fighting the hydra – cut off one ugly head, and eight formalizations take its place. In this situation the only answer is superficiality: when sophistication loses content then the only way of keeping in touch with reality is to be crude and superficial. This is what I intend to be.

Against method

There is a method, says part (1) of the argument. What is it? How does it work?

One answer which is no longer as popular as it used to be is that science works by collecting facts and inferring theories from them. The answer is unsatisfactory as theories never *follow* from facts in the strict logical sense. To say that they may yet be *supported* by facts assumes a notion of support that (a) does now show this defect and is (b) sufficiently sophisticated to permit us to say to what extent, say, the theory of relativity is supported by the facts. No such notion exists today nor is it likely that it will ever be found (one of the problems is that we need a notion of support in which grey ravens can be said to support 'All Ravens are Black'). This was realised by conventionalists and transcendental idealists who pointed out that theories *shape* and *order* facts and can therefore be retained come what may. They can be retained because the human mind either consciously or unconsciously carried out its ordering function. The trouble with these views is that they assume for the mind what they want to explain for the world, viz. that it works in a regular fashion. There is only one view which overcomes all these difficulties. It was invented twice in the 19th century, by Mill, in his immortal essay *On Liberty*, and by some Darwinists who extended Darwinism to the battle of ideas. This view takes the bull by the horns: theories cannot be justified and their excellence cannot be shown without reference to other theories. We may explain the *success* of a theory by reference to a more comprehensive theory (we may explain the success of Newton's theory by using the general theory of relativity); and we may explain our *preference* for it by comparing it with other theories. Such a comparison does not establish the intrinsic excellence of the theory we have chosen. As a matter of fact, the theory we have chosen may be pretty lousy. It may contain contradictions, it may conflict with well-known facts, it may be cumbersome, unclear, ad hoc in decisive places and so on. But it may still be better than any other theory that is available at the time. It may in fact be the best lousy theory there is. Nor are the standards of judgement chosen in an absolute manner. Our sophistication increases with every choice we make, and so do our standards. Standards compete just as theories compete and we choose the standards most appropriate to the historical situation in which the choice occurs. The rejected alternatives (theories; standards; 'facts') are not eliminated. They serve as correctives (after all, we may have made the wrong choice) and they also explain the content of the preferred views (we understand relativity better when we understand the structure of its competitors; we know the full meaning of freedom only when we have an idea of life in a totalitarian state, of its advantages – and there are many advantages – as well as of its disadvantages). Knowledge so conceived is an ocean of alternatives channelled and subdivided by an ocean of standards. It forces our mind to make imaginative choices and thus makes it grow. It makes our mind capable of choosing, imagining, criticisms.

Today this view is often connected with the name of Karl Popper. But there are some very decisive differences between Popper and Mill. To start with, Popper developed his view to solve a special problem of epistemology – he wanted to solve 'Hume's problem'. Mill, on the other hand, is interested in conditions favourable to human growth. His epistemology is the result of a certain theory of man, and not the other way around. Also Popper, being influenced by the Vienna Circle, improves on the logical form of a theory before discussing it while Mill uses every theory in the form in which it occurs in science. Thirdly, Popper's standards of comparison are rigid and fixed while Mill's standards are permitted to change with the historical situation. Finally, Popper's standards eliminate competitors once and for all: theories that are either not falsifiable, or falsifiable and falsified have no place in science. Popper's criteria are clear, unambiguous, precisely formulated; Mill's criteria are not. This would be an advantage if science itself were clear, unambiguous, and precisely formulated. Fortunately, it is not.

To start with, no new and revolutionary scientific theory is ever formulated in a manner that permits us to say under what circumstances we must regard it as endangered: many revolutionary theories are unfalsifiable. Falsifiable versions do exist, but they are hardly ever in agreement with accepted basic statements: every moderately interesting theory is falsified. Moreover, theories have formal flaws, many of them contain contradictions, ad hoc adjustments, and so on and so forth. Applied resolutely, Popperian criteria would eliminate science without replacing it by anything comparable. They are useless as an aid to science.

In the past decade this has been realised by various thinkers, Kuhn and Lakatos among them. Kuhn's ideas are interesting but, alas, they are much too vague to give rise to anything but lots of hot air. If you don't believe me, look at the literature. Never before has the literature on the philosophy of science been invaded by so many creeps and incompetents. Kuhn encourages people who have no idea why a stone falls to the ground to talk with assurance about scientific method. Now I have no objection to incompetence but I do object when incompetence is accompanied by boredom and self-righteousness. And this is exactly what happens. We do not get interesting false ideas, we get boring ideas or words connected with no ideas at all. Secondly, wherever one tries to make Kuhn's ideas more definite one finds that they are *false*. Was there ever a period of normal science in the history of thought? No – and I challenge anyone to prove the contrary.

Lakatos is immeasurably more sophisticated than Kuhn. Instead of theories he considers research programmes which are sequences of theories connected by methods of modification, so-called heuristics. Each theory in the sequence may be full of faults. It may be beset by anomalies, contradictions, ambiguities. What counts is not the shape of the single theories, but the tendency exhibited by the sequence. We judge historical developments, achievements over a period of time, rather than the situation at a particular time. History and methodology are combined into a single enterprise. A research programme is said to progress if the sequence of theories leads to novel predictions. It is said to degenerate if it is reduced to absorbing facts that have been discovered without its help. A decisive feature of Lakatos' methodology is that such evaluations are no longer tied to methodological rules which tell the scientist to either retain or to abandon a research programme. Scientists may stick to a degenerating programme, they may even succeed in making the programme overtake its rivals and they therefore proceed rationally with whatever they are doing (provided they continue calling degenerating programmes degenerating and progressive programmes progressive). This means that Lakatos offers *words* which *sound* like the elements of a methodology; he does not offer a methodology. There is no method according to the most advanced and sophisticated methodology in existence today. This finishes my reply to part (1) of the specific argument.

Against results

According to part (2), science deserves a special position because it has produced *results*. This is an argument only if it can be taken for granted that nothing else has ever produced results. Now it may be admitted that almost everyone who discusses the matter makes such an assumption. It may also be admitted that it is not easy to show that the assumption is false. Forms of life different from science have either disappeared or have degenerated to an extent that makes a fair comparison impossible. Still, the situation is not as hopeless as it was only a decade ago. We have become acquainted with methods of medical diagnosis and therapy which are effective (and perhaps even more effective than the corresponding parts of Western medicine) and which are yet based on an ideology that is radically different from the ideology of Western science. We have learned that there are phenomena such as telepathy and telekinesis which are obliterated by a scientific approach and which could be used to do research in an entirely novel way (earlier thinkers such as Agrippa of Nettesheim, John Dee, and even Bacon were aware of these phenomena). And then – is it not the case that the Church saved souls while science often does the very opposite? Of course, nobody now believes in the ontology that underlies this judgement. Why? Because of ideological pressures identical with those which today make us listen to science to the exclusion of everything else. It is also true that phenomena such as telekinesis and acupuncture may eventually be absorbed into the body of science and may therefore be called 'scientific'. But note that this happens only *after* a long period of

295

resistance during which a science *not yet* containing the phenomena wants to get the upper hand over forms of life that contain them. And this leads to a further objection against part (2) of the specific argument. The fact that science has results counts in its favour only if these results were achieved by science alone, and without any outside help. A look at history shows that science hardly ever gets its results in this way. When Copernicus introduced a new view of the universe, he did not consult *scientific* predecessors, he consulted a crazy Pythagorean such as Philolaos. He adopted his ideas and he maintained them in the face of all sound rules of scientific method. Mechanics and optics owe a lot to artisans, medicine to midwives and witches. And in our own day we have seen how the interference of the state can advance science: when the Chinese communists refused to be intimidated by the judgement of experts and ordered traditional medicine back into universities and hospitals there was an outcry all over the world that science would now be ruined in China. The very opposite occurred: Chinese science advanced and Western science learned from it. Wherever we look we see that great scientific advances are due to outside interference which is made to prevail in the face of the most basic and most 'rational' methodological rules. The lesson is plain: there does not exist a single argument that could be used to support the exceptional role which science today plays in society. Science has done many things, but so have other ideologies. Science often proceeds systematically, but so do other ideologies (just consult the records of the many doctrinal debates that took place in the Church) and, besides, there are no overriding rules which are adhered to under any circumstances; there is no 'scientific methodology' that can be used to separate science from the rest. *Science is just one of the many ideologies that propel society and it should be treated as such* (this statement applies even to the most progressive and most dialectical sections of science). What consequences can we draw from this result?

The most important consequence is that there must be a *formal separation between state and science* just as there is now a formal separation between state and church. Science may influence society but only to the extent to which any political or other pressure group is permitted to influence society. Scientists may be consulted on important projects but the final judgement must be left to the democratically elected consulting bodies. These bodies will consist mainly of laymen. Will the laymen be able to come to a correct judgement? Most certainly, for the competence, the complications and the successes of science are vastly exaggerated. One of the most exhilarating experiences is to see how a lawyer, who is a layman, can find holes in the testimony, the technical testimony of the most advanced expert and thus prepare the jury for its verdict. Science is not a closed book that is understood only after years of training. It is an intellectual discipline that can be examined and criticised by anyone who is interested and that looks difficult and profound only because of a system-atic campaign of obfuscation carried out by many scientists (though, I am happy to say, not by all). Organs of the state should never hesitate to reject the judgement of scientists when they have reason for doing so. Such rejec-tion will educate the general public, will make it more confident and it may even lead to improvement. Considering the sizeable chauvinism of the scientific establishment we can say: the more Lysenko affairs the better (it is not the *interference* of the state that is objectionable in the case of Lysenko, but the *totalitarian* interference which kills the opponent rather than just neglecting his advice). Three cheers to the fundamentalists in California who succeeded in having a dogmatic formulation of the theory of evolution removed from the text books and an account of Genesis included (but I know that they would become as chauvinistic and totali-tarian as scientists are today when given the chance to run society all by themselves. Ideologies are marvellous when used in the company of other ideologies. They become boring and doctrinaire as soon as their merits lead to the removal of their opponents). The most important change, however, will have to occur in the field of *education.*

Education and myth

The purpose of education, so one would think, is to introduce the young into life, and that means: into the *society* where they are born and into the *physical universe* that surrounds the society. The method of education often consists in the reaching of some *basic myth.* The myth is available in various versions. More advanced versions may be taught by initiation rites which firmly implant them into the mind. Knowing the myth the grown-up can explain almost everything (or else he can turn to experts for more detailed information). He is the master of Nature and of Society. He under-stands them both and he knows how to interact with them. However, *he is not the master of the myth that guides his understanding.*

Such further mastery was aimed at, and was partly achieved, by the Presocratics. The Presocratics not only tried to understand the *world.* They also tried to understand, and thus to become the masters of, the *means of understanding the world.* Instead of being content with a single myth they developed many and so diminished the power which a well-told story has over the minds of men. The sophists introduced still further methods for reducing the debilitating effect of interesting, coherent, 'empirically adequate' etc. etc. tales. The achievements of these thinkers were not appreciated and they certainly are not understood today. When teaching a myth we want to increase the chance that it will be understood (i.e. no puzzlement about any feature of the myth), believed, *and accepted.* This does not do any harm when the myth is counterbalanced by other myths:

297

even the most dedicated (i.e. totalitarian) instructor in a certain version of Christianity cannot prevent his pupils from getting in touch with Buddhists, Jews and other disreputable people. It is very different in the case of science, or of rationalism where the field is almost completely dominated by the believers. In this case it is of paramount importance to strengthen the minds of the young and 'strengthening the minds of the young' means strengthening them *against* any easy acceptance of comprehensive views. What we need here is an education that makes people *contrary, counter-suggestive without* making them incapable of devoting themselves to the elaboration of any single view. How can this aim be achieved?

It can be achieved by protecting the tremendous imagination which children possess and by developing to the full the spirit of contradiction that exists in them. On the whole children are much more intelligent than their teachers. They succumb, and give up their intelligence because they are bullied, or because their teachers get the better of them by emotional means. Children can learn, understand, and keep separate two to three different languages ('children' and by this I mean 3 to 5 year olds, NOT eight year olds who were experimented upon quite recently and did not come out too well; why? because they were already loused up by incompetent teaching at an earlier age). Of course, the languages must be introduced in a more interesting way than is usually done. There are marvellous writers in all languages who have told marvellous stories – let us begin our language teaching with *them* and not with 'der Hund hat einen Schwanz' and similar inanities. Using stories we may of course also introduce 'scientific' accounts, say, of the origin of the world and thus make the children acquainted with science as well. But science must not be given any special position except for pointing out that there are lots of people who believe in it. Later on the stories which have been told will be supplemented with 'reasons' where by reasons I mean further accounts of the kind found in the tradition to which the story belongs. And, of course, there will also be contrary reasons. Both reasons and contrary reasons will be told by the experts in the fields and so the young generation becomes acquainted with all kinds of sermons and all types of wayfarers. It becomes acquainted with them, it becomes acquainted with their stories and every individual can make up his mind which way to go. By now everyone knows that you can earn a lot of money and respect and perhaps even a Nobel Prize by becoming a scientist, so, many will become scientists. They will *become* scientists *without having been taken in by the ideology of science*, they will *be* scientists *because they have made a free choice*. But has not much time been wasted on unscientific subjects and will this not detract from their competence once they have become scientists? Not at all! The progress of science, of good science, depends on novel ideas and on intellectual freedom: science has very often been advanced by outsiders (remember that Bohr and Einstein regarded themselves as outsiders). Will not many people make the wrong choice and end up in a dead end? Well, that depends on what you mean by a 'dead end'. Most scientists today are devoid of ideas, full of fear, intent on producing some paltry result so that they can add to the flood of inane papers that now constitutes 'scientific progress' in many areas. And, besides, what is more important? To lead a life which one has chosen with open eyes, or to spend one's time in the nervous attempt of avoiding what some not so intelligent people call 'dead ends'? Will not the number of scientists decrease so that in the end there is nobody to run our precious laboratories? I do not think so. Given a choice many people may choose science, for a science that is run by free agents looks much more attractive than the science of today which is run by slaves, slaves of institutions and slaves of 'reason'. And if there is a temporary shortage of scientists the situation may always be remedied by various kinds of incentives. Of course, scientists will not play any predominant role in the society I envisage. They will be more than balanced by magicians, or priests, or astrologers. Such a situation is unbearable for many people, old and young, right and left. Almost all of you have the firm belief that at least *some* kind of truth has been found, that it must be preserved, and that the method of teaching I advocate and the form of society I defend will dilute it and make it finally disappear. You have this firm belief; many of you may even have reasons. *But what you have to consider is that the absence of good contrary reasons is due to a historical accident*; it does *not* lie in the nature of things. Build up the kind of society I recommend and the views you now despise (without knowing them, to be sure) will return in such splendour that you will have to work hard to maintain your own position and will perhaps be entirely unable to do so. You do not believe me? Then look at history. Scientific astronomy was firmly founded on Ptolemy and Aristotle, two of the greatest minds in the history of Western Thought. Who upset their well argued, empirically adequate and precisely formulated system? Philolaos the mad and antediluvian Pythagorean. How was it that Philolaos could stage such a comeback? Because he found an able defender: Copernicus. Of course, you may follow your intuitions as I am following mine. But remember that your intuitions are the result of your 'scientific' training where by science I also mean the science of Karl Marx. My training, or, rather, my non-training, is that of a journalist who is interested in strange and bizarre events. Finally, is it not utterly irresponsible, in the present world situation, with millions of people starving, others enslaved, downtrodden, in abject misery of body and mind, to think luxurious thoughts such as these? Is not freedom of choice a luxury under such circumstances; Is not the flippancy and the humour I want to see combined with the freedom of choice a luxury under such circumstances? Must we not give up all self-indulgence and *act*? Join together, and *act*? That is the most important objection which today is raised against an approach such as the one recommended by me. It has tremendous appeal, it has the appeal of unselfish dedication. Unselfish dedication – to what? Let us see!

We are supposed to give up our selfish inclinations and dedicate ourselves to the liberation of the oppressed. And selfish inclinations are what? They are our wish for maximum liberty of thought in the society in which we live *now*, maximum liberty not only of an abstract kind, but expressed in appropriate institutions and methods of teaching. This wish for concrete intellectual and physical liberty in our own surroundings is to be put aside, for the time being. This assumes, first, that we do not need this liberty for our task. It assumes that we can carry out our task with a mind that is firmly closed to some alternatives. It assumes that the correct way of liberating others *has already been found* and that all that is needed is to carry it out. I am sorry, I cannot accept such doctrinaire self-assurance in such extremely important matters. Does this mean that we cannot act at all? It does not. But it means that *while acting we have to try to realise as much of the freedom I have recommended so that our actions may be corrected in the light of the ideas we get while increasing our freedom.* This will slow us down, no doubt, but are we supposed to charge ahead simply because some people tell us that they have found an explanation for all the misery and an excellent way out of it? Also we want to liberate people not to make them succumb to a new kind of slavery, *but to make them realise their own wishes*, however different these wishes may be from our own. Self-righteous and narrow minded liberators cannot do this. As a rule they soon impose a slavery that is worse, because more systematic, than the very sloppy slavery they have removed. And as regards humour and flippancy the answer should be obvious. Why would anyone want to liberate anyone else? Surely not because of some *abstract* advantage of liberty but because liberty is the best way to free development *and thus to happiness.* We want to liberate people *so that they can smile.* Shall we be able to do this if we ourselves have forgotten how to smile and are frowning on those who still remember? Shall we then not spread another disease, comparable to the one we want to remove, the disease of puritanical self-righteousness? Do not object that dedication and humour do not go together – Socrates is an excellent example to the contrary. *The hardest task needs the lightest hand or else its completion will not lead to freedom but to a tyranny much worse than the one it replaces.*

34

Feyerabend: anything goes
Alan Sokal and
Jean Bricmont

As part of a general attack on relativism in the philosophy of science, Alan Sokal and Jean Bricmont analyse and criticize Paul Feyerabend's radical position (for an example of Feyerabend's approach, see the previous reading, 'How to defend society against science'). They succinctly demonstrate the flaws in his argument, whilst acknowledging that he is basically correct to maintain that science does not progress by following a well-defined method. Ultimately, though, Feyerabend has been carried away by his own rhetoric, and has made claims that he cannot justify and which are really evasions of the truth.

From Alan Sokal and Jean Bricmont, *Intellectual Impostures*

_____

The main problem in reading Feyerabend is to know when to take him seriously. On the one hand, he is often considered as a sort of court jester in the philosophy of science, and he seems to have taken some pleasure in playing this role.[1] At times he himself emphasized that his words ought not be taken literally.[2] On the other hand, his writings are full of references to specialized works in the history and philosophy of science, as well as in physics; and this aspect of his work has greatly contributed to his reputation as a major philosopher of science. Bearing all this in mind, we shall discuss what seem to us to be his fundamental errors, and illustrate the excesses to which they can lead.

We fundamentally agree with what Feyerabend says about the scientific method, considered in the abstract:

> The idea that science can, and should, be run according to fixed and universal rules, is both unrealistic and pernicious.
>
> (Feyerabend 1975: 295)

He criticizes at length the 'fixed and universal rules' through which earlier philosophers thought that they could express the essence of the scientific method. As we have said, it is extremely difficult, if not impossible, to codify the scientific method, though this does not prevent the development of certain rules, with a more-or-less general degree of validity, on the basis of previous experience. If Feyerabend had limited himself to showing, through historical examples, the limitations of any general and universal codification of the scientific method, we could only agree with him.[3] Unfortunately, he goes much further:

> All methodologies have their limitations and the only 'rule' that survives is 'anything goes'.
>
> (Feyerabend 1975: 296)

This is an erroneous inference that is typical of relativist reasoning. Starting from a correct observation – 'all methodologies have their limitations' – Feyerabend jumps to a totally false conclusion: 'anything goes'. There are several ways to swim, and all of them have their limitations, but it is not true that all bodily movements are equally good (if one prefers not to sink). There is no unique method of criminal investigation, but this does not mean that all methods are equally reliable (think about trial by fire). The same is true of scientific methods.

In the second edition of his book, Feyerabend tries to defend himself against a literal reading of 'anything goes'. He writes:

> A naive anarchist says (a) that both absolute rules and context-dependent rules have their limits and infers (b) that all rules and standards are worthless and should be given up. Most reviewers regard me as a naive anarchist in this sense . . . [But] while I agree with (a) I do not agree with (b). I argue that all rules have their limits and that there is no comprehensive 'rationality', I do not argue that we should proceed without rules and standards.
>
> (Feyerabend 1993: 231)

The problem is that Feyerabend gives little indication of the *content* of these 'rules and standards'; and unless they are constrained by some notion of rationality, one arrives easily at the most extreme form of relativism.

When Feyerabend addresses concrete issues, he frequently mixes reasonable observations with rather bizarre suggestions:

> [T]he first step in our criticism of customary concepts and customary reactions is to step outside the circle and either to invent a new conceptual system, for example a new theory, that clashes with the most carefully established observational results and confounds the most plausible theoretical principles, or to import such a system from

outside science, from religion, from mythology, from the ideas of incompetents, or the ramblings of madmen.

(Feyerabend 1993: 52–3)[4]

One could defend these assertions by invoking the classical distinction between the context of *discovery* and the context of *justification*. Indeed, in the idiosyncratic process of inventing scientific theories, all methods are in principle admissible – deduction, induction, analogy, intuition and even hallucination[5] – and the only real criterion is pragmatic. On the other hand, the justification of theories must be rational, even if this rationality cannot be definitively codified. One might be tempted to think that Feyerabend's admittedly extreme examples concern solely the context of discovery, and that there is thus no real contradiction between his viewpoint and ours.

But the problem is that Feyerabend explicitly *denies* the validity of the distinction between discovery and justification.[6] Of course, the sharpness of this distinction was greatly exaggerated in traditional epistemology. We always come back to the same problem: it is naive to believe that there exist general, context-independent rules that allow us to verify or falsify a theory; otherwise put, the context of justification and the context of discovery evolve historically in parallel.[7] Nevertheless, at each moment of history, such a distinction exists. If it didn't, the justification of theories would be unconstrained by any considerations of rationality. Let us think again about criminal investigations: the culprit can be discovered thanks to all sorts of fortuitous events, but the evidence put forward to prove his guilt does not enjoy such a freedom (even if the standards of evidence also evolve historically).[8]

Once Feyerabend has made the leap to 'anything goes', it is not surprising that he constantly compares science with mythology or religion, as, for example, in the following passage:

Newton reigned for more than 150 years, Einstein briefly introduced a more liberal point of view only to be succeeded by the Copenhagen Interpretation. The similarities between science and myth are indeed astonishing.

(Feyerabend 1975: 298)

Here Feyerabend is suggesting that the so-called Copenhagen interpretation of quantum mechanics, due principally to Niels Bohr and Werner Heisenberg, was accepted by physicists in a rather dogmatic way, which is not entirely false. (It is less clear which point of view of Einstein he is alluding to.) But what Feyerabend does not give are examples of myths that change because experiments contradict them, or that suggest experiments aimed at discriminating between earlier and later versions of the myth. It is only for this reason – which is crucial – that the 'similarities between science and myth' are superficial.

This analogy occurs again when Feyerabend suggests separating Science and the State:

> While the parents of a six-year-old child can decide to have him instructed in the rudiments of Protestantism, or in the rudiments of the Jewish faith, or to omit religious instruction altogether, they do not have a similar freedom in the case of the sciences. Physics, astronomy, history *must* be learned. They cannot be replaced by magic, astrology, or by a study of legends.
>
> Nor is one content with a merely *historical* presentation of physical (astronomical, historical, etc.) facts and principles. One does not say: *some people believe* that the earth moves round the sun while others regard the earth as a hollow sphere that contains the sun, the planets, the fixed stars. One says: the earth *moves* round the sun – everything else is sheer idiocy.
>
> (Feyerabend 1975: 301)

In this passage Feyerabend reintroduces, in a particularly brutal form, the classical distinction between 'facts' and 'theories' – a basic tenet of the Vienna Circle epistemology he rejects. At the same time he appears to use implicitly in the social sciences a naively realist epistemology that he rejects for the natural sciences. How, after all, does one find out exactly what 'some people believe', if not by using methods analogous to those of the sciences (observations, polls, etc.)? If, in a survey of Americans' astronomical beliefs, the sample were limited to physics professors, there would probably be no one who 'regards the earth as a hollow sphere'; but Feyerabend could respond, quite rightly, that the poll was poorly designed and the sampling biased (would he dare say that it is unscientific?). The same goes for an anthropologist who stays in New York and invents in his office the myths of other peoples. But which criteria acceptable to Feyerabend would be violated? Doesn't anything go? Feyerabend's methodological relativism, if taken literally, is so radical that it becomes self-refuting. Without a minimum of (rational) method, even a 'merely historical presentation of facts' becomes impossible.

What is striking in Feyerabend's writings is, paradoxically, their abstractness and generality. His arguments show, at best, that science does not progress by following a well-defined method, and with that we basically agree. But Feyerabend never explains in what sense atomic theory or evolution theory might be *false*, despite all that we know today. And if he does not say that, it is probably because he does not believe it, and shares (at least in part) with most of his colleagues the scientific view of the world, namely that species evolved, that matter is made of atoms, etc.

And if he shares those ideas, it is probably because he has good reasons to do so. Why not think about those reasons and try to make them explicit, rather than just repeating over and over again that they are not justifiable by some universal rules of method? Working case by case, he could show that there are indeed solid empirical arguments supporting those theories.

Of course, this may or may not be the kind of question that interests Feyerabend. He often gives the impression that his opposition to science is not of a cognitive nature but follows rather from a choice of lifestyle, as when he says: 'love becomes impossible for people who insist on "objectivity" i.e. who live entirely in accordance with the spirit of science.'[9] The trouble is that he fails to make a clear distinction between factual judgments and value judgments. He could, for example, maintain that evolution theory is infinitely more plausible than any creationist myth, but that parents nevertheless have a right to demand that schools teach false theories to their children. We would disagree, but the debate would no longer be purely on the cognitive level, and would involve political and ethical considerations.

In the same vein, Feyerabend writes in the introduction to the Chinese edition of *Against Method*:[10]

> *First-world science is one science among many* . . . My main motive in writing the book was humanitarian, not intellectual. I wanted to support people, not to 'advance knowledge'.
> (Feyerabend 1988: 3 and 1993: 3, italics in original)

The problem is that the first thesis is of a purely cognitive nature (at least if he is speaking of science and not of technology), while the second is linked to practical goals. But if, in reality, there are no 'other sciences' really distinct from those of the 'first world' that are nevertheless equally powerful at the cognitive level, in what way would asserting the first thesis (which would be false) allow him to 'support people'? The problems of truth and objectivity cannot be evaded so easily.

Notes

1   For example, he writes: 'Imre Lakatos, somewhat jokingly, called me an anarchist and I had no objection to putting on the anarchist's mask' (Feyerabend 1993, p. vii).

2   For example: 'The main ideas of [this] essay . . . are rather trivial and appear trivial when expressed in suitable terms. I prefer more paradoxical formulations, however, for nothing dulls the mind as thoroughly as hearing familiar words and slogans' (Feyerabend 1993, p. xiv). And also: 'Always remember that the demonstrations and the rhetorics used do not express any "deep

convictions" of mine. They merely show how easy it is to lead people by the nose in a rational way. An anarchist is like an undercover agent who plays the game of Reason in order to undercut the authority of Reason (Truth, Honesty, Justice, and so on)' (ibid., p. 23). This passage is followed by a footnote referring to the Dadaist movement.

3   However, we take no position on the validity of the details of his historical analyses. See, for example, Clavelin 1994 for a critique of Feyerabend's theses concerning Galileo.

Let us note also that several of his discussions of problems in modern physics are erroneous or grossly exaggerated: see, for example his claims concerning Brownian motion (Feyerabend 1993, pp. 27–9), renormalization (p. 46), the orbit of Mercury (pp. 47–9), and scattering in quantum mechanics (pp. 49–50n). to disentangle all these confusions would take too much space; but see Bricmont 1995, p. 184 for a brief analysis of Feyerabend's claims concerning Brownian motion and the second law of thermodynamics.

4   For a similar statement, see Feyerabend 1993, p. 33.

5   For example, it is said that the chemist Kekule (1829–96) was led to conjecture (correctly) the structure of benzene as the result of a dream.

6   Feyerabend 1993, pp. 147–9.

7   For example, the anomalous behavior of Mercury's orbit acquired a different epistemological status with the advent of general relativity . . .

8   A similar remark can be made about the classical distinction, also criticized by Feyerabend, between observational and theoretical statements. One should not be naive when saying that one 'measures' something; nevertheless, there do exist 'facts' – for example, the position of a needle on a screen or the characters on a computer printout – and these facts do not always coincide with our desires.

9   Feyerabend 1987, p. 263.

10   Reproduced in the second and third English editions.

References

Bricmont, Jean (1995) 'Science of chaos or chaos of science?', *Physicalia magazine* 17/3–4 (available on-line as publication UCL-IPT-96–03 at http://www.fyma.ucl.ac.be/reche/1996/1996.html; a slightly earlier version of this article appeared in P. R. Gross, N. Levitt and M. W. Lewis (eds) (1996) *The Flight from Science and Reason, Annals of the New York Academy of Sciences* 775, pp. 131–75).

Clavelin, Maurice (1994) 'L'histoire des sciences devant la sociologie de la science', in Raymond Boudon and Maurice Clavelin (eds) *Le Relativisme est-il résistible? Regards sur la sociologie des sciences*, Paris: Presses Universitaires de France, pp. 229–47.

Feyerabend, Paul (1975) *Against Method*, London: New Left Books. Second edition, London: Verso, 1988; third edition, London: Verso, 1993.

—— (1987) *Farewell to Reason*, London: Verso.

Mind

35

'The diary' and 'The beetle in the box'
Ludwig Wittgenstein

These two sections from Ludwig Wittgenstein's (1889–1951) posthumous *Philosophical Investigations* (1953) suggest that the traditional picture of the relationship between language and experience is fundamentally flawed. The case of the diary (section 258) illustrates the impossibility of reliably labelling one's own experiences since there is no criterion of correctness; the beetle in the box example (section 293) makes the point that we cannot learn the meaning of such terms as 'pain' through reflection on our own private experiences.

From Ludwig Wittgenstein, *Philosophical Investigations*

---

258. Let us imagine the following case. I want to keep a diary about the recurrence of a certain sensation. To this end I associate it with the sign "S" and write this sign in a calendar for every day on which I have the sensation.—I will remark first of all that a definition of the sign cannot be formulated.—But still I can give myself a kind of ostensive definition.—How? Can I point to the sensation? Not in the ordinary sense. But I speak, or write the sign down, and at the same time I concentrate my attention on the sensation—and so, as it were, point to it inwardly.—But what is this ceremony for? for that is all it seems to be! A definition surely serves to establish the meaning of a sign.—Well, that is done precisely by the concentrating of my attention; for in this way I impress on myself the connexion between the sign and the sensation.—But "I impress it on myself" can only mean: this process brings it about that I remember the connexion *right* in the future. But in the present case I have no criterion of correctness. One would like to say: whatever is going to seem right to me is right. And that only means that here we can't talk about 'right'.

[. . .]

293. If I say of myself that it is only from my own case that I know what the word "pain" means—must I not say the same of other people too? And how can I generalize the *one* case so irresponsibly?

Now someone tells me that *he* knows what pain is only from his own case!—Suppose everyone had a box with something in it: we call it a "beetle". No one can look into anyone else's box, and everyone says he knows what a beetle is only by looking at *his* beetle.—Here it would be quite possible for everyone to have something different in his box. One might even imagine such a thing constantly changing.—But suppose the word "beetle" had a use in these people's language?—If so it would not be used as the name of a thing. The thing in the box has no place in the language-game at all; not even as a *something*: for the box might even be empty.—No, one can 'divide through' by the thing in the box; it cancels out, whatever it is.

That is to say: if we construe the grammar of the expression of sensation on the model of 'object and designation' the object drops out of consideration as irrelevant.

36

Sensations and brain
processes
J. J. C. Smart

The basic question in the philosophy of mind is that of the relation between mind and body: the mental and the physical. In this paper J. J. C. Smart (1920–) robustly defends the notion that sensations are identical with brain processes. When I get a sensation of a yellowish-orange after-image this just is a brain process, nothing more. This view, the mind–brain identity thesis, is open to a wide range of objections; Smart replies to most of them here.

From J. J. C. Smart, 'Sensations and brain processes',
Philosophical Review, vol. LXVIII (revised)

This paper[1] takes its departure from arguments to be found in U. T. Place's 'Is Consciousness a Brain Process?'[2] I have had the benefit of discussing Place's thesis in a good many universities in the United States and Australia, and I hope that the present paper answers objections to his thesis which Place has not considered and that it presents his thesis in a more nearly unobjectionable form. This paper is meant also to supplement the paper 'The "Mental" and the "Physical"' by H. Feigl,[3] which in part argues for a similar thesis to Place's.

Suppose that I report that I have at this moment a roundish, blurry-edged after-image which is yellowish towards its edge and is orange towards its center. What is it that I am reporting? One answer to this question might be that I am not reporting anything, that when I say that it looks to me as though there is a roundish yellowy-orange patch of light on the wall I am expressing some sort of *temptation,* the temptation to say that there *is* a roundish yellowy-orange patch on the wall (though I may know that there is not such a patch on the wall). This is perhaps Wittgenstein's view in the *Philosophical Investigations* (see §§367, 370). Similarly, when I 'report' a pain, I am not really reporting anything (or, if you like, I am reporting in a queer sense of 'reporting'), but am doing a sophisticated sort of wince (see §244: 'The verbal expression of pain replaces crying and does not describe it.' Nor does it describe anything else?).[4] I prefer most of the time to discuss an after-image rather than a pain, because the word 'pain' brings in something which is irrelevant to my purpose: the notion of 'distress'. I think that 'he is in pain' entails 'he is in distress', that is, that he is in a certain agitation-condition.[5] Similarly, to say 'I am in pain' may be to do more than 'replace pain behavior': it may be partly to report something, though this something is quite nonmysterious, being an agitation-condition, and so susceptible of behavioristic analysis. The suggestion I wish if possible to avoid is a different one, namely that 'I am in pain' is a genuine report, and that what it reports is an irreducibly psychical something. And similarly the suggestion I wish to resist is also that to say 'I have a yellowish-orange after-image' is to report something irreducibly psychical.

Why do I wish to resist this suggestion? Mainly because of Occam's razor. It seems to me that science is increasingly giving us a viewpoint whereby organisms are able to be seen as physicochemical mechanisms:[6] it seems that even the behavior of man himself will one day be explicable in mechanistic terms. There does seem to be, so far as science is concerned, nothing in the world but increasingly complex arrangements of physical constituents. All except for one place: in consciousness. That is, for a full description of what is going on in a man you would have to mention not only the physical processes in his tissues, glands, nervous system, and so forth, but also his states of consciousness: his visual, auditory, and tactual sensations, his aches and pains. That these should be *correlated* with brain processes does not help, for to say that they are *correlated* is to say that they are something 'over and above'. You cannot correlate something with itself. You correlate footprints with burglars, but not Bill Sikes the burglar with Bill Sikes the burglar. So sensations, states of consciousness, do seem to be the one sort of thing left outside the physicalist picture, and for various reasons I just cannot believe that this can be so. That everything should be explicable in terms of physics (together of course with descriptions of the ways in which the parts are put together – roughly, biology is to physics as radio-engineering is to electromagnetism) except the occurrence of sensations seems to me to be frankly unbelievable. Such sensations would be 'nomological danglers', to use Feigl's expression.[7] It is not often realized how odd would be the laws whereby these nomological danglers would dangle. It is sometimes asked, 'Why can't there be psychophysical laws which are of a novel sort, just as the laws of electricity and magnetism were novelties from the standpoint of Newtonian mechanics?' Certainly we are pretty sure in the future to come across new ultimate laws of a novel type, but I expect them to relate simple constituents: for example, whatever ultimate particles are then in vogue. I cannot believe that ultimate laws of nature could relate simple constituents to configurations consisting of perhaps billions of neurons (and goodness knows how many billion billions of ultimate particles) all put together for all the world as though their main purpose in life was to be a negative feedback mechanism of a complicated sort. Such ultimate laws would be like nothing so far known in science. They have a queer 'smell' to them. I am just unable to believe in the nomological danglers themselves, or in the laws whereby they would dangle. If any philosophical arguments seemed to compel us to believe in such things, I would suspect a catch in the argument. In any case it is the object of this paper to show that there are no philosophical arguments which compel us to be dualists.

The above is largely a confession of faith, but it explains why I find Wittgenstein's position (as I construe it) so congenial. For on this view there are, in a sense, no sensations. A man is a vast arrangement of physical particles, but there are not, over and above this, sensations or states of consciousness. There are just behavioral facts about this vast mechanism, such as that it expresses a temptation (behavior disposition) to say 'there is a yellowish-red patch on the wall' or that it goes through a sophisticated sort of wince, that is, says 'I am in pain.' Admittedly Wittgenstein says that though the sensation 'is not a something', it is nevertheless 'not a nothing either' (§304), but this need only mean that the word 'ache' has a use. An ache is a thing, but only in the innocuous sense in which the plain man, in the first paragraph of Frege's *Foundations of Arithmetic,* answers the question 'What is the number one?' by 'a thing'. It should be noted that when I assert that to say 'I have a yellowish-orange after-image' is to express a temptation to assert the physical-object statement 'There is a yellowish-orange patch on the wall,' I mean that saying 'I have a yellowish-orange after-image' is (partly) the exercise of the disposition[8] which is the temptation. It is not to *report* that I have the temptation, any more than is 'I love you' normally a report that I love someone. Saying 'I love you' is just part of the behavior which is the exercise of the disposition of loving someone.

Though for the reasons given above, I am very receptive to the above 'expressive' account of sensation statements, I do not feel that it will quite do the trick. Maybe this is because I have not thought it out sufficiently, but it does seem to me as though, when a person says 'I have an after-image,' he *is* making a genuine report, and that when he says 'I have a pain,' he *is* doing more than 'replace pain-behavior', and that 'this more' is not just to say that he is in distress. I am not so sure, however, that to admit this is to admit that there are nonphysical correlates of brain processes. Why should not sensations just be brain processes of a certain sort? There are, of course, well-known (as well as lesser-known) philosophical objections to the view that reports of sensations are reports of brain-processes, but I shall try to argue that these arguments are by no means as cogent as is commonly thought to be the case.

Let me first try to state more accurately the thesis that sensations are brain-processes. It is not the thesis that, for example, 'after-image' or 'ache' means the same as 'brain process of sort X' (where 'X' is replaced by a description of a certain sort of brain process). It is that, in so far as 'after-image' or 'ache' is a report of a process, it is a report of a process that *happens to be* a brain process. It follows that the thesis does not claim that sensation statements can be *translated* into statements about brain processes.[9] Nor does it claim that the logic of a sensation statement is the same as that of a brain-process statement. All it claims is that in so far as a sensation statement is a report of something, that something is in fact a brain process. Sensations are nothing over and above brain processes. Nations are nothing 'over and above' citizens, but this does not prevent the logic of nation statements being very different from the logic of citizen statements, nor does it insure the translatability of nation statements into citizen statements. (I do not, however, wish to assert that the relation of sensation statements to brain-process statements is very like that of nation statements to citizen statements. Nations do not just *happen to be* nothing over and above citizens, for example. I bring in the 'nations' example merely to make a negative point: that the fact that the logic of A-statements is different from that of B-statements does not insure that A's are anything over and above B's.)

Remarks on identity

When I say that a sensation is a brain process or that lightning is an electric discharge, I am using 'is' in the sense of strict identity. (Just as in the – in this case necessary – proposition '7 is identical with the smallest prime number greater than 5.') When I say that a sensation is a brain process or that lightning is an electric discharge I do not mean just that the sensation is somehow spatially or temporally continuous with the brain process or that the lightning is just spatially or temporally continuous with the discharge. When on the other hand I say that the successful general is the same person as the small boy who stole the apples I mean only that the successful general I see before me is a time slice[10] of the same four-dimensional object of which the small boy stealing apples is an earlier time slice. However, the four-dimensional object which has the general-I-see-before-me for its late time slice is identical in the strict sense with the four-dimensional object which has the small-boy-stealing-apples for an early time slice. I distinguish these two senses of 'is identical with' because I wish to make it clear that the brain-process doctrine asserts identity in the *strict* sense.

I shall now discuss various possible objections to the view that the processes reported in sensation statements are in fact processes in the brain. Most of us have met some of these objections in our first year as philosophy students. All the more reason to take a good look at them. Others of the objections will be more recondite and subtle.

Objection 1 Any illiterate peasant can talk perfectly well about his after-images, or how things look or feel to him, or about his aches and pains, and yet he may know nothing whatever about neurophysiology. A man may, like Aristotle, believe that the brain is an organ for cooling the body without any impairment of his ability to make true statements about his sensations. Hence the things we are talking about when we describe our sensations cannot be processes in the brain.

Reply You might as well say that a nation of slugabeds, who never saw the Morning Star or knew of its existence, or who had never thought of the expression 'the Morning Star', but who used the expression 'the Evening Star' perfectly well, could not use this expression to refer to the same entity as we refer to (and describe as) 'the Morning Star'[11]

You may object that the Morning Star is in a sense not the very same thing as the Evening Star, but only something spatiotemporally continuous with it. That is, you may say that the Morning Star is not the Evening Star in the strict sense of 'identity' that I distinguished earlier.

There is, however, a more plausible example. Consider lightning.[12] Modern physical science tells us that lightning is a certain kind of electrical discharge due to ionization of clouds of water vapor in the atmosphere. This, it is now believed, is what the true nature of lightning is. Note that there are not two things: a flash of lightning and an electrical discharge. There is one thing, a flash of lightning, which is described scientifically as an electrical discharge to the earth from a cloud of ionized water molecules. The case is not at all like that of explaining a footprint by reference to a burglar. We say that what lightning really is, what its true nature as revealed by science is, is an electrical discharge. (It is not the true nature of a footprint to be a burglar.)

To forestall irrelevant objections, I should like to make it clear that by 'lightning' I mean the publicly observable physical object, lightning, not a visual sense-datum of lightning. I say that the publicly observable physical object lightning is in fact the electrical discharge, not just a correlate of it. The sense-datum, or rather the having of the sense-datum, the 'look' of lightning, may well in my view be a correlate of the electrical discharge. For in my view it is a brain state *caused* by the lightning. But we should no more confuse sensations of lightning with lightning than we confuse sensations of a table with the table.

In short, the reply to Objection 1 is that there can be contingent statements of the form 'A is identical with B,' and a person may well know that something is an A without knowing that it is a B. An illiterate peasant might well be able to talk about his sensations without knowing about his brain processes, just as he can talk about lightning though he knows nothing of electricity.

Objection 2   It is only a contingent fact (if it is a fact) that when we have a certain kind of sensation there is a certain kind of process in our brain. Indeed it is possible, though perhaps in the highest degree unlikely, that our present physiological theories will be as out of date as the ancient theory connecting mental processes with goings on in the heart. It follows that when we report a sensation we are not reporting a brain-process.

Reply   The objection certainly proves that when we say 'I have an after-image' we cannot *mean* something of the form 'I have such and such a brain-process.' But this does not show that what we report (having an after-image) is not *in fact* a brain-process. 'I see lightning' does not *mean* 'I see an electrical discharge.' Indeed, it is logically possible (though highly unlikely) that the electrical discharge account of lightning might one day be given up. Again, 'I see the Evening Star' does not *mean* the same as 'I see the Morning Star,' and yet 'The Evening Star and the Morning Star are one and the same thing' is a contingent proposition. Possibly Objection 2 derives some of its apparent strength from a 'Fido'-Fido theory of meaning. If the meaning of an expression were what the expression named, then of course it *would* follow from the fact that 'sensation' and 'brain-process' have different meanings that they cannot name one and the same thing.

Objection 3[13]   Even if Objections 1 and 2 do not prove that sensations are something over and above brain-processes, they do prove that the qualities of sensations are something over and above the qualities of brain-processes. That is, it may be possible to get out of asserting the existence of irreducibly psychic processes, but not out of asserting the existence of irreducibly psychic *properties*. For suppose we identify the Morning Star with the Evening Star. Then there must be some properties which logically imply that of being the Morning Star, and quite distinct properties which entail that of being the Evening Star. Again, there must be some properties (for example, that of being a yellow flash) which are logically distinct from those in the physicalist story.

Indeed, it might be thought that the objection succeeds at one jump. For consider the property of 'being a yellow flash'. It might seem that this property lies inevitably outside the physicalist framework within which I am trying to work (either by 'yellow' being an objective emergent property of physical objects, or else by being a power to produce yellow sense-data where 'yellow', in this second instantiation of the word, refers to a purely phenomenal or introspectible quality). I must therefore digress for a moment and indicate how I deal with secondary qualities. I shall concentrate on color.

First of all, let me introduce the concept of a normal percipient. One person is more a normal percipient than another if he can make color discriminations that the other cannot. For example, if A can pick a lettuce leaf out of a heap of cabbage leaves, whereas B cannot though he can pick a lettuce leaf out of a heap of beetroot leaves, then A is more normal than B. (I am assuming that A and B are not given time to distinguish the leaves by their slight difference in shape, and so forth.) From the concept of 'more normal than' it is easy to see how we can introduce the concept of 'normal'. Of course, Eskimos may make the finest discriminations at the blue end of the spectrum, Hottentots at the red end. In this case the concept of a normal percipient is a slightly idealized one, rather like that of 'the mean sun' in astronomical chronology. There is no need to go into such subtleties now. I say that 'This is red' means something roughly like 'A normal percipient would not easily pick this out of a clump of geranium petals though he would pick it out of a clump of lettuce leaves.' Of course it does not exactly mean this: a person might know the meaning of 'red' without knowing anything about geraniums, or even about normal percipients. But the point is that a person can be *trained* to say 'This is red' of objects which would not easily be picked out of geranium petals by a normal percipient, and so on. (Note that even a color-blind person can reasonably assert that something is red, though of course he needs to use another human being, not just himself, as his 'color meter'.) This account of secondary qualities explains their unimportance in physics. For obviously the discriminations and lack of discriminations made by a very complex neurophysiological mechanism are hardly likely to correspond to simple and nonarbitrary distinctions in nature.

I therefore elucidate colors as powers, in Locke's sense, to evoke certain sorts of discriminatory responses in human beings. They are also, of course, powers to cause sensations in human beings (an account still nearer Locke's). But these sensations, I am arguing, are identifiable with brain processes.

Now how do I get over the objection that a sensation can be identified with a brain process only if it has some phenomenal property, not possessed by brain processes, whereby one-half of the identification may be, so to speak, pinned down?

Reply My suggestion is as follows. When a person says, 'I see a yellowish-orange after-image,' he is saying something like this: '*There is something going on which is like what is going on when* I have my eyes open, am awake, and there is an orange illuminated in good light in front of me, that is, when I really see an orange.' (And there is no reason why a person should not say the same thing when he is having a veridical sense-datum, so long as we construe 'like' in the last sentence in such a sense that something can be like itself.) Notice that the italicized words, namely 'there is something going on which is like what is going on when,' are all quasilogical or topic-neutral words. This explains why the ancient Greek peasant's reports about his sensations can be neutral between dualistic metaphysics or my materialistic metaphysics. It explains how sensations can be brain-processes and yet how a man who reports them need know nothing about brain-processes. For he reports them only very abstractly as 'something going on which is like what is going on when . . .' Similarly, a person may say 'someone is in the room,' thus reporting truly that the doctor is in the room, even though he has never heard of doctors. (There are not two people in the room: 'someone' *and* the doctor.) This account of sensation statements also explains the singular elusiveness of 'raw feels' – why no one seems to be able to pin any properties on them.[14] Raw feels, in my view, are colorless for the very same reason that *something* is colorless. This does not mean that sensations do not have plenty of properties, for if they are brain-processes they certainly have lots of neurological properties. It only means that in speaking of them as being like or unlike one another we need not know or mention these properties.

This, then, is how I would reply to Objection 3. The strength of my reply depends on the possibility of our being able to report that one thing is like another without being able to state the respect in which it is like. I do not see why this should not be so. If we think cybernetically about the nervous system we can envisage it as able to respond to certain likenesses of its internal processes without being able to do more. It would be easier to build a machine which would tell us, say on a punched tape, whether or not two objects were similar, than it would be to build a machine which would report wherein the similarities consisted.

Objection 4   The after-image is not in physical space. The brain-process is. So the after-image is not a brain-process.

Reply   This is an *ignoratio elenchi. I* am not arguing that the after-image is a brain-process, but that the experience of having an after-image is a brain-process. It is the *experience* which is reported in the introspective report. Similarly, if it is objected that the after-image is yellowy-orange, my reply is that it is the experience of seeing yellowy-orange that is being described, and this experience is not a yellowy-orange something. So to say that a brain-process cannot be yellowy-orange is not to say that a brain-process cannot in fact be the experience of having a yellowy-orange after-image. There is, in a sense, no such thing as an after-image or a sense-datum, though there is such a thing as the experience of having an image, and this experience is described indirectly in material object language, not in phenomenal language, for there is no such thing.[15] We describe the experience by saying, in effect, that it is like the experience we have when, for example, we really see a yellowy-orange patch on the wall. Trees and wallpaper can be green, but not the experience of seeing or imagining a tree or wallpaper. (Or if they are described as green or yellow this can only be in a derived sense.)

Objection 5 It would make sense to say of a molecular movement in the brain that it is swift or slow, straight or circular, but it makes no sense to say this of the experience of seeing something yellow.

Reply So far we have not given sense to talk of experiences as swift or slow, straight or circular. But I am not claiming that 'experience' and 'brain-process' mean the same or even that they have the same logic. 'Somebody' and 'the doctor' do not have the same logic, but this does not lead us to suppose that talking about somebody telephoning is talking about someone over and above, say, the doctor. The ordinary man when he reports an experience is reporting that something is going on, but he leaves it open as to what sort of thing is going on, whether in a material solid medium or perhaps in some sort of gaseous medium, or even perhaps in some sort of nonspatial medium (if this makes sense). All that I am saying is that 'experience' and 'brain-process' may in fact refer to the same thing, and if so we may easily adopt a convention (which is not a change in our present rules for the use of experience words but an addition to them) whereby it would make sense to talk of an experience in terms appropriate to physical processes.

Objection 6 Sensations are private, brain-processes are *public*. If I sincerely say, 'I see a yellowish-orange after-image,' and I am not making a verbal mistake, then I cannot be wrong. But I can be wrong about a brain-process. The scientist looking into my brain might be having an illusion. Moreover, it makes sense to say that two or more people are observing the same brain-process but not that two or more people are reporting the same inner experience.

Reply This shows that the language of introspective reports has a different logic from the language of material processes. It is obvious that until the brain-process theory is much improved and widely accepted there will be no *criteria* for saying 'Smith has an experience of such-and-such a sort' *except* Smith's introspective reports. So we have adopted a rule of language that (normally) what Smith says goes.

Objection 7 1 can imagine myself turned to stone and yet having images, aches, pains, and so on.

Reply I can imagine that the electrical theory of lightning is false, that lightning is some sort of purely optical phenomenon. I can imagine that lightning is not an electrical discharge. I can imagine that the Evening

Star is not the Morning Star. But it is. All the objection shows is that 'experience' and 'brain-process' do not have the same meaning. It does not show that an experience is not in fact a brain-process.

This objection is perhaps much the same as one which can be summed up by the slogan: 'What can be composed of nothing cannot be composed of anything.'[16] The argument goes as follows: on the brain-process thesis' the identity between the brain-process and the experience is a contingent one. So it is logically possible that there should be no brain-process, and no process of any other sort either (no heart process, no kidney process, no liver process). There would be the experience but no 'corresponding' physiological process with which we might be able to identify it empirically.

I suspect that the objector is thinking of the experience as a ghostly entity. So it is composed of something, not of nothing, after all. On his view it is composed of ghost stuff, and on mine it is composed of brain stuff. Perhaps the counter-reply will be[17] that the experience is simple and uncompounded, and so it is not composed of anything after all. This seems to be a quibble, for, if it were taken seriously, the remark 'What can be composed of nothing cannot be composed of anything' could be recast as an a priori argument against Democritus and atomism and for Descartes an infinite divisibility. And it seems odd that a question of this sort could be settled a priori. We must therefore construe the word 'composed' in a very weak sense, which would allow us to say that even an indivisible atom is composed of something (namely, itself). The dualist cannot really say that an experience can be composed of nothing. For he holds that experiences are something over and above material processes, that is, that they are a sort of ghost stuff. (Or perhaps ripples in an underlying ghost stuff.) I say that the dualist's hypothesis is a perfectly intelligible one. But I say that experiences are not to be identified with ghost stuff but with brain stuff. This is another hypothesis, and in my view a very plausible one. The present argument cannot knock it down a priori.

Objection 8 The 'beetle in the box' objection (see Wittgenstein, *Philosophical Investigations*, §293). How could descriptions of experiences, if these are genuine reports, get a foothold in language? For any rule of language must have public criteria for its correct application.

Reply The change from describing how things are to describing how we feel is just a change from uninhibitedly saying 'this is so' to saying 'this looks so.' That is, when the naïve person might be tempted to say, 'There is a patch of light on the wall which moves whenever I move my eyes' or 'A pin is being stuck into me,' we have learned how to resist this temptation and say 'It *looks as though* there is a patch of light on the wall-paper' or 'It *feels as though* someone were sticking a pin into me.' The introspective account tells us about the individual's state of consciousness in the same way as does 'I see a patch of light' or 'I feel a pin being stuck into me': it differs from the corresponding perception statement in so far as it withdraws any claim about what is actually going on in the external world. From the point of view of the psychologist, the change from talking about the environment to talking about one's perceptual sensations is simply a matter of disinhibiting certain reactions. These are reactions which one normally suppresses because one has learned that in the prevailing circumstances they are unlikely to provide a good indication of the state of the environment.[18] To say that something looks green to me is simply to say that my experience is like the experience I get when I see something that really is green. In my reply to Objection 3, I pointed out the extreme openness or generality of statements which report experiences. This explains why there is no language of private qualities. (Just as 'someone', unlike 'the doctor', is a colorless word.)[19]

If it is asked what is the difference between those brain-processes which, in my view, are experiences and those brain-processes which are not, I can only reply that it is at present unknown. I have been tempted to conjecture that the difference may in part be that between perception and reception (in D. M. MacKay's terminology) and that the type of brain-process which is an experience might be identifiable with MacKay's active 'matching response'.[20] This, however, cannot be the whole story because sometimes I can perceive something unconsciously, as when I take a handkerchief out of a drawer without being aware that I am doing so. But at the very least, we can classify the brain-processes which are experiences as those brain-processes which are, or might have been, causal conditions of those pieces of verbal behavior which we call reports of immediate experience.

I have now considered a number of objections to the brain-process thesis. I wish now to conclude with some remarks on the logical status of the thesis itself. U. T. Place seems to hold that it is a straight-out scientific hypothesis.[21] If so, he is partly right and partly wrong. If the issue is between (say) a brain-process thesis and a heart thesis, or a liver thesis, or a kidney thesis, then the issue is a purely empirical one, and the verdict is overwhelmingly in favor of the brain. The right sorts of things don't go on in the heart, liver, or kidney, nor do these organs possess the right sort of complexity of structure. On the other hand, if the issue is between a brain-or-liver-or-kidney thesis (that is, some form of materialism) on the one hand and epiphenomenalism on the other hand, then the issue is not an empirical one. For there is no conceivable experiment which could decide between materialism and epiphenomenalism. This latter issue is not like the average straight-out empirical issue in science, but like the issue between the nineteenth-century English naturalist Philip Gosse[22] and the orthodox geologists and paleontologists of his day. According to Gosse, the earth was created about 4000 BC exactly as described in *Genesis*, with twisted rock strata, 'evidence' of erosion, and so forth, and all sorts of fossils, all in their appropriate strata, just as if the usual evolutionist story had been true. Clearly this theory is in a sense irrefutable: no evidence can possibly tell against it. Let us ignore the theological setting in which Philip Gosse's hypothesis had been placed, thus ruling out objections of a theological kind, such as 'what a queer God who would go to such elaborate lengths to deceive us'. Let us suppose that it is held that the universe just *began* in 4004 BC with the initial conditions just everywhere as they were in 4004 BC and in particular that our own planet began with sediment in the rivers, eroded cliffs, fossils in the rocks, and so on. No scientist would ever entertain this as a serious hypothesis, consistent though it is with all possible evidence. The hypothesis offends against the principles of parsimony and simplicity. There would be far too many brute and inexplicable facts. Why are pterodactyl bones just as they are? No explanation in terms of the evolution of pterodactyls from earlier forms of life would any longer be possible. We would have millions of facts about the world as it was in 4004 BC that just have to be *accepted*.

The issue between the brain-process theory and epiphenomenalism seems to be of the above sort. (Assuming that a behavioristic reduction of introspective reports is not possible.) If it be agreed that there are no cogent philosophical arguments which force us into accepting dualism, and if the brain-process theory and dualism are equally consistent with the facts, then the principles of parsimony and simplicity seem to me to decide overwhelmingly in favor of the brain-process theory. As I pointed out earlier, dualism involves a large number of irreducible psycho-physical laws (whereby the 'nomological danglers' dangle) of a queer sort, that just have to be taken on trust, and are just as difficult to swallow as the irreducible facts about the paleontology of the earth with which we are faced on Philip Gosse's theory.

Notes

1   This is a very slightly revised version of a paper which was first published in the *Philosophical Review* LXVIII (1959), pp. 141–56. Since that date there have been criticisms of my paper by J. T. Stevenson, *Philosophical Review* LXIX (1960), pp. 505–10, to which I have replied in *Philosophical Revies* LXX (1961), pp. 406–7, and by G. Pitcher and by W. D. Joske, *Australasian Journal of Philosophy* XXXVIII (1960), pp. 150–60, to which I have replied in the same volume of that journal, pp. 252–4.
2   *British Journal of Psychology* XLVII (1956), pp. 44–50; reprinted in William Lyons (ed.) *Modern Philosophy of Mind* (London: Dent, 1995).

3   *Minnesota Studies in the Philosophy of Science*, vol. II (Minneapolis: University of Minnesota Press, 1958), pp. 370–497.

4   Some philosophers of my acquaintance, who have the advantage over me of having known Wittgenstein, would say that this interpretation of him is too behavioristic. However, it seems to me a very natural interpretation of his printed words, and whether or not it is Wittgenstein's real view it is certainly an interesting and important one. I wish to consider it here as a possible rival to the 'brain-process' thesis and to straight-out old-fashioned dualism.

5   See Gilbert Ryle, *The Concept of Mind* (London: Hutchinson's University Library, 1949), p. 93.

6   On this point see Paul Oppenheim and Hilary Putnam, 'Unity of science as a working hypothesis', in *Minnesota Studies in the Philosophy of Science*, vol. II (Minneapolis: University of Minnesota Press, 1958), pp. 3–36.

7   H. Feigl, 'The "mental" and the "physical"', op. cit., p. 428. Feigl uses the expression 'nomological danglers' for the laws whereby the entities dangle: I have used the expression to refer to the dangling entities themselves.

8   Wittgenstein did not like the word 'Disposition'. I am using it to put in a nutshell (and perhaps inaccurately) the view which I am attributing to Wittgenstein. I should like to repeat that I do not wish to claim that my interpretation of Wittgenstein is correct. Some of those who knew him do not interpret him in this way. It is merely a view which I find myself extracting from his printed words and which I think is important and worth discussing for its own sake.

9   See U. T. Place, 'Is consciousness a brain process?', op. cit., p. 107, and Feigl, 'The "mental" and the "physical"', p. 390, near top.

10   See J. H. Woodger, *Theory Construction*, International Encyclopedia of Unified Science, II, no. 5 (Chicago: University of Chicago Press, 1939), p. 38. I here permit myself to speak loosely. For warnings against possible ways of going wrong with this sort of talk, see my note 'Spatialising time', *Mind* LXIV (1955), pp. 239–41.

11   Cf. Feigl, 'The "mental" and the "physical"'.

12   See Place, 'Is consciousness a brain process?', p. 106; also Feigl, 'The "mental" and the "physical"', p. 438.

13   I think this objection was first put to me by Professor Max Black. I think it is the most subtle of any of those I have considered, and the one which I am least confident of having satisfactorily met.

14   See B. A. Farrell, 'Experience', *Mind* LIX (1950), pp. 170–98.

15   Dr J. R. Smythies claims that a sense-datum language could be taught independently of the material object language ('A note on the fallacy of the "Phenomenological Fallacy"', *British Journal of Psychology* XLVII (1957), 141–4). I am not so sure of this: there must be some public criteria for a person having got a rule wrong before we can teach him the rule. I suppose someone might *accidently* learn color words by Dr Smythies' procedure. I am not, of course, denying that we can learn a sense-datum language in the sense that we can learn to report our experience. Nor would Place deny it.

16   I owe this objection to Dr C. B. Martin. I gather that he no longer wishes to maintain this objection, at any rate in its present form.

17   Martin did not make this reply, but one of his students did.
18   I owe this point to Place, in correspondence.
19   The 'beetle in the box' objection is, *if it is sound*, an objection to *any* view, and in particular the Cartesian one, that introspective reports are genuine reports. So it is no objection to a weaker thesis that I would be concerned to uphold, namely, that if introspective reports of 'experiences' are genuinely reports, then the things they are reports of are in fact brain processes.
20   See his article 'Towards an information-flow model of human behaviour', *British Journal of Psychology* XLVII (1956), pp. 30–43.
21   'Is consciousness a brain process?'. For a further discussion of this, in reply to the original version of the present paper, see Place's note 'Materialism as a scientific hypothesis', *Philosophical Review* LXIX (1960), pp. 101–4.
22   See the entertaining account of Gosse's book *Omphalos* by Martin Gardner in *Fads and Fallacies in the Name of Science*, 2nd edn (New York: Dover, 1957), pp. 124–7.

37

Minds, brains, and programs
John R. Searle

Could a machine think? In science fiction stories there are many examples of machines which can think. But what would be involved? Is there any reason to believe that some machines can already think? Computers seem the most plausible candidates. Those who defend a position known as Strong AI ('AI' stands for artificial intelligence) believe that artificial intelligence is a genuine possibility, not simply a metaphorical use of language. In this ingenious paper John Searle (1932–) concocts a thought experiment designed to refute Strong AI. His conclusion is that computers can manipulate symbols, but there is more to thinking than this. This is not to say that no machine can think: we are in a sense machines ourselves.

From John R. Searle, 'Minds, brains, and programs', *Behavioral and Brain Sciences*, vol. 3

What psychological and philosophical significance should we attach to recent efforts at computer simulations of human cognitive capacities? In answering this question, I find it useful to distinguish what I will call "strong" AI from "weak" or "cautious" AI. According to weak AI, the principal value of the computer in the study of the mind is that it gives us a very powerful tool. For example, it enables us to formulate and test hypotheses in a more rigorous and precise fashion. But according to strong AI, the computer is not merely a tool in the study of the mind; rather, the appropriately programmed computer really *is* a mind, in the sense that computers given the right programs can be literally said to *understand* and have other cognitive states. In strong AI, because the programmed computer has cognitive states, the programs are not mere tools that enable us to test psychological explanations; rather, the programs are themselves the explanations.

I have no objection to the claims of weak AI, at least as far as this article is concerned. My discussion here will be directed at the claims I have defined as those of strong AI, specifically the claim that the appropriately programmed computer literally has cognitive states and that the programs thereby explain human cognition. When I hereafter refer to AI, I have in mind the strong version, as expressed by these two claims.

I will consider the work of Roger Schank and his colleagues at Yale (Schank and Abelson 1977), because I am more familiar with it than I am with any other similar claims, and because it provides a very clear example of the sort of work I wish to examine. But nothing that follows depends upon the details of Schank's programs. The same arguments would apply to Winograd's SHRDLU, Weizenbaum's ELIZA, and indeed any Turing machine simulation of human mental phenomena.

Very briefly, and leaving out the various details, one can describe Schank's program as follows: The aim of the program is to simulate the human ability to understand stories. It is characteristic of human beings' story-understanding capacity that they can answer questions about the story even though the information that they give was never explicitly stated in the story. Thus, for example, suppose you were given the following story: "A man went into a restaurant and ordered a hamburger. When the hamburger arrived it was burned to a crisp, and the man stormed out of the restaurant angrily, without paying for the hamburger or leaving a tip." Now, if you are asked "Did the man eat the hamburger?" you will presumably answer, "No, he did not." Similarly, if you are given the following story: "A man went into a restaurant and ordered a hamburger; when the hamburger came he was very pleased with it; and as he left the restaurant he gave the waitress a large tip before paying his bill," and you are asked the question, "Did the man eat the hamburger?" you will presumably answer, "Yes, he ate the hamburger." Now Schank's machines can similarly answer questions about restaurants in this fashion. To do this, they have a "representation" of the sort of information that human beings have about restaurants, which enables them to answer such questions as those above, given these sorts of stories. When the machine is given the story and then asked the question, the machine will print out answers of the sort that we would expect human beings to give if told similar stories. Partisans of strong AI claim that in this question and answer sequence the machine is not only simulating a human ability but also (1) that the machine can literally be said to *understand* the story and provide the answers to questions, and (2) that what the machine and its program do *explains* the human ability to understand the story and answer questions about it.

Both claims seem to me to be totally unsupported by Schank's work, as I will attempt to show in what follows. I am not, of course, saying that Schank himself is committed to these claims.

One way to test any theory of the mind is to ask oneself what it would be like if my mind actually worked on the principles that the theory says all minds work on. Let us apply this test to the Schank program with the following *Gedankenexperiment.* Suppose that I'm locked in a room and given a large batch of Chinese writing. Suppose furthermore (as is indeed the case) that I know no Chinese, either written or spoken, and that I'm not even confident that I could recognize Chinese writing as Chinese writing distinct from, say, Japanese writing or meaningless squiggles. To me, Chinese writing is just so many meaningless squiggles. Now suppose further that after this first batch of Chinese writing I am given a second batch of Chinese script together with a set of rules for correlating the second batch with the first batch. The rules are in English, and I understand these rules as well as any other native speaker of English. They enable me to correlate one set of formal symbols with another set of formal symbols, and all that "formal" means here is that I can identify the symbols entirely by their shapes. Now suppose also that I am given a third batch of Chinese symbols together with some instructions, again in English, that enable me to correlate elements of this third batch with the first two batches, and these rules instruct me how to give back certain Chinese symbols with certain sorts of shapes in response to certain sorts of shapes given me in the third batch. Unknown to me, the people who are giving me all of these symbols call the first batch a "script," they call the second batch a "story," and they call the third batch "questions." Furthermore, they call the symbols I give them back in response to the third batch "answers to the questions," and the set of rules in English that they gave me, they call the "program." Now just to complicate the story a little, imagine that these people also give me stories in English, which I understand, and they then ask me questions in English about these stories, and I give them back answers in English. Suppose also that after a while I get so good at following the instructions for manipulating the Chinese symbols and the programmers get so good at writing the programs that from the external point of view – that is, from the point of view of somebody outside the room in which I am locked – my answers to the questions are absolutely indistinguishable from those of native Chinese speakers. Nobody just looking at my answers can tell that I don't speak a word of Chinese. Let us also suppose that my answers to the English questions are, as they no doubt would be, indistinguishable from those of other native English speakers, for the simple reason that I am a native English speaker. From the external point of view – from the point of view of someone reading my "answers" – the answers to the Chinese questions and the English questions are equally good. But in the Chinese case, unlike the English case, I produce the answers by manipulating uninterpreted formal symbols. As far as the Chinese is concerned, I simply behave like a computer; I perform computational operations on formally specified elements. For the purposes of the Chinese, I am simply an instantiation of the computer program.

Now the claims made by strong AI are that the programmed computer understands the stories and that the program in some sense explains human understanding. But we are now in a position to examine these claims in light of our thought experiment.

(1)   As regards the first claim, it seems to me quite obvious in the example that I do not understand a word of the Chinese stories. I have inputs and outputs that are indistinguishable from those of the native Chinese speaker, and I can have any formal program you like, but I still understand nothing. For the same reasons, Schank's computer understands nothing of any stories, whether in Chinese, English, or whatever, since in the Chinese case the computer is me, and in cases where the computer is not me, the computer has nothing more than I have in the case where I understand nothing.

(2)   As regards the second claim, that the program explains human under-standing, we can see that the computer and its program do not provide sufficient conditions of understanding since the computer and the program are functioning, and there is no understanding. But does it even provide a necessary condition or a significant contribution to understanding? One of the claims made by the supporters of strong AI is that when I understand a story in English, what I am doing is exactly the same – or perhaps more of the same – as what I was doing in manipulating the Chinese symbols. It is simply more formal symbol manipulation that distinguishes the case in English, where I do understand, from the case in Chinese, where I don't. I have not demonstrated that this claim is false, but it would certainly appear an incredible claim in the example. Such plausibility as the claim has derives from the supposition that we can construct a program that will have the same inputs and outputs as native speakers, and in addition we assume that speakers have some level of description where they are also instantiations of a program. On the basis of these two assumptions we assume that even if Schank's program isn't the whole story about under-standing, it may be part of the story. Well, I suppose that is an empirical possibility, but not the slightest reason has so far been given to believe that it is true, since what is suggested – though certainly not demonstrated – by the example is that the computer program is simply irrelevant to my understanding of the story. In the Chinese case I have everything that arti-ficial intelligence can put into me by way of a program, and I understand nothing; in the English case I understand everything, and there is so far no reason at all to suppose that my understanding has anything to do with computer programs, that is, with computational operations on purely formally specified elements. As long as the program is defined in terms of computational operations on purely formally defined elements, what the example suggests is that these by themselves have no interesting connec-tion with understanding. They are certainly not sufficient conditions, and not the slightest reason has been given to suppose that they are necessary

conditions or even that they make a significant contribution to under-standing. Notice that the force of the argument is not simply that different machines can have the same input and output while operating on different formal principles – that is not the point at all. Rather, whatever purely formal principles you put into the computer, they will not be sufficient for understanding, since a human will be able to follow the formal principles without understanding anything. No reason whatever has been offered to suppose that such principles are necessary or even contributory, since no reason has been given to suppose that when I understand English I am operating with any formal program at all.

Well, then, what is it that I have in the case of the English sentences that I do not have in the case of the Chinese sentences? The obvious answer is that I know what the former mean, while I haven't the faintest idea what the latter mean. But in what does this consist and why couldn't we give it to a machine, whatever it is? I will return to this question later, but first I want to continue with the example.

I have had the occasions to present this example to several workers in artificial intelligence, and, interestingly, they do not seem to agree on what the proper reply to it is. I get a surprising variety of replies, and in what follows I will consider the most common of these (specified along with their geographic origins).

But first I want to block some common misunderstandings about "understanding": In many of these discussions one finds a lot of fancy footwork about the word "understanding." My critics point out that there are many different degrees of understanding; that "understanding" is not a simple two-place predicate; that there are even different kinds and levels of understanding, and often the law of excluded middle doesn't even apply in a straightforward way to statements of the form "x understands y"; that in many cases it is a matter for decision and not a simple matter of fact whether x understands y; and so on. To all of these points I want to say: of course, of course. But they have nothing to do with the points at issue. There are clear cases in which "understanding" literally applies and clear cases in which it does not apply; and these two sorts of cases are all I need for this argument.[1] I understand stories in English; to a lesser degree I can understand stories in French; to a still lesser degree, stories in German; and in Chinese, not at all. My car and my adding machine, on the other hand, understand nothing: they are not in that line of business. We often attribute "understanding" and other cognitive predicates by metaphor and analogy to cars, adding machines, and other artifacts, but nothing is proved by such attributions. We say, "The door *knows* when to open because of its photoelectric cell. The adding machine *knows how* (*understands how*, is *able*) to do addition and subtraction but not division," and "The thermostat *perceives* changes in the temperature." The reason we make these attributions is quite interesting, and it has to do with the fact that in artifacts we extend our own intentionality;[2] our tools are extensions of our purposes, and so we find it natural to make metaphorical attributions of intentionality to them; but I take it no philosophical ice is cut by such examples. The sense in which an automatic door "understands instructions" from its photoelectric cell is not at all the sense in which I understand English. If the sense in which Schank's programmed computers understand stories is supposed to be the metaphorical sense in which the door understands, and not the sense in which I understand English, the issue would not be worth discussing. But Newell and Simon (1963) write that the kind of cognition they claim for computers is exactly the same as for human beings. I like the straightforwardness of this claim, and it is the sort of claim I will be considering. I will argue that in the literal sense the programmed computer understands what the car and the adding machine understand, namely, exactly nothing. The computer understanding is not just (like my understanding of German) partial or incomplete; it is zero.

Now to the replies:

1. The systems reply (Berkeley)

"While it is true that the individual person who is locked in the room does not understand the story, the fact is that he is merely part of a whole system, and the system does understand the story. The person has a large ledger in front of him in which are written the rules, he has a lot of scratch paper and pencils for doing calculations, he has 'data banks' of sets of Chinese symbols. Now, understanding is not being ascribed to the mere individual; rather it is being ascribed to this whole system of which he is a part."

My response to the systems theory is quite simple: Let the individual internalize all of these elements of the system. He memorizes the rules in the ledger and the data banks of Chinese symbols, and he does all the calculations in his head. The individual then incorporates the entire system. There isn't anything at all to the system that he does not encompass. We can even get rid of the room and suppose he works outdoors. All the same, he understands nothing of the Chinese, and a fortiori neither does the system, because there isn't anything in the system that isn't in him. If he doesn't understand, then there is no way the system could understand because the system is just a part of him.

Actually I feel somewhat embarrassed to give even this answer to the systems theory because the theory seems to me so implausible to start with. The idea is that while a person doesn't understand Chinese, somehow the *connection* of that person and bits of paper might understand Chinese. It is not easy for me to imagine how someone who was not in the grip of an ideology would find the idea at all plausible. Still, I think many people who are committed to the ideology of strong AI will in the end be inclined to say something very much like this; so let us pursue it a bit further. According to one version of this view, while the man in the internalized systems example doesn't understand Chinese in the sense that a native Chinese speaker does (because, for example, he doesn't know that the story refers to restaurants and hamburgers, etc.), still "the man as a formal symbol manipulation system" *really does understand Chinese*. The subsystem of the man that is the formal symbol manipulation system for Chinese should not be confused with the subsystem for English.

So there are really two subsystems in the man; one understands English, the other Chinese, and "it's just that the two systems have little to do with each other." But, I want to reply, not only do they have little to do with each other, they are not even remotely alike. The subsystem that understands English (assuming we allow ourselves to talk in this jargon of "subsystems" for a moment) knows that the stories are about restaurants and eating hamburgers, he knows that he is being asked questions about restaurants and that he is answering questions as best he can by making various inferences from the content of the story, and so on. But the Chinese system knows none of this. Whereas the English subsystem knows that "hamburgers" refers to hamburgers, the Chinese subsystem knows only that "squiggle squiggle" is followed by "squoggle squoggle." All he knows is that various formal symbols are being introduced at one end and manipulated according to rules written in English, and other symbols are going out at the other end. The whole point of the original example was to argue that such symbol manipulation by itself couldn't be sufficient for understanding Chinese in any literal sense because the man could write "squoggle squoggle" after "squiggle squiggle" without understanding anything in Chinese. And it doesn't meet that argument to postulate subsystems within the man, because the subsystems are no better off than the man was in the first place; they still don't have anything even remotely like what the English-speaking man (or subsystem) has. Indeed, in the case as described, the Chinese subsystem is simply a part of the English subsystem, a part that engages in meaningless symbol manipulation according to rules in English.

Let us ask ourselves what is supposed to motivate the systems reply in the first place; that is, what *independent* grounds are there supposed to be for saying that the agent must have a subsystem within him that literally understands stories in Chinese? As far as I can tell the only grounds are that in the example I have the same input and output as native Chinese speakers and a program that goes from one to the other. But the whole point of the examples has been to try to show that that couldn't be sufficient for understanding, in the sense in which I understand stories in English, because a person, and hence the set of systems that go to make up a person, could have the right combination of input, output, and program and still not understand anything in the relevant literal sense in which I understand English. The only motivation for saying there *must* be a subsystem in me that understands Chinese is that I have a program and I can pass the Turing test; I can fool native Chinese speakers. But precisely one of the points at issue is the adequacy of the Turing test. The example shows that there could be two "systems," both of which pass the Turing test, but only one of which understands; and it is no argument against this point to say that since they both pass the Turing test they must both understand, since this claim fails to meet the argument that the system in me that understands English has a great deal more than the system that merely processes Chinese. In short, the systems reply simply begs the question by insisting without argument that the system must understand Chinese.

Furthermore, the systems reply would appear to lead to consequences that are independently absurd. If we are to conclude that there must be cognition in me on the grounds that I have a certain sort of input and output and a program in between, then it looks like all sorts of noncognitive subsystems are going to turn out to be cognitive. For example, there is a level of description at which my stomach does information processing, and it instantiates any number of computer programs, but I take it we do not want to say that it has any understanding. But if we accept the systems reply, then it is hard to see how we avoid saying that stomach, heart, liver, and so on are all understanding subsystems, since there is no principled way to distinguish the motivation for saying the Chinese subsystem understands from saying that the stomach understands. It is, by the way, not an answer to this point to say that the Chinese system has information as input and output and the stomach has food and food products as input and output, since from the point of view of the agent, from my point of view, there is no information in either the food or the Chinese – the Chinese is just so many meaningless squiggles. The information in the Chinese case is solely in the eyes of the programmers and the interpreters, and there is nothing to prevent them from treating the input and output of my digestive organs as information if they so desire.

This last point bears on some independent problems in strong AI, and it is worth digressing for a moment to explain it. If strong AI is to be a branch of psychology, then it must be able to distinguish those systems that are genuinely mental from those that are not. It must be able to distinguish the principles on which the mind works from those on which nonmental systems work; otherwise it will offer us no explanations of what is specifically mental about the mental. And the mental-nonmental distinction cannot be just in the eye of the beholder but it must be intrinsic to the systems; otherwise it would be up to any beholder to treat people as nonmental and, for example, hurricanes as mental if he likes. But quite often in the AI literature the distinction is blurred in ways that would in the long run prove disastrous to the claim that AI is a cognitive inquiry.

McCarthy, for example, writes. "Machines as simple as thermostats can be said to have beliefs, and having beliefs seems to be a characteristic of most machines capable of problem solving performance" (McCarthy 1979). Anyone who thinks strong AI has a chance as a theory of the mind ought to ponder the implications of that remark. We are asked to accept it as a discovery of strong AI that the hunk of metal on the wall that we use to regulate the temperature has beliefs in exactly the same sense that we, our spouses, and our children have beliefs, and furthermore that "most" of the other machines in the room – telephone, tape recorder, adding machine, electric light switch – also have beliefs in this literal sense. It is not the aim of this article to argue against McCarthy's point, so I will simply assert the following without argument. The study of the mind starts with such facts as that humans have beliefs, while thermostats, telephones, and adding machines don't. If you get a theory that denies this point you have produced a counterexample to the theory and the theory is false. One gets the impression that people in AI who write this sort of thing think they can get away with it because they don't really take it seriously, and they don't think anyone else will either. I propose, for a moment at least, to take it seriously. Think hard for one minute about what would be necessary to establish that that hunk of metal on the wall over there had real beliefs, beliefs with direction of fit, propositional content, and conditions of satisfaction; beliefs that had the possibility of being strong beliefs or weak beliefs; nervous, anxious, or secure beliefs; dogmatic, rational, or superstitious beliefs; blind faiths or hesitant cogitations; any kind of beliefs. The thermostat is not a candidate. Neither is stomach, liver, adding machine, or telephone. However, since we are taking the idea seriously, notice that its truth would be fatal to strong AI's claim to be a science of the mind. For now the mind is everywhere. What we wanted to know is what distinguishes the mind from thermostats and livers. And if McCarthy were right, strong AI wouldn't have a hope of telling us that.

2. The robot reply (Yale)

"Suppose we wrote a different kind of program from Shank's program. Suppose we put a computer inside a robot, and this computer would not just take in formal symbols as input and give out formal symbols as output, but rather would actually operate the robot in such a way that the robot does something very much like perceiving, walking, moving about, hammering nails, eating, drinking – anything you like. The robot would, for example, have a television camera attached to it that enabled it to see, it would have arms and legs that enabled it to 'act,' and all of this would be controlled by its computer 'brain.' Such a robot would, unlike Schank's computer, have genuine understanding and other mental states."

333

The first thing to notice about the robot reply is that it tacitly concedes that cognition is not solely a matter of formal symbol manipulation, since this reply adds a set of causal relations with the outside world (cf. Fodor 1980). But the answer to the robot reply is that the addition of such "perceptual" and "motor" capacities adds nothing by way of understanding, in particular, or intentionality, in general, to Schank's original program. To see this, notice that the same thought experiment applies to the robot case. Suppose that instead of the computer inside the robot, you put me inside the room and, as in the original Chinese case, you give me more Chinese symbols with more instructions in English for matching Chinese symbols to Chinese symbols and feeding back Chinese symbols to the outside. Suppose, unknown to me, some of the Chinese symbols that come to me come from a television camera attached to the robot and other Chinese symbols that I am giving out serve to make the motors inside the robot move the robot's legs or arms. It is important to emphasize that all I am doing is manipulating formal symbols: I know none of these other facts. I am receiving "information" from the robot's "perceptual" apparatus, and I am giving out "instructions" to its motor apparatus without knowing either of these facts. I am the robot's homunculus, but unlike the traditional homunculus, I don't know what's going on. I don't understand anything except the rules for symbol manipulation. Now in this case I want to say that the robot has no intentional states at all; it is simply moving about as a result of its electrical wiring and its program. And furthermore, by instantiating the program I have no intentional states of the relevant type. All I do is follow formal instructions about manipulating formal symbols.

3. The brain simulator reply (Berkeley and MIT)

"Suppose we design a program that doesn't represent information that we have about the world, such as the information in Schank's scripts, but simulates the actual sequence of neuron firings at the synapses of the brain of a native Chinese speaker when he understands stories in Chinese and gives answers to them. The machine takes in Chinese stories and questions about them as input, it simulates the formal structure of actual Chinese brains in processing these stories, and it gives out Chinese answers as outputs. We can even imagine that the machine operates, not with a single serial program, but with a whole set of programs operating in parallel, in the manner that actual human brains presumably operate when they process natural language. Now surely in such a case we would have to say that the machine understood the stories; and if we refuse to say that, wouldn't we also have to deny that native Chinese speakers understood the stories? At the level of the synapses, what would or could be different about the program of the computer and the program of the Chinese brain?"

Before countering this reply I want to digress to note that it is an odd reply for any partisan of artificial intelligence (or functionalism, etc.) to make: I thought the whole idea of strong AI is that we don't need to know how the brain works to know how the mind works. The basic hypothesis, or so I had supposed, was that there is a level of mental operations consisting of computational processes over formal elements that constitute the essence of the mental and can be realized in all sorts of different brain processes, in the same way that any computer program can be realized in different computer hardwares: On the assumptions of strong AI, the mind is to the brain as the program is to the hardware, and thus we can understand the mind without doing neurophysiology. If we had to know how the brain worked to do AI, we wouldn't bother with AI. However, even getting this close to the operation of the brain is still not sufficient to produce understanding. To see this, imagine that instead of a monolingual man in a room shuffling symbols we have the man operate an elaborate set of water pipes with valves connecting them. When the man receives the Chinese symbols, he looks up in the program, written in English, which valves he has to turn on and off. Each water connection corresponds to a synapse in the Chinese brain, and the whole system is rigged up so that after doing all the right firings, that is after turning on all the right faucets, the Chinese answers pop out at the output end of the series of pipes.

Now where is the understanding in this system? It takes Chinese as input, it simulates the formal structure of the synapses of the Chinese brain, and it gives Chinese as output. But the man certainly doesn't understand Chinese, and neither do the water pipes, and if we are tempted to adopt what I think is the absurd view that somehow the *conjunction* of man *and* water pipes understands, remember that in principle the man can internalize the formal structure of the water pipes and do all the "neuron firings" in his imagination. The problem with the brain simulator is that it is simulating the wrong things about the brain. As long as it simulates only the formal structure of the sequence of neuron firings at the synapses, it won't have simulated what matters about the brain, namely its causal properties, its ability to produce intentional states. And that the formal properties are not sufficient for the causal properties is shown by the water pipe example: we can have all the formal properties carved off from the relevant neurobiological causal properties.

4. The combination reply (Berkeley and Stanford)

"While each of the previous three replies might not be completely convincing by itself as a refutation of the Chinese room counterexample, if you take all three together they are collectively much more convincing and even decisive. Imagine a robot with a brain-shaped computer lodged in its cranial cavity, imagine the computer programmed with all the synapses of a human brain, imagine the whole behavior of the robot is indistinguishable from human behavior, and now think of the whole thing as a unified system and not just as a computer with inputs and outputs. Surely in such a case we would have to ascribe intentionality to the system."

I entirely agree that in such a case we would find it rational and indeed irresistible to accept the hypothesis that the robot had intentionality, as long as we knew nothing more about it. Indeed, besides appearance and behavior, the other elements of the combination are really irrelevant. If we could build a robot whose behavior was indistinguishable over a large range from human behavior, we would attribute intentionality to it, pending some reason not to. We wouldn't need to know in advance that its computer brain was a formal analogue of the human brain.

But I really don't see that this is any help to the claims of strong AI, and here's why: According to strong AI, instantiating a formal program with the right input and output is a sufficient condition of, indeed is constitutive of, intentionality. As Newell puts it, the essence of the mental is the operation of a physical symbol system. But the attributions of intentionality that we make to the robot in this example have nothing to do with formal programs. They are simply based on the assumption that if the robot looks and behaves sufficiently like us, then we would suppose, until proven otherwise, that it must have mental states like ours that cause and are expressed by its behavior and it must have an inner mechanism capable of producing such mental states. If we knew independently how to account for its behavior without such assumptions we would not attribute intentionality to it, especially if we knew it had a formal program. And this is precisely the point of my earlier reply to objection 2.

Suppose we knew that the robot's behavior was entirely accounted for by the fact that a man inside it was receiving uninterpreted formal symbols from the robot's sensory receptors and sending out uninterpreted formal symbols to its motor mechanisms, and the man was doing this symbol manipulation in accordance with a bunch of rules. Furthermore, suppose the man knows none of these facts about the robot, all he knows is which operations to perform on which meaningless symbols. In such a case we would regard the robot as an ingenious mechanical dummy. The hypothesis that the dummy has a mind would now be unwarranted and unnecessary, for there is now no longer any reason to ascribe intentionality to the robot or to the system of which it is a part (except of course for the man's intentionality in manipulating the symbols). The formal symbol manipulations go on, the input and output are correctly matched, but the only real locus of intentionality is the man, and he doesn't know any of the relevant intentional states; he doesn't, for example, *see* what comes into the robot's eyes, he doesn't *intend* to move the robot's arm, and he doesn't *understand* any of the remarks made to or by the robot. Nor, for the reasons stated earlier, does the system of which man and robot are a part.

To see this point, contrast this case with cases in which we find it completely natural to ascribe intentionality to members of certain other primate species such as apes and monkeys and to domestic animals such as dogs. The reasons we find it natural are, roughly, two: We can't make sense of the animal's behavior without the ascription of intentionality, and we can see that the beasts are made of similar stuff to ourselves – that is an eye, that a nose, this is its skin, and so on. Given the coherence of the animal's behavior and the assumption of the same causal stuff underlying it, we assume both that the animal must have mental states underlying its behavior, and that the mental states must be produced by mechanisms made out of the stuff that is like our stuff. We would certainly make similar assumptions about the robot unless we had some reason not to, but as soon as we knew that the behavior was the result of a formal program, and that the actual causal properties of the physical substance were irrelevant we would abandon the assumption of intentionality.

There are two other responses to my example that come up frequently (and so are worth discussing) but really miss the point.

5. The other minds reply (Yale)

"How do you know that other people understand Chinese or anything else? Only by their behavior. Now the computer can pass the behavioral tests as well as they can (in principle), so if you are going to attribute cognition to other people you must in principle also attribute it to computers."

This objection really is only worth a short reply. The problem in this discussion is not about how I know that other people have cognitive states, but rather what it is that I am attributing to them when I attribute cognitive states to them. The thrust of the argument is that it couldn't be just computational processes and their output because the computational processes and their output can exist without the cognitive state. It is no answer to this argument to feign anesthesia. In "cognitive sciences" one presupposes the reality and knowability of the mental in the same way that in physical sciences one has to presuppose the reality and knowability of physical objects.

6. The many mansions reply (Berkeley)

Your whole argument presupposes that AI is only about analog and digital computers. But that just happens to be the present state of technology. Whatever these causal processes are that you say are essential for intentionality (assuming you are right), eventually we will be able to build devices that have these causal processes, and that will be artificial intelligence. So your arguments are in no way directed at the ability of artificial intelligence to produce and explain cognition."

I really have no objection to this reply save to say that it in effect trivializes the project of strong AI by redefining it as whatever artificially produces and explains cognition. The interest of the original claim made on behalf of artificial intelligence is that it was a precise, well-defined thesis: mental processes are computational processes over formally defined elements. I have been concerned to challenge that thesis. If the claim is redefined so that it is no longer that thesis, my objections no longer apply because there is no longer a testable hypothesis for them to apply to.

Let us now return to the question I promised I would try to answer: Granted that in my original example I understand the English and I do not understand the Chinese, and granted therefore that the machine doesn't understand either English or Chinese, still there must be something about me that makes it the case that I understand English and a corresponding something lacking in me that makes it the case that I fail to understand Chinese. Now why couldn't we give those somethings, whatever they are, to a machine?

I see no reason in principle why we couldn't give a machine the capacity to understand English or Chinese, since in an important sense our bodies with our brains are precisely such machines. But I do see very strong arguments for saying that we could not give such a thing to a machine where the operation of the machine is defined solely in terms of computational processes over formally defined elements; that is, where the operation of the machine is defined as an instantiation of a computer program. It is not because I am the instantiation of a computer program that I am able to understand English and have other forms of intentionality (I am, I suppose, the instantiation of any number of computer programs), but as far as we know it is because I am a certain sort of organism with a certain biological (i.e., chemical and physical) structure, and this structure, under certain conditions, is causally capable of producing perception, action, understanding, learning, and other intentional phenomena. And part of the point of the present argument is that only something that had those causal powers could have that intentionality. Perhaps other physical and chemical processes could produce exactly these effects; perhaps, for example, Martians also have intentionality but their brains are made of different stuff. That is an empirical question, rather like the question whether photosynthesis can be done by something with a chemistry different from that of chlorophyll.

But the main point of the present argument is that no purely formal model will ever be sufficient by itself for intentionality because the formal properties are not by themselves constitutive of intentionality, and they have by themselves no causal powers except the power, when instantiated, to produce the next stage of the formalism when the machine is running. And any other causal properties that particular realizations of the formal model have, are irrelevant to the formal model because we can always put the same formal model in a different realization where those causal properties are obviously absent. Even if, by some miracle, Chinese speakers exactly realize Schank's program, we can put the same program in English speakers, water pipes, or computers, none of which understand Chinese, the program notwithstanding.

What matters about brain operations is not the formal shadow cast by the sequence of synapses but rather the actual properties of the sequences. All the arguments for the strong version of artificial intelligence that I have seen insist on drawing an outline around the shadows cast by cognition and then claiming that the shadows are the real thing.

By way of concluding I want to try to state some of the general philosophical points implicit in the argument. For clarity I will try to do it in a question-and-answer fashion, and I begin with that old chestnut of a question:

"Could a machine think?"

The answer is, obviously, yes. We are precisely such machines.

"Yes, but could an artifact, a man-made machine, think?"

Assuming it is possible to produce artificially a machine with a nervous system, neurons with axons and dendrites, and all the rest of it, sufficiently like ours, again the answer to the question seems to be obviously, yes. If you can exactly duplicate the causes, you could duplicate the effects. And indeed it might be possible to produce consciousness, intentionality, and all the rest of it using some other sorts of chemical principles than those that human beings use. It is, as I said, an empirical question.

"OK, but could a digital computer think?"

If by "digital computer" we mean anything at all that has a level of description where it can correctly be described as the instantiation of a computer program, then again the answer is, of course, yes, since we are the instantiations of any number of computer programs, and we can think.

"But could something think, understand, and so on *solely* in virtue of being a computer with the right sort of program? Could instantiating a program, the right program of course, by itself be a sufficient condition of understanding?"

This I think is the right question to ask, though it is usually confused with one or more of the earlier questions, and the answer to it is no.

"Why not?"

Because the formal symbol manipulations by themselves don't have any intentionality; they are quite meaningless; they aren't even *symbol* manipulations, since the symbols don't symbolize anything. In the linguistic jargon, they have only a syntax but no semantics. Such intentionality as computers appear to have is solely in the minds of those who program them and those who use them, those who send in the input and those who interpret the output.

The aim of the Chinese room example was to try to show this by showing that as soon as we put something into the system that really does have intentionality (a man), and we program him with the formal program, you can see that the formal program carries no additional intentionality. It adds nothing, for example, to a man's ability to understand Chinese.

Precisely that feature of AI that seemed so appealing – the distinction between the program and the realization – proves fatal to the claim that simulation could be duplication. The distinction between the program and its realization in the hardware seems to be parallel to the distinction between the level of mental operations and the level of brain operations. And if we could describe the level of mental operations as a formal program, then it seems we could describe what was essential about the mind without doing either introspective psychology or neurophysiology of the brain. But the equation "mind is to brain as program is to hardware" breaks down at several points, among them the following three:

First, the distinction between program and realization has the consequence that the same program could have all sorts of crazy realizations that had no form of intentionality. Weizenbaum (1976, ch. 2), for example, shows in detail how to construct a computer using a roll of toilet paper and a pile of small stones. Similarly, the Chinese story understanding program can be programmed into a sequence of water pipes, a set of wind machines, or a monolingual English speaker, none of which thereby acquires an understanding of Chinese. Stones, toilet paper, wind, and water pipes are the wrong kind of stuff to have intentionality in the first place – only something that has the same causal powers as brains can have intentionality – and though the English speaker has the right kind of stuff for intentionality you can easily see that he doesn't get any extra intentionality by memorizing the program, since memorizing it won't teach him Chinese.

Second, the program is purely formal, but the intentional states are not in that way formal. They are defined in terms of their content, not their form. The belief that it is raining, for example, is not defined as a certain formal shape, but as a certain mental content with conditions of satisfaction, a direction of fit (see Searle 1979a, 1979b) and the like. Indeed the belief as such hasn't even got a formal shape in this syntactic sense, since one and the same belief can be given an indefinite number of different syntactic expressions in different linguistic systems.

Third, as I mentioned before, mental states and events are literally a product of the operation of the brain, but the program is not in that way a product of the computer.

"Well if programs are in no way constitutive of mental processes, why have so many people believed the converse? That at least needs some explanation."

I don't really know the answer to that one. The idea that computer simulations could be the real thing ought to have seemed suspicious in the first place because the computer isn't confined to simulating mental operations, by any means. No one supposes that computer simulations of a five-alarm fire will burn the neighborhood down or that a computer simulation of a rainstorm will leave us all drenched. Why on earth would anyone suppose that a computer simulation of understanding actually understood anything? It is sometimes said that it would be frightfully hard to get computers to feel pain or fall in love, but love and pain are neither harder nor easier than cognition or anything else. For simulation, all you need is the right input and output and a program in the middle that transforms the former into the latter. That is all the computer has for anything it does. To confuse simulation with duplication is the same mistake, whether it is pain, love, cognition, fires, or rainstorms.

Still, there are several reasons why AI must have seemed – and to many people perhaps still does seem – in some way to reproduce and thereby explain mental phenomena, and I believe we will not succeed in removing these illusions until we have fully exposed the reasons that give rise to them.

First, and perhaps most important, is a confusion about the notion of "information processing": many people in cognitive science believe that the human brain, with its mind, does something called "information processing," and analogously the computer with its program does information processing; but fires and rainstorms, on the other hand, don't do information processing at all. Thus, though the computer can simulate the formal features of any process whatever, it stands in a special relation to the mind and brain because when the computer is properly programmed, ideally with the same program as the brain, the information processing is identical in the two cases, and this information processing is really the essence of the mental. But the trouble with this argument is that it rests on an ambiguity in the notion of "information." In the sense in which people "process information" when they reflect, say, on problems in arithmetic or when they read and answer questions about stories, the programmed computer does not do "information processing." Rather, what it does is manipulate formal symbols. The fact that the programmer and the interpreter of the computer output use the symbols to stand for objects in the world is totally beyond the scope of the computer. The computer, to repeat, has a syntax but no semantics. Thus, if you type into the computer "2 plus 2 equals ?" it will type out "4." But it has no idea that "4" means 4 or that it means anything at all. And the point is not that it lacks some second-order information about the interpretation of its first-order symbols, but rather that its first-order symbols don't have any interpretations as far as the computer is concerned. All the computer has is more symbols. The introduction of the notion of "information processing" therefore produces a dilemma: either we construe the notion of "information processing" in such a way that it implies intentionality as part of the process or we don't. If the former, then the programmed computer does not do information processing, it only manipulates formal symbols. If the latter, then, though the computer does information processing, it is only doing so in the sense in which adding machines, typewriters, stomachs, thermostats, rainstorms, and hurricanes do information processing; namely, they have a level of description at which we can describe them as taking information in at one end, transforming it, and producing information as output. But in this case it is up to outside observers to interpret the input and output as information in the ordinary sense. And no similarity is established between the computer and the brain in terms of any similarity of information processing.

Second, in much of AI there is a residual behaviorism or operationalism. Since appropriately programmed computers can have input-output patterns similar to those of human beings, we are tempted to postulate mental states in the computer similar to human mental states. But once we see that it is both conceptually and empirically possible for a system to have human capacities in some realm without having any intentionality at all, we should be able to overcome this impulse. My desk adding machine has calculating capacities, but no intentionality, and in this paper I have tried to show that a system could have input and output capabilities that duplicated those of a native Chinese speaker and still not understand Chinese, regardless of how it was programmed. The Turing test is typical of the tradition in being unashamedly behavioristic and operationalistic, and I believe that if AI workers totally repudiated behaviorism and operationalism much of the confusion between simulation and duplication would be eliminated.

Third, this residual operationalism is joined to a residual form of dualism; indeed strong AI only makes sense given the dualistic assumption that, where the mind is concerned, the brain doesn't matter. In strong AI (and in functionalism, as well) what matters are programs, and programs are independent of their realization in machines; indeed, as far as AI is concerned, the same program could be realized by an electronic machine, a Cartesian mental substance, or a Hegelian world spirit. The single most surprising discovery that I have made in discussing these issues is that many AI workers are quite shocked by my idea that actual human mental phenomena might be dependent on actual physical-chemical properties of actual human brains. But if you think about it a minute you can see that I should not have been surprised; for unless you accept some form of dualism, the strong AI project hasn't got a chance. The project is to reproduce and explain the mental by designing programs, but unless the mind is not only conceptually but empirically independent of the brain you couldn't carry out the project, for the program is completely independent of any realization. Unless you believe that the mind is separable from the brain both conceptually and empirically – dualism in a strong form – you cannot hope to reproduce the mental by writing and running programs since programs must be independent of brains or any other particular forms of instantiation. If mental operations consist in computational operations on formal symbols, then it follows that they have no interesting connection with the brain; the only connection would be that the brain just happens to be one of the indefinitely many types of machines capable of instantiating the program. This form of dualism is not the traditional Cartesian variety that claims there are two sorts of *substances*, but it is Cartesian in the sense that it insists that what is specifically mental about the mind has no intrinsic connection with the actual properties of the brain. This underlying dualism is masked from us by the fact that AI literature contains frequent fulminations against "dualism"; what the authors seem to be unaware of is that their position presupposes a strong version of dualism.

"Could a machine think?" My own view is that *only* a machine could think, and indeed only very special kinds of machines, namely brains and machines that had the same causal powers as brains. And that is the main reason strong AI has had little to tell us about thinking, since it has nothing to tell us about machines. By its own definition, it is about programs, and programs are not machines. Whatever else intentionality is, it is a biological phenomenon, and it is as likely to be as causally dependent on the specific biochemistry of its origins as lactation, photosynthesis, or any other biological phenomena. No one would suppose that we could produce milk and sugar by running a computer simulation of the formal sequences in lactation and photosynthesis, but where the mind is concerned many people are willing to believe in such a miracle because of a deep and abiding dualism: the mind they suppose is a matter of formal processes and is independent of quite specific material causes in the way that milk and sugar are not.

In defense of this dualism the hope is often expressed that the brain is a digital computer (early computers, by the way, were often called "electronic brains"). But that is no help. Of course the brain is a digital computer. Since everything is a digital computer, brains are too. The point is that the brain's causal capacity to produce intentionality cannot consist in its instantiating a computer program, since for any program you like it is possible for something to instantiate that program and still not have any mental states. Whatever it is that the brain does to produce intentionality, it cannot consist in instantiating a program since no program, by itself, is sufficient for intentionality.

Notes

1   Also "understanding" implies both the possession of mental (intentional) states and the truth (validity, success) of these states. For the purposes of this discussion we are concerned only with the possession of the states.
2   Intentionality is by definition that feature of certain mental states by which they are directed at or about objects and states of affairs in the world. Thus, beliefs, desires, and intentions are intentional states; undirected forms of anxiety and depression are not.

References

Fodor, Jerry A. (1980) 'Methodological solipsism considered as a research strategy in cognitive psychology', *The Behavioral and Brain Sciences*, vol. 3, no. 1, pp. 63–73.

McCarthy, John (1979) 'Ascribing mental qualities to machines', in Martin Ringle (ed.) *Philosophical Perspectives on Artificial Intelligence*, Atlantic Highlands, NJ: Humanities Press.

Newell, Allen and Simon, Herbert (1963) 'GPS: a program that simulates human thought', in E. Feigenbaum and J. Feldman (eds) *Computers and Thought*, New York: McGraw Hill.

Schank, Roger C. and Abelson, Robert P. (1977) *Scripts, Plans, Goals and Understanding*, Hillsdale, NJ: Erlbaum.

Searle, John R. (1979a) 'Intentionality and the use of language', in A. Margolit (ed.) *Meaning and Use*, Hingham, Mass.: Reidel.

—— (1979b) 'What is an intentional state?', *Mind*, vol. 88, pp. 74–92.

Weizenbaum, Joseph (1976) *Computer Power and Human Reason*, San Francisco: Freeman.

38

What is it like to be a bat?
Thomas Nagel

Through an imaginative investigation of a bat's experience, Thomas Nagel
(1937–) makes the point that physicalist theories of mind don't do justice
to the phenomenon of consciousness. They don't adequately explain how
subjective experience can be identical with physical events. The existence of
consciousness makes the mind–body problem far harder to solve than some
philosophers have imagined. This is not to say that physicalism is false.

From Thomas Nagel, 'What is it like to be a bat?', *Philosophical
Review*, vol. LXXXIII

Consciousness is what makes the mind–body problem really intractable.
Perhaps that is why current discussions of the problem give it little attention or get it obviously wrong. The recent wave of reductionist euphoria
has produced several analyses of mental phenomena and mental concepts
designed to explain the possibility of some variety of materialism,
psychophysical identification, or reduction.[1] But the problems dealt with
are those common to this type of reduction and other types, and what
makes the mind–body problem unique, and unlike the water–H_2O problem
or the Turing machine–IBM machine problem or the lightning–electrical
discharge problem or the gene–DNA problem or the oak tree–hydrocarbon
problem, is ignored.

Every reductionist has his favorite analogy from modern science. It
is most unlikely that any of these unrelated examples of successful reduction will shed light on the relation of mind to brain. But philosophers share
the general human weakness for explanations of what is incomprehensible
in terms suited for what is familiar and well understood, though entirely
different. This has led to the acceptance of implausible accounts of
the mental largely because they would permit familiar kinds of reduction.
I shall try to explain why the usual examples do not help us to understand
the relation between mind and body – why, indeed, we have at present no

conception of what an explanation of the physical nature of a mental phenomenon would be. Without consciousness the mind–body problem would be much less interesting. With consciousness it seems hopeless. The most important and characteristic feature of conscious mental phenomena is very poorly understood. Most reductionist theories do not even try to explain it. And careful examination will show that no currently available concept of reduction is applicable to it. Perhaps a new theoretical form can be devised for the purpose, but such a solution, if it exists, lies in the distant intellectual future.

Conscious experience is a widespread phenomenon. It occurs at many levels of animal life, though we cannot be sure of its presence in the simpler organisms, and it is very difficult to say in general what provides evidence of it. (Some extremists have been prepared to deny it even of mammals other than man.) No doubt it occurs in countless forms totally unimaginable to us, on other planets in other solar systems throughout the universe. But no matter how the form may vary, the fact that an organism has conscious experience *at all* means, basically, that there is something it is like to *be* that organism. There may be further implications about the form of the experience; there may even (though I doubt it) be implications about the behavior of the organism. But fundamentally an organism has conscious mental states if and only if there is something that it is like to *be* that organism – something it is like *for* the organism.

We may call this the subjective character of experience. It is not captured by any of the familiar, recently devised reductive analyses of the mental, for all of them are logically compatible with its absence. It is not analyzable in terms of any explanatory system of functional states, or intentional states, since these could be ascribed to robots or automata that behaved like people though they experienced nothing.[2] It is not analyzable in terms of the causal role of experiences in relation to typical human behavior – for similar reasons.[3] I do not deny that conscious mental states and events cause behavior, nor that they may be given functional characterizations. I deny only that this kind of thing exhausts their analysis. Any reductionist program has to be based on an analysis of what is to be reduced. If the analysis leaves something out, the problem will be falsely posed. It is useless to base the defense of materialism on any analysis of mental phenomena that fails to deal explicitly with their subjective character. For there is no reason to suppose that a reduction which seems plausible when no attempt is made to account for consciousness can be extended to include consciousness. Without some idea, therefore, of what the subjective character of experience is, we cannot know what is required of physicalist theory.

While an account of the physical basis of mind must explain many things, this appears to be the most difficult. It is impossible to exclude the phenomenological features of experience from a reduction in the same way that one excludes the phenomenal features of an ordinary substance from a physical or chemical reduction of it – namely, by explaining them as effects on the minds of human observers.[4] If physicalism is to be defended, the phenomenological features must themselves be given a physical account. But when we examine their subjective character it seems that such a result is impossible. The reason is that every subjective phenomenon is essentially connected with a single point of view, and it seems inevitable that an objective, physical theory will abandon that point of view.

Let me first try to state the issue somewhat more fully than by referring to the relation between the subjective and the objective, or between the *pour soi* and the *en soi*. This is far from easy. Facts about what it is like to be an X are very peculiar, so peculiar that some may be inclined to doubt their reality, or the significance of claims about them. To illustrate the connexion between subjectivity and a point of view, and to make evident the importance of subjective features, it will help to explore the matter in relation to an example that brings out clearly the divergence between the two types of conception, subjective and objective.

I assume we all believe that bats have experience. After all, they are mammals, and there is no more doubt that they have experience than that mice or pigeons or whales have experience. I have chosen bats instead of wasps or flounders because if one travels too far down the phylogenetic tree, people gradually shed their faith that there is experience there at all. Bats, although more closely related to us than those other species, nevertheless present a range of activity and a sensory apparatus so different from ours that the problem I want to pose is exceptionally vivid (though it certainly could be raised with other species). Even without the benefit of philosophical reflection, anyone who has spent some time in an enclosed space with an excited bat knows what it is to encounter a fundamentally alien form of life.

I have said that the essence of the belief that bats have experience is that there is something that it is like to be a bat. Now we know that most bats (the microchiroptera, to be precise) perceive the external world primarily by sonar, or echolocation, detecting the reflections, from objects within range, of their own rapid, subtly modulated, high-frequency shrieks. Their brains are designed to correlate the outgoing impulses with the subsequent echoes, and the information thus acquired enables bats to make precise discriminations of distance, size, shape, motion, and texture comparable to those we make by vision. But bat sonar, though clearly a form of perception, is not similar in its operation to any sense that we possess, and there is no reason to suppose that it is subjectively like anything we can experience or imagine. This appears to create difficulties for the notion of what it is like to be a bat. We must consider whether any method will permit us to extrapolate to the inner life of the bat from our own case,[5] and if not, what alternative methods there may be for understanding the notion.

347

Our own experience provides the basic material for our imagination, whose range is therefore limited. It will not help to try to imagine that one has webbing on one's arms, which enables one to fly around at dusk and dawn catching insects in one's mouth; that one has very poor vision, and perceives the surrounding world by a system of reflected high-frequency sound signals; and that one spends the day hanging upside down by one's feet in an attic. Insofar as I can imagine this (which is not very far), it tells me only what it would be like for me to behave as a bat behaves. But that is not the question. I want to know what it is like for a *bat* to be a bat. Yet if I try to imagine this, I am restricted to the resources of my own mind, and those resources are inadequate to the task. I cannot perform it either by imagining additions to my present experience, or by imagining segments gradually subtracted from it, or by imagining some combination of additions, subtractions, and modifications.

To the extent that I could look and behave like a wasp or a bat without changing my fundamental structure, my experiences would not be anything like the experiences of those animals. On the other hand, it is doubtful that any meaning can be attached to the supposition that I should possess the internal neurophysiological constitution of a bat. Even if I could by gradual degrees be transformed into a bat, nothing in my present constitution enables me to imagine what the experiences of such a future stage of myself thus metamorphosed would be like. The best evidence would come from the experiences of bats, if we only knew what they were like.

So if extrapolation from our own case is involved in the idea of what it is like to be a bat, the extrapolation must be incompletable. We cannot form more than a schematic conception of what it *is* like. For example, we may ascribe general *types* of experience on the basis of the animal's structure and behavior. Thus we describe bat sonar as a form of three-dimensional forward perception; we believe that bats feel some versions of pain, fear, hunger, and lust, and that they have other, more familiar types of perception besides sonar. But we believe that these experiences also have in each case a specific subjective character, which it is beyond our ability to conceive. And if there is conscious life elsewhere in the universe, it is likely that some of it will not be describable even in the most general experiential terms available to us.[6] (The problem is not confined to exotic cases, however for it exists between one person and another. The subjective character of the experience of a person deaf and blind from birth is not accessible to me, for example, nor presumably is mine to him. This does not prevent us each from believing that the other's experience has such a subjective character.)

If anyone is inclined to deny that we can believe in the existence of facts like this whose exact nature we cannot possibly conceive, he should reflect that in contemplating the bats we are in much the same position that intelligent bats or Martians[7] would occupy if they tried to form a conception of what it was like to be us. The structure of their own minds might make it impossible for them to succeed, but we know they would be wrong to conclude that there is not anything precise that it is like to be us: that only certain general types of mental state could be ascribed to us (perhaps perception and appetite would be concepts common to us both; perhaps not). We know they would be wrong to draw such a skeptical conclusion because we know what it is like to be us. And we know that while it includes an enormous amount of variation and complexity, and while we do not possess the vocabulary to describe it adequately, its subjective character is highly specific, and in some respects describable in terms that can be understood only by creatures like us. The fact that we cannot expect ever to accommodate in our language a detailed description of Martian or bat phenomenology should not lead us to dismiss as meaningless the claim that bats and Martians have experiences fully comparable in richness of detail to our own. It would be fine if someone were to develop concepts and a theory that enabled us to think about those things; but such an understanding may be permanently denied to us by the limits of our nature. And to deny the reality or logical significance of what we can never describe or understand is the crudest form of cognitive dissonance.

This brings us to the edge of a topic that requires much more discussion than I can give it here: namely, the relation between facts on the one hand and conceptual schemes or systems of representation on the other. My realism about the subjective domain in all its forms implies a belief in the existence of facts beyond the reach of human concepts. Certainly it is possible for a human being to believe that there are facts which humans never *will* possess the requisite concepts to represent or comprehend. Indeed, it would be foolish to doubt this, given the finiteness of humanity's expectations. After all, there would have been transfinite numbers even if everyone had been wiped out by the Black Death before Cantor discovered them. But one might also believe that there are facts which *could* not ever be represented or comprehended by human beings, even if the species lasted for ever – simply because our structure does not permit us to operate with concepts of the requisite type. This impossibility might even be observed by other beings, but it is not clear that the existence of such beings, or the possibility of their existence, is a precondition of the significance of the hypothesis that there are humanly inaccessible facts. (After all, the nature of beings with access to humanly inaccessible facts is presumably itself a humanly inaccessible fact.) Reflection on what it is like to be a bat seems to lead us, therefore, to the conclusion that there are facts that do not consist in the truth of propositions expressible in a human language. We can be compelled to recognize the existence of such facts without being able to state or comprehend them.

I shall not pursue this subject, however. Its bearing on the topic before us (namely, the mind–body problem) is that it enables us to make a general observation about the subjective character of experience, Whatever may be the status of facts about what it is like to be a human being, or a bat, or a Martian, these appear to be facts that embody a particular point of view.

I am not adverting here to the alleged privacy of experience to its possessor. The point of view in question is not one accessible only to a single individual. Rather it is a *type*. It is often possible to take up a point of view other than one's own, so the comprehension of such facts is not limited to one's own case. There is a sense in which phenomenological facts are perfectly objective: one person can know or say of another what the quality of the other's experience is. They are subjective, however, in the sense that even this objective ascription of experience is possible only for someone sufficiently similar to the object of ascription to be able to adopt his point of view – to understand the ascription in the first person as well as in the third, so to speak. The more different from oneself the other experiencer is, the less success one can expect with this enterprise. In our own case we occupy the relevant point of view, but we will have as much difficulty understanding our own experience properly if we approach it from another point of view as we would if we tried to understand the experience of another species without taking up *its* point of view.[8]

This bears directly on the mind–body problem. For if the facts of experience – facts about what it is like *for* the experiencing organism – are accessible only from one point of view, then it is a mystery how the true character of experiences could be revealed in the physical operation of that organism. The latter is a domain of objective facts *par excellence* – the kind that can be observed and understood from many points of view and by individuals with differing perceptual systems. There are no comparable imaginative obstacles to the acquisition of knowledge about bat neurophysiology by human scientists, and intelligent bats or Martians might learn more about the human brain than we ever will.

This is not by itself an argument against reduction. A Martian scientist with no understanding of visual perception could understand the rainbow, or lightning, or clouds as physical phenomena, though he would never be able to understand the human concepts of rainbow, lightning, or cloud, or the place these things occupy in our phenomenal world. The objective nature of the things picked out by these concepts could be apprehended by him because, although the concepts themselves are connected with a particular point of view and a particular visual phenomenology, the things apprehended from that point of view are not: they are observable from the point of view but external to it; hence they can be comprehended from other points of view also, either by the same organisms or by others. Lightning has an objective character that is not exhausted by its visual appearance, and this can be investigated by a Martian without vision. To be precise, it has a more objective character than is revealed in its visual appearance. In speaking of the move from subjective to objective characterization, I wish to remain noncommittal about the existence of an end point, the completely objective intrinsic nature of the thing, which one might or might not be able to reach. It may be more accurate to think of objectivity as a direction in which the understanding can travel. And in understanding a phenomenon like lightning, it is legitimate to go as far away as one can from a strictly human viewpoint.[9]

In the case of experience, on the other hand, the connexion with a particular point of view seems much closer. It is difficult to understand what could be meant by the *objective* character of an experience, apart from the particular point of view from which its subject apprehends it. After all, what would be left of what it was like to be a bat if one removed the viewpoint of the bat? But if experience does not have, in addition to its subjective character, an objective nature that can be apprehended from many different points of view, then how can it be supposed that a Martian investigating my brain might be observing physical processes which were my mental processes (as he might observe physical processes which were bolts of lightning), only from a different point of view? How, for that matter, could a human physiologist observe them from another point of view?[10]

We appear to be faced with a general difficulty about psychophysical reduction. In other areas the process of reduction is a move in the direction of greater objectivity, toward a more accurate view of the real nature of things. This is accomplished by reducing our dependence on individual or species-specific points of view toward the object of investigation. We describe it not in terms of the impressions it makes on our senses, but in terms of its more general effects and of properties detectable by means other than the human senses. The less it depends on a specifically human viewpoint, the more objective is our description. It is possible to follow this path because although the concepts and ideas we employ in thinking about the external world are initially applied from a point of view that involves our perceptual apparatus, they are used by us to refer to things beyond themselves – toward which we *have* the phenomenal point of view. Therefore we can abandon it in favor of another, and still be thinking about the same things.

Experience itself, however, does not seem to fit the pattern. The idea of moving from appearance to reality seems to make no sense here. What is the analogue in this case to pursuing a more objective understanding of the same phenomena by abandoning the initial subjective viewpoint toward them in favour of another that is more objective but concerns the same thing? Certainly it *appears* unlikely that we will get closer to the real nature of human experience by leaving behind the particularity of our human point of view and striving for a description in terms accessible to beings that could not imagine what it was like to be us. If the subjective character of experience is fully comprehensible only from one point of view, then any shift to greater objectivity – that is, less attachment to a specific viewpoint – does not take us nearer to the real nature of the phenomenon: it takes us farther away from it.

In a sense, the seeds of this objection to the reducibility of experience are already detectable in successful cases of reduction; for in discovering sound to be, in reality, a wave phenomenon in air or other media, we leave behind one viewpoint to take up another, and the auditory, human or animal viewpoint that we leave behind remains unreduced. Members of radically different species may both understand the same physical events in objective terms, and this does not require that they understand the phenomenal forms in which those events appear to the senses of members of the other species. Thus it is a condition of their referring to a common reality that their more particular viewpoints are not part of the common reality that they both apprehend. The reduction can succeed only if the species-specific viewpoint is omitted from what is to be reduced.

But while we are right to leave this point of view aside in seeking a fuller understanding of the external world, we cannot ignore it permanently, since it is the essence of the internal world, and not merely a point of view on it. Most of the neobehaviorism of recent philosophical psychology results from the effort to substitute an objective concept of mind for the real thing, in order to have nothing left over which cannot be reduced. If we acknowledge that a physical theory of mind must account for the subjective character of experience, we must admit that no presently available conception gives us a clue how this could be done. The problem is unique. If mental processes are indeed physical processes, then there is something it is like, intrinsically,[11] to undergo certain physical processes. What it is for such a thing to be the case remains a mystery.

What moral should be drawn from these reflections, and what should be done next? It would be a mistake to conclude that physicalism must be false. Nothing is proved by the inadequacy of physicalist hypotheses that assume a faulty objective analysis of mind. It would be truer to say that physicalism is a position we cannot understand because we do not at present have any conception of how it might be true. Perhaps it will be thought unreasonable to require such a conception as a condition of understanding. After all, it might be said, the meaning of physicalism is clear enough: mental states are states of the body; mental events are physical events. We do not know *which* physical states and events they are, but that should not prevent us from understanding the hypothesis. What could be clearer than the words 'is' and 'are'?

But I believe it is precisely this apparent clarity of the word 'is' that is deceptive. Usually, when we are told that X is Y we know *how* it is supposed to be true, but that depends on a conceptual or theoretical background and is not conveyed by the 'is' alone. We know how both 'X' and 'Y' refer, and the kinds of things to which they refer, and we have a rough idea how the two referential paths might converge on a single thing, be it an object, a person, a process, an event or whatever. But when the two terms of the identification are very disparate it may not be so clear how it could be true. We may not have even a rough idea of how the two referential paths could converge, or what kind of things they might converge on, and a theoretical framework may have to be supplied to enable us to understand this. Without the framework, an air of mysticism surrounds the identification.

This explains the magical flavor of popular presentations of fundamental scientific discoveries, given out as propositions to which one must subscribe without really understanding them. For example, people are now told at an early age that all matter is really energy. But despite the fact that they know what 'is' means, most of them never form a conception of what makes this claim true, because they lack the theoretical background.

At the present time the status of physicalism is similar to that which the hypothesis that matter is energy would have had if uttered by a pre-Socratic philosopher. We do not have the beginnings of a conception of how it might be true. In order to understand the hypothesis that a mental event is a physical event, we require more than an understanding of the word 'is'. The idea of how a mental and a physical term might refer to the same thing is lacking, and the usual analogies with theoretical identification in other fields fail to supply it. They fail because if we construe the reference of mental terms to physical events on the usual model, we either get a reappearance of separate subjective events as the effects through which mental reference to physical events is secured, or else we get a false account of how mental terms refer (for example, a causal behaviorist one).

Strangely enough, we may have evidence for the truth of something we cannot really understand. Suppose a caterpillar is locked in a sterile safe by someone unfamiliar with insect metamorphosis, and weeks later the safe is reopened, revealing a butterfly. If the person knows that the safe has been shut the whole time, he has reason to believe that the butterfly is or was once the caterpillar, without having any idea in what sense this might be so. (One possibility is that the caterpillar contained a tiny winged parasite that devoured it and grew into the butterfly.)

It is conceivable that we are in such a position with regard to physicalism. Donald Davidson has argued that if mental events have physical causes and effects, they must have physical descriptions. He holds that we have reason to believe this even though we do not – and in fact *could* not – have a general psychophysical theory.[12] His argument applies to intentional mental events, but I think we also have some reason to believe that sensations are physical processes, without being in a position to understand how. Davidson's position is that certain physical events have irreducibly mental properties, and perhaps some view describable in this way is correct. But nothing of which we can now form a conception corresponds to it; nor have we any idea what a theory would be like that enabled us to conceive of it.[13]

Very little work has been done on the basic question (from which mention of the brain can be entirely omitted) whether any sense can be made of experiences' having an objective character at all. Does it make sense, in other words, to ask what my experiences are *really* like, as opposed to how they appear to me? We cannot genuinely understand the hypothesis that their nature is captured in a physical description unless we understand the more fundamental idea that they *have* an objective nature (or that objective processes can have a subjective nature).[14]

I should like to close with a speculative proposal. It may be possible to approach the gap between subjective and objective from another direction. Setting aside temporarily the relation between the mind and the brain, we can pursue a more objective understanding of the mental in its own right. At present we are completely unequipped to think about the subjective character of experience without relying on the imagination – without taking up the point of view of the experiential subject. This should be regarded as a challenge to form new concepts and devise a new method – an objective phenomenology not dependent on empathy or the imagination. Though presumably it would not capture everything, its goal would be to describe, at least in part, the subjective character of experiences in a form comprehensible to beings incapable of having those experiences.

We would have to develop such a phenomenology to describe the sonar experiences of bats; but it would also be possible to begin with humans. One might try, for example, to develop concepts that could be used to explain to a person blind from birth what it was like to see. One would reach a blank wall eventually, but it should be possible to devise a method of expressing in objective terms much more than we can at present, and with much greater precision. The loose intermodal analogies – for example, 'Red is like the sound of a trumpet' – which crop up in discussions of this subject are of little use. That should be clear to anyone who has both heard a trumpet and seen red. But structural features of perception might be more accessible to objective description, even though something would be left out. And concepts alternative to those we learn in the first person may enable us to arrive at a kind of understanding even of our own experience which is denied us by the very ease of description and lack of distance that subjective concepts afford.

Apart from its own interest, a phenomenology that is in this sense objective may permit questions about the physical[15] basis of experience to assume a more intelligible form. Aspects of subjective experience that admitted this kind of objective description might be better candidates for objective explanations of a more familiar sort. But whether or not this guess is correct, it seems unlikely that any physical theory of mind can be contemplated until more thought has been given to the general problem of subjective and objective. Otherwise we cannot even pose the mind–body problem without sidestepping it.

Notes

1 Examples are J. J. C. Smart, *Philosophy and Scientific Realism* (London: Routledge & Kegan Paul, 1963); David K. Lewis, 'An argument for the identity theory', *Journal of Philosophy* LXIII (1966), reprinted with addenda in David M. Rosenthal, *Materialism and the Mind–Body Problem* (Engelwood Cliffs, NJ: Prentice-Hall, 1971); Hilary Putnam, 'Psychological predicates', in W. H. Capitan and D. D. Merrill (eds) *Art, Mind and Religion* (Pittsburg: University of Pittsburgh Press, 1967), reprinted in Rosenthal, *Materialism* as 'The nature of mental states'; D. M. Armstrong, *A Materialist Theory of the Mind* (London: Routledge & Kegan Paul, 1968); D. C. Dennett, *Content and Consciousness* (London: Routledge & Kegan Paul, 1969). I have expressed earlier doubts in 'Armstrong on the mind', *Philosophical Review* LXXIX (1970), pp. 394–403; a review of Dennett, *Journal of Philosophy*, LXIX (1972); and ch. 11 in my *Mental Questions*. See also Saul Kripke, 'Naming and necessity', in D. Davidson and G. Harmon (eds) *Semantics of Natural Language* (Dordrecht: Reidel, 1972), esp. pp. 334–42; and M. T. Thornton, 'Ostensive terms and materialism' *The Monist* LVI (1972), pp. 193–214.

2 Perhaps there could not actually be such robots. Perhaps anything complex enough to behave like a person would have experiences. But that, if true, is a fact which cannot be discovered merely by analyzing the concept of experience.

3 It is not equivalent to that about which we are incorrigible, both because we are not incorrigible about experience and because experience is present in animals lacking language and thought, who have no beliefs at all about their experiences.

4 Cf. Richard Rorty, 'Mind–Body identity, privacy, and categories', *Review of Metaphysics* XIX (1965), esp. pp. 37–8.

5 By 'our own case' I do not mean just 'my own case', but rather the mentalistic ideas that we apply unproblematically to ourselves and other human beings.

6 Therefore the analogical form of the English expression 'what it is *like*' is misleading. It does not mean 'what (in our experience) it *resembles*', but rather 'how it is for the subject himself'.

7 Any intelligent extraterrestrial beings totally different from us.

8 It may be easier than I suppose to transcend inter-species barriers with the aid of the imagination. For example, blind people are able to detect objects near them by a form of sonar, using vocal clicks or taps of a cane. Perhaps

if one knew what that was like, one could by extension imagine roughly what it was like to possess the much more refined sonar of a bat. The distance between oneself and other persons and other species can fall anywhere on a continuum. Even for other persons the understanding of what it is like to be them is only partial, and when one moves to species very different from oneself, a lesser degree of partial understanding may still be available. The imagination is remarkably flexible. My point, however, is not that we cannot *know* what it is like to be a bat. I am not raising that epistemological problem. My point is rather that even to form a *conception* of what it is like to be a bat (and *a fortiori* to know what it is like to be a bat) one must take up the bat's point of view. If one can take it up roughly, or partially, then one's conception will also be rough or partial. Or so it seems in our present state of understanding.

9   The problem I am going to raise can therefore be posed even if the distinction between more subjective and more objective descriptions or viewpoints can itself be made only within a larger human point of view. I do not accept this kind of conceptual relativism, but it need not be refuted to make the point that psychophysical reduction cannot be accommodated by the subjective-to-objective model familiar from other cases.

10   The problem is not just that when I look at the *Mona Lisa*, my visual experience has a certain quality, no trace of which is to be found by someone looking into my brain. For even if he did observe there a tiny image of the *Mona Lisa*, he would have no reason to identify it with the experience.

11   The relation would therefore not be a contingent one, like that of a cause and its distinct effect. It would be necessarily true that a certain physical state felt a certain way. Saul Kripke in *Semantics of Natural Language* (ed. Davidson and Harman) argues that causal behaviorist and related analyses of the mental fail because they construe, e.g. 'pain' as a merely contingent name of pains. The subjective character of an experience ('its immediate phenomenological quality' Kripke calls it (p. 340)) is the essential property left out by such analyses, and the one in virtue of which it is, necessarily, the experience it is. My view is closely related to his. Like Kripke, I find the hypothesis that a certain brain state should *necessarily* have a certain subjective character incomprehensible without further explanation. No such explanation emerges from theories which view the mind–brain relation as contingent, but perhaps there are other alternatives, not yet discovered.

A theory that explained how the mind–brain relation was necessary would still leave us with Kripke's problem of explaining why it nevertheless appears contingent. That difficulty seems to me surmountable, in the following way. We may imagine something by representing it to ourselves either perceptually, sympathetically, or symbolically. I shall not try to say how symbolic imagination works, but part of what happens in the other two cases is this. To imagine something perceptually, we put ourselves in a conscious state resembling the state we would be in if we perceived it. To imagine something sympathetically, we put ourselves in a conscious state resembling the thing itself. (This method can be used only to imagine mental events and states – our own or another's.) When we try to imagine a mental state occurring without its associated brain state, we first sympathetically imagine the occurrence of the mental state: that is, we put ourselves into a state that resembles it mentally. At the same time, we attempt perceptually to imagine the nonoccurrence of the associated physical state, by putting ourselves into another state unconnected with the first: one resembling that which we would be in if we perceived the nonoccurrence of the physical state. Where the imagination of physical features is perceptual and the imagination of mental features is sympathetic, it appears to us that we can imagine any experience occurring without its associated brain state, and vice versa. The relation between them will appear contingent even if it is necessary, because of the independence of the disparate types of imagination.

(Solipsism, incidentally, results if one misinterprets sympathetic imagination as if it worked like perceptual imagination: it then seems impossible to imagine any experience that is not one's own.)

12   See 'Mental events' in Lawrence Foster and J. W. Swanson (eds) *Experience and Theory* (Amherst, Mass: University of Massachusetts Press, 1970); though I do not understand the argument against psychophysical laws.

13   Similar remarks apply to my paper 'Physicalism', *Philosophical Review*, LXXIV (1965) pp. 339–56, reprinted with postscript in John O'Connor (ed.) *Modern Materialism* (New York: Harcourt Brace Jovanovich, 1969).

14   This question also lies at the heart or the problem of other minds, whose close connection with the mind-body problem is often overlooked. If one understood how subjective experience could have an objective nature, one would understand the existence of subjects other than oneself.

15   I have not defined the term 'physical'. Obviously it does not apply to what can be described by the concepts of contemporary physics, since we expect further developments. Some may think there is nothing to prevent mental phenomena from eventually being recognized as physical in their own right. But whatever else may be said of the physical, it has to be objective. So if our idea of the physical ever expands to include mental phenomena, it will have to assign them an objective character – whether or not this is done by analyzing them in terms of other phenomena already regarded as physical. It seems to me more likely, however, that mental–physical relations will eventually be expressed in a theory whose fundamental terms cannot be placed clearly in either category.

39

Where am I?
Daniel C. Dennett

Although light-hearted in tone, this story by the eminent philosopher Daniel
C. Dennett (1942–   ) raises and explores a number of important issues about
the nature of personal identity.

From Daniel C. Dennett, *Brainstorms*

Now that I've won my suit under the Freedom of Information Act, I am
at liberty to reveal for the first time a curious episode in my life that may
be of interest not only to those engaged in research in the philosophy of
mind, artificial intelligence and neuroscience but also to the general public.

Several years ago I was approached by Pentagon officials who asked
me to volunteer for a highly dangerous and secret mission. In collaboration with NASA and Howard Hughes, the Department of Defense was
spending billions to develop a Supersonic Tunneling Underground Device,
or STUD. It was supposed to tunnel through the earth's core at great speed
and deliver a specially designed atomic warhead "right up the Red's missile
silos," as one of the Pentagon brass put it.

The problem was that in an early test they had succeeded in lodging
a warhead about a mile deep under Tulsa, Oklahoma, and they wanted me
to retrieve it for them. "Why me?" I asked. Well, the mission involved
some pioneering applications of current brain research, and they had heard
of my interest in brains and of course my Faustian curiosity and great
courage and so forth. . . . Well, how could I refuse? The difficulty that
brought the Pentagon to my door was that the device I'd been asked to
recover was fiercely radioactive, in a new way. According to monitoring
instruments, something about the nature of the device and its complex
interactions with pockets of material deep in the earth had produced radi-
ation that could cause severe abnormalities in certain tissues of the brain.
No way had been found to shield the brain from these deadly rays, which
were apparently harmless to other tissues and organs of the body. So it

358

had been decided that the person sent to recover the device should *leave his brain behind*. It would be kept in a safe place where it could execute its normal control functions by elaborate radio links. Would I submit to a surgical procedure that would completely remove my brain, which would then be placed in a life-support system at the Manned Spacecraft Center in Houston? Each input and output pathway, as it was severed, would be restored by a pair of microminiaturized radio transceivers, one attached precisely to the brain, the other to the nerve stumps in the empty cranium. No information would be lost, all the connectivity would be preserved. At first I was a bit reluctant. Would it really work? The Houston brain surgeons encouraged me. "Think of it," they said, "as a mere *stretching* of the nerves. If your brain were just moved over an *inch* in your skull, that would not alter or impair your mind. We're simply going to make the nerves indefinitely elastic by splicing radio links into them."

I was shown around the life-support lab in Houston and saw the sparkling new vat in which my brain would be placed, were I to agree. I met the large and brilliant support team of neurologists, hematololgists, biophysicists, and electrical engineers, and after several days of discussions and demonstrations, I agreed to give it a try. I was subjected to an enormous array of blood tests, brain scans, experiments, interviews, and the like. They took down my autobiography at great length, recorded tedious lists of my beliefs, hopes, fears, and tastes. They even listed my favorite stereo recordings and gave me a crash session of psychoanalysis.

The day for surgery arrived at last and of course I was anesthetized and remember nothing of the operation itself. When I came out of anesthesia, I opened my eyes, looked around, and asked the inevitable, the traditional, the lamentably hackneyed post-operative question: "Where am I?" The nurse smiled down at me. "You're in Houston," she said, and I reflected that this still had a good chance of being the truth one way or another. She handed me a mirror. Sure enough, there were the tiny antennae poking up through their titanium ports cemented into my skull.

"I gather the operation was a success," I said, "I want to go see my brain." They led me (I was a bit dizzy and unsteady) down a long corridor and into the life-support lab. A cheer went up from the assembled support team, and I responded with what I hoped was a jaunty salute. Still feeling lighthearted, I was helped over to the life-support vat. I peered through the glass. There, floating in what looked like ginger-ale, was undeniably a human brain, though it was almost covered with printed circuit chips, plastic tubules, electrodes, and other paraphernalia. "Is that mine?" I asked. "Hit the output transmitter switch there on the side of the vat and see for yourself," the project director replied. I moved the switch to OFF, and immediately slumped, groggy and nauseated, into the arms of the technicians, one of whom kindly restored the switch to its ON position. While I recovered my equilibrium and composure, I thought to myself: "Well, here I am, sitting on a folding chair, staring through a piece of plate glass at my own brain. . . . But wait," I said to myself, "shouldn't I have thought, 'Here I am, suspended in a bubbling fluid, being stared at by my own eyes'?" I tried to think this latter thought. I tried to project it into the tank, offering it hopefully to my brain, but I failed to carry off the exercise with any conviction. I tried again. "Here am I, Daniel Dennett, suspended in a bubbling fluid, being stared at by my own eyes." No, it just didn't work. Most puzzling and confusing. Being a philosopher of firm physicalist conviction, I believed unswervingly that the tokening of my thoughts was occurring somewhere in my brain: yet, when I thought "Here I am," where the thought occurred to me was here, outside the vat, where I, Dennett, was standing staring at my brain.

I tried and tried to think myself into the vat, but to no avail. I tried to build up to the task by doing mental exercises. I thought to myself, "The sun is shining *over there*," five times in rapid succession, each time mentally ostending a different place: in order, the sun-lit corner of the lab, the visible front lawn of the hospital, Houston, Mars, and Jupiter. I found I had little difficulty in getting my "there's" to hop all over the celestial map with their proper references. I could loft a "there" in an instant through the farthest reaches of space, and then aim the next "there" with pinpoint accuracy at the upper left quadrant of a freckle on my arm. Why was I having such trouble with "here"? "Here in Houston" worked well enough, and so did "here in the lab," and even "here in this part of the lab," but "here in the vat" always seemed merely an unmeant mental mouthing. I tried closing my eyes while thinking it. This seemed to help, but still I couldn't manage to pull it off, except perhaps for a fleeting instant. I couldn't be sure. The discovery that I couldn't be sure was also unsettling. How did I know *where* I meant by "here" when I thought "here"? Could I *think* I meant one place when in fact I meant another? I didn't see how that could be admitted without untying the few bonds of intimacy between a person and his own mental life that had survived the onslaught of the brain scientists and philosophers, the physicalists and behaviorists. Perhaps I was incorrigible about where I *meant* when I said "here." But in my present circumstances it seemed that either I was doomed by sheer force of mental habit to thinking systematically false indexical thoughts, or where a person is (and hence where his thoughts are tokened for purposes of semantic analysis) is not necessarily where his brain, the physical seat of his soul, resides. Nagged by confusion, I attempted to orient myself by falling back on a favorite philosopher's ploy. I began naming things.

"Yorick," I said aloud to my brain, "you are my brain. The rest of my body, seated in this chair, I dub 'Hamlet.'" So here we all are: Yorick's my brain, Hamlet's my body, and I am Dennett. *Now*, where am I? And when I think "where am I?" where's that thought tokened? Is it tokened in my brain, lounging about in the vat, or right here between my ears where it *seems* to be tokened? Or nowhere? Its *temporal* coordinates give me no trouble; must it not have spatial coordinates as well? I began making a list of the alternatives.

(1) *Where Hamlet goes, there goes Dennett.* This principle was easily refuted by appeal to the familiar brain transplant thought experiments so enjoyed by philosophers. If Tom and Dick switch brains, Tom is the fellow with Dick's former body – just ask him; he'll claim to be Tom, and tell you the most intimate details of Tom's autobiography. It was clear enough, then, that my current body and I could part company, but not likely that I could be separated from my brain. The rule of thumb that emerged so plainly from the thought experiments was that in a brain-transplant operation, one wanted to be the *donor*, not the recipient. Better to call such an operation a *body*-transplant, in fact. So perhaps the truth was,

(2) *Where Yorick goes, there goes Dennett.* This was not at all appealing, however. How could I be in the vat and not about to go anywhere, when I was so obviously outside the vat looking in and beginning to make guilty plans to return to my room for a substantial lunch? This begged the question I realized, but it still seemed to be getting at something important. Casting about for some support for my intuition, I hit upon a legalistic sort of argument that might have appealed to Locke.

Suppose, I argued to myself, I were now to fly to California, rob a bank, and be apprehended. In which state would I be tried: In California, where the robbery took place, or in Texas, where the brains of the outfit were located? Would I be a California felon with an out-of-state brain, or a Texas felon remotely controlling an accomplice of sorts in California? It seemed possible that I might beat such a rap just on the undecidability of that jurisdictional question, though perhaps it would be deemed an inter-state, and hence Federal, offense. In any event, suppose I were convicted. Was it likely that California would be satisfied to throw Hamlet into the brig, knowing that Yorick was living the good life and luxuriously taking the waters in Texas? Would Texas incarcerate Yorick, leaving Hamlet free to take the next boat to Rio? This alternative appealed to me. Barring capital punishment or other cruel and unusual punishment, the state would be obliged to maintain the life-support system for Yorick though they might move him from Houston to Leavenworth, and aside from the unpleasant-ness of the opprobrium, I, for one, would not mind at all and would consider myself a free man under those circumstances. If the state has an interest in forcibly relocating persons in institutions, it would fail to relocate me in any institution by locating Yorick there. If this were true, it suggested a third alternative.

(3) *Dennett is wherever he thinks he is.* Generalized, the claim was as follows: At any given time a person has a *point of view*, and the location of the point of view (which is determined internally by the content of the point of view) is also the location of the person.

Such a proposition is not without its perplexities, but to me it seemed a step in the right direction. The only trouble was that it seemed to place one in a heads-I-win/tails-you-lose situation of unlikely infallibility as regards location. Hadn't I myself often been wrong about where I was, and at least as often uncertain? Couldn't one get lost? Of course, but getting lost *geographically* is not the only way one might get lost. If one were lost in the woods one could attempt to reassure oneself with the consolation that at least one knew where one was: one was right *here* in the familiar surroundings of one's own body. Perhaps in this case one would not have drawn one's attention to much to be thankful for. Still, there were worse plights imaginable, and I wasn't sure I wasn't in such a plight right now.

Point of view clearly had something to do with personal location, but it was itself an unclear notion. It was obvious that the content of one's point of view was not the same as or determined by the content of one's beliefs or thoughts. For example, what should we say about the point of view of the Cinerama viewer who shrieks and twists in his seat as the roller-coaster footage overcomes his psychic distancing? Has he forgotten that he is safely seated in the theater? Here I was inclined to say that the person is experiencing an illusory shift in point of view. In other cases, my inclination to call such shifts illusory was less strong. The workers in laboratories and plants who handle dangerous materials by operating feed-back-controlled mechanical arms and hands undergo a shift in point of view that is crisper and more pronounced than anything Cinerama can provoke. They can feel the heft and slipperiness of the containers they manipulate with their metal fingers. They know perfectly well where they are and are not fooled into false beliefs by the experience, yet it is as if they were inside the isolation chamber they are peering into. With mental effort, they can manage to shift their point of view back and forth, rather like making a transparent Neckar cube or an Escher drawing change orientation before one's eyes. It does seem extravagant to suppose that in performing this bit of mental gymnastics, they are transporting *themselves* back and forth.

Still their example gave me hope. If I was in fact in the vat in spite of my intuitions, I might be able to train myself to adopt that point of view even as a matter of habit. I should dwell on images of myself comfortably floating in my vat, beaming volitions to that familiar body *out there*. I reflected that the ease or difficulty of this task was presumably independent of the truth about the location of one's brain. Had I been practicing before the operation, I might now be finding it second nature. You might now yourself try such a *tromp l'oeil*. Imagine you have written an inflammatory letter which has been published in the *Times*, the result of which is that the Government has chosen to impound your brain for a probationary period of three years in its Dangerous Brain Clinic in Bethesda, Maryland. Your body of course is allowed freedom to earn a salary and thus to continue its function of laying up income to be taxed. At this moment, however, your body is seated in an auditorium listening to a peculiar account by Daniel Dennett of his own similar experience. Try it. Think yourself to Bethesda, and then hark back longingly to your body, far away, and yet *seeming* so near. It is only with long-distance restraint (yours? the Government's?) that you can control your impulse to get those hands clapping in polite applause before navigating the old body to the rest room and a well-deserved glass of evening sherry in the lounge. The task of imagination is certainly difficult, but if you achieve your goal the results might be consoling.

Anyway, there I was in Houston, lost in thought as one might say, but not for long. My speculations were soon interrupted by the Houston doctors, who wished to test out my new prosthetic nervous system before sending me off on my hazardous mission. As I mentioned before, I was a bit dizzy at first, and not surprisingly, although I soon habituated myself to my new circumstances (which were, after all, well nigh indistinguishable from my old circumstances). My accommodation was not perfect, however, and to this day I continue to be plagued by minor coordination difficulties. The speed of light is fast, but finite, and as my brain and body move farther and farther apart, the delicate interaction of my feedback systems is thrown into disarray by the time lags. Just as one is rendered close to speechless by a delayed or echoic hearing of one's speaking voice so, for instance, I am virtually unable to track a moving object with my eyes whenever my brain and my body are more than a few miles apart. In most matters my impairment is scarcely detectable, though I can no longer hit a slow curve ball with the authority of yore. There are some compensations of course. Though liquor tastes as good as ever, and warms my gullet while corroding my liver, I can drink it in any quantity I please, without becoming the slightest bit inebriated, a curiosity some of my close friends may have noticed (though I occasionally have *feigned* inebriation, so as not to draw attention to my unusual circumstances). For similar reasons, I take aspirin orally for a sprained wrist, but if the pain persists I ask Houston to administer codeine to me *in vitro*. In times of illness the phone bill can be staggering.

But to return to my adventure. At length, both the doctors and I were satisfied that I was ready to undertake my subterranean mission. And so I left my brain in Houston and headed by helicopter for Tulsa. Well, in any case, that's the way it seemed to me. That's how I would put it, just off the top of my head as it were. On the trip I reflected further about my earlier anxieties and decided that my first postoperative speculations had been tinged with panic. The matter was not nearly as strange or meta-physical as I had been supposing. Where was I? In two places, clearly: both inside the vat and outside it. Just as one can stand with one foot in Connecticut and the other in Rhode Island, I was in two places at once. I had become one of those scattered individuals we used to hear so much about. The more I considered this answer, the more obviously true it appeared. But, strange to say, the more true it appeared, the less impor-tant the question to which it could be the true answer seemed. A sad, but not unprecedented, fate for a philosophical question to suffer. This answer did not completely satisfy me, of course. There lingered some question to which I should have liked an answer, which was neither "Where are all my various and sundry parts?" nor "What is my current point of view?" Or at least there seemed to be such a question. For it did seem undeniable that in some sense *I* and not merely *most of me* was descending into the earth under Tulsa in search of an atomic warhead.

When I found the warhead, I was certainly glad I had left my brain behind, for the pointer on the specially built Geiger counter I had brought with me was off the dial. I called Houston on my ordinary radio and told the operation control center of my position and my progress. In return, they gave me instructions for dismantling the vehicle, based upon my on-site observations. I had set to work with my cutting torch when all of a sudden a terrible thing happened. I went stone deaf. At first I thought it was only my radio earphones that had broken, but when I tapped on my helmet, I heard nothing. Apparently the auditory transceivers had gone on the fritz. I could no longer hear Houston or my own voice, but I could speak, so I started telling them what had happened. In mid-sentence, I knew something else had gone wrong. My vocal apparatus had become paralyzed. Then my right hand went limp – another transceiver had gone. I was truly in deep trouble. But worse was to follow. After a few more minutes, I went blind. I cursed my luck, and then I cursed the scientists who had led me into this grave peril. There I was, deaf, dumb, and blind, in a radioactive hole more than a mile under Tulsa. Then the last of my cerebral radio links broke, and suddenly I was faced with a new and even more shocking problem: whereas an instant before I had been buried alive in Oklahoma, now I was disembodied in Houston. My recognition of my new status was not immediate. It took me several very anxious minutes before it dawned on me that my poor body lay several hundred miles away, with heart pulsing and lungs respiring, but otherwise as dead as the body of any heart transplant donor, its skull packed with useless, broken electronic gear. The shift in perspective I had earlier found well nigh impossible now seemed quite natural. Though I could think myself back into my body in the tunnel under Tulsa, it took some effort to sustain the illusion. For surely it was an illusion to suppose I was still in Oklahoma: I had lost all contact with that body.

It occurred to me then, with one of those rushes of revelation of which we should be suspicious, that I had stumbled upon an impressive demonstration of the immateriality of the soul based upon physicalist principles and premises. For as the last radio signal between Tulsa and Houston died away, had I not changed location from Tulsa to Houston at the speed of light? And had I not accomplished this without any increase in mass? What moved from A to B at such speed was surely myself, or at any rate my soul or mind – the massless center of my being and home of my consciousness. My *point of view* had lagged somewhat behind, but I had already noted the indirect bearing of point of view on personal location. I could not see how a physicalist philosopher could quarrel with this except by taking the dire and counter-intuitive route of banishing all talk of persons. Yet the notion of personhood was so well entrenched in everyone's world view, or so it seemed to me, that any denial would be as curiously unconvincing, as systematically disingenuous, as the Cartesian negation, "non sum."[1]

The joy of philosophic discovery thus tided me over some very bad minutes or perhaps hours as the helplessness and hopelessness of my situation became more apparent to me. Waves of panic and even nausea swept over me, made all the more horrible by the absence of their normal body-dependent phenomenology. No adrenalin rush of tingles in the arms, no pounding heart, no premonitory salivation. I did feel a dread sinking feeling in my bowels at one point, and this tricked me momentarily into the false hope that I was undergoing a reversal of the process that landed me in this fix – a gradual undisembodiment. But the isolation and uniqueness of that twinge soon convinced me that it was simply the first of a plague of phantom body hallucinations that I, like any other amputee, would be all too likely to suffer.

My mood then was chaotic. On the one hand, I was fired up with elation at my philosophic discovery and was wracking my brain (one of the few familiar things I could still do), trying to figure out how to communicate my discovery to the journals; while on the other, I was bitter, lonely, and filled with dread and uncertainty. Fortunately, this did not last long, for my technical support team sedated me into a dreamless sleep from which I awoke, hearing with magnificent fidelity the familiar opening strains of my favorite Brahms piano trio. So that was why they had wanted a list of my favorite recordings! It did not take me long to realize that I was hearing the music without ears. The output from the stereo stylus was being fed through some fancy rectification circuitry directly into my auditory nerve. I was mainlining Brahms, an unforgettable experience for any stereo buff. At the end of the record it did not surprise me to hear the reassuring voice of the project director speaking into a microphone that was now my prosthetic ear. He confirmed my analysis of what had gone wrong and assured me that steps were being taken to re-embody me. He did not elaborate, and after a few more recordings, I found myself drifting off to sleep. My sleep lasted, I later learned, for the better part of a year, and when I awoke, it was to find myself fully restored to my senses. When I looked into the mirror, though, I was a bit startled to see an unfamiliar face. Bearded and a bit heavier, bearing no doubt a family resemblance to my former face, and with the same look of spritely intelligence and resolute character, but definitely a new face. Further self-explorations of an intimate nature left me no doubt that this was a new body and the project director confirmed my conclusions. He did not volunteer any information on the past history of my new body and I decided (wisely, I think in retrospect) not to pry. As many philosophers unfamiliar with my ordeal have more recently speculated, the acquisition of a new body leaves one's *person* intact. And after a period of adjustment to a new voice, new muscular strengths and weaknesses, and so forth, one's *personality* is by and large also preserved. More dramatic changes in personality have been routinely observed in people who have undergone extensive plastic surgery, to say nothing of sex change operations, and I think no one contests the survival of the person in such cases. In any event I soon accommodated to my new body, to the point of being unable to recover any of its novelties to my consciousness or even memory. The view in the mirror soon became utterly familiar. That view, by the way, still revealed antennae, and so I was not surprised to learn that my brain had not been moved from its haven in the life-support lab.

I decided that good old Yorick deserved a visit. I and my new body, whom we might as well call Fortinbras, strode into the familiar lab to another round of applause from the technicians, who were of course congratulating themselves, not me. Once more I stood before the vat and contemplated poor Yorick, and on a whim I once again cavalierly flicked off the output transmitter switch. Imagine my surprise when nothing unusual happened. No fainting spell, no nausea, no noticeable change. A technician hurried to restore the switch to ON, but still I felt nothing. I demanded an explanation, which the project director hastened to provide. It seems that before they had even operated on the first occasion, they had constructed a computer duplicate of my brain, reproducing both the complete information processing structure and the computational speed of my brain in a giant computer program. After the operation, but before they had dared to send me off on my mission to Oklahoma, they had run this computer system and Yorick side by side. The incoming signals from Hamlet were sent simultaneously to Yorick's transceivers and to the computer's array of inputs. And the outputs from Yorick were not only beamed back to Hamlet, my body; they were recorded and checked against the simultaneous output of the computer program, which was called "Hubert" for reasons obscure to me. Over days and even weeks, the outputs were identical and synchronous, which of course did not *prove* that they had succeeded in copying the brain's functional structure, but the empirical support was greatly encouraging.

Hubert's input, and hence activity, had been kept parallel with Yorick's during my disembodied days. And now, to demonstrate this, they had actually thrown the master switch that put Hubert for the first time in on-line control of my body – not Hamlet, of course, but Fortinbras. (Hamlet, I learned, had never been recovered from its underground tomb and could be assumed by this time to have largely returned to the dust. At the head of my grave still lay the magnificent bulk of the abandoned device, with the word STUD emblazoned on its side in large letters – a circumstance which may provide archeologists of the next century with a curious insight into the burial rites of their ancestors.)

The laboratory technicians now showed me the master switch, which had two positions, labeled B, for Brain (they didn't know my brain's name was Yorick) and H, for Hubert. The switch did indeed point to H, and they explained to me that if I wished, I could switch it back to B. With my heart in my mouth (and my brain in its vat), I did this. Nothing happened. A click, that was all. To test their claim, and with the master switch now set at B, I hit Yorick's output transmitter switch on the vat and sure enough, I began to faint. Once the output switch was turned back on and I had recovered my wits, so to speak, I continued to play with the master switch, flipping it back and forth. I found that with the exception of the transitional click, I could detect no trace of a difference. I could switch in mid-utterance, and the sentence I had begun speaking under the control of Yorick was finished without a pause or hitch of any kind under the control of Hubert. I had a spare brain, a prosthetic device which might some day stand me in very good stead, were some mishap to befall Yorick. Or alternatively, I could keep Yorick as a spare and use Hubert. It didn't seem to make any difference which I chose, for the wear and tear and fatigue on my body did not have any debilitating effect on either brain, whether or not it was actually causing the motions of my body, or merely spilling its output into thin air.

The one truly unsettling aspect of this new development was the prospect, which was not long in dawning on me, of someone detaching the spare – Hubert or Yorick, as the case might be – from Fortinbras and hitching it to yet another body – some Johnny-come-lately Rosencrantz or Guildenstern. Then (if not before) there would be *two* people, that much was clear. One would be me, and the other would be a sort of super-twin brother. If there were two bodies, one under the control of Hubert and the other being controlled by Yorick, then which would the world recognize as the true Dennett? And whatever the rest of the world decided, which one would be me? Would I be the Yorick-brained one, in virtue of Yorick's causal priority and former intimate relationship with the original Dennett body, Hamlet? That seemed a bit legalistic, a bit too redolent of the arbitrariness of consanguinity and legal possession, to be convincing at the metaphysical level. For, suppose that before the arrival of the second body on the scene, I had been keeping Yorick as the spare for years, and letting Hubert's output drive my body – that is, Fortinbras – all that time. The Hubert-Fortinbras couple would seem then by squatter's rights (to combat one legal intuition with another) to be the true Dennett and the lawful inheritor of everything that was Dennett's. This was an interesting question, certainly, but not nearly so pressing as another question that bothered me. My strongest intuition was that in such an eventuality *I* would survive so long as *either* brain-body couple remained intact, but I had mixed emotions about whether I should want both to survive.

I discussed my worries with the technicians and the project director. The prospect of two Dennetts was abhorrent to me, I explained, largely for social reasons. I didn't want to be my own rival for the affections of my wife, nor did I like the prospect of the two Dennetts sharing my modest professor's salary. Still more vertiginous and distasteful, though, was the idea of knowing *that much* about another person, while he had the very same goods on me. How could we ever face each other? My colleagues in the lab argued that I was ignoring the bright side of the matter. Weren't there many things I wanted to do but, being only one person, had been unable to do? Now one Dennett could stay at home and be the professor and family man, while the other could strike out on a life of travel and adventurer – missing the family of course, but happy in the knowledge that the other Dennett was keeping the home fires burning. I could be faithful and adulterous at the same time. I could even cuckold myself – to say nothing of other more lurid possibilities my colleagues were all too ready to force upon my overtaxed imagination. But my ordeal in Oklahoma (or was it Houston?) had made me less adventurous, and I shrank from this opportunity that was being offered (though of course I was never quite sure it was being offered to *me* in the first place).

There was another prospect even more disagreeable – that the spare, Hubert or Yorick as the case might be, would be detached from any input from Fortinbras and just left detached. Then, as in the other case, there would be two Dennetts, or at least two claimants to my name and possessions, one embodied in Fortinbras, and the other sadly, miserably disembodied. Both selfishness and altruism bade me take steps to prevent this from happening. So I asked that measures be taken to ensure that no one could ever tamper with the transceiver connections or the master switch without my (our? no, *my*) knowledge and consent. Since I had no desire to spend my life guarding the equipment in Houston, it was mutually decided that all the electronic connections in the lab would be carefully locked: both those that controlled the life-support system for Yorick and those that controlled the power supply for Hubert would be guarded with fail-safe devices, and I would take the only master switch, outfitted for radio remote control with me wherever I went. I carry it strapped around my waist and – wait a moment – *here it is*. Every few months I reconnoiter the situation by switching channels. I do this only in the presence of friends of course, for if the other channel were, heaven forbid, either dead or otherwise occupied, there would have to be somebody who had my interests at heart to switch it back, to bring me back from the void. For while I could feel, see, hear and otherwise sense whatever befell my body, subsequent to such a switch, I'd be unable to control it. By the way, the two positions on the switch are intentionally unmarked, so I never have the faintest idea whether I am switching from Hubert to Yorick or *vice versa*. (Some of you may think that in this case I really don't know *who* I am, let alone where I am. But such reflections no longer make much of a dent on my essential Dennettness, on my own sense of who I am. If it is true that in one sense I don't know who I am then that's another one of your philosophical truths of underwhelming significance.)

In any case, every time I've flipped the switch so far, nothing has happened. *So let's give it a try . . .*

"THANK GOD! I THOUGHT YOU'D NEVER FLIP THAT SWITCH! You can't imagine how horrible it's been these last two weeks – but now you know, it's your turn in purgatory. How I've longed for this moment! You see, about two weeks ago – excuse me, ladies and gentlemen, but I've got to explain this to my . . . um, brother, I guess you could say, but he's just told you the facts, so you'll understand – about two weeks ago our two brains drifted just a bit out of synch. I don't know whether *my* brain is now Hubert or Yorick, any more than you do, but in any case, the two brains drifted apart, and of course once the process started, it snowballed, for I was in a slightly different receptive state for the input we both received, a difference that was soon magnified. In no time at all the illusion that I was in control of my body – our body – was completely dissipated. There was nothing I could do – no way to call you. YOU DIDN'T EVEN KNOW I EXISTED! It's been like being carried around in a cage, or better, like being possessed – hearing my own voice say things I didn't mean to say, watching in frustration as my own hands performed deeds I hadn't intended. You'd scratch our itches, but not the way I would have, and you kept me awake, with your tossing and turning. I've been totally exhausted, on the verge of a nervous breakdown, carried around helplessly by your frantic round of activities, sustained only by the knowledge that some day you'd throw the switch.

"Now it's your turn, but at least you'll have the comfort of knowing *I* know you're in there. Like an expectant mother, I'm eating – or at any rate tasting, smelling, seeing – for *two* now, and I'll try to make it easy for you. Don't worry. Just as soon as this colloquium is over, you and I will fly to Houston, and we'll see what can be done to get one of us another body. You can have a female body – your body could be any color you like. But let's think it over. I tell you what – to be fair, if we both want this body, I promise I'll let the project director flip a coin to settle which of us gets to keep it and which then gets to choose a new body. That should guarantee justice, shouldn't it? In any case, I'll take care of you, I promise. These people are my witnesses.

"Ladies and gentlemen, this talk we have just heard is not exactly the talk *I* would have given, but I assure you that everything he said was perfectly true. And now if you'll excuse me, I think I'd – we'd – better sit down."[2]

Notes

1   C.F. Jaakko Hintikka, "Conito ergo sum: inference of performance?", *Philosophical Review* LXXI (1962) pp. 3–32.

2   Anyone familiar with the literature on this topic will recognize that my remarks owe a great deal to the explorations of Sydney Shoemaker, John Perry, David Lewis and Derek Parfit, and in particular to their papers in Amélie Rorty (ed.) *The Identities of Persons* (Berkeley, Calif.: University of California Press, 1976).

Art

40

Significant form
Clive Bell

In this extract from his book *Art* (first published in 1914), Clive Bell (1881–1964) sets out his view that art is significant form: patterns of lines, shapes and colours which have the power to evoke the aesthetic emotion in the sensitive viewer. Representation is largely irrelevant to a painting's status as art: it is form that matters above all. Although he concentrates on painting, the general theory of art that he outlines is supposed to apply to all art.

From Clive Bell, *Art*

For either all works of visual art have some common quality, or when we speak of "works of art" we gibber. Everyone speaks of "art," making a mental classification by which he distinguishes the class "works of art" from all other classes. What is the justification of this classification? What is the quality common and peculiar to all members of this class? Whatever it be, no doubt it is often found in company with other qualities; but they are adventitious – it is essential. There must be some one quality without which a work of art cannot exist; possessing which, in the least degree, no work is altogether worthless. What is this quality? What quality is shared by all objects that provoke our aesthetic emotions? What quality is common to Sta. Sophia and the windows at Chartres, Mexican sculpture, a Persian bowl, Chinese carpets, Giotto's frescoes at Padua, and the master-pieces of Poussin, Piero della Francesca, and Cézanne? Only one answer seems possible – significant form. In each lines and colours combined in a particular way, certain forms and relations of forms, stir our aesthetic emotions. These relations and combinations of lines and colours, these aesthetically moving forms, I call "Significant Form"; and "Significant Form" is the one quality common to all works of visual art. [...]

To appreciate a work of art we need bring with us nothing but a sense of form and colour and a knowledge of three-dimensional space.

That bit of knowledge, I admit, is essential to the appreciation of many great works, since many of the most moving forms ever created are in three dimensions. To see a cube or a rhomboid as a flat pattern is to lower its significance, and a sense of three-dimensional space is essential to the full appreciation of most architectural forms. Pictures which would be insignificant if we saw them as flat patterns are profoundly moving because, in fact, we see them as related planes. If the representation of three-dimensional space is to be called "representation," then I agree that there is one kind of representation which is not irrelevant. Also, I agree that along with our feeling for line and colour we must bring with us our knowledge of space if we are to make the most of every kind of form. Nevertheless, there are magnificent designs to an appreciation of which this knowledge is not necessary: so, though it is not irrelevant to the appreciation of some works of art it is not essential to the appreciation of all. What we must say is that the representation of three-dimensional space is neither irrelevant nor essential to all art, and that every other sort of representation is irrelevant.

That there is an irrelevant representative or descriptive element in many great works of art is not in the least surprising. Why it is not surprising I shall try to show elsewhere. Representation is not of necessity baneful, and highly realistic forms may be extremely significant. Very often, however, representation is a sign of weakness in an artist. A painter too feeble to create forms that provoke more than a little aesthetic emotion will try to eke that little out by suggesting the emotions of life. To evoke the emotions of life he must use representation. Thus a man will paint an execution, and, fearing to miss with his first barrel of significant form, will try to hit with his second by raising an emotion of fear or pity. But if in the artist an inclination to play upon the emotions of life is often the sign of a flickering inspiration, in the spectator a tendency to seek, behind form, the emotions of life is a sign of defective sensibility always. It means that his aesthetic emotions are weak or, at any rate, imperfect. Before a work of art people who feel little or no emotion for pure form find themselves at a loss. They are deaf men at a concert. They know that they are in the presence of something great, but they lack the power of apprehending it. They know that they ought to feel for it a tremendous emotion, but it happens that the particular kind of emotion it can raise is one that they can feel hardly or not at all. And so they read into the forms of the work those facts and ideas for which they are capable of feeling emotion, and feel for them the emotions that they can feel – the ordinary emotions of life. When confronted by a picture, instinctively they refer back its forms to the world from which they came. They treat created form as though it were imitated form, a picture as though it were a photograph. Instead of going out on the stream of art into a new world of aesthetic experience, they turn a sharp corner and come straight home to the world of human interests. For them the significance of a work of art depends on what they bring to it; no new thing is added to their lives, only the old material is stirred. A good work of visual art carries a person who is capable of appreciating it out of life into ecstasy: to use art as a means to the emotions of life is to use a telescope for reading the news. You will notice that people who cannot feel pure aesthetic emotions remember pictures by their subjects; whereas people who can, as often as not, have no idea what the subject of a picture is. They have never noticed the representative element, and so when they discuss pictures they talk about the shapes of forms and the relations and quantities of colours. Often they can tell by the quality of a single line whether or not a man is a good artist. They are concerned only with lines and colours, their relations and quantities and qualities; but from these they win an emotion more profound and far more sublime than any that can be given by the description of facts and ideas.

This last sentence has a very confident ring – over-confident, some may think. Perhaps I shall be able to justify it, and make my meaning clearer too, if I give an account of my own feelings about music. I am not really musical. I do not understand music well. I find musical form exceedingly difficult to apprehend, and I am sure that the profounder subtleties of harmony and rhythm more often than not escape me. The form of a musical composition must be simple indeed if I am to grasp it honestly. My opinion about music is not worth having. Yet, sometimes, at a concert, though my appreciation of the music is limited and humble, it is pure. Sometimes, though I have a poor understanding, I have a clean palate. Consequently, when I am feeling bright and clear and intent, at the beginning of a concert for instance, when something that I can grasp is being played, I get from music that pure aesthetic emotion that I get from visual art. It is less intense, and the rapture is evanescent; I understand music too ill for music to transport me far into the world of pure aesthetic ecstasy. But at moments I do appreciate music as pure musical form, as sounds combined according to the laws of a mysterious necessity, as pure art with a tremendous significance of its own and no relation whatever to the significance of life; and in those moments I lose myself in that infinitely sublime state of mind to which pure visual form transports me. How inferior is my normal state of mind at a concert. Tired or perplexed, I let slip my sense of form, my aesthetic emotion collapses, and I begin weaving into the harmonies, that I cannot grasp, the ideas of life. Incapable of feeling the austere emotions of art, I begin to read into the musical forms human emotions of terror and mystery, love and hate, and spend the minutes, pleasantly enough, in a world of turbid and inferior feeling. At such times, were the grossest pieces of onomatopoeic representation – the song of a bird, the galloping of horses, the cries of children, or the laughing of demons – to be introduced into the symphony, I should not be offended. Very likely I should be pleased; they would afford new points

375

of departure for new trains of romantic feeling or heroic thought. I know very well what has happened. I have been using art as a means to the emotions of life and reading into it the ideas of life. I have been cutting blocks with a razor. I have tumbled from the superb peaks of aesthetic exaltation to the snug foothills of warm humanity. It is a jolly country. No one need be ashamed of enjoying himself there. Only no one who has ever been on the heights can help feeling a little crestfallen in the cosy valleys. And let no one imagine, because he has made merry in the warm tilth and quaint nooks of romance, that he can even guess at the austere and thrilling raptures of those who have climbed the cold, white peaks of art.

About music most people are as willing to be humble as I am. If they cannot grasp musical form and win from it a pure aesthetic emotion, they confess that they understand music imperfectly or not at all. They recognise quite clearly that there is a difference between the feeling of the musician for pure music and that of the cheerful concert-goer for what music suggests. The latter enjoys his own emotions, as he has every right to do, and recognises their inferiority. Unfortunately, people are apt to be less modest about their powers of appreciating visual art. Everyone is inclined to believe that out of pictures, at any rate, he can get all that there is to be got; everyone is ready to cry "humbug" and "impostor" at those who say that more can be had. The good faith of people who feel pure aesthetic emotions is called in question by those who have never felt anything of the sort. It is the prevalence of the representative element, I suppose, that makes the man in the street so sure that he knows a good picture when he sees one. For I have noticed that in matters of architecture, pottery, textiles, etc., ignorance and ineptitude are more willing to defer to the opinions of those who have been blest with peculiar sensibility. It is a pity that cultivated and intelligent men and women cannot be induced to believe that a great gift of aesthetic appreciation is at least as rare in visual as in musical art. A comparison of my own experience in both has enabled me to discriminate very clearly between pure and impure appreciation. Is it too much to ask that others should be as honest about their feelings for pictures as I have been about mine for music? For I am certain that most of those who visit galleries do feel very much what I feel at concerts. They have their moments of pure ecstasy; but the moments are short and unsure. Soon they fall back into the world of human interests and feel emotions, good no doubt, but inferior. I do not dream of saying that what they get from art is bad or nugatory; I say that they do not get the best that art can give. I do not say that they cannot understand art; rather I say that they cannot understand the state of mind of those who understand it best. I do not say that art means nothing or little to them; I say they miss its full significance. I do not suggest for one moment that their appreciation of art is a thing to be ashamed of; the majority of the charming and intelligent people with whom I am acquainted appreciate visual art impurely; and, by the way, the appreciation of almost all great writers has been impure. But provided that there be some fraction of pure aesthetic emotion, even a mixed and minor appreciation of art is, I am sure, one of the most valuable things in the world – so valuable, indeed, that in my giddier moments I have been tempted to believe that art might prove the world's salvation.

Yet, though the echoes and shadows of art enrich the life of the plains, her spirit dwells on the mountains. To him who woos, but woos impurely, she returns enriched what is brought. Like the sun, she warms the good seed in good soil and causes it to bring forth good fruit. But only to the perfect lover does she give a new strange gift – a gift beyond all price. Imperfect lovers bring to art and take away the ideas and emotions of their own age and civilisation. In twelfth-century Europe a man might have been greatly moved by a Romanesque church and found nothing in a T'ang picture. To a man of a later age, Greek sculpture meant much and Mexican nothing, for only to the former could he bring a crowd of associated ideas to be the objects of familiar emotions. But the perfect lover, he who can feel the profound significance of form, is raised above the accidents of time and place. To him the problems of archaeology, history, and hagiography are impertinent. If the forms of a work are significant its provenance is irrelevant. Before the grandeur of those Sumerian figures in the Louvre he is carried on the same flood of emotion to the same aesthetic ecstasy as, more than four thousand years ago, the Chaldean lover was carried. It is the mark of great art that its appeal is universal and eternal.[1] Significant form stands charged with the power to provoke aesthetic emotion in anyone capable of feeling it. The ideas of men go buzz and die like gnats; men change their institutions and their customs as they change their coats; the intellectual triumphs of one age are the follies of another; only great art remains stable and unobscure. Great art remains stable and unobscure because the feelings that it awakens are independent of time and place, because its kingdom is not of this world. To those who have and hold a sense of the significance of form what does it matter whether the forms that move them were created in Paris the day before yesterday or in Babylon fifty centuries ago? The forms of art are inexhaustible; but all lead by the same road of aesthetic emotion to the same world of aesthetic ecstasy.

Note

1   Mr Roger Fry permits me to make use of an interesting story that will illustrate my view. When Mr. Okakura, the Government editor of *The Temple Treasures of Japan*, first came to Europe, he found no difficulty in appreciating the pictures of those who from want of will or want of skill did

not create illusions but concentrated their energies on the creation of form. He understood immediately the Byzantine masters and the French and Italian Primitives. In the Renaissance painters, on the other hand, with their descriptive pre-occupations, their literary and anecdotic interests, he could see nothing but vulgarity and muddle. The universal and essential quality of art, significant form, was missing, or rather had dwindled to a shallow stream, overlaid and hidden beneath weeds, so the universal response, aesthetic emotion, was not evoked. It was not till he came on to Henri Matisse that he again found himself in the familiar world of pure art. Similarly, sensitive Europeans who respond immediately to the significant forms of great Oriental art, are left cold by the trivial pieces of anecdote and social criticism so lovingly cherished by Chinese dilettanti. It would be easy to multiply instances did not decency forbid the labouring of so obvious a truth.

41

The intentional fallacy
W. K. Wimsatt Jr and
Monroe C. Beardsley

It might seem obvious that when interpreting a work of art the author's or artist's intentions are relevant. However, in their important article 'The intentional fallacy' (originally published in 1946), W. K. Wimsatt Jr (1907–) and Monroe C. Beardsley (1915–85) put the case against this. The success or failure of a work of art is independent of what an artist or author says he or she was trying to do; furthermore, a work of art can be interpreted without recourse to artist biography. They dub the alleged mistake of going outside the work the 'intentional fallacy'. They do, however, acknowledge that intentions which are realized in the work (what they call 'internal evidence') have their part to play in interpretation and evaluation.

From W. K. Wimsatt Jr and Monroe C. Beardsley, *The Verbal Icon*

He owns with toil he wrote the following scenes;
But, if they're naught, ne'er spare him for his pains:
Damn him the more; have no commiseration
For Dullness on mature deliberation

> William Congreve
> Prologue to *The Way of the World*

I

The claim of the author's "intention" upon the critic's judgment has been challenged in a number of recent discussions, notably in the debate entitled *The Personal Heresy*, between Professors Lewis and Tillyard. But it seems doubtful if this claim and most of its romantic corollaries are as yet subject to any widespread questioning. The present writers, in a short article entitled "Intention" for a *Dictionary*[1] of literary criticism, raised the issue but were unable to pursue its implications at any length. We argued that the design or intention of the author is neither available nor desirable as a standard for judging the success of a work of literary art, and it seems to us that this is a principle which goes deep into some differences in the history of critical attitudes. It is a principle which accepted or rejected points to the polar opposites of classical "imitation" and romantic expression. It entails many specific truths about inspiration, authenticity, biography, literary history and scholarship, and about some trends of contemporary poetry, especially its allusiveness. There is hardly a problem of literary criticism in which the critic's approach will not be qualified by his view of "intention."

"Intention," as we shall use the term, corresponds to *what he intended* in a formula which more or less explicitly has had wide acceptance. "In order to judge the poet's performance, we must know *what he intended*." Intention is design or plan in the author's mind. Intention has obvious affinities for the author's attitude toward his work, the way he felt, what made him write.

We begin our discussion with a series of propositions summarized and abstracted to a degree where they seem to us axiomatic.

1. A poem does not come into existence by accident. The words of a poem, as Professor Stoll has remarked, come out of a head, not out of a hat. Yet to insist on the designing intellect as a *cause* of a poem is not to grant the design or intention as a *standard* by which the critic is to judge the worth of the poet's performance.

2. One must ask how a critic expects to get an answer to the question about intention. How is he to find out what the poet tried to do? If the poet succeeded in doing it, then the poem itself shows what he was trying to do. And if the poet did not succeed, then the poem is not adequate evidence, and the critic must go outside the poem – for evidence of an intention that did not become effective in the poem. "Only one *caveat* must be borne in mind," says an eminent intentionalist[2] in a moment when his theory repudiates itself; "the poet's aim must be judged at the moment of the creative act, that is to say, by the art of the poem itself."

3. Judging a poem is like judging a pudding or a machine. One demands that it work. It is only because an artifact works that we infer the intention of an artificer. "A poem should not mean but be." A poem can *be* only through its *meaning* – since its medium is words – yet it *is*, simply *is*, in the sense that we have no excuse for inquiring what part is intended or meant. Poetry is a feat of style by which a complex of meaning is handled all at once. Poetry succeeds because all or most of what is said or implied is relevant; what is irrelevant has been excluded, like lumps from pudding and "bugs" from machinery. In this respect poetry differs

from practical messages, which are successful if and only if we correctly infer the intention. They are more abstract than poetry.

4. The meaning of a poem may certainly be a personal one, in the sense that a poem expresses a personality or state of soul rather than a physical object like an apple. But even a short lyric poem is dramatic, the response of a speaker (no matter how abstractly conceived) to a situation (no matter how universalized). We ought to impute the thoughts and attitudes of the poem immediately to the dramatic *speaker*, and if to the author at all, only by an act of biographical inference.

5. There is a sense in which an author, by revision, may better achieve his original intention. But it is a very abstract sense. He intended to write a better work, or a better work of a certain kind, and now has done it. But it follows that his former concrete intention was not his intention. "He's the man we were in search of, that's true," says Hardy's rustic constable, "and yet he's not the man we were in search of. For the man we were in search of was not the man we wanted."

"Is not a critic," asks Professor Stoll, "a judge, who does not explore his own consciousness, but determines the author's meaning or intention, as if the poem were a will, a contract, or the constitution? The poem is not the critic's own." He has accurately diagnosed two forms of irresponsibility, one of which he prefers. Our view is yet different. The poem is not the critic's own and not the author's (it is detached from the author at birth and goes about the world beyond his power to intend about it or control it). The poem belongs to the public. It is embodied in language, the peculiar possession of the public, and it is about the human being, an object of public knowledge. What is said about the poem is subject to the same scrutiny as any statement in linguistics or in the general science of psychology.

A critic of our *Dictionary* article, Ananda K. Coomaraswamy, has argued[3] that there are two kinds of inquiry about a work of art: (1) whether the artist achieved his intentions; (2) whether the work of art "ought ever to have been undertaken at all" and so "whether it is worth preserving." Number (2), Coomaraswamy maintains, is not "criticism of any work of art *qua* work of art," but is rather moral criticism; number (1) is artistic criticism. But we maintain that (2) need not be moral criticism: that there is another way of deciding whether works of art are worth preserving and whether, in a sense, they "ought" to have been undertaken, and this is the way of objective criticism of works of art as such, the way which enables us to distinguish between a skillful murder and a skillful poem. A skillful murder is an example which Coomaraswamy uses, and in his system the difference between the murder and the poem is simply a "moral" one, not an "artistic" one, since each if carried out according to plan is "artistically" successful. We maintain that (2) is an inquiry of more worth than (1), and since (2) and not (1) is capable of distinguishing poetry from murder, the name "artistic criticism" is properly given to (2).

II

It is not so much a historical statement as a definition to say that the intentional fallacy is a romantic one. When a rhetorician of the first century AD writes: "Sublimity is the echo of a great soul," or when he tells us that "Homer enters into the sublime actions of his heroes" and "shares the full inspiration of the combat," we shall not be surprised to find this rhetorician considered as a distant harbinger of romanticism and greeted in the warmest terms by Saintsbury. One may wish to argue whether Longinus should be called romantic, but there can hardly be a doubt that in one important way he is.

Goethe's three questions for "constructive criticism" are "What did the author set out to do? Was his plan reasonable and sensible, and how far did he succeed in carrying it out?" If one leaves out the middle question, one has in effect the system of Croce – the culmination and crowning philosophic expression of romanticism. The beautiful is the successful intuition-expression, and the ugly is the unsuccessful; the intuition or private part of art is *the* aesthetic fact, and the medium or public part is not the subject of aesthetic at all.

> The Madonna of Cimabue is still in the Church of Santa Maria Novella; but does she speak to the visitor of to-day as to the Florentines of the thirteenth century?
>
> *Historical interpretation* labors ... to reintegrate in us the psychological conditions which have changed in the course of history. It ... enables us to see a work of art (a physical object) as its *author saw* it in the moment of production.[4]

The first italics are Croce's, the second ours. The upshot of Croce's system is an ambiguous emphasis on history. With such passages as a point of departure a critic may write a nice analysis of the meaning or "spirit" of a play by Shakespeare or Corneille – a process that involves close historical study but remains aesthetic criticism – or he may, with equal plausibility, produce an essay in sociology, biography, or other kinds of non-aesthetic history.

I went to the poets; tragic, dithyrambic, and all sorts. . . . I took them some of the most elaborate passages in their own writings, and asked what was the meaning of them. . . . Will you believe me? . . . there is hardly a person present who would not have talked better about their poetry than they did themselves. Then I knew that not by wisdom do poets write poetry, but by a sort of genius and inspiration.

That reiterated mistrust of the poets which we hear from Socrates may have been part of a rigorously ascetic view in which we hardly wish to participate, yet Plato's Socrates saw a truth about the poetic mind which the world no longer commonly sees – so much criticism, and that the most inspirational and most affectionately remembered, has proceeded from the poets themselves.

Certainly the poets have had something to say that the critic and professor could not say; their message has been more exciting: that poetry should come as naturally as leaves to a tree, that poetry is the lava of the imagination, or that it is emotion recollected in tranquillity. But it is necessary that we realize the character and authority of such testimony. There is only a fine shade of difference between such expressions and a kind of earnest advice that authors often give. Thus Edward Young, Carlyle, Walter Pater:

I know two golden rules from *ethics*, which are no less golden in *Composition*, than in life. 1. *Know thyself*; 2dly, *Reverence thyself*.

This is the grand secret for finding readers and retaining them: let him who would move and convince others, be first moved and convinced himself. Horace's rule, *Si vis me flere*, is applicable in a wider sense than the literal one. To every poet, to every writer, we might say: Be true, if you would be believed.

Truth! there can be no merit, no craft at all, without that. And further, all beauty is in the long run only *fineness* of truth, or what we call expression, the finer accommodation of speech to that vision within.

And Housman's little handbook to the poetic mind yields this illustration:

Having drunk a pint of beer at luncheon – beer is a sedative to the brain, and my afternoons are the least intellectual portion of my life – I would go out for a walk of two or three hours. As I went along, thinking of nothing in particular, only looking at things around me

> and following the progress of the seasons, there would flow into my mind, with sudden and unaccountable emotion, sometimes a line or two of verse, sometimes a whole stanza at once.

This is the logical terminus of the series already quoted. Here is a confession of how poems were written which would do as a definition of poetry just as well as "emotion recollected in tranquillity" – and which the young poet might equally well take to heart as a practical rule. Drink a pint of beer, relax, go walking, think on nothing in particular, look at things, surrender yourself to yourself, search for the truth in your own soul, listen to the sound of your own inside voice, discover and express the *vraie vérité*.

It is probably true that all this is excellent advice for poets. The young imagination fired by Wordsworth and Carlyle is probably closer to the verge of producing a poem than the mind of the student who has been sobered by Aristotle or Richards. The art of inspiring poets, or at least of inciting something like poetry in young persons, has probably gone further in our day than ever before. Books of creative writing such as those issued from the Lincoln School are interesting evidence of what a child can do.[5] All this, however, would appear to belong to an art separate from criticism – to a psychological discipline, a system of self-development, a yoga, which the young poet perhaps does well to notice, but which is something different from the public art of evaluating poems.

Coleridge and Arnold were better critics than most poets have been, and if the critical tendency dried up the poetry in Arnold and perhaps in Coleridge, it is not inconsistent with our argument, which is that judgment of poems is different from the art of producing them. Coleridge has given us the classic "anodyne" story, and tells what he can about the genesis of a poem which he calls a "psychological curiosity," but his definitions of poetry and of the poetic quality "imagination" are to be found elsewhere and in quite other terms.

It would be convenient if the passwords of the intentional school, "sincerity," "fidelity," "spontaneity," "authenticity," "genuineness," "originality," could be equated with terms such as "integrity," "relevance," "unity," "function," "maturity," "subtlety," "adequacy," and other more precise terms of evaluation – in short, if "expression" always meant aesthetic achievement. But this is not so.

"Aesthetic" art, says Professor Curt Ducasse, an ingenious theorist of expression, is the conscious objectification of feelings, in which an intrinsic part is the critical moment. The artist corrects the objectification when it is not adequate. But this may mean that the earlier attempt was not successful in objectifying the self, or "it may also mean that it was a successful objectification of a self which, when it confronted us clearly, we disowned and repudiated in favor of another."[6] What is the standard by which we disown or accept the self? Professor Ducasse does not say.

Whatever it may be, however, this standard is an element in the definition of art which will not reduce to terms of objectification. The evaluation of the work of art remains public; the work is measured against something outside the author.

There is criticism of poetry and there is author psychology, which when applied to the present or future takes the form of inspirational promotion; but author psychology can be historical too, and then we have literary biography, a legitimate and attractive study in itself, one approach, as Professor Tillyard would argue, to personality, the poem being only a parallel approach. Certainly it need not be with a derogatory purpose that one points out personal studies, as distinct from poetic studies, in the realm of literary scholarship. Yet there is danger of confusing personal and poetic studies; and there is the fault of writing the personal as if it were poetic.

There is a difference between internal and external evidence for the meaning of a poem. And the paradox is only verbal and superficial that what is (1) internal is also public: it is discovered through the semantics and syntax of a poem, through our habitual knowledge of the language, through grammars, dictionaries, and all the literature which is the source of dictionaries, in general through all that makes a language and culture; while what is (2) external is private or idiosyncratic; not a part of the work as a linguistic fact: it consists of revelations (in journals, for example, or letters or reported conversations) about how or why the poet wrote the poem – to what lady, while sitting on what lawn, or at the death of what friend or brother. There is (3) an intermediate kind of evidence about the character of the author or about private or semiprivate meanings attached to words or topics by the author or by a coterie of which he is a member. The meaning of words is the history of words, and the biography of an author, his use of a word, and the associations which the word had for *him*, are part of the word's history and meaning.[7] But the three types of evidence, especially (2) and (3), shade into one another so subtly that it is not always easy to draw a line between examples, and hence arises the difficulty for criticism. The use of biographical evidence need not involve intentionalism, because while it may be evidence of what the author intended, it may also be evidence of the meaning of his words and the dramatic character of his utterance. On the other hand, it may not be all this. And a critic who is concerned with evidence of type (1) and moderately with that of type (3) will in the long run produce a different sort of comment from that of the critic who is concerned with (2) and with (3) where it shades into (2).

The whole glittering parade of Professor Lowes' *Road to Xanadu*, for instance, runs along the border between types (2) and (3) or boldly traverses the romantic region of (2). " 'Kubla Khan' " says Professor Lowes, "is the fabric of a vision, but every image that rose up in its weaving had passed that way before. And it would seem that there is nothing haphazard or fortuitous in their return." This is not quite clear – not even when Professor Lowes explains that there were clusters of associations, like hooked atoms, which were drawn into complex relation with other clusters in the deep well of Coleridge's memory, and which then coalesced and issued forth as poems. If there was nothing "haphazard or fortuitous" in the way the images returned to the surface, that may mean (1) that Coleridge could not produce what he did not have, that he was limited in his creation by what he had read or otherwise experienced, or (2) that having received certain clusters of associations, he was bound to return them in just the way he did, and that the value of the poem may be described in terms of the experiences on which he had to draw. The latter pair of propositions (a sort of Hartleyan associationism which Coleridge himself repudiated in the *Biographia*) may not be assented to. There were certainly other combinations, other poems, worse or better, that might have been written by men who had read Bartram and Purchas and Bruce and Milton. And this will be true no matter how many times we are able to add to the brilliant complex of Coleridge's reading. In certain flourishes (such as the sentence we have quoted) and in chapter headings like "The Shaping Spirit," "The Magical Synthesis," "Imagination Creatrix," it may be that Professor Lowes pretends to say more about the actual poems than he does. There is a certain deceptive variation in these fancy chapter titles; one expects to pass on to a new stage in the argument, and one finds – more and more sources, more and more about "the streamy nature of association."[8]

"Wohin der Weg?" quotes Professor Lowes for the motto of his book. "Kein Weg! Ins Unbretretene." Precisely because the way is *unbetreten*, we should say, it leads away from the poem. Bartram's *Travels* contains a good deal of the history of certain words and of certain romantic Floridian conceptions that appear in "Kubla Khan." And a good deal of that history has passed and was then passing into the very stuff of our language. Perhaps a person who has read Bartram appreciates the poem more than one who has not. Or, by looking up the vocabulary of "Kubla Khan" in the *Oxford English Dictionary*, or by reading some of the other books there quoted, a person may know the poem better. But it would seem to pertain little to the poem to know that *Coleridge* had read Bartram. There is a gross body of life, of sensory and mental experience, which lies behind and in some sense causes every poem, but can never be and need not be known in the verbal and hence intellectual composition which is the poem. For all the objects of our manifold experience, for every unity, there is an action of the mind which cuts off roots, melts away context – or indeed we should never have objects or ideas or anything to talk about.

It is probable that there is nothing in Professor Lowes' vast book which could detract from anyone's appreciation of either *The Ancient Mariner* or "Kubla Khan." We next present a case where preoccupation with evidence of type (3) has gone so far as to distort a critic's view of a poem (yet a case not so obvious as those that abound in our critical journals).

In a well-known poem by John Donne appears this quatrain:

> Moving of th'earth brings harmes and feares,
>   Men reckon what it did and meant,
> But trepidation of the spheares,
>   Though greater farre, is innocent.

A recent critic in an elaborate treatment of Donne's learning has written of this quatrain as follows:

> He touches the emotional pulse of the situation by a skillful allusion to the new and the old astronomy. . . . Of the new astronomy, the "moving of the earth" is the most radical principle; of the old, the "trepidation of the spheares" is the motion of the greatest complexity. . . . The poet must exhort his love to quietness and calm upon his departure; and for this purpose the figure based upon the latter motion (trepidation), long absorbed into the traditional astronomy, fittingly suggests the tension of the moment without arousing the "harmes and feares" implicit in the figure of the moving earth.[9]

The argument is plausible and rests on a well substantiated thesis that Donne was deeply interested in the new astronomy and its repercussions in the theological realm. In various works Donne shows his familiarity with Kepler's *De Stella Nova*, with Galileo's *Siderius Nuncius*, with William Gilbert's *De Magnete*, and with Clavius' commentary on the *De Sphaera* of Sacrobosco. He refers to the new science in his Sermon at Paul's Cross and in a letter to Sir Henry Goodyer. In *The First Anniversary* he says the "new philosophy calls all in doubt." In the *Elegy* on *Prince Henry* he says that the "least moving of the center" makes "the world to shake."

It is difficult to answer argument like this, and impossible to answer it with evidence of like nature. There is no reason why Donne might not have written a stanza in which the two kinds of celestial motion stood for two sorts of emotion at parting. And if we become full of astronomical ideas and see Donne only against the background of the new science, we may believe that he did. But the text itself remains to be dealt with, the analyzable vehicle of a complicated metaphor. And one may observe: (1) that the movement of the earth according to the Copernican theory is a celestial motion, smooth and regular, and while it might cause religious or philosophic fears, it could not be associated with the crudity and earthiness of the kind of commotion which the speaker in the poem wishes to discourage; (2) that there is another moving of the earth, an earthquake, which has just these qualities and is to be associated with the tear-floods and sigh-tempests of the second stanza of the poem; (3) that "trepidation" is an appropriate opposite of earthquake, because each is a shaking or vibratory motion; and "trepidation of the spheares" is "greater farre" than an earthquake, but not much greater (if two such motions can be compared as to greatness) than the annual motion of the earth; (4) that reckoning what it "did and meant" shows that the event has passed, like an earthquake, not like the incessant celestial movement of the earth. Perhaps a knowledge of Donne's interest in the new science may add another shade of meaning, an overtone to the stanza in question, though to say even this runs against the words. To make the geocentric and heliocentric antithesis the core of the metaphor is to disregard the English language, to prefer private evidence to public, external to internal.

V

If the distinction between kinds of evidence has implications for the historical critic, it has then no less for the contemporary poet and his critic. Or, since every rule for a poet is but another side of a judgment by a critic, and since the past is the realm of the scholar and critic, and the future and present that of the poet and the critical leaders of taste, we may say that the problems arising in literary scholarship from the intentional fallacy are matched by others which arise in the world of progressive experiment.

The question of "allusiveness," for example, as acutely posed by the poetry of Eliot, is certainly one where a false judgment is likely to involve the intentional fallacy. The frequency and depth of literary allusion in the poetry of Eliot and others has driven so many in pursuit of full meanings to the *Golden Bough* and the Elizabethan drama that it has become a kind of commonplace to suppose that we do not know what a poet means unless we have traced him in his reading – supposition redolent with intentional implications. The stand taken by F. O. Matthiessen is a sound one and partially forestalls the difficulty.

> If one reads these lines with an attentive ear and is sensitive to their sudden shifts in movement, the contrast between the actual Thames and the idealized vision of it during an age before it flowed through

a megalopolis is sharply conveyed by that movement itself, whether or not one recognizes the refrain to be from Spenser.

Eliot's allusions work when we know them – and to a great extent when we do not know them – through their suggestive power.

But sometimes we find allusions supported by notes, and it is a nice question whether the notes function more as guides to send us where we may be educated, or more as indications in themselves about the character of the allusions. "Nearly everything of importance . . . that is apposite to an appreciation of 'The Waste Land,' " writes Matthiessen of Miss Weston's book, "has been incorporated into the structure of the poem itself, or into Eliot's Notes." And with such an admission it may begin to appear that it would not much matter if Eliot invented his sources (as Sir Walter Scott invented chapter epigraphs from "old plays" and "anonymous" authors, or as Coleridge wrote marginal glosses for *The Ancient Mariner*). Allusions to Dante, Webster, Marvell, or Baudelaire doubtless gain something because these writers existed, but it is doubtful whether the same can be said for an allusion to an obscure Elizabethan:

> The sound of horns and motors, which shall bring Sweeney to
>   Mrs. Porter in the spring.

"Cf. Day, *Parliament of Bees*": says Eliot,

> When of a sudden, listening, you shall hear,
> A noise of horns and hunting, which shall bring
> Actaeon to Diana in the spring,
> Where all shall see her naked skin.

The irony is completed by the quotation itself; had Eliot, as is quite conceivable, composed these lines to furnish his own background, there would be no loss of validity. The conviction may grow as one reads Eliot's next note: "I do not know the origin of the ballad from which these lines are taken: it was reported to me from Sydney, Australia." The important word in this note – on Mrs. Porter and her daughter who washed their feet in soda water – is "ballad." And if one should feel from the lines themselves their "ballad" quality, there would be little need for the note. Ultimately, the inquiry must focus on the integrity of such notes as parts of the poem, for where they constitute special information about the meaning of phrases in the poem, they ought to be subject to the same scrutiny as any of the other words in which it is written. Matthiessen believes the notes were the price Eliot "had to pay in order to avoid what he would have considered muffling the energy of his poem by extended connecting links in the text itself." But it may be questioned whether the notes and the need for them are not equally muffling. F. W. Bateson has plausibly argued that Tennyson's "The Sailor Boy" would be better if half the stanzas were omitted, and the best versions of ballads like "Sir Patrick Spens" owe their power to the very audacity with which the minstrel has taken for granted the story upon which he comments. What then if a poet finds he cannot take so much for granted in a more recondite context and rather than write informatively, supplies notes? It can be said in favor of this plan that at least the notes do not pretend to be dramatic, as they would if written in verse. On the other hand, the notes may look like unassimilated material lying loose beside the poem, necessary for the meaning of the verbal symbol, but not integrated, so that the symbol stands incomplete.

We mean to suggest by the above analysis that whereas notes tend to seem to justify themselves as external indexes to the author's *intention*, yet they ought to be judged like any other parts of a composition (verbal arrangement special to a particular context), and when so judged their reality as parts of the poem, or their imaginative integration with the rest of the poem, may come into question. Matthiessen, for instance, sees that Eliot's titles for poems and his epigraphs are informative apparatus, like the notes. But while he is worried by some of the notes and thinks that Eliot "appears to be mocking himself for writing the note at the same time that he wants to convey something by it," Matthiessen believes that the "device" of epigraphs "is not at all open to the objection of not being sufficiently structural." "The *intention*," he says, "is to enable the poet to secure a condensed expression in the poem itself." "In each case the epigraph *is designed* to form an integral part of the effect of the poem." And Eliot himself, in his notes, has justified his poetic practice in terms of intention.

> The Hanged Man, a member of the traditional pack, fits my purpose in two ways: because he is associated in my mind with the Hanged God of Frazer, and because I associate him with the hooded figure in the passage of the disciples to Emmaus in Part V. . . . The man with Three Staves (an authentic member of the Tarot pack) I associate, quite arbitrarily, with the Fisher King himself.

And perhaps he is to be taken more seriously here, when off guard in a note, than when in his Norton Lectures he comments on the difficulty of saying what a poem means and adds playfully that he thinks of prefixing to a second edition of *Ash Wednesday* some lines from *Don Juan*:

> I don't pretend that I quite understand
> My own meaning when I would be *very* fine;
> But the fact is that I have nothing planned
> Unless it were to be a moment merry.

If Eliot and other contemporary poets have any characteristic fault, it may be in *planning* too much.

Allusiveness in poetry is one of several critical issues by which we have illustrated the more abstract issue of intentionalism, but it may be for today the most important illustration. As a poetic practice allusiveness would appear to be in some recent poems an extreme corollary of the romantic intentionalist assumption, and as a critical issue it challenges and brings to light in a special way the basic premise of intentionalism. The following instance from the poetry of Eliot may serve to epitomize the practical implications of what we have been saying. In Eliot's "Love Song of J. Alfred Prufrock," toward the end, occurs the line: "I have heard the mermaids singing, each to each," and this bears a certain resemblance to a line in a Song by John Donne, "Teach me to heare Mermaides singing," so that for the reader acquainted to a certain degree with Donne's poetry, the critical question arises: Is Eliot's line an allusion to Donne's? Is Prufrock thinking about Donne? Is Eliot thinking about Donne? We suggest that there are two radically different ways of looking for an answer to this question. There is (1) the way of poetic analysis and exegesis, which inquires whether it makes any sense if Eliot-Prufrock is thinking about Donne. In an earlier part of the poem, when Prufrock asks, "Would it have been worth while, . . . To have squeezed the universe into a ball," his words take half their sadness and irony from certain energetic and passionate lines of Marvell's "To His Coy Mistress." But the exegetical inquirer may wonder whether mermaids considered as "strange sights" (to hear them is in Donne's poem analogous to getting with child a mandrake root) have much to do with Prufrock's mermaids, which seem to be symbols of romance and dynamism, and which incidentally have literary authentication, if they need it, in a line of a sonnet by Gérard de Nerval. This method of inquiry may lead to the conclusion that the given resemblance between Eliot and Donne is without significance and is better not thought of, or the method may have the disadvantage of providing no certain conclusion. Nevertheless, we submit that this is the true and objective way of criticism, as contrasted to what the very uncertainty of exegesis might tempt a second kind of critic to undertake: (2) the way of biographical or genetic inquiry, in which, taking advantage of the fact that Eliot is still alive, and in the spirit of a man who would settle a bet, the critic writes to Eliot and asks him what he meant, or if he had Donne in mind. We shall not here weigh the probabilities – whether Eliot would answer that he meant nothing at all, had nothing at all in mind – a sufficiently good answer to such a question – or in an unguarded moment might furnish a clear and, within its limit, irrefutable answer. Our point is that such an answer to such an inquiry would have nothing to do with the poem "Prufrock"; it would not be a critical inquiry. Critical inquiries, unlike bets, are not settled in this way. Critical inquiries are not settled by consulting the oracle.

Notes

1 Joseph T. Shipley (ed.) *Dictionary of World Literature* (New York, 1942), pp. 326–9.
2 J. E. Spingarn, "The new criticism," in *Criticism in America* (New York, 1924), pp. 24–5.
3 Ananda K. Coomaraswamy, "Intention," in *American Bookman*, I (1944) pp. 41–8.
4 It is true that Croce himself in his *Aristo, Shakespeare and Corneille* (London, 1920), ch. 7, "The practical personality and the poetical personality," and in his *Defence of Poetry* (Oxford, 1934), p. 24, and elsewhere, early and late, has delivered telling attacks on emotive geneticism, but the main drive of the *Aesthetic* is surely toward a kind of cognitive intentionalism.
5 See Hughes Mearns, *Creative Youth* (Garden City, 1925), esp. pp. 27–9. The technique of inspiring poems has apparently been outdone more recently by the study of inspiration in successful poets and other artists. See, for instance, Rosamond E. M. Hading, *An Anatomy of Inspiration* (Cambridge, 1940); Julius Portnoy, *A Psychology of Art Creation* (Philadelphia, 1942); Rudolf Arnheim and others, *Poets at Work* (New York, 1947); Phyllis Bartlett, *Poems in Process* (New York, 1951); Brewer Ghiselin, ed., *The Creative Process: A Symposium* (Berkeley and Los Angeles, 1952).
6 Curt Ducasse, *The Philosophy of Art* (New York, 1929), p. 116.
7 And the history of words *after* a poem is written may contribute meanings which if relevant to the original pattern should not be ruled out by a scruple about intention.
8 Chs. 8, "The pattern," and 16, "The known and familiar landscape," will be found of most help to the student of the poem.
9 Charles M. Coffin, *John Donne and the New Philosophy* (New York, 1927), pp. 97–8.

42

Of the standard of taste
David Hume

In this classic essay, first published in 1757, David Hume (1711–76) addresses the apparent paradox of taste: many people argue that taste is purely subjective yet at the same time want to claim that particular judgements that they make, such as that one writer is far superior to another, are objective. What we need is some kind of standard by which to measure different judgements of taste. Hume provides a set of criteria by which we can judge whether or not a critic's judgement should be respected.

From David Hume, *Four Dissertations*

The great variety of Taste, as well as of opinion, which prevails in the world, is too obvious not to have fallen under every one's observation. Men of the most confined knowledge are able to remark a difference of taste in the narrow circle of their acquaintance, even where the persons have been educated under the same government, and have early imbibed the same prejudices. But those who can enlarge their view to contemplate distant nations and remote ages, are still more surprised at the great inconsistence and contrariety. We are apt to call *barbarous* whatever departs widely from our own taste and apprehension; but soon find the epithet of reproach retorted on us. And the highest arrogance and self-conceit is at last startled, on observing an equal assurance on all sides, and scruples, amidst such a contest of sentiment, to pronounce positively in its own favour.

As this variety of taste is obvious to the most careless inquirer, so will it be found, on examination, to be still greater in reality than in appearance. The sentiments of men often differ with regard to beauty and deformity of all kinds, even while their general discourse is the same. There are certain terms in every language which import blame, and others praise; and all men who use the same tongue must agree in their application of them. Every voice is united in applauding elegance, propriety, simplicity, spirit in writing; and in blaming fustian, affectation, coldness, and a false, brilliancy. But when critics come to particulars, this seeming unanimity vanishes; and it is found, that they had affixed a very different meaning to their expressions. In all matters of opinion and science, the case is opposite; the difference among men is there oftener found to lie in generals than in particulars, and to be less in reality than in appearance. An explanation of the terms commonly ends the controversy: and the disputants are surprised to find that they had been quarrelling, while at bottom they agreed in their judgment.

Those who found morality on sentiment, more than on reason, are inclined to comprehend ethics under the former observation, and to maintain, that, in all questions which regard conduct and manners, the difference among men is really greater than at first sight it appears. It is indeed obvious, that writers of all nations and all ages concur in, applauding justice, humanity, magnanimity, prudence, veracity; and in blaming the opposite qualities. Even poets and other authors, whose compositions are chiefly calculated to please the imagination, are yet found, from HOMER down to FENELON, to inculcate the same moral precepts, and to bestow their applause and blame on the same virtues and vices. This great unanimity is usually ascribed to the influence of plain reason, which, in all these cases, maintains similar sentiments in all men, and prevents those controversies to which the abstract sciences are so much exposed. So far as the unanimity is real, this account may be admitted as satisfactory. But we must also allow, that some part of the seeming harmony in morals may be accounted for from the very nature of language. The word *virtue*, with its equivalent in every tongue, implies praise, as that of *vice* does blame; and no one, without the most obvious and grossest impropriety, could affix reproach to a term, which in general acceptation is understood in a good sense; or bestow applause, where the idiom requires disapprobation. HOMER's general precepts, where he delivers any such, will never be controverted; but it is obvious, that, when he draws particular pictures of manners, and represents heroism in ACHILLES, and prudence in ULYSSES, he intermixes a much greater degree of ferocity in the former, and of cunning and fraud in the latter, than FENELON would admit of. The sage ULYSSES, in the GREEK poet, seems to delight in lies and fictions, and often employs them without any necessity, or even advantage. But his more scrupulous son, in the FRENCH epic writer, exposes himself to the most imminent perils, rather than depart from the most exact line of truth and veracity.

The admirers and followers of the ALCORAN insist on the excellent moral precepts interspersed throughout that wild and absurd performance. But it is to be supposed, that the ARABIC words, which correspond to the ENGLISH, equity, justice, temperance, meekness, charity, were such as, from the constant use of that tongue, must always be taken in a good sense:

and it would have argued the greatest ignorance, not of morals, but of language, to have mentioned them with any epithets, besides those of applause and approbation. But would we know, whether the pretended prophet had really attained a just sentiment of morals, let us attend to his narration, and we shall soon find, that he bestows praise on such instances of treachery, inhumanity, cruelty, revenge, bigotry, as are utterly incompatible with civilized society. No steady rule of right seems there to be attended to; and every action is blamed or praised, so far only as it is beneficial or hurtful to the true believers.

The merit of delivering true general precepts in ethics is indeed very small. Whoever recommends any moral virtues, really does no more than is implied in the terms themselves. That people who invented the word *charity*, and used it, in a good sense, inculcated more clearly, and much more efficaciously, the precept, *be charitable*, than any pretended legislator or prophet, who should insert such a *maxim* in his writings. Of all expressions, those which, together with their other meaning, imply a degree either of blame or approbation, are the least liable to be perverted or mistaken.

It is natural for us to seek a *Standard of Taste*; a rule by which the various sentiments of men may be reconciled; at least a decision afforded confirming one sentiment, and condemning another.

There is a species of philosophy, which cuts off all hopes of success in such an attempt, and represents the impossibility of ever attaining any standard of taste. The difference, it is said, is very wide between judgment and sentiment. All sentiment is right; because sentiment has a reference to nothing beyond itself, and is always real, wherever a man is conscious of it. But all determinations of the understanding are not right; because they have a reference to something beyond themselves, to wit, real matter of fact; and are not always conformable to that standard. Among a thousand different opinions which different men may entertain of the same subject, there is one, and but one, that is just and true: and the only difficulty is to fix and ascertain it. On the contrary, a thousand different sentiments, excited by the same object, are all right; because no sentiment represents what is really in the object. It only marks a certain conformity or relation between the object and the organs or faculties of the mind; and if that conformity did not really exist, the sentiment could never possibly have being. Beauty is no quality in things themselves: it exists merely in the mind which contemplates them; and each mind perceives a different beauty. One person may even perceive deformity, where another is sensible of beauty; and every individual ought to acquiesce in his own sentiment, without pretending to regulate those of others. To seek the real beauty, or real deformity, is as fruitless an inquiry, as to pretend to ascertain the real sweet or real bitter. According to the disposition of the organs, the same object may be both sweet and bitter; and the proverb has justly determined it to be fruitless to dispute concerning tastes. It is very natural, and even quite necessary, to extend this axiom to mental, as well as bodily taste; and thus common sense, which is so often at variance with philosophy, especially with the sceptical kind, is found, in one instance at least, to agree in pronouncing the same decision.

But though this axiom, by passing into a proverb, seems to have attained the sanction of common sense; there is certainly a species of common sense, which opposes it, at least serves to modify and restrain it. Whoever would assert an equality of genius and elegance between OGILBY and MILTON, or BUNYON and ADDISON would be thought to defend no less an extravagance, than if he had maintained a mole-hill to be as high as TENERIFFE, or a pond as extensive as the ocean. Though there may be found persons, who give the preference to the former authors; no one pays attention to such a taste; and we pronounce, without scruple, the sentiment of these pretended critics to be absurd and ridiculous. The principle of the natural equality of tastes is then totally forgot, and while we admit it on some occasions, where the objects seem near an equality, it appears an extravagant paradox, or rather a palpable absurdity, where objects so disproportioned are compared together.

It is evident that none of the rules of composition are fixed by reasonings *a priori*, or can be esteemed abstract conclusions of the understanding, from comparing those habitudes and relations of ideas, which are eternal and immutable. Their foundation is the same with that of all the practical sciences, experience; nor are they any thing but general observations, concerning what has been universally found to please in all countries and in all ages. Many of the beauties of poetry, and even of eloquence, are founded on falsehood and fiction, on hyperboles, metaphors, and an abuse or perversion of terms from their natural meaning. To check the sallies of the imagination, and to reduce every expression to geometrical truth and exactness, would be the most contrary to the laws of criticism; because it would produce a work, which, by universal experience, has been found the most insipid and disagreeable. But though poetry can never submit to exact truth, it must be confined by rules of art, discovered to the author either by genius or observation. If some negligent or irregular writers have pleased, they have not pleased by their transgressions of rule or order, but in spite of these transgressions: they have possessed other beauties, which were conformable to just criticism; and the force of these beauties has been able to overpower censure, and give the mind a satisfaction superior to the disgust arising from the blemishes. Ariosto pleases; but not by his monstrous and improbable fictions, by his bizarre mixture of the serious and comic styles, by the want of coherence in his stories, or by the continual interruptions of his narration. He charms by the force and clearness of his expression, by the readiness and variety of his inventions, and by his natural pictures of the passions, especially those of the gay and amorous kind: and, however his faults may diminish our satisfaction, they are not able entirely to destroy it. Did our pleasure really arise from those parts of his poem, which we denominate faults, this would be no objection to criticism in general: it would only be an objection to those particular rules of criticism, which would establish such circumstances to be faults, and would represent them as universally blamable. If they are found to please, they cannot be faults, let the pleasure which they produce be ever so unexpected and unaccountable.

But though all the general rules of art are founded only on experience, and on the observation of the common sentiments of human nature, we must not imagine, that, on every occasion, the feelings of men will be conformable to these rules. Those finer emotions of the mind are of a very tender and delicate nature, and require the concurrence of many favourable circumstances to make them play with facility and exactness, according to their general and established principles. The least exterior hindrance to such small springs, or the least internal disorder, disturbs their motion, and confounds the operations of the whole machine. When we would make an experiment of this nature, and would try the force of any beauty or deformity, we must choose with care a proper time and place, and bring the fancy to a suitable situation and disposition. A perfect serenity of mind, a recollection of thought, a due attention to the object; if any of these circumstances be wanting, our experiment will be fallacious, and we shall be unable to judge of the catholic and universal beauty. The relation, which nature has placed between the form and the sentiment, will at least be more obscure; and it will require greater accuracy to trace and discern it. We shall be able to ascertain its influence, not so much from the operation of each particular beauty, as from the durable admiration which attends those works that have survived all the caprices of mode and fashion, all the mistakes of ignorance and envy.

The same HOMER who pleased at ATHENS and ROME two thousand years ago, is still admired at PARIS and LONDON. All the changes of climate, government, religion, and language, have not been able to obscure his glory. Authority or prejudice may give a temporary vogue to a bad poet or orator; but his reputation will never be durable or general. When his compositions are examined by posterity or by foreigners, the enchantment is dissipated, and his faults appear in their true colours. On the contrary, a real genius, the longer his works endure, and the more wide they are spread, the more sincere is the admiration which he meets with. Envy and jealousy have too much place in a narrow circle; and even familiar acquaintance with his person may diminish the applause due to his performances: but when these obstructions are removed, the beauties, which are naturally fitted to excite agreeable sentiments, immediately display their energy; and while the world endures, they maintain their authority over the minds of men.

It appears, then, that amidst all the variety and caprice of taste, there are certain general principles of approbation or blame, whose influence a careful eye may trace in all operations of the mind. Some particular forms or qualities, from the original structure of the internal fabric are calculated to please, and others to displease; and if they fail of their effect in any particular instance, it is from some apparent defect or imperfection in the organ. A man in a fever would not insist on his palate as able to decide concerning flavours; nor would one affected with the jaundice pretend to give a verdict with regard to colours. In each creature there is a sound and a defective state; and the former alone can be supposed to afford us a true standard of taste and sentiment. If, in the sound state of the organ, there be an entire or a considerable uniformity of sentiment among men, we may thence derive an idea of the perfect beauty; in like manner as the appearance of objects in daylight, to the eye of a man in health, is denominated their true and real colour, even while colour is allowed to be merely a phantasm of the senses.

Many and frequent are the defects in the internal organs, which prevent or weaken the influence of those general principles, on which depends our sentiment of beauty or deformity. Though some objects, by the structure of the mind, be naturally calculated to give pleasure, it is not to be expected that in every individual the pleasure will be equally felt. Particular incidents and situations occur, which either throw a false light on the objects, or hinder the true from conveying to the imagination the proper sentiment and perception.

One obvious cause why many feel not the proper sentiment of beauty, is the want of that *delicacy* of imagination which is requisite to convey a sensibility of those finer emotions. This delicacy every one pretends to: every one talks of it; and would reduce every kind of taste or sentiments to its standard. But as our intention in this essay is to mingle some light of the understanding with the feelings of sentiment, it will be proper to give a more accurate definition of delicacy than has hitherto been attempted. And not to draw our philosophy from too profound a source, we shall have recourse to a noted story in DON QUIXOTE.

It is with good reason, says SANCHO to the squire with the great nose, that I pretend to have a judgment in wine: this is a quality hereditary in our family. Two of my kinsmen were once called to give their opinion of a hogshead, which was supposed to be excellent, being old and of a good vintage. One of them tastes it, considers it; and, after mature reflection, pronounces the wine to be good, were it not for a small taste of leather which he perceived in it. The other, after using the same precautions, gives also his verdict in favour of the wine; but with the reserve of a taste of iron, which he could easily distinguish. You cannot imagine how much they were both ridiculed for their judgment. But who laughed in the end? On emptying the hogshead, there was found at the bottom an old key with a leathern thong tied to it.

The great resemblance between mental and bodily taste will easily teach us to apply this story. Though it be certain that beauty and deformity, more than sweet and bitter, are not qualities in objects, but belong entirely to the sentiment, internal or external, it must be allowed, that there are certain qualities in objects which are fitted by nature to produce those particular feelings. Now, as these qualities may be found in a small degree, or may be mixed and confounded with each other, it often happens that the taste is not affected with such minute qualities, or is not able to distinguish all the particular flavours, amidst the disorder in which they are presented. Where the organs are so fine as to allow nothing to escape them, and at the same time so exact as to perceive every ingredient in the composition, this we call delicacy of taste, whether we employ these terms in the literal or metaphorical sense. Here then the general rules of beauty are of use, being drawn from established models, and from the observation of what pleases or displeases, when presented singly and in a high degree; and if the same qualities, in a continued composition, and in a smaller degree, affect not the organs with a sensible delight or uneasiness, we exclude the person from all pretensions to this delicacy. To produce these general rules or avowed patterns of composition, is like finding the key with the leathern thong, which justified the verdict of SANCHO'S kinsmen, and confounded those pretended judges who had condemned them. Though the hogshead had never been emptied, the taste of the one was still equally delicate, and that of the other equally dull and languid; but it would have been more difficult to have proved the superiority of the former, to the conviction of every bystander. In like manner, though the beauties of writing had never been methodized, or reduced to general principles; though no excellent models had ever been acknowledged, the different degrees of taste, would still have subsisted, and the judgment of one man been preferable to that of another; but it would not have been so easy to silence the bad critic, who might always insist upon his particular sentiment, and refuse to submit to his antagonist. But when we show him an avowed principle of art; when we illustrate this principle by examples, whose operation, from his own particular taste, he acknowledges to be conformable to the principle; when we prove that the same principle may be applied to the present case, where he did not perceive or feel its influence: he must conclude, upon the whole, that the fault lies in himself, and that he wants the delicacy which is requisite to make him sensible of every beauty and every blemish in any composition or discourse.

It is acknowledged to be the perfection of every sense or faculty, to perceive with exactness its most minute objects, and allow nothing to escape its notice and observation. The smaller the objects are which become sensible to the eye, the finer is that organ, and the more elaborate its make and composition. A good palate is not tried by strong flavours, but by a mixture of small ingredients, where we are still sensible of each part, notwithstanding its minuteness and its confusion with the rest. In like manner, a quick and acute perception of beauty and deformity must be the perfection of our mental taste; nor can a man be satisfied with himself while he suspects that any excellence or blemish in a discourse has passed him unobserved. In this case, the perfection of the man, and the perfection of the sense of feeling, are found to be united. A very delicate palate, on many occasions, may be a great inconvenience both to a man himself and to his friends. But a delicate taste of wit or beauty must always be a desirable quality, because it is the source of all the finest and most innocent enjoyments of which human nature is susceptible. In this decision the sentiments of all mankind are agreed. Wherever you can ascertain a delicacy of taste, it is sure to meet with approbation; and the best way of ascertaining it is, to appeal to those models and principles which have been established by the uniform consent and experience of nations and ages.

But though there be naturally a wide difference, in point of delicacy, between one person and another, nothing tends further to increase and improve this talent, than *practice* in a particular art, and the frequent survey or contemplation of a particular species of beauty. When objects of any kind are first presented to the eye or imagination, the sentiment which attends them is obscure and confused; and the mind is, in a great measure, incapable of pronouncing concerning their merits or defects. The taste cannot perceive the several excellences of the performance, much less distinguish the particular character of each excellency, and ascertain its quality and degree. If it pronounce the whole in general to be beautiful or deformed, it is the utmost that can be expected; and even this judgment, a person so unpractised will be apt to deliver with great hesitation and reserve. But allow him to acquire experience in those objects, his feeling becomes more exact and nice: he not only perceives the beauties and defects of each part, but marks the distinguishing species of each quality, and assigns it suitable praise or blame. A clear and distinct sentiment attends him through the whole survey of the objects; and he discerns that very degree and kind of approbation or displeasure which each part is naturally fitted to produce. The mist dissipates which seemed formerly to hang over the object; the organ acquires greater perfection in its operations, and can pronounce, without danger of mistake, concerning the merits of every performance. In a word, the same address and dexterity which practice gives to the execution of any work, is also acquired by the same means in the judging of it.

So advantageous is practice to the discernment of beauty, that, before we can give judgment on any work of importance, it will even be requisite that that very individual performance be more than once perused by us, and be surveyed in different lights with attention and deliberation. There is a flutter or hurry of thought which attends the first perusal of any piece, and which confounds the genuine sentiment of beauty. The relation of the parts is not discerned: the true characters of style are little distinguished. The several perfections and defects seem wrapped up in a species of confusion, and present themselves indistinctly to the imagination. Not to mention, that there is a species of beauty, which, as it is florid and superficial, pleases at first; but being found incompatible with a just expression either of reason or passion, soon palls upon the taste, and is then rejected with disdain, at least rated at a much lower value.

It is impossible to continue in the practice of contemplating any order of beauty, without being frequently obliged to form *comparisons* between the several species and degrees of excellence, and estimating their proportion to each other. A man who has had no opportunity of comparing the different kinds of beauty, is indeed totally unqualified to pronounce an opinion with regard to any object presented to him. By comparison alone we fix the epithets of praise or blame, and learn how to assign the due degree of each. The coarsest daubing contains a certain lustre of colours and exactness of imitation, which are so far beauties, and would affect the mind of a peasant or Indian with the highest admiration. The most vulgar ballads are not entirely destitute of harmony or nature; and none but a person familiarized to superior beauties would pronounce their members harsh, or narration uninteresting. A great inferiority of beauty gives pain to a person conversant in the highest excellence of the kind, and is for that reason pronounced a deformity; as the most finished object with which we are acquainted is naturally supposed to have reached the pinnacle of perfection, and to be entitled to the highest applause. One accustomed to see, and examine, and weigh the several performances, admired in different ages and nations, can alone rate the merits of a work exhibited to his view, and assign its proper rank among the productions of genius.

But to enable a critic the more fully to execute this undertaking, he must preserve his mind free from all *prejudice*, and allow nothing to enter into his consideration, but the very object which is submitted to his examination. We may observe, that every work of art, in order to produce its due effect on the mind, must be surveyed in a certain point of view, and cannot be fully relished by persons whose situation, real or imaginary, is not conformable to that which is required by the performance. An orator addresses himself to a particular audience, and must have a regard to their particular genius, interests, opinions, passions, and prejudices; otherwise he hopes in vain to govern their resolutions, and inflame their affections. Should they even have entertained some prepossessions against him, however unreasonable, he must not overlook this disadvantage: but, before he enters upon the subject, must endeavour to conciliate their affection, and acquire their good graces. A critic of a different age or nation, who should peruse this discourse, must have all these circumstances in his eye, and must place himself in the same situation as the audience, in order to form a true judgment of the oration. In like manner, when any work is addressed to the public, though I should have a friendship or enmity with the author, I must depart from this situation, and, considering myself as a man in general, forget, if possible, my individual being, and my peculiar circumstances. A person influenced by prejudice complies not with this condition, but obstinately maintains his natural position, without placing himself in that point of view which the performance supposes. If the work be addressed to persons of a different age or nation, he makes no allowance for their peculiar views and prejudices; but, full of the manners of his own age and country, rashly condemns what seemed admirable in the eyes of those for whom alone the discourse was calculated. If the work be executed for the public, he never sufficiently enlarges his comprehension, or forgets his interest as a friend or enemy, as a rival or commentator. By this means his sentiments are perverted; nor have the same beauties and blemishes the same influence upon him, as if he had imposed a proper violence on his imagination, and had forgotten himself for a moment. So far his taste evidently departs from the true standard, and of consequence loses all credit and authority.

It is well known, that, in all questions submitted to the understanding, prejudice is destructive of sound judgment, and perverts all operations of the intellectual faculties: it is no less contrary to good taste; nor has it less influence to corrupt our sentiment of beauty. It belongs to *good sense* to check its influence in both cases; and in this respect, as well as in many others, reason, if not an essential part of taste, is at least requisite to the operations of this latter faculty. In all the nobler productions of genius, there is a mutual relation and correspondence of parts; nor can either the beauties or blemishes be perceived by him whose thought is not capacious enough to comprehend all those parts, and compare them with each other, in order to perceive the consistence and uniformity of the whole. Every work of art has also a certain end or purpose for which it is calculated; and is to be deemed more or less perfect, as it is more or less fitted to attain this end. The object of eloquence is to persuade, of history to instruct, of poetry to please, by means of the passions and the imagination. These ends we must carry constantly in our view when we peruse any performance; and we must be able to judge how far the means employed are adapted to their respective purposes. Besides, every kind of composition, even the most poetical, is nothing but a chain of propositions and reasonings; not always, indeed, the justest and most exact, but still plausible and specious, however disguised by the colouring of the imagination. The persons introduced in tragedy and epic poetry must be represented as reasoning, and thinking and concluding, and acting, suitably to their character and circumstances; and without judgment, as well as taste and invention, a poet can never hope to succeed in so delicate an undertaking. Not to mention, that the same excellence of faculties which contributes to the improvement of reason, the same clearness of conception, the same exactness of distinction, the same vivacity of apprehension, are essential to the operations of true taste, and are its infallible concomitants. It seldom or never happens, that a man of sense, who has experience in any art, cannot judge of its beauty; and it is no less rare to meet with a man who has a just taste without a sound understanding.

Thus, though the principles of taste be universal, and nearly, if not entirely, the same in all men; yet few are qualified to give judgment on any work of art, or establish their own sentiment as the standard of beauty. The organs of internal sensation are seldom so perfect as to allow the general principles their full play, and produce a feeling correspondent to those principles. They either labour under some defect, or are vitiated by some disorder; and by that means excite a sentiment, which may be pronounced erroneous. When the critic has no delicacy, he judges without any distinction, and is only affected by the grosser and more palpable qualities of the object: the finer touches pass unnoticed and disregarded. Where he is not aided by practice, his verdict is attended with confusion and hesitation. Where no comparison has been employed, the most frivolous beauties, such as rather merit the name of defects, are the object of his admiration. Where he lies under the influence of prejudice, all his natural sentiments are perverted. Where good sense is wanting, he is not qualified to discern the beauties of design and reasoning, which are the highest and most excellent. Under some or other of these imperfections, the generality of men labour, and hence a true judge in the finer arts is observed, even during the most polished ages, to be so rare a character: strong sense, united to delicate sentiment, improved by practice, perfected by comparison, and cleared of all prejudice, can alone entitle critics to this valuable character; and the joint verdict of such, wherever they are to be found, is the true standard of taste and beauty.

But where are such critics to be found? By what marks are they to be known? How distinguish them from pretenders? These questions are embarrassing; and seem to throw us back into the same uncertainty from which, during the course of this essay, we have endeavoured to extricate ourselves.

But if we consider the matter aright, these are questions of fact, not of sentiment. Whether any particular person be endowed with good sense and a delicate imagination, free from prejudice, may often be the subject of dispute, and be liable to great discussion and inquiry: but that such a character is valuable and estimable, will be agreed in by all mankind. Where these doubts occur, men can do no more than in other disputable questions which are submitted to the understanding: they must produce the best arguments that their invention suggests to them; they

403

must acknowledge a true and decisive standard to exist somewhere, to wit, real existence and matter of fact; and they must have indulgence to such as differ from them in their appeals to this standard. It is sufficient for our present purpose, if we have proved, that the taste of all individuals is not upon an equal footing, and that some men in general, however difficult to be particularly pitched upon, will be acknowledged by universal sentiment to have a preference above others.

But, in reality, the difficulty of finding, even in particulars, the standard of taste, is not so great as it is represented. Though in speculation we may readily avow a certain criterion in science, and deny it in sentiment, the matter is found in practice to be much more hard to ascertain in the former case than in the latter. Theories of abstract philosophy, systems of profound theology, have prevailed during one age: in a successive period these have been universally exploded: their absurdity has been detected: other theories and systems have supplied their place, which again gave place to their successors: and nothing has been experienced more liable to the revolutions of chance and fashion than these pretended decisions of science. The case is not the same with the beauties of eloquence and poetry. Just expressions of passion and nature are sure, after a little time, to gain public applause, which they maintain for ever. ARISTOTLE, and PLATO, and EPICURUS and DESCARTES, may successively yield to each other: but TERENCE and VIRGIL maintain an universal, undisputed empire over the minds of men. The abstract philosophy of CICERO has lost its credit: the vehemence of his oratory is still the object of our admiration.

Though men of delicate taste be rare, they are easily to be distinguished in society by the soundness of their understanding, and the superiority of their faculties above the rest of mankind. The ascendant, which they acquire, gives a prevalence to that lively approbation with which they receive any productions of genius, and renders it generally predominant. Many men, when left to themselves, have but a faint and dubious perception of beauty, who yet are capable of relishing any fine stroke which is pointed out to them. Every convert to the admiration of the real poet or orator, is the cause of some new conversion. And though prejudices may prevail for a time, they never unite in celebrating any rival to the true genius, but yield at last to the force of nature and just sentiment. Thus, though a civilized nation may easily be mistaken in the choice of their admired philosopher, they never have been found long to err, in their affection for a favourite epic or tragic author.

But notwithstanding all our endeavours to fix a standard of taste, and reconcile the discordant apprehensions of men, there still remain two sources of variation, which are not sufficient indeed to confound all the boundaries of beauty and deformity, but will often serve to produce a difference in the degrees of our approbation or blame. The one is the different humours of particular men; the other, the particular manners and opinions of our age and country. The general principles of taste are uniform in human nature: where men vary in their judgments, some defect or perversion in the faculties may commonly be remarked; proceeding either from prejudice, from want of practice, or want of delicacy: and there is just reason for approving one taste, and condemning another. But where there is such a diversity in the internal frame or external situation as is entirely blameless on both sides, and leaves no room to give one the preference above the other; in that case a certain degree of diversity in judgment is unavoidable, and we seek in vain for a standard, by which we can reconcile the contrary sentiments.

A young man, whose passions are warm, will be more sensibly touched with amorous and tender images, than a man more advanced in years, who takes pleasure in wise, philosophical reflections, concerning the conduct of life, and moderation of the passions. At twenty, OVID may be the favourite author, HORACE at forty, and perhaps TACITUS at fifty. Vainly would we, in such cases, endeavour to enter into the sentiments of others, and divest ourselves of those propensities which are natural to us. We choose our favourite author as we do our friend, from a conformity of humour and disposition. Mirth or passion, sentiment or reflection; whichever of these most predominates in our temper, it gives us a peculiar sympathy with the writer who resembles us.

One person is more pleased with the sublime, another with the tender, a third with raillery. One has a strong sensibility to blemishes, and is extremely studious of correctness; another has a more lively feeling of beauties, and pardons twenty absurdities and defects for one elevated or pathetic stroke. The ear of this man is entirely turned towards conciseness and energy; that man is delighted with a copious, rich, and harmonious expression. Simplicity is affected by one; ornament by another. Comedy, tragedy, satire, odes, have each its partisans, who prefer that particular species of writing to all others. It is plainly an error in a critic, to confine his approbation to one species or style of writing, and condemn all the rest. But it is almost impossible not to feel a predilection for that which suits our particular turn and disposition. Such performances are innocent and unavoidable, and can never reasonably be the object of dispute, because there is no standard by which they can be decided.

For a like reason, we are more pleased, in the course of our reading, with pictures and characters that resemble objects which are found in our own age and country, than with those which describe a different set of customs. It is not without some effort that we reconcile ourselves to the simplicity of ancient manners, and behold princesses carrying water from the spring, and kings and heroes dressing their own victuals. We may allow in general, that the representation of such manners is no fault in the author, nor deformity in the piece; but we are not so sensibly touched with them.

405

For this reason, comedy is not easily transferred from one age or nation to another. A FRENCHMAN or ENGLISHMAN is not pleased with the ANDRIA of TERENCE, or CLITIA of MACHIAVEL; where the fine lady, upon whom all the play turns, never once appears to the spectators, but is always kept behind the scenes, suitably to the reserved humour of the ancient GREEKS and modern ITALIANS. A man of learning and reflection can make allowance for these peculiarities of manners; but a common audience can never divest themselves so far of their usual ideas and sentiments, as to relish pictures which nowise resemble them.

But here there occurs a reflection, which may, perhaps, be useful in examining the celebrated controversy concerning ancient and modern learning; where we often find the one side excusing any seeming absurdity in the ancients from the manners of the age, and the other refusing to admit this excuse, or at least admitting it only as an apology for the author, not for the performance. In my opinion, the proper boundaries in this subject have seldom been fixed between the contending parties. Where any innocent peculiarities of manners are represented, such as those above mentioned, they ought certainly to be admitted; and a man who is shocked with them, gives an evident proof of false delicacy and refinement. The poet's *monument more durable than brass*, must fall to the ground like common brick or clay, were men to make no allowance for the continual revolutions of manners and customs, and would admit of nothing but what was suitable to the prevailing fashion. Must we throw aside the pictures of our ancestors, because of their ruffs and farthingales? But where the ideas of morality and decency alter from one age to another, and where vicious manners are described, without being marked with the proper characters of blame and disapprobation, this must be allowed to disfigure the poem, and to be a real deformity. I cannot, nor is it proper I should, enter into such sentiments; and however I may excuse the poet, on account of the manners of his age, I can never relish the composition. The want of humanity and of decency, so conspicuous in the characters drawn by several of the ancient poets, even sometimes by HOMER and the GREEK tragedians, diminishes considerably the merit of their noble performances, and gives modern authors an advantage over them. We are not interested in the fortunes and sentiments of such rough heroes; we are displeased to find the limits of vice and virtue so much confounded; and whatever indulgence we may give to the writer on account of his prejudices, we cannot prevail on ourselves to enter into his sentiments, or bear an affection to characters which we plainly discover to be blamable.

The case is not the same with moral principles as with speculative opinions of any kind. These are in continual flux and revolution. The son embraces a different system from the father. Nay, there scarcely is any man, who can boast of great constancy and uniformity in this particular. Whatever speculative errors may be found in the polite writings of any age or country, they detract but little from the value of those compositions. There needs but a certain turn of thought or imagination to make us enter into all the opinions which then prevailed, and relish the sentiments or conclusions derived from them. But a very violent effort is requisite to change our judgment of manners, and excite sentiments of approbation or blame, love or hatred, different from those to which the mind, from long custom, has been familiarized. And where a man is confident of the rectitude of that moral standard by which he judges, he is justly jealous of it, and will not pervert the sentiments of his heart for a moment, in complaisance to any writer whatsoever.

Of all speculative errors, those which regard religion are the most excusable in compositions of genius; nor is it ever permitted to judge of the civility or wisdom of any people, or even of single persons, by the grossness or refinement of their theological principles. The same good sense that directs men in the ordinary occurrences of life, is not hearkened to in religious matters, which are supposed to be placed altogether above the cognizance of human reason. On this account, all the absurdities of the pagan system of theology must be overlooked by every critic, who would pretend to form a just notion of ancient poetry; and our posterity, in their turn, must have the same indulgence to their forefathers. No religious principles can ever be imputed as a fault to any poet, while they remain merely principles, and take not such strong possession of his heart as to lay him under the imputation of *bigotry* or *superstition*. Where that happens, they confound the sentiments of morality, and alter the natural boundaries of vice and virtue. They are therefore eternal blemishes, according to the principle above mentioned; nor are the prejudices and false opinions of the age sufficient to justify them.

It is essential to the ROMAN catholic religion to inspire a violent hatred of every other worship, and to represent all pagans, mahometans, and heretics, as the objects of divine wrath and vengeance. Such sentiments, though they are in reality very blamable, are considered as virtues by the zealots of that communion, and are represented in their tragedies and epic poems as a kind of divine heroism. This bigotry has disfigured two very fine tragedies of the FRENCH theatre, POLIEUCTE and ATHALIA; where an intemperate zeal for particular modes of worship is set off with all the pomp imaginable, and forms the predominant character of the heroes. 'What is this,' says the sublime JOAD to JOSABET, finding her in discourse with MATHAN the priest of BAAL, 'Does the daughter of DAVID speak to this traitor? Are you not afraid lest the earth should open, and pour forth flames to devour you both? Or lest these holy walls should fall and crush you together? What is his purpose? Why comes that enemy of God hither to poison the air, which we breathe, with his horrid presence?' Such sentiments are received with great applause on the theatre of PARIS; but at LONDON the spectators would be full as much pleased to hear

ACHILLES tell AGAMEMNON, that he was a dog in his forehead, and a deer in his heart; or JUPITER threaten JUNO with a sound drubbing, if she will not be quiet.

RELIGIOUS principles are also a blemish in any polite composition, when they rise up to superstition, and intrude themselves into every sentiment, however remote from any connection with religion. It is no excuse for the poet, that the customs of his country had burdened life with so many religious ceremonies and observances, that no part of it was exempt from that yoke. It must for ever be ridiculous in PETRARCH to compare his mistress, LAURA, to JESUS CHRIST. Nor is it less ridiculous in that agreeable libertine, BOCCACE, very seriously to give thanks to GOD ALMIGHTY; and the ladies, for their assistance in defending him against his enemies.

43

What is wrong with a forgery?
Alfred Lessing

The question of the artistic status of good forgeries is a vexing one. If two paintings are indistinguishable, why should it matter that one is a forgery? Here Alfred Lessing (1936–) argues that what a forgery lacks is a particular kind of originality, one that is particularly valued in the western artistic tradition. Nevertheless, from an aesthetic point of view, it makes no difference whether or not a painting is authentic. Lessing makes his case through an analysis of the work of the most famous forger this century: Han van Meegeren, whose forgeries convinced experts that they were by Vermeer.

From Alfred Lessing, 'What is wrong with a forgery?', *Journal of Aesthetics and Art Criticism*, vol. 23

This chapter attempts to answer the simple question: What is wrong with a forgery? It assumes, then, that something is wrong with a forgery. This is seen to be a reasonable assumption when one considers that the term *forgery* can be defined only in reference to a contrasting phenomenon which must somehow include the notion of genuineness or authenticity. When thus defined there can be little doubt that the concept of forgery is a normative one. It is clear, moreover, that it is a negative concept implying the absence or negation of value. But a problem arises when we ask what kind of value we are speaking of. It appears to be generally assumed that in the case of artistic forgeries we are dealing with the absence or negation of *aesthetic* value. If this were so, a forgery would be an aesthetically inferior work of art. But this, as I will show, is not the case. Pure aesthetics cannot explain forgery. Considering a work of art aesthetically superior because it is genuine, or inferior because it is forged, has little or nothing to do with aesthetic judgment or criticism. It is rather a piece of snobbery.[1]

It is difficult to make this position convincing to a person who is convinced that forgery *is* a matter of aesthetics. If a person insists that for him the aesthetic value (i.e., the beauty) of a work of art is affected by the knowledge that it is or is not genuine, there is little one can say to make that fact unreal for him. At most one can try to show that in the area of aesthetics and criticism we are easily confused and that his view, if carried through, leads to absurd or improbable conclusions. It is important that we do this because it is impossible to understand what is wrong with a forgery unless it be first made quite clear that the answer will not be in terms of its aesthetic worth.

Somehow critics have never understood this and have again and again allowed themselves to be forced into an embarrassing position upon the discovery of some forgery or other. Perhaps the classic, certainly the most celebrated case in point, was that of Han van Meegeren, who in 1945 disturbed the complacent tranquility of the world of art and art critics by confessing that he was the artist responsible for eight paintings, six of which had been sold as legitimate Vermeers and two as de Hooghs. It is not hard to imagine the discomfort felt by critics at that time, especially when we recall how thoroughly successful van Meegeren was in perpetrating his fraud. His *Disciples at Emmaus* was subjected to the very highest praise by the noted critic and scholar Abraham Bredius . . . as one of Vermeer's finest achievements, and it hung in the Boymans Museum for seven years. During that time thousands upon thousands admired and praised the painting. There was no doubt in anyone's mind that this was one of the greatest of Vermeer's paintings and, indeed, one of the most beautiful works of art in the world. It was undoubtedly this universal judgment of aesthetic excellence which accounts largely for the sensational effects of van Meegeren's confession in 1945.

It is of course embarrassing and irritating for an expert to make a mistake in his field. And it *was*, as it turned out, a mistake to identify the painting as a Vermeer. But it should be obvious from the words of Bredius that there is more involved here than a mere matter of misidentification. 'The colors are magnificent,' he writes. 'The highest art . . . this magnificent painting . . . the masterpiece of Vermeer': this is more than identification. This clearly is aesthetic praise. And it is just the fact that the critics heaped such lavish praise on a picture which turned out to have been painted by a second-rate contemporary artist that made the van Meegeren case such a painful affair for them. To their way of thinking, which I am trying to show was not very logical, they were now apparently faced with the dilemma of either admitting that they had praised a worthless picture or continuing to do so.

This was, of course, precisely the trap that van Meegeren had laid for the critics. It was, in fact, the whole *raison d'être* of his perpetrating the fraud. He deliberately chose this extreme, perhaps pathological, way of exposing what he considered to be false aesthetic standards of art critics. In this respect his thinking was no more logical than that of the critics. His reasoning, at least about his first forgery, *The Disciples*, was in effect as follows: 'Once my painting has been accepted and admired as a genuine Vermeer, I will confess publicly to the forgery and thus force the critics either to retract their earlier judgments of praise, thereby acknowledging their fallibility, or to recognize that I am as great an artist as Vermeer.' The dilemma as stated contains a difficulty to which we shall return later. What as important historically is that the critics accepted van Meegeren's dilemma as a genuine one (thereby becoming the dupes of a logical forgery as well as an artistic one), although in the public outburst of indignation, condemnation, praise, blame, analysis, investigation, and discussion which followed van Meegeren's confession, it is difficult to determine which horn of this dilemma the critics actually chose to be impaled on.

There existed, in fact, a small group of critics who never for a moment accepted van Meegeren's claim to have painted *The Disciples at Emmaus*. They argued vehemently that whereas all the other paintings in question are easily shown to be forgeries, no convincing evidence had been produced to prove that *The Disciples* (as well as one other painting entitled *The Last Supper*) was not by Vermeer and that, in fact, all evidence pointed to the conclusion that it was a genuine Vermeer. Subsequent laboratory tests using more modern techniques have finally settled the issue against these critics, but that need not concern us.

What should concern us is the fact that aesthetically it would seem to make no difference whatever whether *The Disciples* is a Vermeer or a van Meegeren. Needless to say, this is not the view of the critics. To them apparently it makes all the difference in the world. Consider, for example, the words of J. Decoen, who was one of that aforementioned group of critics that held that *The Disciples* was a genuine Vermeer:

I must recall that the moment of greatest anguish for me was when the verdict [of van Meegeren] was being considered. The Court might, according to an ancient Dutch Law, have ordered the destruction of *all* the pictures. One shudders at the thought that one could, officially, have destroyed two of the most moving works which Vermeer has created. During the trial, at the moment of his indictment, the public prosecutor stated that there was in Court a man who claimed that a number of the paintings were not by van Meegeren. He made this statement because, ever since 1945, he must have realized that my perseverance had not faltered, that my conviction was deep, and that I had never changed my original statements in any respect whatsoever. These words may possibly have influenced the decision of the Court with regard to the application of the Law. If this be so, I should consider myself amply repaid for my efforts and pains, for my tenacity may possibly have ultimately rescued two capital works of the Dutch school of the seventeenth century.[2]

But what does it matter that Decoen is wrong? Could he no longer take pride in having prevented the destruction of these paintings even though they are products of the twentieth instead of the seventeenth century? The answers, it seems to me, are almost self-evident. What, after all, makes these paintings 'capital works'? Surely it is their purely aesthetic qualities, such as the ones mentioned by Bredius in his description of *The Disciples*. But if this is so, then why, even if this painting is a forgery, should Decoen not be justified in his actions, since he has preserved a painting which is aesthetically important for the only reason that a painting can be aesthetically important – namely, its beauty? Are we any more justified in destroying capital paintings of the twentieth century than those of the seventeenth? To this question we are usually given the answer that the one is after all a forgery while the other is genuine. But our question is precisely: What is the difference between a genuine Vermeer and a van Meegeren forgery? It is of no use to maintain that one need but look to see the difference. The fact that *The Disciples* is a forgery (if indeed it is) cannot, so to speak, be read off from its surface, but can finally be proved or disproved only by means of extensive scientific experiments and analyses. Nor are the results of such scientific investigations of any help in answering our question, since they deal exclusively with nonaesthetic elements of the picture, such as its chemical composition, its hardness, its crackle, and so on. The truth is that the difference between a forgery and a genuine work of art is by no means as obvious as critics sometimes make out. In the case of *The Disciples*, at least, it is certainly not a matter of but needing to look in order to see. The actual history of *The Disciples* turns all such attempted *post facto* explanations into a kind of academic sour grapes.

The plain fact is that aesthetically it makes no difference whether a work of art is authentic or a forgery, and, instead of being embarrassed at having praised a forgery, critics should have the courage of their convictions and take pride in having praised a work of beauty. Perhaps if critics did respond in this way we should be less inclined to think that so often their judgments are historical, biographical, economical, or sociological instead of aesthetic. For in a sense, of course, van Meegeren proved his point. Perhaps it is a point for which such radical proof was not even necessary. We all know very well that it is just the preponderance in the art world of nonaesthetic criteria such as fame of the artist and the age or cost of the canvas which is largely responsible for the existence of artistic forgeries in the first place. We all know that a few authentic pen and ink scratches by Picasso are far more valuable than a fine landscape by an unknown artist. If we were offered a choice between an inferior (but genuine) Degas sketch and a beautiful Jones or Smith or X, how many of us would choose the latter? In a museum that did not label its paintings, how many of us would not feel uneasy lest we condemn one of the greats or praise an unknown? But, it may be argued, all this we know. It is simply a fact and, moreover, probably an unavoidable, understandable – even a necessary – fact. Is this so serious or regrettable? The answer, of course, is that it is indeed serious and regrettable that the realm of art should be so infested with nonaesthetic standards of judgment that it is often impossible to distinguish artistic from economic value, taste or fashion from true artistic excellence, and good artists from clever businessmen.

This brings us to the point of our discussion so far. The matter of genuineness versus forgery is but another nonaesthetic standard of judgment. The fact that a work of art is a forgery is an item of information about it on a level with such information as the age of the artist when he created it, the political situation in the time and place of its creation, the price it originally fetched, the kind of materials used in it, the stylistic influences discernible in it, the psychological state of the artist, his purpose in painting it, and so on. All such information belongs to areas of interest peripheral at best to the work of art as aesthetic object, areas such as biography, history of art, sociology, and psychology. I do not deny that such areas of interest may be important and that their study may even help us to become better art appreciators. But I do deny that the information which they provide is of the essence of the work of art or of the aesthetic experience which it engenders.

It would be merely foolish to assert that it is of no interest whatsoever to know that *The Disciples* is a forgery. But to the man who has never heard of either Vermeer or van Meegeren and who stands in front of *The Disciples* admiring it, it can make no difference whether he is told that it is a seventeenth-century Vermeer, or a twentieth-century van Meegeren in the style of Vermeer. And when some deny this and argue vehemently that, indeed, it does make a great deal of difference, they are only admitting that *they* do know something about Vermeer and van Meegeren and the history of art and the value and reputation of certain masters. They are only admitting that *they* do not judge a work of art on purely aesthetic grounds but also take into account when it was created, by whom, and how great a reputation it or its creator has. And instead of seeking justification in the fact that in truth it is difficult to make a pure, aesthetic judgment, unbiased by all our knowledge of the history and criticism of art, they generally confuse matters of aesthetics even more by rationalizing that it is the complexity of the aesthetic experience which accounts for the difference made by the knowledge that a work of art is a forgery. That the aesthetic experience is complex I do not deny. But it is not so complex that such items of information as the place and date of creation or the name of the creator of a work of art have to be considered. The fact that *The Disciples* is a forgery is just that, a fact. It is a fact *about* the painting which stands entirely apart from it as an object for aesthetic contemplation. The knowledge of this fact can neither add anything to nor subtract anything from the aesthetic experience (as aesthetic), except insofar as preoccupation with it or disappointment on its account may in some degree prevent us from having an aesthetic experience at all. Whatever the reasons for the removal of *The Disciples* from the walls of the Boymans Museum in Rotterdam, they were assuredly not aesthetic.

And yet, we can all sympathize with, or at least understand, why *The Disciples* was removed. It was, after all, a forgery, and even if we grant that it is not a matter of aesthetics, it still seems self-evident that forgery remains a normative term implying a defect or absence in its object. In short, we still elect to answer our question: What is wrong with a forgery?

The most obvious answer to this question, after the aesthetic one, is that forgery is a moral or legal normative concept, and that it thus refers to an object which, if not necessarily aesthetically inferior, is always morally offensive. Specifically, the reason forgery is a moral offense, according to this view, is of course that it involves *deception*. Reasonable as this view seems at first, it does not, as I will try to show, answer our question adequately.

Now it cannot be denied, I think, that we do in fact often intend little more than this moral connotation when we speak of forgery. Just because forgery is a normative concept we implicitly condemn any instance of it because we generally assume that it involves the breaking of a legal or moral code. But this assumption is only sometimes correct. It is important to note this because historically by far the majority of artistic fakes or forgeries have not been legal forgeries. Most often they have been the result of simple mistakes, misunderstandings, and lack of information about given works of art. We can, as a point of terminology, exclude all such instances from the category of forgery and restrict the term to those cases involving deliberate deception. There is, after all, a whole class of forgeries, including simple copies, misattributions, composites, and works 'in the manner of' some reputable artist, which represent deliberate frauds. In these cases of forgery, which are undoubtedly the most notorious and disconcerting, someone, e.g., artist or art dealer, has passed off a work of art as being something which it is not. The motive for doing so is almost always economic, but occasionally, as with van Meegeren, there is involved also a psychological motive of personal prestige or revenge. In any case, it seems clear that – if we leave out of consideration the factor of financial loss, which can of course be considerable, as again the van Meegeren case proved – such deliberate forgeries are condemned by us on moral grounds, that is, because they involve conscious deception.

Yet as a final answer to our question as to what is wrong with a forgery, this definition fails. The reason is the following: Although to some extent it is true that passing *anything* off as *anything* that it is not constitutes deception and is thus an undesirable or morally repugnant act, the case of deception we have in mind when we define forgery in terms of it is that of passing off the inferior as the superior. Although, strictly speaking, passing off a genuine de Hoogh as a Vermeer is also an immoral act of deception, it is hard to think of it as a forgery at all, let alone a forgery in the same sense as passing off a van Meegeren as a Vermeer is. The reason is obviously that in the case of the de Hoogh a superior work is being passed off as a superior work (by another artist), while in the van Meegeren case a presumably inferior work is passed off as a superior work.

What is needed, then, to make our moral definition of forgery more accurate is the specification 'passing off the inferior as the superior.' But it is just at this point that this common-sense definition of artistic forgery in moral terms breaks down. For we are now faced with the question of what is meant by superior and inferior in art. The moral definition of forgery says in effect that a forgery is an inferior work passed off as a superior one. But what is meant here by inferior? We have already seen the forgery is not necessarily *aesthetically* inferior. What, then, does it mean? Once again, what is wrong with a forgery?

The attempt to define forgery in moral terms fails because it inevitably already assumes that there exists a difference between genuine works of art and forgeries which makes passing off the latter as the former an offense against a moral or legal law. For only if such a difference does in fact exist can there be any rationale for the law. It is, of course, precisely this assumed real difference which we are trying to discover in this chapter.

It seems to me that the offense felt to be involved in forgery is not so much against the spirit of beauty (aesthetics) or the spirit of the law (morality) as against the spirit of art. Somehow, a work such as *The Disciples* lacks artistic integrity. Even if it is beautiful and even if van Meegeren had not forged Vermeer's signature, there would still be something wrong with *The Disciples. What?* is still our question.

We may approach this problem by considering the following interesting point. The concept of forgery seems to be peculiarly inapplicable to the performing arts. It would be quite nonsensical to say, for example, that the man who played the Bach Suites for unaccompanied cello and whom at the time we took to be Pablo Casals was in fact a forger. Similarly, we should want to argue that the term *forgery* was misused if we should read in the newspaper that Margot Fonteyn's performance in *Swan Lake* last night was a forgery because as a matter of fact it was not Margot Fonteyn who danced last night, but rather some unknown person whom everyone mistook for Margot Fonteyn. Again, it is difficult to see in what sense a performance of, say *Oedipus Rex* or *Hamlet* could be termed a forgery.

Here, however, we must immediately clarify our point, for it is easily misunderstood. There is, of course, a sense in which a performance of

Hamlet or *Swan Lake* or the Bach suites could be called a forgery. If, for example, someone gave a performance of *Hamlet* in which every gesture, every movement, every vocal interpretation had been copied or imitated from the performance of *Hamlet* by Laurence Olivier, we could, I suppose, call the former a forgery of the latter. But notice that in that case we are interpreting the art of acting not as a performing art but as a creative art. For what is meant is that Olivier's interpretation and performance of *Hamlet* is itself an original and creative work of art which can be forged. Similar comments would apply to Margot Fonteyn's *Swan Lake* and Casals's Bach suites and, in fact, to every performance.

My point is, then, that the concept of forgery applies only to the creative and not to the performing arts. It can be denied, of course, that there is any such ultimate distinction between creative and performing arts. But we shall still have to admit, I think, that the duality on which it is based – the duality of creativity or originality on the one hand and reproduction or technique on the other – is real. We shall have to admit that originality and technique are two elements of all art; for it can be argued not only that a performance requires more than technique, namely originality, but also that the creation of a work of art requires more than originality, namely technique.

The truth of the matter is probably that both performances and works of art vary greatly and significantly in the degree to which they possess these elements. In fact, their relative presence in works of art and performances makes an interesting way of categorizing the latter. But it would be wrong to assert that these two elements are inseparable. I can assure the reader that a portrait painted by me would be technically almost totally incompetent, and yet even I would not deny that it might be original. On the other hand, a really skillful copy of, for example, a Rembrandt drawing may be technically perfect and yet lack all originality. These two examples establish the two extreme cases of a kind of continuum. The copy of Rembrandt is, of course, the forgery *par excellence.* My incompetent portrait is as far removed from being a forgery as any work can be. Somewhere in between lies the whole body of legitimate performances and works of art.

The implications of this long and devious argument are as follows: Forgery is a concept that can be made meaningful only by reference to the concept of originality, and hence only to art viewed as a *creative*, not as a reproductive or technical, activity. The element of performance or technique in art cannot be an object for forgery because technique is not the kind of thing that can be forged. Technique is, as it were, public. One does or does not possess it or one acquires it or learns it. One may even pretend to have it. But one cannot forge it because in order to forge it one must already possess it, in which case there is no need to forge it.

It is not Vermeer's technique in painting light which van Meegeren forged. That technique is public and may be had by anyone who is able and willing to learn it. It is rather Vermeer's discovery of this technique and his use of it, that is, Vermeer's originality, which is forged. The light, as well as the composition, the color, and many other features, of course, were original with Vermeer. They are not original with van Meegeren. They are forged.

At this point our argument could conclude were it not for the fact that the case which we have used throughout as our chief example, *Christ and the Disciples at Emmaus*, is not in fact a skillful copy of a Vermeer but a novel painting in the style of Vermeer. This threatens our definition of forgery since this particular forgery (always assuming it *is* a forgery) obviously possesses originality in some sense of the word.

The problem of forgery, in other words, is a good deal more complex than might at first be supposed, and before we can rest content with our definition of forgery as the lack of originality in works of art, we must show that the concept of originality can indeed account for the meaning of forgery as an untrue or objectionable thing in all instances, including even such a bizarre case as van Meegeren's *Disciples at Emmaus*. It thus becomes important to examine the various possible meanings that the term *originality* may have in the context of art in order to determine in what sense *The Disciples* does and does not possess it, and hence in what sense it can meaningfully and justifiably be termed a forgery.

1. A work of art may be said to be original in the sense of being a particular object not identical with any other object. But this originality is trivial since it is a quality possessed by all things. *Particularity* or *self-identity* would be better names for it.

2. By originality in a work of art we may mean that it possesses a certain superficial individuality which serves to distinguish it from other works of art. Thus, for example, a certain subject matter in a particular arrangement painted in certain colors may serve to identify a painting and mark it as an original work of art in the sense that its subject matter is unique. Probably the term *individuality* specifies this quality more adequately than *originality*.

It seems safe to assert that this quality of individuality is a necessary condition for any work of art to be called original in any significant sense. It is, however, not a necessary condition for a work to be called beautiful or to be the object of an aesthetic experience. A good reproduction or copy of a painting may be the object of aesthetic contemplation yet lack all originality in the sense which we are here considering. Historically many forgeries are of this kind, i.e., more or less skillful copies of existing works of art. They may be described as being forgeries just because they lack this kind of originality and hence any other kind of originality as well. Notice that the quality which makes such a copy a forgery, i.e., its lack of individuality, is not a quality which exists in the work of art as such. It is a fact about the work of art which can be known only by placing the latter in the context of the history of art and observing whether any identical work predates it.

As we said above, it is not this kind of originality which is lacking in *The Disciples*.[3]

3. By originality in art we may mean the kind of imaginative novelty or spontaneity which is a mark of every good work of art. It is the kind of originality which attaches to individual works of art and which can be specified in formal or technical terms such as composition, balance, color intensity, perspective, harmony, rhythm, tempo, texture, rhyme, alliteration, suspense, character, plot, structure, choice of subject matter, and so on. Here again, however, in order for this quality to be meaningfully called originality, a reference must be made to a historical context in terms of which we are considering the particular work of art in question, e.g., this work of art is original because the artist has done something with the subject and its treatment which has never been done before, or this work is not original because many others just like it predate it.

In any case, *The Disciples* does, by common consent, possess this kind of originality and is therefore, in this sense at least, not a forgery.

4. The term *originality* is sometimes used to refer to the great artistic achievement of a specific work of art. Thus we might say that whereas nearly all of Milton's works are good and original in the sense of (3) above, *Paradise Lost* has a particularly profound originality possessed only by really superlative works of art. It is hard to state precisely what is meant by this use of the term *originality*. In justifying it we should probably point to the scope, profundity, daring, and novelty of the conception of the work of art in question as well as to the excellence of its execution. No doubt this kind of originality differs from that discussed under (3) above only in degree.

It is to be noted that it cannot be the lack of this kind of originality which defines a forgery since, almost by definition, it is a quality lacking in many – maybe the majority of legitimate works of art. Moreover, judging from the critical commentary with which *The Disciples* was received at the time of its discovery – commentary unbiased by the knowledge that it was a forgery – it seems reasonable to infer that the kind of originality meant here is in fact one which *The Disciples* very likely possesses.

5. Finally, it would seem that by originality in art we can and often do mean the artistic novelty and achievement not of one particular work of

art but of the totality of artistic productions of one man or even one school. Thus we may speak of the originality of Vermeer or El Greco or Mozart or Dante or Impressionism or the Metaphysical Poets or even the Greeks or the Renaissance, always referring, I presume, to the artistic accomplishments achieved and embodied in the works of art belonging to the particular man, movement, or period. In the case of Vermeer we may speak of the originality of the artist's sense of design in the genre picture, the originality of his use of bright and pure colors, and of the originality of his treatment and execution of light.

We must note first of all that this meaning of originality, too, depends entirely on a historical context in which we are placing and considering the accomplishment of one man or one period. It would be meaningless to call Impressionism original, in the sense here considered, except in reference to the history of art which preceded it. Again, it is just because Vermeer's sense of pictorial design, his use of bright colors, and his mastery of the technique of painting light are not found in the history of art before him that we call these things original in Vermeer's work. Originality, even in this more profound sense, or rather especially in this more profound sense, is a quality definable only in terms of the history of art.

A second point of importance is that while originality as here considered is a quality which attaches to a whole corpus or style of works of art, it can be considered to exist in one particular work of art in the sense that that work of art is a typical example of the style or movement to which it belongs and therefore embodies the originality of that style or movement. Thus we may say that Vermeer's *A Painter in his Studio* is original because in this painting (as well as in several others, of course) we recognize those characteristics mentioned earlier (light, design, color, etc.) which are so typical of Vermeer's work as a whole and which, when we consider the whole of Vermeer's work in the context of the history of art, allow us to ascribe originality to it.

Turning our attention once more to *The Disciples*, we are at last in a position to provide an adequate answer to our question as to the meaning of the term forgery when applied to a work of art such as *The Disciples*. We shall find, I think, that the fraudulent character of this painting is adequately defined by stating that it lacks originality in the fifth and final sense which we have here considered. Whatever kinds of originality it can claim – and we have seen that it possesses all the kinds previously discussed – it is *not* original in the sense of being the product of a style, period, or technique which, when considered in its appropriate historical context, can be said to represent a significant achievement. It is just this fact which differentiates this painting from a genuine Vermeer! The latter, when considered in its historical context, i.e., the seventeenth century, possesses the qualities of artistic or creative novelty which justify us in calling it original. *The Disciples*, on the other hand, in *its* historical context, i.e., the twentieth century, is not original, since it presents nothing new or creative to the history of art even though, as we have emphasized earlier, it may well be as beautiful as the genuine Vermeer pictures.

It is to be noted that in this definition of forgery the phrase 'appropriate historical context' refers to the date of production of the particular work of art in question, not the date which in the history of art is appropriate to its style or subject matter.[4] In other words, what makes *The Disciples* a forgery is precisely the disparity or gap between its stylistically appropriate features and its actual date of production. It is simply this disparity which we have in mind when we say that forgeries such as *The Disciples* lack integrity.

It is interesting at this point to recall van Meegeren's reasoning in perpetrating the Vermeer forgeries. 'Either,' he reasoned, 'the critics must admit their fallibility or else acknowledge that I am as great an artist as Vermeer.' We can see now that this reasoning is not sound. For the notion of greatness involved in it depends on the same concept of historical originality which we have been considering. The only difference is that we are now thinking of it as an attribute of the artist rather than of the works of art. Van Meegeren's mistake was in thinking that Vermeer's reputation as a great artist depended on his ability to paint beautiful pictures. If this were so, the dilemma which van Meegeren posed to the critics would have been a real one, for his picture is undeniably beautiful. But, in fact, Vermeer is *not* a great artist only because he could paint beautiful pictures. He is great for that reason plus something else. And that something else is precisely the fact of his originality, i.e., the fact that he painted certain pictures in a certain manner *at a certain time in history and development of art*. Vermeer's art represents a genuine creative achievement in the history of art. It is the work not merely of a master craftsman or technician but of a creative genius as well. And it is for the latter rather than for the former reason that we call Vermeer great.

Van Meegeren, on the other hand, possessed only craftsmanship or technique. His works lack the historical originality of Vermeer's and it is for this reason that we should not want to call him great as we call Vermeer great.[5] At the same time it must be recalled that van Meegeren's forgeries are not forgeries *par excellence*. *The Disciples*, though not original in the most important sense, possesses, as we have seen, degrees of originality generally lacking in forgeries.

In this connection it is interesting to speculate on the relations between originality and technique in the creative continuum which we came upon earlier. A totally original work is one which lacks all technique. A forgery *par excellence* represents the perfection of technique with the absence of all originality. True works of art are somewhere in between.

Perhaps the really great works of art, such as Vermeer's, are those which embody a maximum of both originality and technique: van Meegeren's forgeries can never be in this last category, for, as we have seen, they lack the most important kind of originality.

Finally, the only question that remains is why originality is such a significant aspect of art. Now we need to note, of course, that the concern with originality is not a universal characteristic of art or artists. Yet the fact that the search for originality is perhaps typical only of modern Western art tends to strengthen the presumption of its fundamental relation to the concept of forgery. For it is also just in the modern Western tradition that the problem of forgery has taken on the kind of economic and aesthetic significance which warrants our concern with it here. But why, even in modern Western art, should the importance of originality be such that the concepts of greatness and forgery in art are ultimately definable only by reference to it? The answer is, I believe, not hard to find. It rests on the fact that art has and must have a history. If it did not, if artists were concerned only with making beautiful pictures, poems, symphonies, etc., the possibilities for the creation of aesthetically pleasing works of art would soon be exhausted. We would (perhaps) have a number of lovely paintings, but we should soon grow tired of them, for they would all be more or less alike. But artists do not seek merely to produce works of beauty. They seek to produce *original* works of beauty. And when they succeed in achieving this originality we call their works great not only because they are beautiful but because they have also unlocked, both to artists and to appreciators, unknown and unexplored realms of beauty. Men like Leonardo, Rembrandt, Haydn, Goethe, and Vermeer are great not merely because of the excellence of their works, but also because of their creative originality which goes on to inspire other artists and leads through them to new and aesthetically valuable developments in the history of art. It is, in fact, this search for creative originality which insures the continuation and significance of such a history in the first place

It is for this reason that the concept of originality has become inseparable from that of art. It is for this reason too that aesthetics has traditionally concerned itself with topics such as the inspiration of the artist, the mystery of the creative act, the intense and impassioned search of the artist, the artist as the prophet of his times, the artistic struggle after expression, art as the chronicle of the emotional life of a period in history, art as a product of its time, and so on. All such topics are relevant not to art as the production of works of beauty but to art as the production of *original* works of beauty, or, more accurately, works of original beauty. As such they are perfectly legitimate topics of discussion. But we must not forget that the search for originality is, or ought to be, but the means to an end. That end is, presumably, the production of aesthetically valuable or beautiful works of art; that is, works which are to become the object of an aesthetic experience. That experience is a wholly autonomous one. It does not and cannot take account of any entity or fact which is not aesthetically perceivable in the work of art itself. The historical context in which that work of art stands is just such a fact. It is wholly irrelevant to the pure aesthetic appreciation and judgment of the work of art. And because the fact of forgery – together with originality and greatness – can be ultimately defined only in terms of this historical context, it too is irrelevant to the aesthetic appreciation and judgment of *The Disciples at Emmaus* or any other work of art. The fact of forgery is important historically, biographically, perhaps legally, or, as the van Meegeren case proved, financially; but not, strictly speaking, aesthetically.

In conclusion, let us consider the following paradoxical result. We have seen in what sense Vermeer is considered to be a great artist. We have also seen that although *The Disciples* is indistinguishable from a genuine Vermeer, van Meegeren cannot be thus called great. And yet we would suppose that Vermeer's greatness is somehow embodied in his work, that his paintings are proof of and monuments to his artistic genius. What are we to say, then, of this van Meegeren forgery which hung in a museum for seven years as an embodiment and proof of Vermeer's genius? Are we to say that it now no longer embodies anything at all except van Meegeren's skillful forging technique? Or are we to grant after all that this painting proves van Meegeren's greatness as Vermeer's paintings do his? The answer is, I think, surprising but wholly appropriate. Paradoxically, *The Disciples at Emmaus* is as much a monument to the artistic genius of Vermeer as are Vermeer's own paintings. Even though it was painted by van Meegeren in the twentieth century, it embodies and bears witness to the greatness of the seventeenth-century art of Vermeer.

Notes

1. Cf. Arthur Koestler, 'The anatomy of snobbery,' *The Anchor Review* 1 (Garden City, NY: Doubleday Anchor Books, 1955), pp. 1–25.
2. J. Decoen, *Vermeer–Van Meegeren Back to the Truth*, trans. E.J. Labarre (London: Donker, 1951), p. 60.
3. A slightly more complex case is offered by forgeries (including probably some of van Meegeren's less carefully executed Vermeer forgeries) which are not simple copies of other paintings but which are composites of other paintings. While such forgeries clearly have a measure of individuality totally lacking in the simple copy, I should want to maintain that they lack only superficially the kind of originality here discussed.
4. To avoid all ambiguity in my definition of forgery, I need to specify whether 'actual date of production' refers to the completion of the finished, concrete work of art or only to the productive means of such works. This question bears on the legitimacy of certain works in art forms where the means of

production and the finished product are separable. Such works include lithographs, etchings, woodcuts, cast sculptures, etc. What, for example, are we to say of a modern bronze cast made from a mold taken directly from an ancient bronze cast or a modern print made from an eighteenth-century block? Are such art objects forgeries? The answer, it seems to me, is largely a matter of convenience and terminology. Assuming that there is no moral fraud, i.e., deception, involved, whether or not to call such cases instances of forgery becomes an academic question. It depends entirely on what we take to be 'the work of art.' In the case of lithography or etching there may be some ambiguity about this. I myself would define 'the work of art' as the finished concrete product and hence I would indeed call modern prints from old litho stones forgeries, though, assuming no deception is involved, forgeries of a peculiarly amoral, nonoffensive sort. In other arts, such as music, there is little or no ambiguity on this point. Clearly, no one would want to label the first performance of a newly discovered Beethoven symphony a forgery. In still other, e.g., the literary, arts, due to the absolute inseparability of the concrete work of art and the means of its production, this problem cannot arise at all.

5. Unless it be argued that van Meegeren derives *his* greatness from the originality of his works when considered in the context not of the history of art but of the history of forgery!

44

Pierre Menard, author of
the Quixote
Jorge Luis Borges

Can indistinguishable works of art have different aesthetic qualities? In this brilliant short story the Argentinian writer Jorge Luis Borges (1899–1986) investigates this question.

From Jorge Luis Borges, *Labyrinths*

The *visible* work left by this novelist is easily and briefly enumerated. Impardonable, therefore, are the omissions and additions perpetrated by Madame Henri Bachelier in a fallacious catalogue which a certain daily, whose *Protestant* tendency is no secret, has had the inconsideration to inflict upon its deplorable readers – though these be few and Calvinist, if not Masonic and circumcized. The true friends of Menard have viewed this catalogue with alarm and even with a certain melancholy. One might say that only yesterday we gathered before his final monument, amidst the lugubrious cypresses, and already Error tries to tarnish his Memory. . . . Decidedly, a brief rectification is unavoidable.

I am aware that it is quite easy to challenge my slight authority. I hope, however, that I shall not be prohibited from mentioning two eminent testimonies. The Baroness de Bacourt (at whose unforgettable *vendredis* I had the honour of meeting the lamented poet) has seen fit to approve the pages which follow. The Countess de Bagnoregio, one of the most delicate spirits of the Principality of Monaco (and now of Pittsburgh, Pennsylvania, following her recent marriage to the international philanthropist Simon Kautzsch, who has been so inconsiderately slandered, alas! by the victims of his disinterested manoeuvres) has sacrificed 'to veracity and to death' (such were her words) the stately reserve which is her distinction, and, in an open letter published in the magazine *Luxe*, concedes me her approval as well. These authorizations, I think, are not entirely insufficient.

I have said that Menard's visible work can be easily enumerated. Having examined with care his personal files, I find that they contain the following items:

(a)   A Symbolist sonnet which appeared twice (with variants) in the review *La conque* (issues of March and October 1899).

(b)   A monograph on the possibility of constructing a poetic vocabulary of concepts which would not be synonyms or periphrases of those which make up our everyday language, 'but rather ideal objects created according to convention and essentially designed to satisfy poetic needs' (Nîmes, 1901).

(c)   A monograph on 'certain connexions or affinities' between the thought of Descartes, Leibniz and John Wilkins (Nîmes, 1903).

(d)   A monograph on Leibniz's *Characteristica universalis* (Nîmes, 1904).

(e)   A technical article on the possibility of improving the game of chess, eliminating one of the rook's pawns. Menard proposes, recommends, discusses and finally rejects this innovation.

(f)   A monograph on Raymond Lully's *Ars magna generalis* (Nîmes, 1906).

(g)   A translation, with prologue and notes, of Ruy López de Segura's *Libro de la invención liberal y arte del juego del axedrez* (Paris, 1907).

(h)   The work sheets of a monograph on George Boole's symbolic logic.

(i)   An examination of the essential metric laws of French prose, illustrated with examples taken from Saint-Simon *(Revue des langues romanes*, Montpellier, October 1909).

(j)   A reply to Luc Durtain (who had denied the existence of such laws), illustrated with examples from Luc Durtain *(Revue des langues romanes*, Montpellier, December 1909).

(k)   A manuscript translation of the *Aguia de navegar cultos* of Quevedo, entitled *La Boussole des précieux*.

(l)   A preface to the Catalogue of an exposition of lithographs by Carolus Hourcade (Nîmes, 1914).

(m)   The work *Les problèmes d'un problème* (Paris, 1917), which discusses, in chronological order, the different solutions given to the illustrious problem of Achilles and the tortoise. Two editions of this book have appeared so far; the second bears as an epigraph Leibniz's recommendation *'Ne craignez point, monsieur, la tortue'* and revises the chapters dedicated to Russell and Descartes.

(n)   A determined analysis of the 'syntactical customs' of Toulet (*N. R. F.*, March 1921). Menard – I recall – declared that censure and praise are sentimental operations which have nothing to do with literary criticism.

(o) A transposition into alexandrines of Paul Valéry's *Le cimetière marin* (*N. R. F.*, January 1928).

(p) An invective against Paul Valéry, in the *Papers for the Suppression of Reality* of Jacques Reboul. (This invective, we might say parenthetically, is the exact opposite of his true opinion of Valéry. The latter understood it as such and their old friendship was not endangered.)

(q) A 'definition' of the Countess de Bagnoregio, in the 'victorious volume' – the locution is Gabriele d'Annunzio's, another of its collaborators – published annually by this lady to rectify the inevitable falsifications of journalists and to present 'to the world and to Italy' an authentic image of her person, so often exposed (by very reason of her beauty and her activities) to erroneous or hasty interpretations.

(r) A cycle of admirable sonnets for the Baroness de Bacourt (1934).

(s) A manuscript list of verses which owe their efficacy to their punctuation.[1]

This, then, is the *visible* work of Menard, in chronological order (with no omission other than a few vague sonnets of circumstance written for the hospitable, or avid, album of Madame Henri Bachelier). I turn now to his other work: the subterranean, the interminably heroic, the peerless. And – such are the capacities of man! – the unfinished. This work, perhaps the most significant of our time, consists of the ninth and thirty-eighth chapters of the first part of *Don Quixote* and a fragment of chapter twenty-two. I know such an affirmation seems an absurdity; to justify this 'absurdity' is the primordial object of this note.[2]

Two texts of unequal value inspired this undertaking. One is that philological fragment by Novalis – the one numbered 2005 in the Dresden edition – which outlines the theme of a *total* identification with a given author. The other is one of those parasitic books which situate Christ on a boulevard, Hamlet on La Cannebière or Don Quixote on Wall Street. Like all men of good taste, Menard abhorred these useless carnivals, fit only – as he would say – to produce the plebeian pleasure of anachronism or (what is worse) to enthral us with the elementary idea that all epochs are the same or are different. More interesting, though contradictory and superficial of execution, seemed to him the famous plan of Daudet: to conjoin the Ingenious Gentleman and his squire in *one* figure, which was Tartarin. . . . Those who have insinuated that Menard dedicated his life to writing a contemporary *Quixote* calumniate his illustrious memory.

He did not want to compose another *Quixote* – which is easy – but *the Quixote itself*. Needless to say, he never contemplated a mechanical transcription of the original; he did not propose to copy it. His admirable intention was to produce a few pages which would coincide – word for word and line for line – with those of Miguel de Cervantes.

'My intent is no more than astonishing,' he wrote me the 30 September 1934, from Bayonne. 'The final term in a theological or meta-physical demonstration – the objective world, God, causality, the forms of the universe – is no less previous and common than my famed novel. The only difference is that the philosophers publish the intermediary stages of their labour in pleasant volumes and I have resolved to do away with those stages.' In truth, not one worksheet remains to bear witness to his years of effort.

The first method he conceived was relatively simple. Know Spanish well, recover the Catholic faith, fight against the Moors or the Turk, forget the history of Europe between the years 1602 and 1918, *be* Miguel de Cervantes. Pierre Menard studied this procedure (I know he attained a fairly accurate command of seventeenth-century Spanish) but discarded it as too easy. Rather as impossible! my reader will say. Granted, but the undertaking was impossible from the very beginning and of all the impos-sible ways of carrying it out, this was the least interesting. To be, in the twentieth century, a popular novelist of the seventeenth seemed to him a diminution. To be, in some way, Cervantes and reach the *Quixote* seemed less arduous to him – and, consequently, less interesting – than to go on being Pierre Menard and reach the *Quixote* through the experiences of Pierre Menard. (This conviction, we might say in passing, made him omit the autobiographical prologue to the second part of *Don Quixote*. To include that prologue would have been to create another character – Cervantes – but it would also have meant presenting the *Quixote* in terms of that character and not of Menard. The latter, naturally, declined that facility.) 'My undertaking is not difficult, essentially,' I read in another part of his letter. 'I should only have to be immortal to carry it out.' Shall I confess that I often imagine he did finish it and that I read the *Quixote* – all of it – as if Menard had conceived it? Some nights past, while leafing through chapter XXVI – never essayed by him – I recognized our friend's style and something of his voice in this exceptional phrase: 'the river nymphs and the dolorous and humid Echo.' This happy conjunction of a spiritual and a physical adjective brought to my mind a verse by Shakespeare which we discussed one afternoon:

Where a malignant and a turbaned Turk . . .

But why precisely the *Quixote*? our reader will ask. Such a prefer-ence, in a Spaniard, would not have been inexplicable; but it is, no doubt, in a Symbolist from Nîmes, essentially a devoté of Poe, who engendered Baudelaire, who engendered Mallarmé, who engendered Valéry, who engendered Edmond Teste. The aforementioned letter illuminates this point. 'The *Quixote*,' clarifies Menard, 'interests me deeply, but it does not seem – how shall I say it? – inevitable. I cannot imagine the universe without Edgar Allan Poe's exclamation:

Ah, bear in mind this garden was enchanted!

or without the *Bateau ivre* or the *Ancient Mariner*, but I am quite capable of imagining it without the *Quixote*. (I speak, naturally, of my personal capacity and not of those works' historical resonance.) The *Quixote* is a contingent book; the *Quixote* is unnecessary. I can premeditate writing it, I can write it, without falling into a tautology. When I was ten or twelve years old, I read it, perhaps in its entirety. Later, I have reread closely certain chapters, those which I shall not attempt for the time being. I have also gone through the interludes, the plays, the *Galatea*, the exemplary novels, the undoubtedly laborious tribulations of Persiles and Segismunda and the *Viaje del Parnaso* . . . My general recollection of the *Quixote*, simplified by forgetfulness and indifference, can well equal the imprecise and prior image of a book not yet written. Once that image (which no one can legitimately deny me) is postulated, it is certain that my problem is a good bit more difficult than Cervantes' was. My obliging predecessor did not refuse the collaboration of chance: he composed his immortal work somewhat *à la diable*, carried along by the inertias of language and invention. I have taken on the mysterious duty of reconstructing literally his spontaneous work. My solitary game is governed by two polar laws. The first permits me to essay variations of a formal or psychological type; the second obliges me to sacrifice these variations to the "original" text and reason out this annihilation in an irrefutable manner. . . . To these artificial hindrances, another – of a congenital kind – must be added. To compose the *Quixote* at the beginning of the seventeenth century was a reasonable undertaking, necessary and perhaps even unavoidable; at the beginning of the twentieth, it is almost impossible. It is not in vain that three hundred years have gone by, filled with exceedingly complex events. Among them, to mention only one, is the *Quixote* itself.'

In spite of these three obstacles, Menard's fragmentary *Quixote* is more subtle than Cervantes'. The latter, in a clumsy fashion, opposes to the fictions of chivalry the tawdry provincial reality of his country; Menard selects as his 'reality' the land of Carmen during the century of Lepanto and Lope de Vega. What a series of *espagnolades* that selection would have suggested to Maurice Barrès or Dr Rodríguez Larreta! Menard eludes them with complete naturalness. In his work there are no gipsy flourishes or conquistadors or mystics or Philip the Seconds or *autos da fé*. He neglects or eliminates local colour. This disdain points to a new conception of the historical novel. This disdain condemns *Salammbô*, with no possibility of appeal.

It is no less astounding to consider isolated chapters. For example, let us examine Chapter XXXVIII of the first part, 'which treats of the curious discourse of Don Quixote on arms and letters'. It is well known that Don Quixote (like Quevedo in an analogous and later passage in *La hora de todos*) decided the debate against letters and in favour of arms. Cervantes was a former soldier: his verdict is understandable. But that Pierre Menard's Don Quixote – a contemporary of *La trahison des clercs* and Bertrand Russell – should fall prey to such nebulous sophistries! Madame Bachelier has seen here an admirable and typical subordination on the part of the author to the hero's psychology; others (not at all perspicaciously), a *transcription* of the *Quixote*; the Baroness de Bacourt, the influence of Nietzsche. To this third interpretation (which I judge to be irrefutable) I am not sure I dare to add a fourth, which concords very well with the almost divine modesty of Pierre Menard: his resigned or ironical habit of propagating ideas which were the strict reverse of those he preferred. (Let us recall once more his diatribe against Paul Valéry in Jacques Reboul's ephemeral Surrealist sheet.) Cervantes's text and Menard's are verbally identical, but the second is almost infinitely richer. (More ambiguous, his detractors will say, but ambiguity is richness.)

It is a revelation to compare Menard's *Don Quixote* with Cervantes's. The latter, for example, wrote (part one, chapter nine):

> . . . truth, whose mother is history, rival of time, depository of deeds, witness of the past, exemplar and adviser to the present, and the future's counsellor.

Written in the seventeenth century, written by the 'lay genius' Cervantes, this enumeration is a mere rhetorical praise of history. Menard, on the other, writes:

> . . . truth, whose mother is history, rival of time, depository of deeds, witness of the past, exemplar and adviser to the present, and the future's counsellor.

History, the *mother* of truth: the idea is astounding. Menard, a contemporary of William James, does not define history as an inquiry into reality but as its origin. Historical truth, for him, is not what has happened; it is what we judge to have happened. The final phrases – *exemplar and adviser to the present, and the future's counsellor* – are brazenly pragmatic.

The contrast in style is also vivid. The archaic style of Menard – quite foreign, after all – suffers from a certain affectation. Not so that of his forerunner, who handles with ease the current Spanish of his time.

There is no exercise of the intellect which is not, in the final analysis, useless. A philosophical doctrine begins as a plausible description of the universe; with the passage of the years it becomes a mere chapter – if not a paragraph or a name – in the history of philosophy. In literature, this eventual caducity is even more notorious. The *Quixote* – Menard told me – was, above all, an entertaining book; now it is the occasion for patriotic toasts, grammatical insolence and obscene de luxe editions. Fame is a form of incomprehension, perhaps the worst.

There is nothing new in these nihilistic verifications; what is singular is the determination Menard derived from them. He decided to anticipate the vanity awaiting all man's efforts; he set himself to an undertaking which was exceedingly complex and, from the very beginning, futile. He dedicated his scruples and his sleepless nights to repeating an already extant book in an alien tongue. He multiplied draft upon draft, revised tenaciously and tore up thousands of manuscript pages.[3] He did not let anyone examine these drafts and took care they should not survive him. In vain have I tried to reconstruct them.

I have reflected that it is permissible to see in this 'final' *Quixote* a kind of palimpsest, through which the traces – tenuous but not indecipherable – of our friend's 'previous' writing should be translucently visible. Unfortunately, only a second Pierre Menard, inverting the other's work, would be able to exhume and revive those lost Troys . . .

'Thinking, analysing, inventing (he also wrote me) are not anomalous acts; they are the normal respiration of the intelligence. To glorify the occasional performance of that function, to hoard ancient and alien thoughts, to recall with incredulous stupor what the *doctor universalis* thought, is to confess our laziness or our barbarity. Every man should be capable of all ideas and I understand that in the future this will be the case.'

Menard (perhaps without wanting to) has enriched, by means of a new technique, the halting and rudimentary art of reading: this new technique is that of the deliberate anachronism and the erroneous attribution. This technique, whose applications are infinite, prompts us to go through the *Odyssey* as if it were posterior to the *Aeneid* and the book *Le jardin du Centaure* of Madame Henri Bachelier as if it were by Madame Henri Bachelier. This technique fills the most placid works with adventure. To attribute the *Imitatio Christi* to Louis Ferdinand Céline or to James Joyce, is this not a sufficient renovation of its tenuous spiritual indications?

1   Madame Henri Bachelier also lists a literal translation of Quevedo's literal translation of the *introduction à la vie dévote* of St Francis of Sales. There are no traces of such a work in Menard's library. It must have been a jest of our friend, misunderstood by the lady.

2   I also had the secondary intention of sketching a personal portrait of Pierre Menard. But how could I dare to compete with the golden pages which, I am told, the Baroness de Bacourt is preparing or with the delicate and punctual pencil of Carolus Hourcade?

3   I remember his quadricular notebooks, his black crossed-out passages, his peculiar typographical symbols and his insect-like handwriting. In the afternoons he liked to go out for a walk around the outskirts of Nîmes; he would take a notebook with him and make a merry bonfire.

Appendix 1: suggestions for further reading

I have deliberately kept this list of further reading very brief. I have only included books that I believe to be genuinely useful for someone coming to philosophy for the first time.

What is philosophy?

Most general introductions to Philosophy address the question 'What is Philosophy?' – either directly or indirectly. *Philosophy: Basic Readings* is designed to complement my own book, *Philosophy: The Basics* (London: Routledge, 3rd edn, 1999). Although there is not a complete overlap between the two books, they follow a similar section structure. They are both topic-based in approach. For a text-based approach, see my *Philosophy: The Classics* (London: Routledge, 1998); this provides a critical introduction to twenty key works in the history of philosophy, from Plato's *Republic* to Wittgenstein's *Philosophical Investigations.*

For an introduction to critical thinking – the basic method of philosophy – see my *Thinking from A to Z* (London: Routledge, 1996). On any particular topic in philosophy, the *Routledge Encyclopedia of Philosophy*, edited by Edward Craig (London: Routledge, 1998), is an excellent place to start.

God

There are several good introductions to the philosophy of religion available. From a sceptical angle, J. L. Mackie, *The Miracle of Theism* (Oxford: Clarendon Press, 1982) and Robin Le Poidevin, *Arguing for Atheism* (London: Routledge 1996) are both excellent. Brian Davies, *An Introduction to the Philosophy of Religion* (Oxford: Oxford University Press, 2nd edn, 1993) surveys the main arguments in this area from a Christian perspective.

Right and wrong

Richard Norman, *The Moral Philosophers* (Oxford: Clarendon Press, 2nd edn, 1997) provides a clear introduction to the major thinkers in this area. Jonathan Glover, *Causing Death and Saving Lives* (Harmondsworth: Penguin Books, 1977) is an interesting investigation of a number of issues in applied ethics. Peter Singer (ed.), *A Companion to Ethics* (Oxford: Blackwell Publishers, 1991) is a very useful collection of articles on a wide range of topics.

Politics

Jonathan Wolff, *An Introduction to Political Philosophy* (Oxford: Oxford University Press, 1996) is the best available introduction to political philosophy. Quentin Skinner, Richard Tuck, William Thomas and Peter Singer, *Great Political Thinkers* (Oxford: Oxford University Press, 1992) provides a good introduction to the work of Machiavelli, Hobbes, Mill and Marx – some of the most important political philosophers of all time.

The external world

Adam Morton, *A Guide through the Theory of Knowledge* (Oxford: Blackwell Publishers, 2nd edn, 1997) is highly recommended.

Science

A. F. Chalmers, *What Is This Thing Called Science?* (Milton Keynes: Open University Press, 1978) is a very clear introduction, C. G. Hempel, *Philosophy of Natural Science* (Englewood Cliffs, NJ: Prentice Hall, 1966) is also recommended.

Mind

Peter Smith and O. R. Jones, *The Philosophy of Mind* (Cambridge:

Cambridge University Press, 1986) provides a clear introduction. Stephen Priest, *Theories of Mind* (Harmondsworth: Penguin Books, 1991) is a critical survey of the major approaches to the philosophy of mind.

Art

Anne Sheppard, *Aesthetics: An Introduction to the Philosophy of Art* (Oxford: Oxford University Press, 1987) and Gordon Graham, *Philosophy of the Arts* (London: Routledge, 1997) are both good general introductions to the philosophical questions which arise from considering works of art. Alex Neill and Aaron Ridley (eds), *Arguing about Art* (New York: McGraw-Hill, 1995) is an excellent anthology.

Appendix 2: acknowledgements and sources

I would like to thank Caroline Dawnay, Adrian Driscoll, Oswald Hanfling, Alex Orenstein, Miriam Selwyn, and several publisher's readers for the help they gave me in selecting, organising and editing these readings.

The readings in this book were taken from the following sources:

Mary Warnock, 'What makes someone a philosopher?', taken from *Women Philosophers*, Everyman, 1996, pp. xxix–xxx. Reprinted by permission of the Orion Publishing Group Ltd.

D. H. Mellor, 'Analytic philosophy', taken from *Matters of Metaphysics*, 1991, pp. 1–4. Reprinted by permission of Cambridge University Press and the author.

A. J. Ayer, 'The method of philosophy', taken from *The Problem of Knowledge*, 1956, pp. 7–9. Reprinted by permission of Penguin Books.

Bertrand Russell, 'The value of philosophy', taken from *The Problems of Philosophy*, 1912, pp. 89–94. Reprinted by permission of Oxford University Press.

Blaise Pascal, 'The wager', taken from *Pensées*, translated and with an introduction by A. J. Krailsheimer, 1966, pp. 150–153. Reprinted by permission of Penguin Books.

Martin Gardner, 'Proofs of God', taken from *The Night is Large*, Penguin, 1996, pp. 533–547. Originally published in *Whys of a Philosophical Scrivener*. Reprinted by permission of St Martin's Press/Martin Gardner, Woods End, Inc.

J. L. Mackie, 'Evil and omnipotence', taken from Basil Mitchell (ed.), *The Philosophy of Religion*, 1971, pp. 92–104. Originally published in *Mind*, vol. 64, 1965. Reprinted by permission of Oxford University Press.

Richard Swinburne, 'Why God allows evil', taken from *Is There a God?*, 1996, pp. 95–113. Reprinted by permission of Oxford University Press.

David Hume, 'Of miracles', taken from *Enquiries Concerning Human Understanding and Concerning the Principles of Morals*, 1975, pp. 17–22, 110–131. Reprinted by permission of Oxford University Press.

Richard Dawkins, 'Viruses of the mind', taken from Bo Dahlbom (ed.), *Dennett and His Critics: Demystifying mind*, 1993, pp. 13–27. Reprinted by kind permission of Blackwell Publishers.

Immanuel Kant, 'The Categorical Imperative', taken from *The Moral Law*, translated and analysed by H. J. Paton, 1948, pp. 67–68. Reprinted by permission of Routledge and HarperCollins Publishers.

Robert Nozick, 'The experience machine', taken from *Anarchy, State and Utopia*, 1978, pp. 42–45. Reprinted by kind permission of Blackwell Publishers.

Bernard Williams, 'A critique of utilitarianism', taken from J. J. C. Smart and Bernard Williams (eds), *Utilitarianism: For and against*, 1963, pp. 96–118. Reprinted by permission of Cambridge University Press and Professor Bernard Williams.

Jonathan Glover, 'The Solzhenitsyn principle', taken from 'It makes no difference whether or not I do it', in P. Singer (ed.), *Applied Ethics*, Oxford University Press, 1986, pp. 138–142. Originally published in *Proceedings of the Aristotelian Society*, suppl. vol. XLIX, 1975. Reprinted by permission of The Aristotelian Society.

Rosalind Hursthouse, 'Neo-Aristotelianism', taken from *Beginning Lives*, 1987, pp. 220, 221–237. Reprinted by kind permission of Blackwell Publishers.

Judith Jarvis Thompson, 'A defence of abortion', taken from P. Singer (ed.), *Applied Ethics*, Oxford University Press, 1986, pp. 37–56. Originally published in *Philosophy and Public Affairs*, vol. 1, no. 1. Reprinted by permission of Princeton University Press.

Thomas Nagel, 'Moral luck', taken from *Mortal Questions*, 1979, pp. 24–38. Reprinted by permission of Cambridge University Press and the author. Originally published in *Proceedings of the Aristotelian Society*, suppl. vol. L, 1976.

Bernard Williams, 'Relativism', taken from Bernard Williams, *Morality: An introduction to ethics*, 1972, pp. 34–39. Reprinted by permission of Cambridge University Press and the author.

Thomas Hobbes, 'Of the natural condition of mankind', taken from *Leviathan*, edited with an introduction by J. C. A. Gaskin, 1996, pp. 82–86. Reprinted by permission of Oxford University Press.

Isaiah Berlin, 'Two concepts of liberty', taken from *Four Essays on Liberty*, 1968. Reprinted by permission of Oxford University Press.

Nigel Warburton, 'Freedom to box', taken from *Journal of Medical Ethics*, 1998, vol. 24, pp. 56–60. Reprinted by permission from the BMJ Publishing Group.

Janet Radcliffe Richards, 'Discrimination and sexual justice', taken from *The Sceptical Feminist: A philosophical inquiry*, Penguin, 1982, pp. 127–143. Copyright © Janet Radcliffe Richards.

Martin Luther King Jr, 'Letter from Birmingham City Jail', taken from Hugo Adam Bedau (ed.), *Civil Disobedience in Focus*, Routledge, 1991, pp. 68–76. Originally published in *Why We Can't Wait*, Harper & Row, 1963. Reprinted by permission of HarperCollins.

Peter Singer, 'All animals are equal', taken from P. Singer (ed.), *Applied Ethics*, Oxford University Press, 1986, pp. 215–228. Reprinted by permission of The New York Review of Books, NYREV Inc., 5 April 1973.

René Descartes, 'About the things we may doubt', taken from *Discourse on Method and the Meditations*, translated with an introduction by F. E. Sutcliffe, 1968, pp. 95–105. Reprinted by permission of Penguin Books.

Bernard Williams and Brian Magee, 'Descartes', taken from Brian Magee, *The Great Philosophers: An introduction to western philosophy*, 1987, pp. 78–95. Reprinted by permission of BBC Worldwide Limited.

George Berkeley, 'Colours', taken from *Three Dialogues Between Hylas and Philonous*, edited by J. Dancy, 1998, pp. 70–73. Reprinted by permission of Oxford University Press.

David Hume, 'Of the origin of ideas', taken from *Enquiries Concerning Human Understanding and Concerning the Principles of Morals*, 1975, pp. 17–22, 110–131. Reprinted by permission of Oxford University Press.

Alex Orenstein, 'Epistemology naturalized - nature know thyself', taken from E. Craig (ed.), *The Routledge Encyclopedia of Philosophy*, 1998, vol. 8, pp. 5–6. Reprinted by permission of Routledge.

Karl Popper, 'The problem of demarcation', taken from D. Miller (ed.), *Popper Selections*, Princeton University Press, 1985, pp. 118–130. Originally published 1974. Reprinted by kind permission of the Estate of Sir Karl Popper.

Alfred Lessing, 'What is wrong with a forgery?', taken from *Journal of Aesthetics and Art Criticism*, vol. 23, 1964. Reprinted by permission of The Journal of Aesthetics and Art Criticism.

Jorge Luis Borges, 'Pierre Menard, author of the Quixote', from *Labyrinths: Selected stories and other writings*, translated by J. E. Irby, pp. 62–71. Copyright © 1962, 1964 by New Directions Publishing Corp. Reprinted by permission of New Directions Publishing Corp and Gerald Pollinger.

The publishers have made every effort to contact copyright holders of material reprinted in *Philosophy: Basic Readings*. However, this has not been possible in every case and we would welcome correspondence from those individuals or companies we have been unable to trace.

Index